A masterly piece of writing and a riveting story, based on meticulous research, by award winning author, William Scott. This tale captures the reader and transports him back three and a half centuries to dark and dangerous days, with a compelling solution to the mystery of the witches of Bute.

David Torrie, an editor, D.C. Thomson Publications

I must give you all praise for your imaginative interpretation and fleshing out of the account in the archives. I can't fault your logical explanation of the witches' "evidence" and the return of Jonet McNicoll. Your novel is enthralling and would surely stand alone as historical fiction.

Tom McCallum, MA hons Classics, St Andrews

THE BUTE WITCHES

The Town of Rothesay, 1780

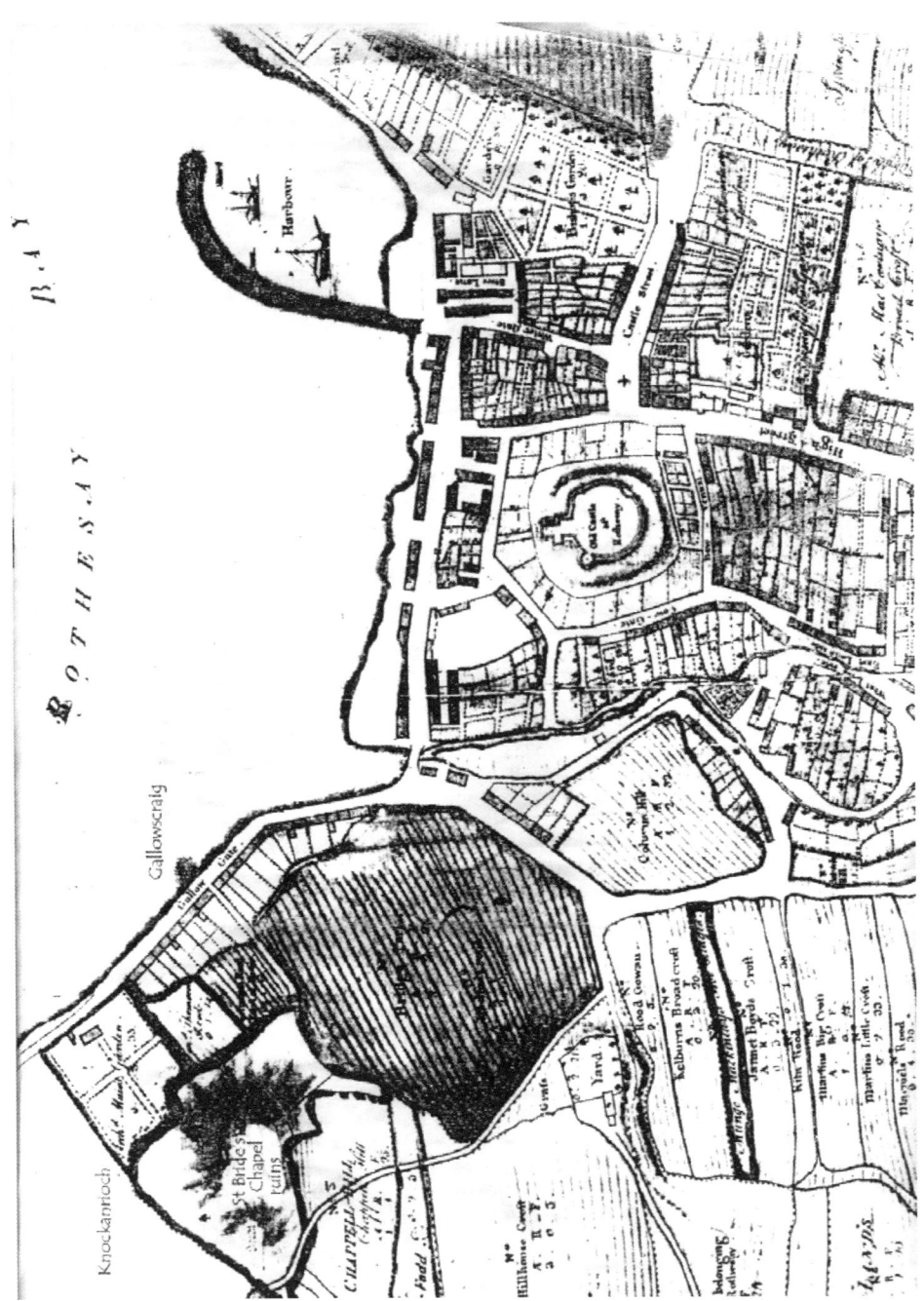

The Island of Bute c1600, by Timothy Pont

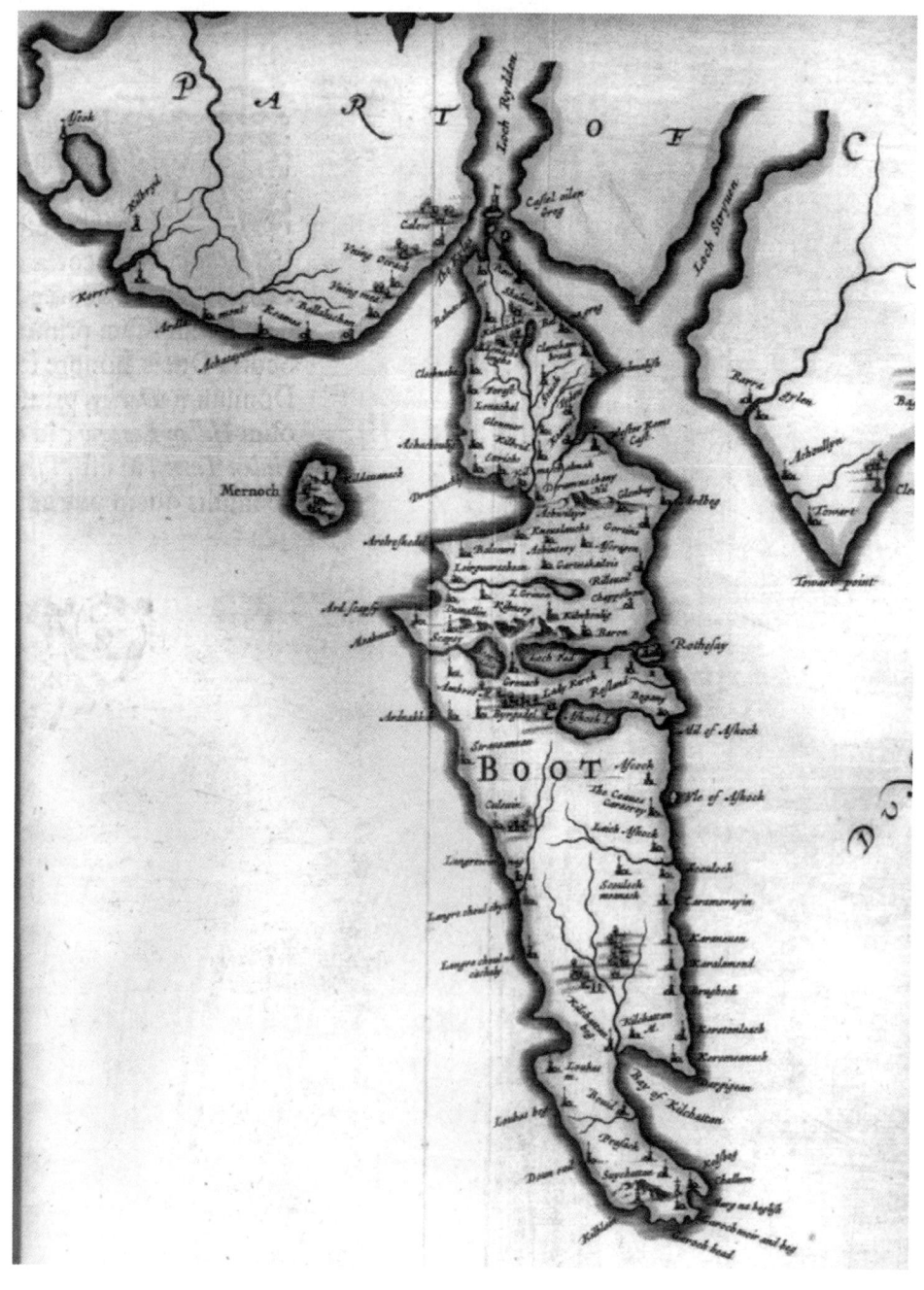

THE BUTE WITCHES

by

William Scott

BA,BSc,MEd,FIMA,FSAScot

History, Reconstruction of Events, Historical Records and Inferences

ELENKUS

MMVII

First Published in Great Britain in August 2007 by
Elenkus

PO BOX 9807,
Rothesay,
Isle of Bute,
PA20 9YA,
Scotland,
United Kingdom

email: elenkus@yahoo.com
website: www.elenkus.com
telephone: 01700505439
mobile: 07842 404268

© William Wallace Cunningham Scott

All rights reserved. No part of this publication may be copied or transmitted in any way without the permission of the author.

ISBN 978-0-9521910-7-0

The right of William Wallace Cunningham Scott to be identified as the author of this work has been asserted by him in accordance with the Copyright, Design and Patent Act 1988

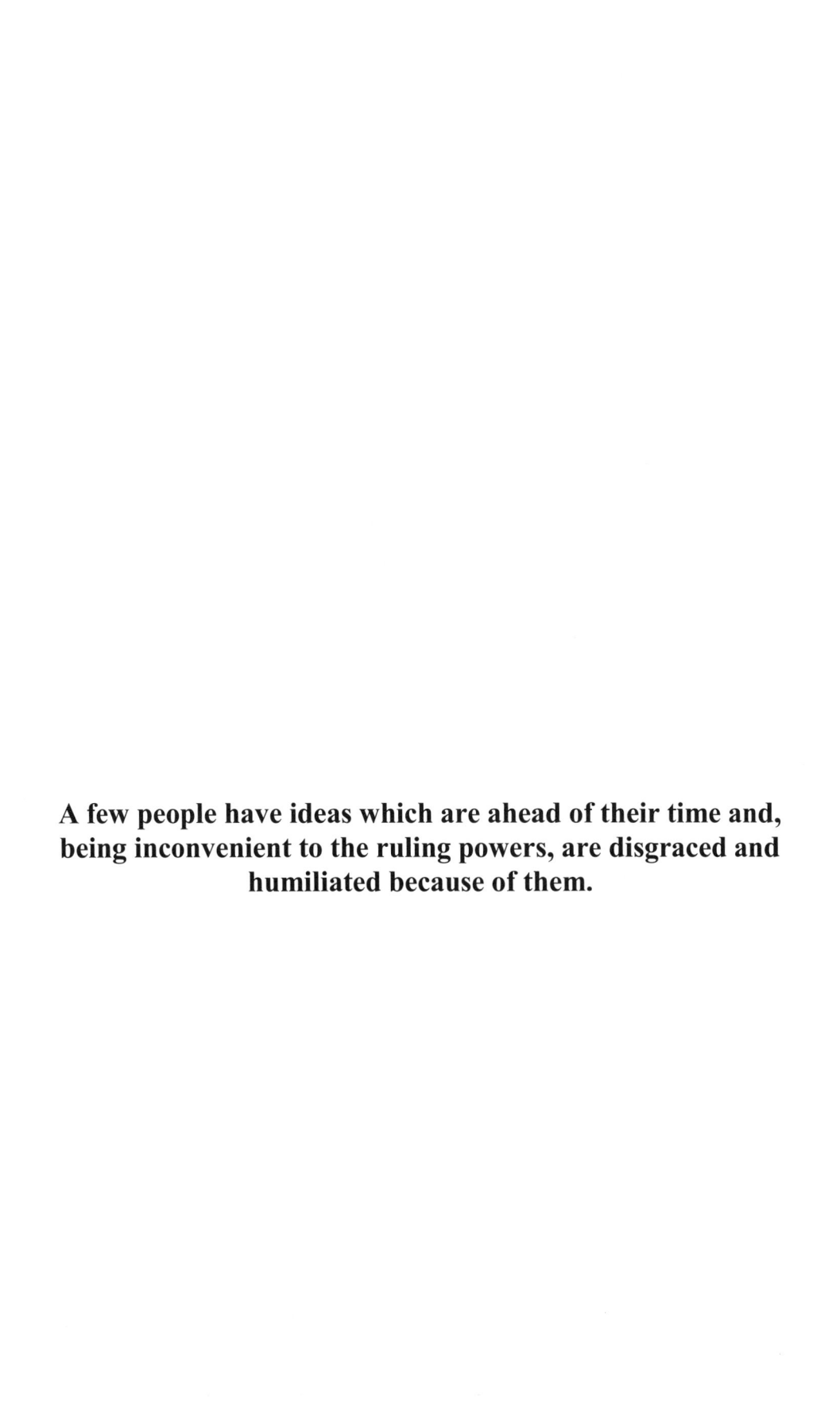

A few people have ideas which are ahead of their time and, being inconvenient to the ruling powers, are disgraced and humiliated because of them.

In 1662, on the Island of Bute, 4 women were executed for witchcraft. Another, who would have been convicted but escaped, returned to the island 12 years later, was recognised and then executed with a sixth. The women were mostly burnt at the stake, latterly, strangled first.

What follows is an investigation into these events. What caused them? Who were responsible? And what can be learned from them?

There are not many records to guide us, the reason for which will eventually become clear. The investigation is therefore imaginative in places, based on what is known to have happened elsewhere in Scotland at that time. It will be necessary to try to understand the kind of society in which such things could happen and what the island looked like then. The voluminous pre trial 'confessions' of the witches have also been discovered and printed. These have been used to provide a reconstruction of events. Every relevant historical document is printed and analysed, with inferences, in appendices at the end of the work, for the sake of scholars.

There is, even in an imaginative reconstruction of events, an underlying logic which, far better than any history, governed by what humans are likely to do, can lead us inexorably to the truth— even going beyond the supposed facts of the history by correcting mistakes in it. The question: why did this woman, Jonet McNicoll, return to the Island of Bute 12 years after she escaped, having apparently lived in safety on the mainland? is a puzzle resolved here. So is the question: how did she manage to escape from prison? And why only her? But the principal question is: why of all periods in history was there a witch hunt in Bute which resulted in two dozen trials and 5 executions, in that particular year of 1662? What caused it and who caused it?

The witch craze, even after 4 centuries of investigation is not well understood, though a great deal has been written on the subject. There is, for example, a mountain of literature on the Witches of Salem but no full understanding even then. The Scottish experience, when an estimated 3,000 to 4,000 witches were publicly killed, most of them in 1662, is far less clear. There has been no serious attempt to understand the problems posed by the Witches of Bute before and the outcome of this research is surprising. It may be that other witch hunts in Scotland at that time have a similar cause.

In 1661, Isaac Newton entered Trinity College, Cambridge and the dawn of science in these islands was at hand. By the time he left in 1696, after publishing Principia Mathematica Philosophiae Naturalis[1] the world had been transformed by his new system.

But he was not alone. Other minds in 1661 were stirring....

The cause of the witch craze in Britain has never been understood. In the Island of Bute it can be traced to a man, wealthy, well educated and distinguished, who would hardly have realised that he was discovering a new world of another kind: a world of love. The ultimate cause of the witch trials in Bute is love: the romantic love rampantly and vibrantly expressed by this man—which he was powerless to prevent—and, after his humiliation and disgrace, which he knew to be inevitable, that other, nobler form of love which the Greeks called agape: the disinterested love of everyone.
He discovered the second because of the first.
Had he not become the fallen angel, he would have failed to recognise that the Kirk Session—which punished the most trivial offence harshly with fines, sackcloth humiliation and penance chained to a wall—still followed the Old Testament; that nothing had been learned from the Life of Christ about forgiveness and unconditional love, the main discoveries of Jesus about how men and women should live.
Cast out of society, he found companionship with the people on the periphery and, because of his stature, soon became their leader. He had the ability, as well as the message, to draw people to him in prospect of a happier life. Threatened by his goodness and the originality of his insights, afraid a new church was starting up and unwilling to make another Jesus out of him and a Nazareth out of Rothesay, the Kirk Session attacked the splinter group at its weakest points: the witches, all of whom were on the periphery. The witch-burnings were the reaction of the Kirk to the inevitable demand on the periphery for a more forgiving way of life, one compatible with the best teachings of Jesus.

---

[1] *The Mathematical Principles of Natural Philosophy*. The first of the 3 volumes was published in 1684. Its alternative title: *A System of the World*, the heading under the Contents in the edition of 1819 et al.

PREFACE

Why is the witch hunt in Bute of interest and concern? Because it tells us about ourselves. Those who do not wish to know the awful truth— and some would rather not know it—have the same mindset as those others now in Germany who would rather not know about the Holocaust. 'It was not in my time, I had nothing to do with it, I am not responsible. Therefore, it is of no interest or concern to me,' is their refrain.
And yet the Holocaust is arguably the most important event in the history of the world. Understand it—fully— and you just might be able to help prevent an equivalent disaster in the future.
The witch hunt in Bute is a local disaster—one assuredly repeated elsewhere. It has lessons for us about how we should live, how we should treat differences of opinion and differences of values; and perhaps, above all, about the need to stand up against the evil that can sometimes get a grip of a community and a society. Some very good Germans, like Dietrich Bonhoeffer, died fighting that evil. But there were not enough to prevent it or even moderate it very much.

How should history be written? As a dry-as-dust account of the facts with references or an invention which pays little attention to the facts, most of which have never been ascertained? Or something in between? And what is it for? Is it to present the reader with a sweet smelling gilded lily which will encourage him to turn the pages and recommend the book to others so that it enjoys good sales and profits for its author and publisher?
These, I believe, are all unworthy aims. What is wanted, instead—at least what should be wanted—is the truth, as far as it can be discovered. And if this means offending sensitive souls by the inclusion of swearing or descriptions of the shit running down the legs of women about to be burnt at the stake or the sexual adventures of a man driven to take enormous risks, I believe we should have it warts and all.
President Clinton's behaviour with Monica Lewinsky—among others!— was over the top so far as many people were concerned. But would we be better off never to have read about it? Since his office was degraded by it and failed in as high-minded a task as this world offers anyone and for which he was supremely qualified—it matters! How could such a thing be explained without the details, sordid as they were, being made clear?

In this case, we need to know the truth or as much of it as can be fathomed after a lapse of 4 centuries.

Would a woman—full of righteous indignation all her life—being murdered because of it— would she—just before burning at the stake— desist from cursing her executioners to protect their feelings? Of course not! She would protest to the limit of her invective and inventiveness and wish to shock them in compensation for her own agony. It was her character. It is what she would do and anyone who would sanitise her words for the sake of sensitive souls does a disservice to that character and her courage. Lions roar in that situation and she was a lion.

A critical reader asked me who I was writing for: where was my market? And my answer was: no one in particular. If there was a particular reader in mind it could only serve to distort the truth being pursued. My one concern is to do my best: to reveal the events and the time.

In contrast to every tenet of creative or other writing, I have no target reader. My aim is simple: to add to the good literature of my country and my community and for the sake of them and my family, usually by solving very difficult problems. Whether this is appreciated or perceived successful is irrelevant. If it pleased everyone, it could not be original: it would already be available. Nor is it for profit: nothing is ever done really well if that is the object: commerce demands compromise. Virtue is a sufficient reward in itself. If I were to worry in advance about how things will be received, I would limit the possibilities of reaching a deeper truth than is usual. Restriction—of any kind—is anathema to the enquiring mind. How can the truth be reached if whether it is sweet smelling and pleasant to the ear are issues? You would, unconsciously at least, forget the natural, nauseous, odours of impoverished, suffering society, the discordant thunder of their oppressors and the pitiful, heart scorching lamentations of their victims. Why should reality be dumbed down and sanitised because some readers might be offended by it?

The truth is hard enough to discover without such limitations; can only be found without them and risks must be taken for there to be any hope of achieving it.

And how can the truth be reached?

With sufficient insight, it can be found in the documents of the time (if there are enough) but not in every case directly, for the people in the past who wrote them did not always have the truth, only an interpretation of it. Sometimes they got it wrong. Sometimes they knew it was wrong and the distortion was deliberate! The solution to one of the puzzles herein is precisely that the people of the time made a mistake and it may have been deliberate— probably was—for the prosecution case was stronger then and no defence was allowed to counter it. Once this is realised—and why—the answer can then be seen.

So the notion that one must stick to 'the facts' as if we knew what they are, is juvenile: some of the things taken to be facts at the time are not. The idea that everything else is speculation is equally foolish. A great deal can be inferred from the documents, from the records of the Kirk Session and Town Council and the pre-trial inquisition. Moreover, just as in the investigation of a modern crime, it is often worthwhile to reconstruct the events that took place beforehand, a similar procedure, based on what can be gleaned from the available documents, will help us to see what caused the witch hunt. This reconstruction is imaginative. Some readers may think it is over the top. But I am not writing to please, this is not an entertainment. It is a serious effort to understand what happened. I do not mind if you do not like the characters I have created. Some of what people do we might prefer not to know about. Some of the words they use we might prefer not to hear. But if we seek to understand them and their doings we need to enter into their lives as fully as possible. Yet *I* like them! I admire their courage, regret their humiliation and am incensed by their ill treatment and death.

Does this offend taste? Of course some may think so. It will certainly offend some people's ideas of what a book should be. To satisfy everyone would be impossible. Some people's doings **are** distasteful. But this is not about pleasing the reader. The aim is to reach the truth, as far as possible. Much of this is about the life of one man. What kind of man he was is very important and can be seen in the records. To understand the witch hunt we need to understand his nature and his world for he is the key to the executions. As never before, there is such a variety of taste that the word is virtually meaningless. Many— and it is many— make a life out of pornography; many—still many—eschew bodily pleasure in their pursuit of spiritual enlightenment. Between, is a huge range of what is acceptable.

Whether the reader agrees that the behaviour attributed to the characters here, based on the records, is likely, will depend upon his experience and it may be inadequate to the task. People do develop, they make surprising moves and changes of direction and they learn or do not learn and sometimes they fail in courage or perception. They are not, as a rule, very predictable. If they were, they would not be human. Yet these characters herein have got to be as they are portrayed—at least approximately—for the records tell us enough to demand it.

The reader who disagrees with the reconstruction is at liberty to read the records which are printed in the Appendices and then say: I do not believe this is how it was. If he does, he will be left with a deep mystery, which I believe I have solved.

Some readers will think that a book must be either fact or fiction. Why should this be? Because it is usual? Not good enough! There is a great advantage in being able to provide both within the same volume. The facts are all here—literally, in the Appendix with analyses. These are used to provide markers for the reconstruction which is imaginative. Of course this is original and it has this added value: the momentum generated by the evolving story carries us naturally into solutions for the problems: what caused the witch hunt? How did one witch escape? And why only one? Where did she spend the next twelve years? And why did she return when it was inevitable that she would be recognised and executed? In this way, the facts, added to imagination, have driven us by the imperceptible, transcendental logic which governs human affairs, to the answers.

Every writer ought to try to advance his subject, not merely by adding to the language— for of course there is no standard English[2], it is constantly evolving— but also by providing new kinds of book. That is what is attempted here. A new kind of book which answers questions no historian could answer if following the usual procedures.

William Scott,
Rothesay, April, 2007

---

[2] As Professor Randolph Quirk of London University explained in 1967 or thereby.

CONTENTS

1. The Island of Bute in 1662
   - (i) Places on the Island — 1
   - (ii) What was life like in Bute then? — 6
2. What was a witch in Scotland anyway?
   - (i) Generally — 17
   - (ii) Witch hunts in Bute — 20
3. The Inverary Document: elements of — 30
4. The Story of Master Robert Stewart of Scarrell — 48
   - I Education — 48
   - II Wanting Widows — 61
   - III Marriage — 68
   - IV Schoolmastering — 74
   - V Nancy — 84
   - VI Dinner with the Devil — 92
   - VII Defences for Deception — 102
   - VIII Nancy and the Kirk Session — 114
   - IX Sunday Service at the Kirk — 118
   - X Evidence of Lechery — 121
   - XI Meetings with Witches — 124
   - XII To Pray or Seek for Prey? — 137
   - XIII Disgrace at the Kirk Session — 139
   - XIV Consequences of Disgrace: Original Insights — 152
   - XV Two Scenes from the Play — 154
   - XVI The Witch Hunt Begins — 159
   - XVII Nightwalkers in the Prison — 168
   - XVIII Jonet McNicoll's Trial — 175
   - XIX Planning Escape — 180
   - XX The Trial of Jonet Morison — 186
   - XXI Jonet Morison Exposed — 191
   - XXII The Devil Exposed — 195
   - XXIII Jonet McNicoll's Departure from Bute — 204
   - XXIV The Burning of the Witches — 209
5. Jonet McNicoll's Story — 216
6. Aftermath — 237
7. Questions — 237
8. Cause of the Witch hunt
   - (i) General — 240
- (ii) Particular [The Main Argument] — 242

9. APPENDICES

(i) Inventory of Persons accused of Witchcraft in Bute County with charges	246
(ii) Witches' confessions in the Document in Inverary, analysed	252
(iii) What was the outcome of the investigations in the Inverary Document?	277
(iv) Justiciary Record at Rothesay, 1673	277
(v) Who were executed in 1662?	279
(vi) Did the accused commit murder?	282
(vii) Why is Robert Stewart of Scarrell taken to be the devil?	284
(viii) Why is the devil taken to be a cat, dog or heather-stalk?	285
(ix) Why were McLevin and Morison psychotic?	285
(x) What did Robert Stewart do about his predicament?	286
(xi) The Character of Robert and Nancy	286
(xii) Did the women kill the children?	287
(xiii) Why did the women say that murder had been done?	287
(xiv) Were the four said to be burnt in the reconstruction the ones involved?	288
(xv) Records about Robert Stewart of Scarrell	288
(xvi) Statements from the Session Book of Rothesay 1658-1750	289
(a) Going with the fairies	289
(b) The Process against Nancy Throw	290
(xvii) Would Robert Stewart have remained as Session Clerk?	294
(xviii) Inferences	295
(xix) What triggers the witch hunt?	297
(xx) Robert Stewart's possible excommunication	298
(a) Acts of the General Assembly of the Church of Scotland	298
(b) Inferences	298
(xxi) Was Argyll at the trials?	299
(xxii) The age of Ninian Bannatyne younger in 1673?	299
(xxiii) The Relationship between Rev Patrick Stewart and Rev John Stewart	300
(xxiv) Was the spouse at the trial and confession?	300
(xxv) What became of Jonet McNicoll's child?	300
(xxvi) Records of Jean Colquhoun and Robert Stewart	301
(xxvii) They had tar in Bute in 1662	302
(xxviii) Were the trials held in the Kirk or Tolbooth?	302
(xxix) Would Jean Colquhoun have remained with Robert Stewart after the trials?	302

(xxx) The Status of conclusions reached	303
(xxxi) Robert Stewart of Kilchattan	306
(xxxii) Deceased Rev Patrick Stewart's Estate	306
(xxxiii) Bute in 1662	
(a) Maps	307
(b) The Population of Bute in 1662	312
(xxxiv) Incomplete Research	319
10. Acknowledgements	320
11. Bibliography	321

DEDICATION

This is for my friend, the late Robert Davison, of the Royal Scots and King's African Rifles, educated in a British School in Shanghai, followed by 4 years of finishing school in a Japanese Prison. He became a distinguished exciseman, planter and tea-maker who, protecting his workforce, killed snakes, tigers and sharks in India, Africa and New Guinea; a generous, noble-hearted and courageous man whom you could count on in all seasons.

The Island of Bute in 1662

(the maps can be referred to with a magnifier or left to a second reading)

This book is about the devil.
In 1662, on this island, everybody knew the devil. Soon, you will know him too: who he was, what he was like, what evil he was capable of and what he actually did.

(i) Places on the Island

The settlements in country districts would be little different from what they were in 1750, which we can see in General Roy's map[1] made about that time (on the cover[2])— except for fewer buildings. Notice Scarrell, a settlement near the shore close to what is now and was then called the farm of Kildavanan. This place has particular significance for what follows. Notice also Chapelton, a place to the west of the causeway at Loch Fad on the north side of the bridle path. (There were no roads then). At this place, in the kaleyard, occurred an important incident involving a woman, Margaret McWilliam, afterwards convicted of witchcraft. She met the devil there and made a covenant with him to do whatever he wanted. Kilmory is also important, not merely the farm but the settlement or fermtoun[3] nearby at which lived Jonet Morrison, another witch. Since she was employed as a servant at Wester Kames, her journey, every working day, can be plotted on the map. As we will discover, she had an encounter with the devil near Gortans which is between the two, probably after a whole day of work.
Another place mentioned in the historical record is Barmore, still remembered today in a farm of that name between the Quien and Loch Fad but not shown as such by Roy a century later; meaning: it may have been destroyed as a witch's place or missed by the surveyor. But there

---

[1] The genius of Roy and his maps are celebrated in an appendix herein. That is, the map is very accurate in its details as any Brandane (native) can immediately see.
[2] With the permission of the British Library.
[3] Often a group of two or four houses with adjoining walls, used by farm labourers.

was another settlement at Barmore at which John Galie and his wife lived, both of them members of the witch folk. His home, which was not at the farm (the farmer's name was McConnachie), was probably on the hill a little to the south, where there is, even today, a ruined house which Roy shows as the place: Quien, a name that may have been applied later. The hill above Kilmory and south of Barone Hill was a place where witches' meetings were held, as the record will eventually tell us, when consulted. An important meeting is mentioned there in 1661, involving the devil. Two other meetings of witches are mentioned particularly: one at St Bride's Chapel which can be seen both on Roy's map of 1750 and also on the map of 1780; the other at Bute Quay. Again, the devil was present at both meetings. What was his role? What was he up to? We will eventually discover a great deal about this personage and even that he was there for a very remarkable purpose. Imagine it! Here is a book which tells us a great deal about the devil.

Notice Dunagoil where Patrick McKaw lived and Inchmarnock (spelled: Elanshemaroke in the historical record) where Patrick is said to have killed Donald McKirdy's bairn. Knockanrioch is important. There it was that Jonet Morison had doings with the devil. Knockanrioch is on the 1780 map. In 1662, the name would have been applied to a large area which included the farm of today, Ballochgoy and Skeoch Woods and probably Larkhall. It is hardly surprising that Jonet Morison should have met the devil here in a tryst, since she would be on her way home from the town, as she tells us she was. The Loaning is another place she mentions. A loaning is a path for animals and is probably roughly where Barone Road is now and Columshill Street, for animals from the north of the island would naturally have been led into the Cowgate from that direction, for Montague Street did not exist then.

As you can see in Roy's map, there is hardly any housing across the Lade on the north side of the town in 1750 and therefore in 1662. Another place often mentioned is Roseland, a name which remains today as the site of a former holiday camp beside the golf course. In 1662, Roseland included the grounds occupied by the present golf course, the hill above the Bush (even in Roy's map) and probably the upper reaches of the Serpentine. Since it is called in 1750 'New Roseland', there was probably an older place, Roseland, either destroyed or ruined (because of satanic associations) or omitted. The Serpentine, proper, as the 1780 map shows, was also called The Loaning, a different one, however. Major Ramsay (who had a grievance against Margaret McWilliam for turning the evil eye on his cows) farmed at Roseland in 1662, and the Rev Patrick Stewart came from there and probably owned a house there, the one removed.

One place of significance not shown on the maps is Corsmore, where Margaret McWilliam also lived before she removed to Chapelton. Corsmore (which became Crossmore) was between Kerrycresach (modern spelling) and Lochley (Lochend, today). This is immediately clear on reading the historical record of her resistance (heroic resistance!) to the flitting of the McFie family from their former house at Kerryscresach to Lochley across her fields. But Corsmore is very close to a place Roy shows: Crossbeg or maybe Grassbeg, as it seems instead, on Roy's map (cf Ambrismore and Ambrisbeg, close together).

Margaret McWilliam mentions meeting the devil at a field called Faldtombuie near Corsmore which can be exactly identified. 'Faldtombuie' means: field of the yellow knoll. On the north side of the road from Rothesay southwards today, there is indeed a knoll between Kerrycresach and Lochend (Lochley). In 1662, that knoll would have been covered in whins. In May and June these would have been bright yellow. Hence the name: the field of the yellow knoll. Ambrismore, near Scalpsie, is mentioned, for in 1661, Jean Campbell, the farmer's wife, was accused of going with the fairies, a serious offence. There is even a glen which was sometimes called the Fairy Glen, in the escarpment near the shore where, perhaps, Jean Campbell had hidden herself for a few days, perhaps to escape the unwelcome attentions of her family. As we will soon learn, any woman who went missing for any length of time and could not account for herself, was assumed to 'have been with the fairies'. Ambrisbeg is the scene of an act of malefice by Margaret McWilliam, convicted witch, who gave the evil eye to the tenant farmer's wife, for interfering with McWilliam's cutting rushes for roofing thatch at the edge of the Quien Loch. Edinmore, high up the hill above Kames Castle to the north, is another place mentioned by witches, as is 'Kames' the name then given to Port Bannatyne.

Notice Kelspoke where lived Katherine McIlmartin, a convicted witch, very young and beautiful, probably, (though that may have been her mother) for she was maiden (Queen) at witches meetings. This is south of Kilchattan Bay. Largizean, a farm west of Kilchattan Bay, was the home of Katherine Stewart, another member of the witch group, said to be 'a great witch' by Margaret McLevin, an important witch in her own right who lived at Ardroscadale where she made her covenant with the devil in the barn. Mecknoch is where Robert Stewart, farmer, lived, who first gave evidence against the witches in January 1662. Why did he do this? What prompted him? Since the evidence he gave is very slight, these questions are even more intriguing. The answer is: tracks in the snow. Read on.

Notice also Ascog Island, confirmed as a fact on both Pont's map of c1590 and Roy's of c1750; and the Kirk of Kingarth which is not where expected near Kilchattan Bay but close to Mount Stuart, which suggests that this was the Kirk in 1662. The Middle Kirk, across the road from the present cemetery, where there was until recently a kirk, may be a later addition. In the Kirk Session records, Rev John Stewart—an important figure herein—when Minister of Kingarth Parish, lived far from the Kirk which may mean that he lived in one of the houses at Kilchattan Bay, for he mentions, with regret, the distance between his home and the Kirk. In 1658, this man became Minister of Rothesay Parish and lived there for a time in a house rented to him by Robert Stewart of Scarrell, son of Rev Patrick Stewart, until the manse in the present High Street of Rothesay was refurbished. This manse was close to the High Street on the east side about 50 yds downhill towards the town from Minister's Brae—about where today, there is a bus shelter. An old map in the museum shows it precisely. It was set back about 20 feet from the street.

Only the town would be greatly different in 1662 from how it is shown by Roy, and then not by much. Houses on the periphery of the town shown by the General are the ones likely to have been added between 1662 and 1750.

In 1662, there were three main areas of housing in Rothesay: around the castle, the block to the south which went as far as Russell Street (today's name: there were no street names then) and Balskyte which is the area on both sides of the Balskyte burn which came down the Serpentine, turned right (from west to north) just before the Tolbooth and went down the Watergate to enter the Harbour to the east of the breakwater. Castle Street and Watergate would have large flat stones laid down, some of them shaky, to assist passage across the Balskyte burn into which would be thrown all the waste matter, including excrement, from the houses. *Gardyloo!* was a phrase not confined to Edinburgh.

The Tolbooth is the building where trials were normally held: in the Burgh Court; and the Tolbooth stretched from the present High Street across to the Watergate and took up about half of the block. Upstairs were the cells on the east side and the Court on the west side, overlooking the Castle. Underneath were three shops which were rented out by the town on an annual basis to tenders. Notice that all the housing stopped in 1750 to the SOUTH of the south edge of Montague Street, because in 1662 there was no street there. The sea came right up to within 40 yds of the

Castle moat, as Martin Martin confirms during his visit in 1695, or thereby, and both Roy and Pont confirm in their maps.

What the reader cannot be expected to realise at this stage is that the map of the town given by Roy is wondrously accurate as to details. See appendix. What was the population of the town in 1662? Between 500 and 700, and probably the latter figure is closest. For the island as a whole, the population was between 1300 and 1700, the lower figure again more likely. In 1662, there were about 500 in Kingarth Parish, 500 in Rothesay and 500 in the rest of Rothesay Parish in the country. That is, 500 in the town and 1000 on the island in the country districts. These figures are fully justified in the appendix. Roy's map shows us about 80 buildings in all in the town in 1750; so a few less, say about 75, in 1662. Some of these were workshops and offices like the Tolbooth, few of them were over two stories high (there may have been some: the word 'tenements', is used) and mostly made of the wattle, plaster and wood construction which was then current. Ann Hathaway's cottage, Stratford, is like this, even today. This method of construction was mainly responsible for The Great Fire of London because fire spread so rapidly between such dwellings, which were often close together.

Martin Martin, c1695, also confirms these figures. On his visit, he counted 80 heavy fishing boats in Rothesay Harbour (which stretched from the present mid pier to the Albert, only) which implies at least 160 fishing families given the need for a crew, some of whom would have lived out of town. Martin believed there were only 100 families in the town then which makes a population of 500-600 for that year very likely: about 5 or 6 per family, which would include a few old folks, perhaps. Martin was a very accurate observer. Notice that the population of the town gradually overtook the country districts when the herring fishing expanded. Because it did, the number of boats increased and the harbour, created by the Cromwellians, became cramped for manoeuvring sailing craft. The solution was to infill the sea below the Castle, which was very shallow there, as at Kilchattan, Ettrick Bay and Lochgilphead etc and therefore easily covered over, a process that took place between 1750 and 1780, as the maps reveal. See appendix for details. Infilling allowed boats to dock outside the harbour and buildings for storage and marketing of fish. Some of the fishers lived out of town in every period, farming and fishing being a useful combination of jobs. In the late 18th century, farming suffered because so many left the country districts for the town where cotton mills and fishing provided a better wage.

(ii) What was life in Bute like in 1662?

Since we have few written accounts of that time—Martin's is one of the few— we know very little. But from the Statistical Survey of 1792 a lot can be inferred. Life would not be all that different a century later. The main differences would be far fewer people in 1662, as we have seen and greater poverty. In 1792, 'nearly one half of the rents are paid by barley...to the distillers of the island.'[4] So whisky was made in Bute then. Indeed, one of the witches in 1662, Isobel McNicoll, was a distiller who had even been delated [impeached] for drunkenness at the Kirk Session: the effects of working with a still may have contributed to the stories she told about her meetings with the devil, as we will soon learn.

What did people eat? Potatoes and herring, were the staples in 1792 and it would have been the same in 1662 for Martin mentions the herring in 1695. The waters around the island were full of fish but herrings were the favourite and they were salted and preserved for use throughout the year. The salt would be made locally, perhaps at Ascog where there are signs of salt pans. Porridge made from oats; turnip and probably kale, were also staples of the diet.

In 1772, we learn, from Rev James Thorburn's survey in 1792, that there were no carts in the Parish except at Mount Stewart, which confirms John Blain's statement very largely about the absence of wheeled vehicles on the island when he arrived.

There was little trade with other communities and therefore little in the way of imports, except by the gentry, some of whom were very rich, who might bring in luxuries from the cities at great expense. Even by 1792, we learn that 'few of the inhabitants export their own commodities; buyers come to the island, and are at the expence (sic) of ferrying them over to the other side.'[5] In 1792, there were two packets every week from Rothesay and a ferry boat once every week from Scoulag, near Mount Stuart, to Largs which was the only market for oats.

A better indicator of the moral tenor of the times is the Kirk Session record. In 1641, in Kingarth, we find a woman punished for slander: 'she is esteemed guilty of slandering the said Finlay, of perjuring hir self and him both by hir first confession of fornication and incest with Robert Glass. She is enjoyned to stand between the 2nd and 3rd bell bare footed,

---

[4] Statistical Survey, 1792, p455
[5] ibid p459

bare headed in sackcloth at the Kirk door in the jougs twelve Sabbaths, and being poor to pay but ten pounds of penalty.'[6]

How much is that? A schoolmaster a decade later would be paid £40 a year (excluding fees which were not much). A lot of money to be found by a poor person for slander, then.

Yet consider this, in 1649: 'Every elder who shall reveal an other elder's name delating a fact to the Session, shall stand a Sabbath and pay of penalty 4 pounds for the first time, and for the second time be put out of the Session.'[7]

So the identity of accusers was secret.

And 'Whatsoever parishioner shall upbraid any elder for delating his name to the Session shall stand according to the degree of scandall and pay 4 pounds.'[8]

'It is enacted that every elder who absents himself from intimated sessions without a lawful excuse shall pay 40 shillings.'[9]

What was an elder supposed to do? 'not only to delate gross and public scandalous sins but also all swearers, banners [cursers], ordinary drinkers, all that practises not seemly exercise with their bounds and generally to have a care of their own carriage that they may be a good example to others.'[10]

But it was not all painful cash punishment: Gabriel Walker denied calling Katherine McIlmartin a witch, despite witnesses testimony. 'The Session knowing the woman to be honest and free of all suspicion and brute ordains the said Gabriel to stand three Sabbaths, and the last day to come down off the stool [the cutty stool, of Burns] and sit down upon his knees before the pulpit and take the said Katherine by the hand and crave her mercy, and because he is poor his penalty is forgiven.'[11]

What was a witch? Several criteria can be seen. In May 1649, Margaret McKirdy was delated for charming Robert Hyndman and confessed that she used the charm for the evil eye. Like most charms, it was in the Irish

---

[6] Session Book of Kingarth, 1641, p4; spellings modernised. Jougs: a hinged iron collar, locked round the neck (and sometimes the head too) chained to a wall.
[7] ibid p9
[8] ibid p9
[9] ibid p9, that is £2.
[10] ibid p14
[11] ibid p11, 1649

and it was: Cuirrith mi an obi er hule; a hucht phedir is phoile; An in obi is fear fui na yren; Obi yia o neoth gilar, etc.'[12]

What happened to a suspected witch? In March 1650 Finwell Hyndman 'is delated to the Session as suspect of witchcraft and that she uses to be away from her service about 24 hours every quarter, and that nobody knows where she goes to nor will she confess it, and has been often trapped in a lie in saying that during the time of her absence she had been in such a place.'[13]

In other words, the evidence against her was merely that she had been unaccountable for 24 hours!

All we learn thereafter is that 3 men testify that this is so. We then find that the Session concludes that 'the said Finwell being still bruted for a witch or (as the common people calls it) being with the fairies, they appoint Ninian Stewart of Largizean and John Wallace to apprehend the said Finwell.' The last entry on this subject is: 'The said Finwell Hyndman's confession, as also Margaret McKirdy and Jonet McKamy their confessions, are written at large in a scroll by the self [The Session Clerk, probably] together with the presumptions upon which they were apprehended.'[14]

What is the outcome? The Session records do not say! Usually they do say. There is a fine—a substantial fine and penance on the cutty stool dressed in sackcloth and maybe the jougs. Why is there no conclusion here? Perhaps because the people who dealt with the matter were later ashamed of it and somehow excised the offending lines from the manuscript, perhaps rewriting the entirety with the excisions. We do not hear of Finwell again which suggests that she escaped or she was injured or even died. 'Going with the fairies' was a serious crime. Jean Campbell of Ambrismore was accused of this in 1661 in the Rothesay Records. Had Finwell's punishment been of the ordinary kind we would expect to read what it was in the record. Once begun, the process could not just be dropped. We just do not know what she confessed or how that confession was obtained. As we will eventually learn, the men of the Session were adept at getting confessions and even at determining who were witches by ducking and witch-pricking. But maybe the process against Finwell Hyndman was dropped. We cannot tell.

---

[12] ibid p12. This is, evidently, Irish Gaelic which no Scot consulted can translate. £50 was wanted by a translation service for the 4 lines. This struggling scholar can do without it; having enough charm for his purpose.
[13] ibid p20
[14] ibid p21

Where were these Session meetings held? At the Kirk of Kingarth. But where was that? The Middle Kirk was not built until 1680. Mount Stuart would not be erected at that time: until after the Stewarts became earls of Bute. What Roy shows as the Kirk of Kingarth in 1750 is the Kirk near the shore not far from Scoulag burn foot. This is probably the Kirk that is meant in 1649 and therefore in 1662. St Blane's Chapel at this time was probably a ruin, like St Bride's in Rothesay. By 1792, the Kirk of Kingarth (near Scoulag burn) is described as in use by the family of Stewart when they are at home. What this suggests is that there was a kirk in that place before Mount Stuart existed. In which case, when the 3rd Marquis became a Roman Catholic—around the middle of the 19th century, during the Oxford Movement, while he was a student—there had to be some trouble about that Kirk, which was still Church of Scotland, being on his land.

Now look at this, for it has resonance for us later: In August 1650, 'John McFie [the same John McFie mentioned in the evidence against Margaret McWilliam, the chief witch] in a claim on behalf of his wife Christine Glass, against Finwell Glass, [*declared*] that the said Finwell came to Kerrycresoch to James McFie's house and speired at his mother and his wife if there died a bairn from Christine Glass and how the bairn died and said that the said Christine gave her bairn for an offering to the devil to save her husband, her offspring and means from misfortune.'[15]

This is a charge of murder. You will read such charges again made in the Inverary Document in far more serious circumstances and within the reconstruction.

What was the outcome? The Records do not say. What does a statement like this tell us? That the idea of a child being offered to the devil as a sacrifice for some higher good (such as the lives of the rest of the family) is in the mindset of the people. But notice this: there is nothing in the statement to suggest that there is a scrap of truth in it. People do get odd ideas into their heads and sometimes these have no basis whatever. Notice this, though: accusers like this whose allegations were false are invariably punished as slanderers.

What happened if the accused escaped on the ferry? 'The Session being informed that Isobel More is fugitive out of the country to the Lowlands, they recommend to these that go to the mainland to learn out in what parish there she resides, and especially to the ferryman.'[16]

---

[15] ibid p25
[16] ibid p29

This tells us that people who are wanted by the Session (or the burgh court!) who escape are pursued. This makes escape very difficult from the island especially, for you have to go by boat. Remember this when Jonet McNicol tells her version of events. She would be quite unable to use the ferry: she was known, her trial had been held; the ferryman would have refused to convey her to freedom. Her escape had to be different and it had to be at dead of night to avoid discovery.

Were the people uniformly obnoxious? No, they were good to visitors to the island who had had their goods stolen or people who were in need of alms because they were destitute. On one occasion later, a house was built, probably near Crocanraer [St Colmac's] for a leper. Of course this was partly self interest: they did not want to rub shoulders with him! But they could have killed him out of hand instead, as sometimes must have happened. Money— got by the Session in fines— is continually handed out as alms to the poor. But there is a lot of money for this, because the fines for sin are steep. In Kingarth in 1664, William Boyle was fined ten merks which seems to be £6.13.4 for fornicating with Bessie McKerrel or McKellar who is fined £4 for the same offence[17]. Of course public repentance on the cutty stool in sack cloth was another part of the punishment— and very humiliating that would be. In May 1665, the total of fines paid in Kingarth by just 12 people who have committed offences totalled £71.16.4.

What does the Kingarth Session Record say about 1662? Nothing. There is nothing between April 1651 and March 1664. The Session Records at Rothesay show a similar hiatus, as we will see; except that there the record is complete for almost all of 1661. The record for 1662 is missing and there is nothing else in the Rothesay Records until 1673, at which time Jonet McNicol was executed.

One conclusion that might be possible is that the Kingarth Record up to 1651 shows a harsher application of the rules than after 1664, for in August 1665, Jonat Bannatyne, a confessed adulteress, was merely required 'to stand both in the place of public repentance and at the Kirk door in sackcloth till she give evidence of her repentance'. She was not fined. But then that was because she was a beggar and a fine could not be got out of her. A year later, John Cormick, adulterer with Jonat Bannatyne, was fined £10. If this is so, it could be laid at the door of Rev John Stewart of Rothesay, who, until 1658 had been the Minister at Kingarth. His ministry may have been more severe than others.

---

[17] ibid pp31,35

What was a typical day at that time in the life of an inhabitant?
You would get up very early and dress. By 1662 the gentry, those at least who were royalists, like Sir James Stewart, would wear quite colourful clothing, like the cavaliers of Charles I's time. They would have breeches, stockings and jackets of almost any colour and a hat with a feather. A kirk elder who would be a person of substance, a farmer or burgess or fisherman, would dress in the sober black of the church conformer. A servant or labourer would wear what he could afford and it might only be a kilt of whatever material he could find or a plaid that covered the whole body: a kind of toga made from a long piece of cloth but, judging from the fines paid at the Kirk Session, most people had some money and could therefore afford to buy clothing of some kind. And yet, the decade of English martial law was accompanied by great poverty. The Scots could not afford to pay the money required for the maintenance of the army and it could not be got out of them by any means—because they just did not have the money.

A servant might not own shoes. Even by 1900 some children [18] in Scotland went to school barefoot. But most people would be able to find something to put on their feet even if it was not an article we would recognise as a shoe. A wooden clog would be common, for that was something you could easily fashion out of wood with a knife. Of course there were shoemakers and they might do it for you. You could probably earn enough as a day labourer to buy such essentials. In 1650, John Glass was fined 20 merks: £13.6.8 for fornication: 'his penalty in respect of his poverty is modified by the magistrate to 20 merks.'[19] If that is poverty, even the poor could lay their hands on money. So destitution was rare.

The first thing to be done in the morning was fetch water for the porridge and light the fire. Coal would be imported from time to time but would be expensive. As Roy shows us in 1750 there were few trees left on the island, most having been cut down for fuel and building materials, including boats, by then. The main fuel was peat and the records tell of parishioners being given the task of digging, carrying and stacking peats for the Minister. Both the great moors of Bute in the north and at Scoulag would provide peats. Take off the heather and underneath, especially

---

[18] The author's father in law [born 1889] and his brothers all walked barefoot several miles to school in Lanarkshire. In 1985 in Brunei, an American who had crossed the Pacific in a yacht spent 3 months there and never wore shoes. He even went on *The Hash* (cross country) regularly and always barefoot. The jungle was full of thorns. His feet were evidently impervious to discomfort because they had toughened with time.

[19] ibid p26

when the ground rises on either side so that it collects rain water, peat will often be found: a consequence of old woodlands and vegetation decaying and being compacted. Peats, each a foot or so in length and a few inches in width and depth, were dug and left to dry out for the summer and then lifted and carried to the houses where they were carefully stacked against the outside wall for use as necessary in the fire inside. Handling dry peats is hard on the hands, conveying them without a cart, an arduous matter. There were no wheeled vehicles on the island in 1662, perhaps because of the absence of a wheelwright which means the horse carried a pair of baskets one on either side or dragged a pallet: a couple of lengths of wood with cross pieces which supported the freight.

Water would be got from the nearest place: a well, a spring, a burn or even the loch. Because disease was not understood at all and medicine barely existed, many people would exercise no care in where water was drawn and that would be one of the reasons for illness. If you drank from the loch in summer, you could ingest algae and other matter that was damaging. The tendency would be to use the nearest source of water and not the best. Some people, more ignorant and careless than most, would have used the water from the Lade, mindless of the fact that further upstream animals would pollute it. The effects of pollution were not understood. In the reconstruction, mention is made of the Balskyte burn which carried spring water down the Serpentine and turned down the Watergate to the harbour. People living in the Balskyte, especially near the harbour, after so much piss and shit had come down it from chamber pots emptied every morning higher up, would have used it as a source of water, at least on occasion to save the trouble of the journey to a well. Porridge was oatmeal milled by the miller. Bute had several mills: at Ettrick, at Ascog and in Rothesay, in each case using a water source to move the wheel: the burns at Ettrick, Ascog and the Lade. Wherever on Roy's map you see a burn, there you could, in principle at least, have a mill. In practice the flow needs to be sufficient in all seasons.

After breakfast, which might also include salt herring and eggs and even bread if you lived in the town and could buy it, or make it yourself, or bannocks—a staple among Scottish armies at all times: oatmeal and water mixed and cooked on a griddle—there was work. Work on the farm or the shop in town or at the fishing or the workshop: the joiner, the butcher, the baker, the candlestick-maker, the shoemaker, the builder, the glazier, the weaver, the webster, the boat builder, the nursery—though more people would grow their own vegetables—etc. Any item for which there was a demand which could be made, would be made by someone on the island with the exception of anything requiring unusual skill [like gun, powder or sword making] which could not be learned in Bute.

People walked great distances. Jonet Morison, a witch, probably burnt, walked every day from her home at Kilmory to Wester Kames where she worked as a servant: over 10 miles a day. No wonder she got tired. Her confession shows signs of this on the way home: really tired and maybe seeing things.

Without the advantages of summer time, everything was determined by the light and the light would fail early in winter, by four o'clock at times, which is why dinner was eaten at about that time. Food would be served on wooden platters or off the board in some cases of poverty, though the tradesmen and gentry would have pewter or even silver in the case of great men like Ninian Bannatyne of Kames whose wife inherited a fortune. Knives and forks would be in short supply, obtainable only on the mainland, travel there a serious obstacle. Most people would have a knife of some sort and probably a spoon. There would be some vegetables like turnip and kale as well as potatoes, some locally grown fruits and game, like rabbit, snared for the pot, birds and occasionally venison. Fish would be a staple, herring in various forms much enjoyed. So much, that other fish were ignored even in 1792 when an industry could have been made from them. Ale and aquavitae would be brewed locally in diverse places. Wine would be a rarity, imported for the gentry unless it was elderflower, blaeberry or bramble which could be produced locally.

A very important matter is entertainment. There was none. For the years before the English occupation and during it, since the moral cast of mind was the same, entertainment was effectively banned. Dancing and singing were banned; any kind of licentiousness was banned, such as bawdy stories or flirting with barmaids. What could be done in one's spare time was therefore heavily restricted and wrongdoing fiercely punished when discovered. And the islanders, as never before, had an eye on everything and each other. The elders were required to report all derelictions. The only exception was the tavern, the ale house. These existed and time could be spent in them drinking with a few others in quiet talk. But even here there were restrictions. In 1648 'was delated Patrick McKaw for drinking and other misbehaviores done be him in the toune of Bute.'[20]

Notice that drinking in itself was an offence! And, in 1651, five men were delated for 'drinking upon a Sunday at even, being a fast day.[21]' This was

---

[20] ibid p5
[21] ibid p29

worse and they would be heavily fined. Some days like Christmas day were fast days: you were supposed to eat nothing, out of respect.

What does this all mean? That life was pretty miserable, even for the gentry but especially for the poor. Imagine living on salt herring, potatoes and porridge without much alteration. Imagine working from early in the morning till late afternoon and then cooking one's dinner and going to bed to do the same thing all over again. And on Sundays, the only day that was free from work, going to the Kirk on pain of punishment. Imagine being unable to do work of any kind on Sunday or to travel any distance, for that was Sabbath breaking. People were punished for falling asleep in the Kirk. One woman was delated for sitting at her spinning wheel, observed through a window, the assumption being that she was at work.

There would be few books but some people would be able to read if books could be borrowed. A century later Burns could read and people like him who attended the school and attendance was compulsory and fees were paid. The idea of a free school in Scotland in early times is a myth. Both parishes on the island provided schools overseen by the Kirk Session. There was of course no library, though Sir James Stewart would have the beginnings of the libraries which were eventually established at Mount Stuart and the Ministers, who were university graduates, would have their own libraries, mostly of religious or theological works.

One of the few reliefs from this was market day which was Thursday. Even then, from very early in the morning, anyone involved in trade would be standing at his stall selling in what is now Castle Street, around the Mercat Cross which stood about opposite the door of the present Town Hall in the middle of the space. This is why that street is now so much wider than any other. In 1662, the site line of what became known as Castle Street on the sea side would have been roughly a straight line! That is, the exterior offices of the present Town Hall were built out of the old Tolbooth into the market square at a later period. Why does the landward side (south) of Castle Street turn when approaching the Castle to the south? To make a greater space for the market, a process that would have begun in the 12th century or thereby. When the Town Hall was extended into the space of the market square, that was the time when moving the Mercat Cross could have occurred, for the space was no longer suitable for a market which could be held down on the landfilled area below the escarpment on which the Castle stands. In 1662 there were no street names. In such a small town street names were unnecessary.

Everybody knew everybody else and where they lived. What need of an address?

As we are going to discover, the very lack of entertainment is a key factor in the witch hunt. Of course the trials themselves were entertainment— the best ever— but this is not what is meant. Even before 1660 and the Restoration there were secret meetings of a few folk, less than a dozen, for the Inverary Document tells us about them. These were the witch folk, poor people, people on the periphery of the community, who met in secret out of the way, up this hill or that, in a col between hills or in a glen somewhere—anywhere out of the public eye. They would go to some prearranged place in ones or twos and so attract no attention. They would be assumed to be taking a walk or collecting plants or enjoying the scenery. But what they met for was fun. They met to talk and dance and sing a little—for they had not much in the way of songs to sing—all that would have been lost in the many years of repression by the Kirk and the Westminster Parliament. If songs there were, they would be psalms mostly and pretty dull most of these are. In the 1960's in Sutherland the Free Kirkers there still regarded hymn singing as entertainment. On Sundays, only the psalms were sung, for only these were serious.

Some of the people at the meetings were charmers and knew something of herbs and they could help each other with ailments of one kind and another. They would repeat a charm over a diseased limb or sore place hoping that the charm would have some beneficial effect. Sometimes it seemed to have a good effect. Coincidence was a powerful factor. People do get well all by themselves at times. But if it had been perceived to work for one person that charm might be expected to work for another. And if the distressed person believed in the charm it was like having a placebo from the doctor— a drug that does nothing: at least it made you feel better to think that someone had treated it. And that better feeling might just be enough to cure the problem. Having faith in the cure helped. When most people had not the least idea of the real reasons for their medical problems, what else were they to do but chant spells and brew up combinations of plants in the hope that something worthwhile would occur if applied to the hurt place? And if your friend was ill would you not try anything to help? And if all you knew was herbs and charms and spells of course you tried them. By any modern standard of morality anything else was immoral. But the Kirk Session regarded herbs and charms and spells as superstition—something dangerous and antichristian. That was why women were delated for it: accused of it. And fined and punished.

In Rothesay in 1662 there was a leech ('surgeon')—the only person allowed to practice medicine. But since his skill was limited to extracting blood, thus weakening the patient, it was worth little. And since it cost money the poor could not afford him. The attitude of the Church to illness seems to have been: 'Ok, you have something wrong with you. If God wants to take you now he will do so and there is nothing you can do about it. If you get well it will be because God wants you to go on living.' To chant spells and charms and apply herbal poultices would be taken as interfering in God's work—trying to interfere with his plans for that person. And as the world knows, God sometimes wants nice people to die for some mysterious purpose of his own that we are not entitled to question.

When the Restoration began in 1660 there would be the prospect of a more relaxed attitude to living: the hope that life could be more enjoyable, for it had been much freer under the Monarchy of Charles I. Gradually, there would be a move by those who could afford them towards brighter clothing and greater variety in everything. The stranglehold of the Kirk was under threat from this new menace; and it would respond by increasing its grip. The pro-catholic influences of this new monarch with the prospect again of Episcopal bishops governing the Kirk would be seen as a return to decadence that must be fought. And so, the secret meetings that might have been thought to be allowed to become open—they were but picnics, after all—had to remain secret. If discovered, the Kirk Session would move against them, whose elders would have enquired: What evil was being practised there? If they are secret, of course there must be a reason. And there was: they wanted a little merriment and pleasure in their lives of misery. Some of the women had the name of witches, practised charming and used herbs to cure people, didn't they? Well that had to be stopped, the matter investigated. And the Kirk Session men were already very good at extracting confessions out of people.

But it takes more than this to publicly burn people. A meeting, a picnic, of ten people on a moor miles from anyone, singing songs and roasting bannocks, is not much of a threat. We are going to see what the real threat was.

2. What was a witch in Scotland anyway?

(i) Generally

It varied from country to country, place to place within the same country and tribe to tribe. Christina Larner, in 'The Enemies of God', a wonderful book, has a lot to tell us.

'The women who sought or involuntarily received the accolade of witch were poor but they were not in Scotland always solitary. The women who were the classic focus of witch accusations were frequently impoverished not because they were widows or single women with no supporters or independent means of livelihood, but were simply married to impoverished men... About half of those whose status is recorded were married at the time... Nor does ugliness appear to have been an important element in the composition of the Scottish witch.[22]

'The essential individual personality trait does seem to have been that of a ready, sharp, and angry tongue. The witch had the Scottish female quality of smeddum: spirit, a refusal to be put down, quarrelsomeness. No cursing: no malefice; no witch.[23]

'I hope yer balls is boiled in oil. I pray yer bairns are born deed. I expect yer crops will fail and I hope God in his justice gi'es ye a dose of some pestilence.'

"The richness of language attributed to witches is considerable. Helen Thomas of Dumfries was accused by Agnes Forsyth in August 1657 of having said, 'Ane ill sight to you all, and ane ill sight to them that is foremost, that is Agnes Forsyth.' In similar vein Elspeth Cursetter of Orkney in May 1629 hoped that 'ill might they all thryve and ill might they speid...Agnes Finnie of Potterrow in Edinburgh, who was accused in 1642, was alleged to have said that 'she should gar the Devil take a bite of the said Bessie Currie.'[24]

---

[22] Enemies of God, Larner, p96
[23] ibid p97
[24] ibid p97

But what often resulted in accusation was 'the refusal to bring to this situation the deference and subservience which was deemed appropriate to the role'[25] of a social and economic dependent.

What made the witch hunts possible was the collective rule-making in the statute of 1563 refined during the trials of 1590-91. 'There were charmers, poisoners, owners of the evil eye, sooth-sayers, cursers. Some would have been called witches'[26] The witch hunts introduced a new dimension: the label changed to make the witch not only the enemy of the individual and the community but of the state and of God himself.

Amazingly, according to Larner,

> 'The existence of the third level of social action, the new organisational processes, both **created a demand for the production of witches** and at the same time **made the production more rewarding to the community!**'[27]

This is appalling if true.
It means that people needed somebody to blame for their misfortunes and that taking punitive action against them helped them to cope with these. 'Now we have got rid of the cause, we can with greater hope look to the future.'

People were often labelled as witches because they were linked to those who were. And labels stuck, a trait still seen today.

Many witches died in their beds unmolested. But three to four thousand were killed. 'In the last resort it can only be said that these individuals were in the wrong place at the wrong time.'[28]
   'Witch hunting is the hunting of women who do not fulfil the male view of how women should conduct themselves.'[29]
Before witch hunting, women, who were regarded as inferiors, as chattels, even, were punished by their men for misdemeanours. Once they were

---

[25] ibid p98
[26] ibid
[27] ibid
[28] ibid p100
[29] ibid

taken to be responsible for their own souls they could be punished like anybody else by officialdom.

'They were accused not only by men but by other women because women who conformed to the male image of them felt threatened by any identification with those who did not.

'The pursuit of witches was an end in itself and was directly related to the necessity of enforcing moral and theological conformity.'[30]
So that is why witches were wanted: to reinforce the moral and theological conformity. The women accused were those who did not conform to male ideas of what women should be and efforts were made to extract confessions from them by torture. And if no convictions were achieved what did it matter? At least everyone in the community knew what was expected and the consequences of failure. The threat of burning would have been a curb on many a rebellious female tongue.

So there it is. The Scottish witch was usually an older woman, usually poor, usually married, not necessarily ugly, usually strong-willed and outspoken, given to verbal abuse as a means of defence, especially against men of the pompous sort. It would not have been difficult to manufacture accusations against any female termagant that dared to pluck a proud cock's feathers. And it did not have to go the full term. A bit of fun at the ducking stool and a good fright would be all that was needed, often enough. An oversimplification, surely, but useful.

As I was eventually to discover, Christina Larner's excellent work on witchcraft, though illuminating, is not the key to the witch hunt in Bute.

Let us not forget the symptoms. 'How is your daughter, today?' Answer: 'Better. So and so said a spell over her and gave her the use of a charm.' So and so is thereby branded a witch. Or, 'So and so applied a poultice and healed the sore bit.' Only a witch could have done that. Conclusion: So and so is a witch. Or, 'My cows fell sick when so and so was passing.' Conclusion: So and so is a witch. She gave them the evil eye. 'So and so disappeared for 24 hours and cannot explain her absence. Conclusion: So and so has been with the fairies. 'Margaret McWilliam tried to stop me crossing her fields and my horse fell down and would not get up for half an hour.' Conclusion: 'McWilliam is a witch who put the evil eye on my horse. And since I got an illness a few months later, she must have caused it.'

---

[30] ibid p102

(ii) Witch hunts in Bute

In Scotland the chief opponent of witchcraft was King James VI who wrote a book about it: 'Daemonologie', 1597. The laws against it were mostly framed in his time.

The first record of witchcraft being punished in Bute was 1630 when several women, accused of witchcraft, were locked up in the Castle dungeon in Rothesay, forgotten about and died[31] there, partly because, perhaps, no one knew what to do about them or were even afraid to do anything. They may have been left to starve.

Margaret McWilliam was first accused of witchcraft around 1630 and may have been tried for it. If so, she was acquitted at that time. A few others followed: Finwell Hyndman of Kilchattan Bay in 1649 and Jeane Campbell of Ambrismore who, in 1661, were said to have 'gone with the fairies', having disappeared for a day or two. The outcome of these accusations and trials, if any, is unclear. In all, about 60 names have been listed as tried in Buteshire for witchcraft. However, one or two are repetitions: McCuillem and McWilliam are probably the same person.

The most serious cases occurred in 1662. 24 persons (at least, 51 were accused: 10% of the town) were tried in that year and it is clear that 4 were executed then, one having escaped who would have been executed. In 1673 she returned to the island, was recognised and then was tried again and executed with another. A full list of those tried and what is known about the charges (quite a lot) and the outcome (not much) is printed in the Appendix.

The most interesting and the most difficult question is why there should be so many witch trials in 1662 in Bute and why then (and in 1673) were people executed for it?

This question has never been answered before in connexion with the witch hunts in Scotland. The solution found here was not easily discovered and it is unique. It may have no counterpart anywhere else in Scotland and yet it may be that further investigation will reveal that the witch burnings in Forfar and Haddington, for example, in the same year, have a similar cause.

How do you set out to answer this question?

---

[31] Inverary Document p14 note 2. See Appendix. Also in Highland Papers vol III.

The obvious reply is to try to see what about the year 1662 was unusual. What made that year so different that a witch hunt of this unusual size and deadly consequence, was the result?

For a decade before 1660, after the Scottish failure at the battle of Dunbar, Scotland was ruled by the government of Oliver Cromwell, a process that ended when Cromwell died, his son was unable to continue and the crown was restored to the monarchy under Charles II. All this took place just before the witch hunt in Bute of 1662. For a time in this investigation this looked a likely cause. The island of Bute was occupied by English troops under martial law commanded, first, by General Lilburn and later, General Monck. By 1661 these troops had largely disappeared. Most of the soldiers were shipped off to Spain from the port of Leith to help to fight in an alien war. Even before this, the troops had mostly been withdrawn from Scotland by Monck who sat for several months outside London waiting to see what would transpire out of the confusion after the death of Cromwell.

What effect had the English occupation upon the people of Bute? Not much. Though little is known, this is because there was little friction. Any trouble took place elsewhere, in the Western Highlands mostly, where a royalist force was eventually defeated by the far more effective Ironsides. Because the English were devotedly Christian, there was no difficulty of maltreatment under their rule, at least for those who obeyed, as most people in Bute would do. There were laws prohibiting travel on a Sunday—or any day, indeed, for a time—prohibiting weapons etc, as one might expect. But the poor of Bute would have done better than the gentry, for the cess or tax every community was obliged to pay for the maintenance of the English army, could not be extracted from those without the means. Only the gentry, then, were inconvenienced. They could sell land and goods, if necessary, to pay their share of the cess. In fact, the cess could not be collected in full and remained unpaid in part. Whatever they may have been as an occupying force, the Parliamentarians were at least Christian and fair and so effective as soldiers that opposition, at least within Bute, seems hardly to have been considered. Most other places in Scotland were the same.

Instead of looking for answers in the Cromwellian occupation, therefore, we must look elsewhere: in the Records of the Town Council and the Kirk Session and do so just before 1662. And there we find what we seek.

The first thing to notice is that the records for Rothesay cease at the end of 1661 and do not continue until 1673. Why is this? Obviously someone had something to lose by their existence. But who and what? This is a puzzle which will continue for the length of this book.

In 1660 we find in the Records the beginning of a process of examination by the Kirk Session which continues up to the very end of 1661 and occupies the majority of the entire contents of the Kirk Session Records for this extended period. Almost every meeting mentions it and there are meetings every fortnight and even more often on occasion. What is this extraordinary event?

The young maidservant of Master Robert Stewart of Scarrell[32], a hamlet on the north side of Ettrick Bay, has been got with child. As the moral authority of the island as well as the civil, in some cases, the Kirk Session naturally and vigorously investigated every sin from the merest trifle—as we would think today—from breaking the sabbath by travelling or working or non attendance at the Kirk to far more serious offences such as slander and fornication. For these, offenders could be put in the stocks, fined, tortured in the jougs—iron clamps that went around the neck—and were routinely required to beg forgiveness dressed in nothing but hair shirts (sacks, in effect) from the entire congregation. The penalty, according to a famous verse in Exodus, for sabbath breaking, was death. By this time, such a severe penalty was rarely exercised but the idea was omnipresent. If that was the mentality, what would be the penalty for such a serious sexual offence? But this offence was far worse.

Several men were mentioned and examined as possible fathers of the bairn, among them, Ninian Bannatyne of Kames, one of the richest men on the island, a family soon, along with the Stewarts of Bute, to be ennobled. In each case the accused man was hauled before the Kirk Session and subjected to intensive questioning—an inquisition. It was forceful, relentless and effective. The most determined liar would find it difficult to stand up against this and the Session doubted it could be done. For there was no limit to it: the inquisitions could, in theory, continue ad

---

[32] According to the Transactions XXV published by the Local Natural History Society, Scarrell or Scarrel—spelling was not fixed in 1662—was up on the hill above Drumachcloy where a building can still be seen. However, Roy in 1750, shows no such building and places Scarrell at about where Sheriff Hook's House was, on the shore underneath this hill. Today, there are 5 houses there. Being close to the point of that name, they are known as Kildavanan, [as Sheriff Hook has stated recently to the author] as the nearest farm is known. Since there were several Robert Stewarts on the island, this one is distinguished by the place where he mostly lived, the custom of the time. Both Drumachcloy and Kildavanan farms are shown by Roy. Roy's version is likely to be correct because of the sheer difficulty of getting to the building that the Local Historians identify as Scarrel. It is a severe climb from the shore, especially with goods.

infinitum: until the accused perished because of it, of malnutrition, starvation or disease, even. The threat of hellfire, excommunication and even execution was venomous and sufficient..

The maidservant herself, Nancy Throw, encouraged by her employer, actively tried to put the blame onto other men, one of them Alexander Bannatyne, even going so far as to offer him bribes to admit that he was the father. Alexander and Nancy Throw both compiered (presented themselves), were examined and found to have given contrary evidence which was not believed.

On 5th February 1661, Nancy gave birth to a child which remained unbaptised until the very end of the year because the father had not owned up. On July 4th 1661, after months of spirited defence of him, Nancy admitted that Robert Stewart of Scarrell, her late employer, was the father. For months, he did not appear before the Kirk Session to answer the charge—which everyone knew by now was true. Only on 28th November 1661 did he compier and admit his guilt. What his punishment was is not recorded. The Kirk Session Records cease almost immediately. According to Nancy, she agreed to bribe Alexander to take the blame because Robert Stewart of Scarrell told her if discovered, she would be drowned and he executed for the crime.

There is more. Robert Stewart of Scarrell was one of the best men of the community: a graduate of Glasgow University, son of Rev Patrick Stewart, Minister of Rothesay Parish for many years and before that of Kingarth. Robert was a trained minister who had acted as assistant to his father in the Kirk of Rothesay. In 1658, Robert Stewart of Scarrell, having failed to gain a charge and be ordained in his own right, was appointed schoolmaster at Rothesay, a post he was forced to demit in the summer of 1661 because of his offence. Finally, as schoolmaster, he had also been the Clerk to the Kirk Session: he would have written the Session minutes himself, until asked to stand down at the point where he is recorded or records himself, as the author of 'a public scandal'. Of course he was married at the time he got Nancy Throw with child. An adulterer, then. This meant that the usual way of dealing with such a situation (by marrying him to Nancy) was impossible; divorce was unthinkable: only for Kings like Henry VIII.

This is the only event which stands out and it does so with such intensity that it deserves careful examination. If this is not the reason for the witch-hunt, there is nothing else in the records which will replace it.

Why could this cause the witch hunt? Because this man had to be ostracised as soon as he demitted the post of schoolmaster and even before then. This means that in effect he had been kicked out of the community—shunned totally—by that very severely disapproving society. Denied any society of any kind and expecting to be excommunicated at least and maybe executed as soon as he admitted his guilt which he would have to do, he would be forced to seek the company of the group of people on the very periphery of the community: the people who were collectively known as the witch folk: the poorest in the community.

These people were accustomed to meet, about a dozen or so at a time, in secret places on the island, as an important document[33] which has recently come to light, reveals. On his necessarily solitary walks on the island in its wilder places, he would naturally come upon them and be asked to join.

Why did they meet in secret? To amuse themselves, to dance, to tell stories and sing—all things banned by the Kirk Session who kept a careful watch to see that no one transgressed, which is why the meetings had to be secret. They met to enjoy themselves, to the limit of their poverty. They met in secret because enjoyments of this kind were banned by the Church. If this is thought strange, recognise that even today some of the Free Kirkers still do not allow dancing or music. Even in their church today there are no musical instruments at all.

Why would they accept him? Because he was in difficulty and in need. They would take pity upon him. Because he had status and they would enjoy the association with him. Because he had money—quite a lot of money—and would help them out. Because he had education and knew how to do things that would be useful to them. Probably they liked him.

It is fairly obvious that, denied all conventional society, he would take up with the unconventional. He would have gone mad otherwise. Once in that group and in it for several months, he can be expected to have had an effect upon it. He was a university graduate, a trained minister, a preacher and a schoolmaster. Of course he would become an important leader in it.

His own shortcomings as an adulterer would be well known to the entire group and he can be expected to have been questioned about his actions and even to have wondered at the nature of his moral shortcomings, examining them very carefully to estimate the extent of his wrongdoing and doing so aloud in their company. As a schoolmaster he would naturally have sought to teach what he had learned. And so, as month followed month, he would have become a preacher and teacher on his

---

[33] I have entitled this: the Inverary Document, since it was found there. It was written in Bute in 1662; printed, verbatim, herein in the Appendix.

own account—not in the Church of Scotland but in a Church of his own devising within the secret places of the island, though that might not have been how he viewed his own actions.

It is likely, that in his extreme position, he began to question the teachings of the Church of Scotland and to formulate a better way. Yet, any different way would be seen as heretical by the local Church: its minister and its elders. If this man had any talent as a preacher and schoolmaster it can be expected that people would hear about his meetings and flock to join them. By the end of December 1661, large numbers of people were meeting in secret (when there had been very few before) as we now know they were from the new document. These would be noticed and brought to the attention of the Minister and Kirk Session. How would it be noticed? By the tracks in the snow that fell about that time in every age in centuries gone by.

This is why the witch hunt began in January 1662. The document tells us who first gave evidence: Robert Stewart of Mecknoch, a farmer and an elder, who of all men would have noticed the meetings taking place, as some did, on the moor above his farm. The Parish Minister, Rev John Stewart, felt threatened by the effect of Robert Stewart of Scarrell upon the witch folk, an effect so strong that others were being attracted to it to meet in secret. Before, there had been small meetings of the witch folk which may have gone unnoticed, meetings for dancing and entertainment. This was different. This was a lot of people. People were being attracted to the meetings in large numbers. The danger was that he could lose his entire congregation to a superior preacher, advocating a more compassionate attitude to life and even one far more in keeping with the teachings of Jesus than the Old Testament which governed the mentality of the Kirk Session. How could the Kirk Session be in favour of love and forgiveness when they were so unforgiving in their every practice? How could punishments of standing chained to the wall in the jougs in sackcloth and severe fines be reconciled with the forgiveness in the Sermon on the Mount? Impossible. Yet the spirit of The Sermon on the Mount is likely to have been what Master Robert Stewart of Scarrrell was reproducing at his secret meetings (also on a mount or near one) which is the only possible reason why so many people suddenly began to attend them. He was present, he was preaching and what he preached was relevant to them. And why would he not do just that? He had himself committed a serious offence. Of course he would examine it publicly. People would want to know what he thought about it, why he did it. And of all men he was uniquely driven towards a more compassionate idea of what life was about. In a society as repressive as this one (as the records tell us it was) this was a new departure. That is why suddenly, at the end of 1661, the knowledge that large numbers of people were meeting in secret in the hills, caused the Kirk Session to act against their members. The Inverary document tells us this is so. Margaret McLevin tells us that 'she met the divell <u>and a great company with him</u> about three nights before hallow day, that she saw the same also as she was coming from Ardbeg.'[34] and 'she was at a meeting at Corsmore where there was <u>a great number</u>'[35]. Jonet Morison reported 'coming from Kilmory in the evening there appeared <u>a great number of people</u>'[36] and 'she met with the devil when he was going by with a great number of men'[37]. And, 'about three nights before Hallowday last (October 1661) as she was going out of the town home, at Bute Quay she saw <u>the devil and a company with him</u> coming down the hill side underneath St Bride's Chapel'[38]

How else could the Minister respond to the knowledge of these meetings? Since they were secret they had to be against the teachings of the Kirk. It was his duty and the duty of every elder to act against them. And the way to stop them was to attack the people attending them who were vulnerable under the law: those who used charms and spells and had the reputation of giving the evil eye to those they did not like: the witches. Get some information against them, try a few for witchcraft and the meetings would cease.

Why would they not go for Scarrell himself? Because of the fear that they would make a martyr of him. One Jesus Christ was enough. Better to leave him out of it. If they did kill him, he might become the new Jesus, the focus of a new religion. The very fact that time and again in the confessions in the Inverary document, there is clear mention of the devil and not the least interest in identifying this obviously human personage, tells us that this is so. Jonet Morison even tells us she asked him his name and he replied: 'Klareanough'[39]: ie Clear Enough. This was a real, breathing man! A man whose identity was plain. She asked the question only because it was dark. She knew him. Everybody did. He had been the assistant minister under his father. He would have been observed by

---

[34] ID p7, line 26: Herein p 258, line 17.

[35] ID p8 line 19; Herein p259. Spellings have been modernised for the reader's convenience.

[36] ibid p21 line 8. Herein, p269 para 3. Kilmory is under Barone Hill to the west.

[37] ID p23, line 12. Herein, p271.

[38] ibid p24, line 11. Herein p 272 para4

[39] ID p22, line 18. Herein p270 para3

WHAT WAS A WITCH?

everyone in that pulpit at the Kirk, would have officiated at funerals, which every minister likes to avoid.

Pause and consider this carefully:
1. The devil is plainly an actual person, from the many confessions: a young well-favoured man, as most say.
2. His identity is clear enough to Jonet Morison and therefore everyone else.
3. Who was the known actual devil in that society? Robert Stewart of Scarrell, recently exposed; admitted possession by the devil.
4. Robert Stewart of Scarrell is the devil in the confessions. QED
5. No effort is made to identify him in any of the 28 pages of confessions which were recorded over 3 months in 1662 by the Minister mostly, and elders.
6. Why? Because they had a great deal to lose by the exposure. They could not handle it. Could not kill him and could not think of him as continuing to live among them. They had to think that though he had been the devil (ie the devil had taken possession of him) the devil had left him.

Two other matters are relevant. Rev John Stewart hated Rev Patrick Stewart, Scarrell's father, fought him in the Synod and even in the Burgh Court over the payment of the stipend at Kingarth of which at that time, John Stewart was minister. In 1654, the Synod wrote to Patrick 'to desist from purshewing wrongfullie the said Rev Master John Stewart' for the Kingarth stipend which he claimed in spite of having given up that part of the island in 1640[40]. In 1658, Patrick was found guilty by the Synod of 'his purshew of Mr. Jon {sic} Stewart, Minister at Kingarth, very violently and unjustlie,' and of 'scandalous and deteastable covetousness'[41]

Rev John Stewart is likely to have considered Scarrell as an enemy from the outset. Even so, the idea of taking on Scarrell himself about these meetings might have worried the Minister far more. If it came to a debate, as a man of lesser ability (if, as is likely, he was), he might fear to lose. This is another reason why Scarrell himself was not loaded with this additional crime and why there is no attempt to identify the devil in the witches confessions with him when, time after time, it is perfectly clear that the devil the witches are referring to is a human within the community. The consequences of such identification were very dangerous to the Kirk Session. If that superbly educated, wealthy, fully qualified

---

[40] Whyte, p100; herein appendix (xxiii)

minister—a member of the gentry—was the devil, what about others, especially, lesser examples? This will become clearer in the reconstruction that follows. The recognition that he may even have been preaching a religion of compassion which made better sense than that current, may have been perceived. Further, this man, this very particular disgraced man, had to be preaching something. He had to be in that group meeting in secret. He was the preacher and teacher. What else would he do? What else could he teach but a doctrine of compassion? Of unconditional love and forgiveness. The principal doctrine of the sermon on the Mount. It is the one doctrine which made it possible for him to go on living. The one doctrine that excused his own conduct. And—over and above this— the one doctrine that really was far better than the current one in 1662, as the passage of time has shown. Notice also, that they may have believed that, though he had been the devil in 1661 and, perhaps before, he had ceased to be the devil. This would conform to the notion that he had been possessed by the devil who, having appeared in the form of Scarrell had now left him and gone elsewhere. To believe that Scarrell continued to be the devil would have required them to abandon their concept of the devil, which they were unable to do, partly because it was so central to their view of sin. They needed to retain their concept to justify what had gone before and continue the practices which were standard. They needed to act as if the devil had left Scarrell: the concept required that the devil could enter anybody and then leave him when it suited him to do so.

What we have just seen in these pages is historical fact together with inferences drawn from these facts. The cause of the witch hunt is already explained. In the proposed reconstruction of events this explanation will be given life that should make it more illuminating than the bare facts of history. What sort of man was Master Robert Stewart of Scarrell? That is the question. What sort of man would put himself in a position wherein exposure and dire punishment were inevitable, as he would know they were. This is the kind of character that has to be generated. And yet he is highly educated and intelligent. He is a trained preacher and has the skills thereof, as well as a teacher. He is a natural leader. You, the reader, might not like this man. The confessions tell us he was a bit presumptuous and demanding of the women, on occasion, and even hurtful of them, though these aspects might come under the aegis of embellishment by the recorders or even by the women in their confessions to try to distance themselves from him. That is irrelevant. In the pursuit of the truth we have to try to recreate him. You may think his behaviour is over the top.

You will, I believe, be mistaken. As a man, he is of immense interest but we need to know him, warts and all, if we are to understand him and his effect upon the community. You may think some of his doings are unlikely. If so, remember that his ultimate crime is absolutely unthinkable in that society and that time. Nobody in his right mind would have considered committing such a series of crimes as he committed in full knowledge of the outcome which had to be disastrous for him and for his wife and his lover, Nancy Throw. Thus, when you think that he does not do the things imputed to him in the reconstruction, just remember what he is known to have done and think again. Only a very particular man could have committed such a litany of crimes in such a venomously disapproving society which, he is on record of thinking, would kill him for them. Notice this: Isobel McNicol, a convicted witch, confessed: 'a month thereafter <u>in the night</u> as she went out at her own back door she met the devil and spoke with him.'[42] Jonet Morison, a convicted witch confessed: 'about a fortnight before Hallowday last, as she was going from the town of Bute to her own house <u>in the twilight</u> she foregathered on the way with a black fierce rough man who came to her and desired her to go with him...she refused but trysted to meet him <u>that same night</u> eight nights (later) at Knockanrioch and being enquired by us[43] if she knew what that man was, she said she knew him to be the devil.'[44]

What does this mean? That the man who was the devil was accustomed to accost women at night in the darkness. Remember this when you read the reconstruction.

Several historical questions remain to be answered. One is: how did one woman escape? And why only one? Why not more? And how did she escape and why? Where did she go and why did she return and, inevitably, be recognised just 12 years later to be tried again and burnt? It would be easy to give the answer in the above fashion but I believe it will be far better for the people concerned to tell their stories in as full a manner as can be imagined for then the logic that transcends all human affairs will offer a compulsion no record of the bare facts can provide. It will be shown, not stated: more enlightening, more compelling and more vibrant that way.

Before this process begins, it will, I believe, be productive to investigate the document which has not been seen in Bute before, at least in the local

---

[42] ID p12, line 27 Herein p263. Spelling modernised.
[43] The investigators for the Kirk Session: Rev John Stewart, John Glass, Provost et al.
[44] ID p20 line 18. Herein p269 para 2

museum and among its aficionados. The reconstruction will follow the confessions of the witches which we will find therein. And what these confessions really mean as distinct from what they were taken to mean by the Kirk Session, witnesses and recorders, will be illuminating as the reconstruction unfolds.

3. The Inverary Document: elements of

This document occupies 28 pages and was found in the charter room at Inverary Castle. It was written in 1662, mostly by the Minister of Rothesay at that time, the Rev John Stewart. It consists of the pre-trial confessions of the most important witches. These were written down at the time, in the house of the accused person or in the Tolbooth prison once they had been 'warded', the term used for placed on remand.
How did this document get into Inverary Castle? In 1661 the Duke of Argyll was beheaded at Edinburgh for treason. His son, who had been a royalist supporter, took up the earldom, though he never became Duke. The son presided over the Justice Ayre at Rothesay in 1673 when Jonet McNicoll, the witch who had escaped from the Tolbooth in 1662, was retried and executed. This document would have been used at that second trial, for it contained the confession she had made in 1662. After the trial, the Earl would have taken it back with him to Inverary. He may even have acquired the document during the trials of 1662 and made use of it then, as suggested in the reconstruction; for the earl plays a major role in it as we will see. And there is a reason: he was the only person with the authority to challenge the proceedings and probably the only person with enough ability to do it as well as he is imagined to do so in the reconstruction.

The entire document is printed in the Appendix with commentary and analysis for the sake of the enthusiast. It makes alarming reading when read over many times. Some aspects of it are worthy of note here.
- ∞ 1. The first mentions of witchcraft are harmless and inconsequential. This matters. It means that there was no evidence of witchcraft at the beginning. The witch hunt was initiated for other reasons. A group of people had to be prosecuted for they had taken themselves out of the world of the Church of Scotland and were meeting in secret. These

were mainly poor people, the poorest on the island. What did the community 'have on them'? What about them was known which could be legally attacked? Some of them were known to have practised witchcraft: to have tried to cure ailments with herbs and charms, to have muttered spells, usually in the Irish and to have cast the evil eye on people that opposed them or that they did not like. If your cow died and Margaret McWilliam was passing your field around the time it did so—the day before, say—having no understanding of what had caused the cow to die, you might easily think she had been responsible. If so, because she was content that you should fear her so that you would think twice about crossing her in future, she might even agree that she had the power of malefice: that she could affect you and your animals and crops with the evil eye. And so people like Margaret McWilliam had the reputation of being witches. If you wanted to prosecute that group who were meeting in secret, therefore, it would make good sense to look for evidence of witchcraft among these people, some of whom had the name of being witches. And if you were really determined to destroy the group all you had to do was find good reasons for executing a few of them. The law against witchcraft was very severe. It had been formulated by James VI. It was therefore the perfect instrument to attack this splinter group and destroy it by executing some of its members. Who above all would want to destroy this group? The Minister, because, as he would see it, some of his congregation, simply by meeting in secret, were up to no good. When these meetings were understood to be of large numbers of people, he must have felt that his authority over the people was under threat; even, that he would lose his congregation altogether if the group became large enough and strong enough. The elders of the church would see such meetings as sinful. Inevitably, reports would circulate about what was said and done at them. Since dancing and entertainment were part of it, that in itself was enough to condemn the meetings in their eyes. Since the leader was Robert Stewart of Scarrell, a known adulterer, fornicator and deceiver—no matter that he was an educated wealthy member of the upper class of the island— the meetings would be condemned out of hand by them, no matter what qualities of compassion, decency and originality of mind were exhibited by him in this altered condition of his life.

2. Though most of the confessions of the witches are relatively harmless, two women cause all the damage. These, Margaret McLevin of Ardroscadale and Jonet Morison of Kilmory, tell tales

that involve the witch people in murder; about a dozen murders are mentioned altogether, some of them of children. At first this seems appalling. Yet, it becomes clear that these two women are unusual. They have an urge to confess which is peculiar for they were bound to realise that what they were saying would definitely get them burnt at the stake. The other symptom they reveal is what we would term today, 'the hearing of voices'. Thus the devil appears to Jonet Morison as a voice coming out of a stalk of heather while she is coming home from Wester Kames, where she was employed, when crossing the Gortans. These two symptoms suggest that these women were suffering from what would today be called a psychosis. Close study of their statements has convinced me that their tales of murder are untrue. People died but no one murdered them. Had murder been done to a child the parents would have been badgering the Kirk Session, the Sheriff, Sir James Stewart and the Crowner, Jamieson, as well as the occupying English forces, to have the culprit discovered and punished. But there is no mention in any of the records of anyone, adult or child being murdered, apart from this one, which is unofficial: notes made by and for the Minister for use in the trials, still less of any pursuit of the criminal or his trial. If indeed, their stories of murder were correct, it would mean that about a dozen people would have had to be executed for they were all stated to be associates in the crimes. And yet, only 4 people were executed in 1662—far less than a dozen. This discontinuity can be explained in two ways. Either the other 8 people died in prison, which is possible; or the tales of murder were understood to have been invented by the two women who told them in the Inverary Document. It is hard to believe that every one of the other 8 died in prison. As soon as one or two did, efforts would be made to ensure that no more died. The blame for their deaths would otherwise fall upon the prosecutors. In that case, it is probable that these tales were understood to be inventions. Two other symptoms of psychosis are precisely: the interpretation of real events which is distorted and the invention of events which never took place.

3. Why then were the 4 women convicted and executed for witchcraft, if these tales of murder were untrue? The conviction for witchcraft depended upon a pact being made with the devil. 'A covenant' is the expression that is used constantly in the confessions. In each case, the woman, who is always very poor, is promised that she will want for nothing if the covenant is made. In return, she must do the bidding of the devil. She is required to renounce her baptism and is rebaptised by

the devil. Often, certainly in some of the cases reported in Fife, the devil then has carnal knowledge of the woman. Because of this he must lay hands upon her. In this way, she acquires marks which are the so called 'witches marks'. Some witches, some of the witches involved in Bute for sure, were investigated by a witch pricker to see if they were witches. The witch pricker would take a needle and insert it into a mark on the body of the woman concerned. If the woman felt no pain, this meant that it was a witch's mark. Some marks on the human body are not very sensitive, due to these being birth marks or scars of old wounds or hurts that have healed over. So, quite innocent marks on the body can have this property of insensitivity. In the reconstruction we will see a witchpricker in action. The critical factors which make the difference between an old lady muttering spells and applying herbs and a witch, is the presence or absence of this covenant. One other fact is worth mentioning. During the intercourse between the devil and the new female recruit, his penis is taken to be cold. Though it is not a factor reported in the confessions in the Bute case, it is in the cases in Fife[45] and elsewhere and may have been omitted because of the Minister's distaste for that detail within the concept.

∞ 4. One enduring puzzle is that, in the confessions, evidently 6 women made a covenant with the devil. If so, why were not 6 convicted? That is, why were not 5 burnt in 1662, given that one escaped? The answer may be that the extra one died in prison.

∞ 5. Why would they die in prison? Because the conditions were probably insanitary and very cold, there being no heating. Because the senior people of the town were unwilling to spend money feeding them properly. The town was very poor at this period. Because the accused were poor people almost exclusively who had no money for food, especially when incarcerated for many months in a prison. Another reason is that they would be tortured to reveal details of other people's witchcraft as well as their own. The torture could take many forms. One form, the form probably used in Bute, was sleep deprivation. Deprive someone of sleep and they can be got to reveal almost anything. In this case, the accused had no defenders and no access to supporters. Confessions could be extracted very easily from

---

[45] The Witches of Fife, by Stuart Macdonald p110: "Even the sexual act follows a stereotype: his nature (i.e. penis) was cold, and several echoed Janet Hendrie's comment that he used her 'after the manner of a beast'."

people deprived of sleep who were anxious to be left alone. 'If you agree to this we will let you sleep,' would be an easy way to get an admission and the admissions were all witnessed by several elders in most cases. All the women had to do was agree to what was put to them. The very words they use continually are the same, which means they are the words of the inquisitor. Finally, people would die of disease far more readily when locked up in the prison for months with others, some of whom already suffered from diseases before they were warded. This was a time when disease was not understood. Because of it, women resorted to charms, spells and herbs, some of which may actually have been poisonous; others did help.

∞ 6. One of the puzzles is the identity of the devil. Of course there is no devil, no such person. And yet, the confessions continually mention the devil as being present at the meetings. He is plainly the leader of the band. And since he is engaged in conversation during as well as after the meetings, it is clear that he is a human being. Indeed, Jonet Morison asks his name and his reply is: 'Klareanough', that is, Clear enough. Everybody knows who the devil is, or at least, the name of the human afterwards—after the witch hunt begins—who is taken to be the devil. It is perfectly obvious that this human male is none other than Robert Stewart of Scarrell, the refugee from the gentry who, humiliated, disgraced and shunned, has been admitted to the company of the indigent poor (some of whom have the name of being witches) and because of his obvious advantages of every kind, he has, in effect, been elected leader.

∞ 7. Since this is so, it is clear that the covenants were made with him, though at the time he was known, not as the devil, but as the ex schoolmaster who had committed adultery with the beautiful maid servant half his age and tried to put the blame onto other men. The validity of this inference is, all things considered, very strong.

∞ 8. How can this be explained? Robert Stewart of Scarrell was a very highly sexed male. Humiliated and disgraced, his wife would return to her parents. If he was about to be excommunicated, as seemed inevitable— he thought he would be executed (and worse!), with some reason—she could not continue to act as his wife without herself being shunned. To associate with an excommunicate was to be excommunicated oneself. Without his wife, of course, he was driven to make use of the sexual favours available to him from the witch women, or women with the name of being witches— the people with whom alone now he consorted. He would ask them for sex and promise them rewards if they agreed. Since he was wealthy, owned lands and houses and came from moneyed folk—his grandfather had been Commissary of the Isles—they would know that he could provide what he offered. He was rich, educated, vigorous, well dressed, probably strong and handsome. They were destitute, mostly. Why would they not agree? That is the covenant that was made: 'Let me have my way with you and you will want for nothing.'

∞ 9. The Minister, who has been promulgating the idea of the devil from the pulpit, takes the recollections of these women of these arrangements for sexual favours and reinterprets them. Robert Stewart of Scarrell becomes, for the Minister and others on the Kirk Session, once the witch hunt is on, identical to the devil, the devil the Minister has been warning them against and the person they now learn to identify with the devil, in their confessions which he, as the Minister, is writing down or dictating to another who is the scribe. All you have to do is get the women to agree to what you say. And that is easy if you deprive them of sleep.

∞ 10. So a perfectly ordinary arrangement is altered in the telling so that it becomes an example of the actions of the devil, this mythical being who makes people do wrong.

∞ 11. And it made perfect sense to the Minister to speak of Scarrell as the devil, because Scarrell had admitted to possession by the devil and, plainly, from his appalling and inexplicable conduct, he had been possessed by the devil. Minister:' When you speak of Scarrell, you mean the devil, do you not?' Witch: 'Yes, if you want to put it like that.' Minister: 'I do, oh I do. That is who it was really. We all know he was possessed. The devil had taken possession of Scarrell. We will call him the devil, then, since that is the man he had lodged in.' WRITES IT DOWN IN THAT WAY.

∞ 12. Notice that the Minister cannot split the group up— the secret meetings outwith his control—if all that happened was a series of financial or other arrangements for sexual favours. These were relatively innocent, would not even count as prostitution— at least to a modern mind, for these were one-off transactions, the women did not depend upon them and only one man was involved. But if the devil was involved that was different; the laws of witchcraft applied.

Now, in the reconstruction, you are about to witness these innocent arrangements being made. Each of them is carefully constructed from the confessions in the document of 1662 which is why they have characteristics which may seem peculiar. They are not invented. They are this way because that is how they are reported by the executed women—or at least by the recorder of the confession, a different thing assuredly, including transpositions, confusions and other sorts of errors. The task of making a record within the candle-lit prison under the instruction of the Minister or an elder was difficult.

If the amount of sex in the story seems excessive, remember that sex is what is the basis of these covenants and that the person at the heart of it, Robert Stewart of Scarrell, is quite definitely a very highly sexed male accustomed to take risks in pursuit of sexual gratification or he would not have been capable of adultery in his remarkably advantageous position which he knew would result unavoidably in his utter destruction. Probably he had been making arrangements all his life for sexual favours. Many will have involved no financial inducement. These would not begin after his marriage, but long before.

To make the process clear, we need to examine some of the confessions in detail.

Before doing this recognise that:

Several witches confessions in 1662 mention the devil. He is stated to be an actual person in the community. That person has a name. The name is clear enough. We already have a candidate who shouts aloud to be this person. Nobody else fits. Nobody else is ever going to fit for nobody else is mentioned in these old records. This is correct then. The question is how did this person become associated with the name of the devil? The Minister did it, assisted by the elders. The Minister identified this man as the devil because, as Robert Stewart of Scarrell had so recently shown the entire community, he was a devil, behaved like the devil, did awful things no one would have believed possible, given his class, his education, his wealth, his connexions and his status as a minister, schoolmaster and the Kirk Session Clerk. And most of all, this devil had taken charge of the poorest people of the congregation and people were going in droves to join him and hear what he had to say. The confessions tell of a great crowd of people led by this man. Robert Stewart of Scarrell was a threat to everything the Minister stood for, may have had, probably had, talents and distinctions of character—in spite of his actions—which the Minister feared might overwhelm his own. The idea that what was being started up was a new church, a new religion with a far more compassionate message [born out of this man's very able mind and a consequence of his own nature] than the prevailing Church of Scotland—and that would not be difficult!—may have terrified the Minister.

WHAT WAS A WITCH?

Once the witch trials were started, they could not be stopped. The law, the law of King James VI, would ensure that those who had made a covenant were executed.

Where did the idea of the devil originate? It is mentioned hardly at all in the Bible. Yet in 1662 it was a concept in every mind, especially every uneducated mind. Who put it there? The Minister, every Sunday. It was reinforced by the elders as they went about doing their religious and other works. Everyone had to beware of the devil who would put temptation in your way and if you succumbed you would spend eternity in hell fire with Satan for company. Confessions were plainly tortured out of the persons accused of being witches. All that was wanted was their agreement that certain things were so. If you relentlessly question someone for hours and days, depriving them of sleep, of course in the end they will agree with what you want, admit to anything you say, so that they can be allowed to get back to sleep. What things? The things the Minister and the elders had put there in the first place. The devil is this kind of being and he makes covenants with innocent people in exchange for a better life—food and goods and clothing—and all they have to do in return is do his bidding. And he will rebaptise you and you will become his servant. And in Fife the first act was to provide him with sex. These were what the Minister and elders believed. They put these ideas in the heads of their congregation and got them back, under torture, from the people they wished to condemn. Whatever the women said was reinterpreted by the inquisitors to fit their idea of what had taken place. Since the inquisitors had total control over what was written down, of course their interpretation was the one recorded and read out during the trials. The witches were not given any defence or any opportunity to rebut the accusations or even to query the confessions. For every confession was witnessed by several members of the eldership. All the elders had to do at the trial was agree that the confession was as reported in the document read out. That was enough!

And since, over the years, these particular members of the group meeting secretly already had the name of witches—though their actions were mostly harmless—these were the people chosen as sacrificial victims. This was a group, an increasingly large group, of people meeting in secret outwith the church. Of course, as the Minister and elders would see it, these meetings had to be stopped. Burning a few of them as witches would soon scatter them and meetings would stop.

So what do the confessions say?

Here, first is what Isobel McNicoll is alleged to have confessed.

21 Feb 1662 p12. 'Issobell McNicoll with a great deal of seeming remorse and praying to God to deliver her soule from the power of Satan [This is the motive of confession then: to get rid of the prospect of Hell and maybe yet get to heaven] confessed that as she was in her owne house her alone drawing acquavittie *the devill came to her <u>in the lyknes of a young man</u> and <u>desyred her to goe with him</u> and <u>confesses that she made a covenant with him</u> quhairn he promised that she should not want meanes enough and she promised to be his servand.*
Item *that he baptised her and gave her a new name and called her Caterine.* Item that about a month therafter in the night as she went out at her own back dore she met with the devill and spok with him.
Item that about a moneth therafter the devill came to her again as she was ther alone brewing with quhom she hade made speiches and conference. Item confesses that she was at a meeting with the devill and several other associates about Hallowday at Cregandow or Butt[46] key.'

What do you suppose 'go with him' meant? Half a century ago it meant 'court him' or 'agree to allow him to court her'. Even the courting sometimes led to sexual intercourse. That is probably what it means here too. It is difficult to imagine any other meaning. Where were they to go? And for how long? In every case, the woman is soon away from the devil and about her normal business. Since she goes with him immediately and for a short time, it is very likely that 'go with him' means: consent to perform a sexual act. Since this very act is the usual culmination of the process of the covenant in the Fife cases, it is likely to be the same here.

14 Feb 1662. Confession **Margrat McWilliam**.

'She was duelling in Corsmoire about Candelmes about 12 hours of the day she went owt to a fald beneath her hous called Faldtombuie[47] and out of the furz in the mids of the fald ther appeared a spreit in the lyknes of a litle browne dog and **desyred her to goe with it** which she refused at first, it followed her downe to the fitt [foot] of the fald and **apeared in the lyknes of a wele favored yong man** and dsyred her agane to goe with it and she should want nothing and that tyme griped her about the left

---

[46] Cairndow, Argyll, possibly, and Bute Quay for sure. Herein p262/263.
[47] The field of the yellow knoll. Why? Because, with so many whins thereon, it was yellow in May and June.. It is the knoll between Kerrycresach and Lochend on the east side of Loch Fad, Bute. The story of the McFee's removal in ID makes this clear.:p264/5

WHAT WAS A WITCH?

hensh [*haunch: thigh: a blue mark; there were two others*] quhich pained her sorely and went away as if were a grene smoak.'[48]

What we have here is a well favoured young man walking a little brown dog. She sees the dog first and the man next. The man asks for sexual favours and she declines. He reaches for her and hurts her as she draws away from him.

'(2) That betweixt (sic) and the May therafter she being in a fald above the said house <u>the devill apeired to her</u> **first** <u>in the lyknes of a catt</u> and speired at her How doe ye? **will ye not now goe with me and serve me? at which tyme she promised to be his servand and he said that she should want for nothing and** put his mouth upon the sore and hailled it. Item that she renounced her baptisme and he baptised her and she gave him as a gift a hen or cock.'[49]

How do you give a hen or cock as a gift to a cat? Probably it means that a cat was in the vicinity but it must be very likely that a man was too—our very particular man. It was not a cat who baptised her but a man. It was a 'he'.

28 Jan 1662 p6. **Margaret McLevin.** 'The devill came to her <u>in the</u> **<u>lyknes of a man</u>** and **<u>deseired hir to goe with him</u>** **and that she refusing he said I will not...and she gave him....** she never saw afterward (sic) and that she knew it was the devill and after he went that he came bak and asked hir to give give him hir hand quhich she refusing to doe he took her by the middle finger of the rycht hand quhich he had almost cutt off hir and therwith left hir. Her finger was so sorely pained for the space of a moneth ther after that there was no pain comparable to it, as also took her by the right leg quhich was sorly pained likewayes as also be the devill. Item he came to her again as she was shaking straw in the barne of Ardoscidell in a very ugly shape and that there <u>he desired hir</u> <u>to goe with</u> <u>him</u> and she refusing he said to her I will either have thy self or then thy heart. Item that he healed her sore foot and finger quhich finger is yet be numbed. Item that before he haled her that **she made a covenant with him and promised to doe him any service that he would imploy her in.** Item that he asked quhat was her name. She answered him Margret the name that God gave me, and he said to her I

---
[48] Herein p267, ID p18
[49] ibid p267, ID p18

baptise the Jonat.'[50] [*The hurt here is exaggerated: she would not have 'gone with him' had it been that bad.*]

22 Feb 1662. Confession **Jonet McNicoll**.

'Confesses with remorse praying to God to forgive her [motive again for confession] sins that about hallowday as she was in Mary Moores house that there appeared to her two men the on(e) a gross copperfaced man and the other **a wele favored young man** and that the copperfaced man quhom she knew to be ane evil spirit **bade her goe with him. Item confesses that she made a covenant with him and that he promised she wold not want meines eneugh and she promised to serve him** and that he gave her a new name saying I baptise the(e) Mary[51].'

Again we have a well favoured young man present. This is the version written down by the recorder. It is quite likely that the two men are transposed. That the young well favoured man is the one who was the evil spirit and that with him she made the covenant. Why would the other man be copperfaced? He may have been a tanner or fish curer or a man who had a sun tan. Some of the confessions show very clear transposition[52] and confusion by the recorder of what was said or intended to be taken as the facts reported.

'Item confesses that she was at that meitting with the devill at Butt Key [*Bute Quay*] about hallowday last (which the other witches maks mention off) quhair ther was a company with hir and as she was comeing over the burne that **the yong man quhilk spok to her before** reached her a cog with watter to drink which as she was taking out of his hand her foot slipped and she fell in the burne [*the outlet of the Balskyte burn at the harbour*] and that the said young man lifted her and as she rose the company left her and only the yong man abode with her and convoyed her till the foot of the broad waast [*probably waste ground near the entry of the lade into the Bay*]. ....Item the devill conveyed her be the left arm.'[53]

---

[50] ID p6, Herein p 257
[51] In the 1673 document the name is 'Mary Likeas'. See p278,9 herein. This is on p263.
[52] This is in conformity with Bartlett's experiments at Cambridge into the errors induced by serial transmission of a story. Undergraduates were asked to transmit a story serially. After seven repetitions, it was unrecognisable: events transposed, omitted and inventions to explain them was the rule; and these were the ablest people of that generation.
[53] Herein p263/264

WHAT WAS A WITCH?

19 Jan 1662. Jonet **Morison** p21

'about a fourtnight afore halountayd last, as shee was going from the toune of Boot till her owne house in the twilight she foregathered on the way at the loning foot with **a black rough fierce man** who cam to her and **desired her till goe with him** fer that thou art but a poor womune and are begging amongst harlots and uncharitable people and notheing the better of them and I will make the a Lady.. Item he drew near her and wald have taken her be the hand bot she refused bot traysted to meet him that same night eight nights at Knockanrioch [most of Ballochgoy as far as Skeoch Woods, including the farm of that name, and the old primary school was known as Knockanrioch] and being enqueired be us if shee knew quhat that man was shee said she knew him to be the divill and at first she grew eyry [*anxious, worried, shy*]

2. Item..she declared that according to her promise shee keeped the tryst with him and meet in the place appointed and that he appeared clad with a wheit midell and that he said to her thow art a poor woman and beggar among a cumpanie of harlots, goe with me and I'll make the (sic: thee) a Lady and put the in a brave castall quhair thou shalt want nothing and I will free the of all the poverties and troubles thou art in.'[54]

18 Jan 1662. '**Jonet Morisoune**,

'Shee declared over againe her declaratione made at her owne house the 15 Januar 1662 word be word [NB! supposed to be 18 Jan] and farder declared that that night she traysted with the divill at the Knockanrioch [*the land around the farm and the old Academy*], being the secound tyme of her meeting with him, that **she made a covenant with the divill quhairn the divill promised to give her any thing she desyred ....and woon [*won*} her hayre** [here] **quairin** [wherein] **she promised to be his servant etc.** that she asked quhat was his name his answer was my name is Klareanough and he asked quhat was her name and she answered Jonet Morisoun, the name God gave me and he said belive not in Christ bot belive in me. I baptize the (sic) Margarat.[55]'

It must be very likely that the phrase: 'believe not in Christ but believe in me' is an invention introduced by the recorders, the Session men, for it is

---

[54] Herein p269
[55] Herein p270, ID p22

what they would like to think; especially if they were attacking what they took to be a new church with a different emphasis.

22 January 1662
'Jonet Morisone sent for Mr. John Stewart minister and before James Stewart.....That about three nights before Hallowday last as she was goeing out of the towne home at But Kyie [*Bute Quay*] **She saw the devill and a company with him** comeing down the hill syde underneath Brod cheppell [*St Bride's Chapel, near the old secondary school*] and that himself was foremost and that after him was John Galie in Barmore and his wife Jenat McConachie, Elspat Galie in Ambrisbeg Margaret McWilliam Katrine Moore [blank] McLevin Cristen Banantyne Jonet McNeil her good daughter who came all orderly doune the brae and quhen they came to the craft [*ship*] went in a ring and **himself in the midst** of them and that she hearkened and heard **them speiking to him and that the devill came out from among them to her and convoyed her** to the Loaning fitt [*foot of the way to Kilmory, around Barone Road, Columshill St near the mill*] quhair her and she sett a tryst to meit against that day 8 dayes.'[56]

This devil is a man! He is of the group. They all knew his identity. Only once the witch trials begin, however, is he spoken of as the devil. This man is Master Robert Stewart of Scarrell. To the Minister, Rev John Stewart, he really is the devil for he has been taking away the congregation with promises of help, guidance and even money, all of which as a wealthy, educated person he can easily supply— as well as new ideas about how people ought to live their lives.
He has led his flock down the hill from the ruined St Bride's Chapel where he has been holding one of his meetings and when he reached the shore beside a ship drawn up there, he gathers his flock about him (as a minister or schoolmaster would) and regales them with further reflections which have just come to mind during the journey down the hill—a condition most schoolmasters and ministers will recognise as common.

These are quotations from the confessions. Notice that the spelling is original, unchanged, and that there are occasional blanks in the document due to fading with age.

---

[56] Herein p272, ID p24

WHAT WAS A WITCH? 43

It is already clear that these women are going to be burnt, for they have admitted to (or believed to have admitted, by the recorder in the prison and the witnesses will support it) having made a covenant with the devil, having become his servant and the sign of this, the confirming actions, are that she has been rebaptised (as if it meant anything: what man does not call his lover by a name different from that given?) and finally, she has acceded to his request 'to go with him' (that is have sex with him). By the law of King James VI execution is a certainty, by the customs of the time inevitable, in that very cruel society, so unforgiving of the least misdemeanour.

Thus, Margaret McLevin, Margaret McWilliam, Jonet McNicoll, Isobel McNicoll and Jonet Morison are going to be found guilty.

Then on March 26, 1662, we read: 'Jonet Mcilmertine <u>haveing confessed covenant and baptisme</u> delated Amy Hyndman elder and younger, Katrine Frissell, Marione Frissell and Mary McNivan her dochter, Jonet McIntyre mcNivan's wife.'[57]

In other words, Jonet McIlmartin is also doomed already, even before the trials begin. What has been 'confessed', written down and witnessed, must stand in court as the truth if only because there is no defence lawyer and the accused is given no opportunity to defend herself. That was the practice of the times. Even at Salem in 1692 trials were conducted in this fashion. The details of the Salem trials are very complete.

What about the other women delated [stated to be] as witches? Unless these are very remarkable in withstanding the tortures soon to be applied, they are bound to make the confessions that the inquisitors will relentlessly demand. So they should all have been executed along with Katherine Moore who is accused with her mother Margaret McWilliam of murder, Christine Bannatyne who is alleged to have poisoned the Lady of Kames and many others. And yet only 4 were executed, one having escaped. There ought to be far more. It suggests that many died in prison and perhaps the authorities were afterwards so embarrassed about their neglect and ill treatment of them that the records had to be falsified to cover it up.

How could 24 people be tried all of whom are associates, most of whom are apparently present when murders are planned and all of whom attend meetings, engage in charming, applying herbal cures and acts of malefice: putting the evil eye on people (or their animals or kin) with whom one has

---

[57] ID p28, Herein p 276

a grievance—how could such people survive, given that some were executed? Especially when the procedure for extracting confessions was bound to produce the result wanted from the whole lot, one by one?

What were the circumstances of the confessions? Almost all were made within the Tolbooth of Rothesay, in the jail which was alongside the room used as the Burgh Court. In 1662, most buildings would be partly of wood and maybe mainly of wood together with plaster. The Tolbooth would be like this. This means that everything that was said in one jail cell of the Tolbooth would be heard in every other. So witches were telling tales about each other and being overheard doing so. There can be little doubt that the Minister and others would press the women to tell on each other for the sake of a more lenient sentence. Even within the pre-trial document found in Inverary there are already signs of women trying to get on the good side of the Kirk Session by telling tales about others. Indeed, Jonet Morison has a history of slandering others. And yet, it is not as simple as that. The two women, Margaret McLevin and Jonet Morison have an urge to confess, they really are psychotic and they do hear voices in stalks of heather that tell them to do awful things. But it is significant that their first confessions are not of murders. That comes later, after pressure is applied by the Session men. What this means is that the later confessions of phenomenal wrongdoing on the part of other witches are inventions and distortions to add lustre to their own performances and if they are inter confirming, that is because the circumstances within the prison enabled them to decide upon what they would agree to say.

What we have seen so far is an explanation of what lay behind the witch hunt, what the method of extracting confessions was, the importance of ordinary transactions between a man and several women, a known man of the community, which, once the witch hunt starts, are altered, reinterpreted to imply transactions between the devil and these women. This is the only explanation for these confessions. A human has to be involved and the particular human is very obvious, given the happenings in the town just prior to the witch hunt. It is Master Robert Stewart of Scarrell for sure. No one else comes within a hundred miles of him as a candidate.

Many questions have yet to be answered. How did Jonet McNicol escape? Why did she alone escape? Did she make her way to Kilmarnock, as her trial document in 1673 says? And why did she return 12 years after 1662, when she was likely to be recognised and executed then?

Rather than continue in this fashion, it will be preferable now to begin to try and reconstruct the people and the time. From the tales told by the characters, we are likely to understand their doings far better as well as to answer the remaining questions. The story, it is hoped will be illuminated by the exercise of imagination.

But this is not a novel. The intention is not to produce characters that you will necessarily like as people. These people once lived. Some of them would have been disliked by others. Margaret McWilliam was too formidable a person to be liked. Anyone who crossed her would be sure to suffer for it. Robert Stewart of Scarrell behaved so badly in the terms of that community that he would have been detested by everyone in the Kirk Session and all the gentry of the island, though a few would say to themselves: 'There but for the grace of God go I.' Yet he may have been well enough liked before his fall from grace. He was clearly a highly sexed man, he took a terrible—unbelievable!— risk in mating with Nancy Throw, his maidservant. The outcome—a child—must have been an obvious consequence and his utter destruction once it was known. Some men take terrible risks. President Clinton is such a man[58]. They have ability, energy and decency— very great, indeed—and yet they allow their passions to rule them especially when the sap is rising. Maybe Robert Stewart was of this same stamp as Clinton. This, then is the kind of man we are about to read about. He is bound to reveal his sexual history and some readers may find it too shocking for their tastes. Nothing can be done about that. If we are to have any hope of getting close to the truth (all we can expect) we must take him, warts and all. The same for the witches when they are on the Gallows Craig burning and about to die. Of course what they say will be pretty awful. We can hardly expect them to enjoy the experience and turn a pretty phrase to amuse us with.

The reader then, who has a sensitive nature, who prefers entertainment to knowledge of the truth, had better close this volume and choose another. Like the characters above, this writer is willing to take risks in the effort—the difficult and yet noble effort—to arrive at the truth.

Now, within a few pages, we are going to see an example of an ordinary event which will, eventually, be altered by the Minister and eldership to

---

[58] Julius Caesar was another. He had very many affairs with married women which was, then as now, very dangerous and could have got him killed long before he was. So was President Kennedy who needed a fresh piece of skirt every day.

be extraordinary: to involve a meeting with the devil and a covenant made with him—the defining characteristic of the witch and the one, above all, that she will be executed for. But there is another aspect. A murder, or apparent murder, is confessed to.

Part of this confession was quoted before but to make the point about the devil being an actual human, an extra paragraph which reveals a fresh development was omitted. There is no harm in the repetition. Indeed, in the Bannockburn books repetition of written reports at the battle was one of the keys to success— the first time the matter had been understood in seven centuries. There is much good in it. What these meant: their full implication gradually became compellingly clear. So be patient and understanding, for that is what we are after: understanding: to cast light into this dark time. In just a page or two, the stories will begin and things will become much easier.

Remember that the entire document is printed at the end of this work, verbatim and with added commentary.

To make it easier the spelling will be modernised here.

'Confession of Margaret McWilliam February 14, 1662, before John Glass provost and Mr. John Stewart minister.

Item that the year before the great Snow about 28 years ago when she was dwelling in Corsmore about Candlemas about 12 hours of the day she went out to a field beneath her house called **Faldtombuie**[59] and out of a whin bush in the midst of the field there appeared a little brown dog and desired her to go with it which she refused at first. It followed her down to the foot of the field and appeared in the likeness of a well favoured young man and desired her again to go with it and she should want for nothing and that time gripped her about the left thigh which pained her sorely and went away as if it were a green smoke.

(2) That between then and the May thereafter she being in a field above the said house the devil appeared to her first in the likeness of a cat which asked her: how are you? Will you not now go with me and serve me? At which time she said she made a covenant with him wherein she promised to be his servant and he said that she should want for nothing and put his mouth upon the sore and healed it. Item that she renounced her baptism and he rebaptised her and she gave him as a gift a hen or cock.

---

[59] Field with a yellow knoll: whins are yellow in May, June in Bute. This part of the Inverary Document appears on p267.

[The fact that he appeared to her **first** in the likeness of a cat suggests that he soon after appeared in his normal guise as a well favoured young man. We are reading a listener's record of what she said. It is bound to be inaccurate]

(3) That about 18 years ago, when dwelling in Chapelton, the devil appeared to her at the back of the Kaleyard and she, having sustained loss by the death of horse and cows, was turning to great poverty. He said to her: be not afraid for you will get rings enough and requiring.....he sought her son William, a child of 7 years old, which she promised to him and he gave her an elf arrow stone to shoot him which she did ten days thereafter; that the child died immediately thereafter which grieved her most of anything that she ever did.'[60]

[Remember that this is not what she said but what the inquisitor wanted recorded as having been said by her and what the recorder thought this was— all different things from what she said. Would a woman, any woman, voluntarily admit to having murdered her own son? Under duress, anything can be admitted; especially when it is 'yes' or 'no' answers to questions under torture]

Now the reconstruction can begin. Where references are given to the Inverary Document the words therein which give rise to the scene constructed can be studied. Since the Inverary Document is printed herein after p254, adding the page number of ID to about 250 should take you approximately (a page or two less or more) to the very page in the document where the scene is described by the recorder of the confession in 1662. In addition, great efforts have been made to provide the precise page numbers.

---

[60] ID p18, Herein p 267/8

4. The Story of Master Robert Stewart of Scarrell[61]

'These are the words which the LORD hath commanded, that ye should do them. Six days shall work be done, but on the seventh day there shall be to you an holy day, a sabbath of rest to the LORD: <u>whosoever doeth work therein shall be put to death.</u>'[62]

I Education

My name is Robert Stewart, Master Robert Stewart, for I hold a master's degree from the University of Glasgow. I was born in the year 1620 and attended the university at the age of 14, as usual in those days, where for several years I continued the studies initiated by my father, the Reverend Master Patrick Stewart of Roseland, a hill to the east of the Royal Burgh of Rothesay on the Island of Bute. As there was no parish school in our town in those days my education devolved upon my father who was, first, Minister of Kingarth and later, the minister of the Parish which occupied the town and the north side of the island.

My father was a man inclined to rages, and it was because of one of these that he eventually lost his stipend, having demitted the charge late in life. Though he had effectively retired in 1650, his stipend was still paid for

---

[61] Editor's note: the language and the spelling of this story have been adjusted to modern usage.
[62] Exodus Ch 35 v 1-2; King James version.

seven further years and would have continued had he not been found guilty of swearing at his mother in law[63], my grandmother.

I was myself the butt of many of those rages and my boyhood and young manhood were accordingly carried out in a steel suit of conformity, where to diverge so much as an inch either way was to suffer scrapes and cuffs and bruises, so that at any time I could barely count them, new and on the mend. Being the minister, my father had a lot to do. Sunday services on the Sabbath and a regular crop of funerals, given the poverty, the times and the congregation of about a thousand. And he collected rents from his properties. But he had free time. And so he had time to spend on me.

From my father I learned Latin and then Greek and Arithmetic and writing and even Rhetoric and Mathematics. First I had to learn the declensions, conjugations and the vocabulary—and woe betide me if I failed in any particular, for my father demanded perfection and beat me mercilessly for every infringement. He would keep a careful score on a slate every day and by nightfall it would be totted up and then, last thing at night before turning in, he would lay into my backside with the requisite number of strokes of the cane. Translations, which followed rote learning, were worst of all, for there I made many more mistakes. And yet in time, I became a proficient scholar and even enjoyed reading about the doings of Julius Caesar in de Bello Gallico, and Cicero, Martial and Seneca—my favourite—and all the others whose writings have come down to us. And Catullus, how could one like me not enjoy Catullus?

Every day was the same, except for the weather, of course, which varied from a month of snow and ice in winter to hot summers with a lot of rain in between. The household would rise early at cock crow, I would wash in a basin with water drawn from the spring outside the back door and then there were prayers and readings and then breakfast of porridge and eggs or meat if there was any. And then more readings from the Bible and final prayers and then my father would take us one by one and go through our duties for the day which rarely changed. For me, it was studies and more studies, carefully arranged: so much time for this and so much for that. So much actual instruction and so much memorising and translating and even, in the end, composition in the language itself. Under my father's thumb I was for most of the morning. Only in the afternoon was there any respite when I was allowed to walk down into the town nestling between the hills under its cloud of smoke. There were so many rules. No eating between meals and only 3 meals a day and prayers and Bible readings before and

---

[63] Editor's note: Whyte's Lectures, p87 line 41 confirm this.

after each and before going to bed and even on getting up—though, as it was one thing my father never checked on, this was something I learned to do very quickly and even, latterly, to avoid altogether. The quarrel between my grandmother and my father was surely over me, for by that time he and I had grown very far apart and it was my fault: I did not conform to his idea of what I ought to be.

Now, so many years later, I see that it was not wholly my fault. It was me myself: my constitution. I was just different from most others.

It began when I was nearly 15, just beginning university and still staying with the Jamesons, a family with connexions in Bute where the father was the crownaer or crowner—coroner, the English would call it. But it was different in Scotland where he was something like a Sheriff and in some places might actually be the Sheriff. Mostly, the Sheriff was someone else. Looking out for evildoers and apprehending them and getting them dealt with, often by the Sheriff, was the crowner's role[64].

Every week day I attended lectures at the university, dined and studied in the house close by in which I boarded. The Jamesons were a decent pleasant couple with a single daughter, Jane, about a year older than myself, on whom they doted. She had long chestnut brown hair, blue eyes and a very slender shape with no chest I could see. As time went on, I could see that she was increasingly interested in me, though I was not much bothered about her.

What did trouble me was the sudden problem of projecting flesh for which I had received no warning of any kind. Every morning when I awoke it was to discover this rod of iron standing up the lower part of my body. Worst of all, during the day there were occasions when the object would announce itself, sometimes at the most inconvenient moments. Once, after dinner, when I was seated in the kitchen at the table with the Jamesons having supper before retiring to bed. Fortunately, on that occasion, I still wore my long coat because it was winter and the house was insufficiently warmed by the fire. So my condition was not apparent to my hosts.

A few of my fellow students became aware of my proclivity for arousal and joshed me about it but, so it seemed, we were all the same in this respect. It was just that I was worse than anybody else. I suppose it was my constitution that was to blame. I was certainly well-made and taller than most men. Mostly, it was vigour. I seem to have had a richer infusion

---

[64] Editor's note: Given up in Bute around 1680, ref: Whyte's lectures.

of blood flowing through my veins than other men. This, at least, is what I learned to put it down to.

The trouble with my father began suddenly one morning. I had just got up to dress for the schools when Jane knocked and entered my room. Evidently, her education had not prepared her for these elementary proprieties and—as I was the first lodger the family had ever taken—and that only as a favour to my father—the idea that preparation of her in lodging in the same house, a young man like me, had not occurred to anyone. There was no time to halt her outside the door. She had entered my room innocently, thoughtlessly and stood just inside the room, took in my aroused appearance, put her hand to her mouth and gasped with astonishment. 'Whatever is that?' pointing to the area below my navel.

'You know very well,' I replied, as best I could, out of my red face, though I eventually found that I was mistaken: living in a town, Jane, an only child like me, had never seen the ordinary things that are commonplace in the country: animals mating.

She ran out of the room, in a state of shock, I suppose, and I soon heard crying in the kitchen down below as she gave her version of events.

When eventually I went down to join them for breakfast, her father was waiting for me. There was no sign of Jane. He took me by the collar and glared daggers into my face. 'I will ask you to leave this house this instant and find other accommodation.'

I protested that this was unfair— in vain. He refused to discuss the matter and within the hour I was in the street, bag and baggage, having to lug my traps to the university and carry them around until I had found somewhere else to stay.

Five days later—by which time he had evidently had news of my doings—my father arrived in one of his rages, purple-faced, and met me outside the university building. He took me by the ear and rounded the corner into an alleyway where he stood me up against the wall in a smoky close, stinking with urine.

'You are a disgrace! A disgrace to the family.' A volley of abuse followed.

Finally, having tired himself out, I managed to reply. 'What am I supposed to have done?'

'Done? You exposed yourself to that innocent child! She is made ill with it! Has taken to her bed with a sleeping draught. And you have ruined your reputation! —And mine!'

'I did no such thing. I do not know what you have been told but that is not right! I exposed myself to nobody. I was dressing and she came into my room. What was I supposed to do about that?'

My father's head rocked backwards at my defiance, but only for a moment. 'She tells a different story.'

'You mean her father does? Nasty man, then. How can I be responsible for her entering my room when I am dressing. They had not prepared her for living in a house with a lodger. And they had kept her innocent of these things.'

'That's not the way they tell it.'

'What can I do then?'

'You could marry her.'

'Marry her? Why? I hardly know her.'

'Well, they would like you to do that now. It is all that will mollify them.'

'I will do no such thing. If they think so badly of me, why would they want me to marry her?'

'Because you have as good as polluted her! That is what men do when this happens. They marry to make everything right again.'

'But I never touched her!'

'To them, it is as if you had! You destroyed her innocence.'

'I destroyed nothing! She should not have been so innocent. They have no right to blame me! I am not responsible for her innocence or for its destruction.'

'Well they do blame you!'

My father was as angry as I have ever seen him. He actually struck me a blow which bounced my head off the close-wall. Once I had recovered from the shock, I said: 'Why cannot we return to that house and question them about it? The truth will out.'

'They wouldn't let us in.'

'They would have to if you insist.'

'I won't do that.'

'Why not? My life is at stake.'

'I won't do it because I cannot afford to have another scene.'

It was appalling. My own father would not take the action necessary to clear my name, the only action possible; and he saw nothing amiss in this. That was the worst of it. He thought his action right.

This was the first time I realised that life was not just, that fairness was an ideal, an illusion, rarely achieved. I also lost faith in my father there and then. Though in truth, I had always been sceptical of many things about him, many of them ideas and rules and regulations that he sought to inculcate in me.

My father soon departed and I was left to wonder what the effect of the disgrace would be. Surely the Jamesons would inform their relatives in Bute and my name would be mud there?

Before I was due to return there was a whole term to get through and it was just possible to survive, as the funds for my maintenance had been doled out to me in advance.

It was the worst ten weeks of my life, thus far, though I was to experience worse much later.

At the back of my mind was the thought of what my father would do. He might disown me, though I doubted he would go that far. And this affected my studies which, until then, had gone well, supported by people with a more than average concern for my welfare—until, that is, I spoiled everything or had it spoiled for me.

The only place I could find to live at short notice, every other being taken, was with two other students, neither of whom had any aptitude or inclination for study; both of whom drank to excess and whored with the women of the town whenever they could raise the fees.

Gradually, I am ashamed to say, I was drawn into their company and soon was engaged in every vice available.

The projecting flesh ceased to be a problem for the elementary reason that it was engaged nearly every day and sometimes several times a day. And, unlike some of my fellows, I found that I often did not have to pay for the exercise.

Studies I did little for most of the time and I failed the examination that ended the term.

But it was my attitude to religion that underwent the greatest change. Maybe it was my father's refusal to accept my account of things, maybe it was the disaster itself. Probably, it was the effect of living in a town with a university— even one in which the idea of God and the worship of Jesus Christ was as deep-rooted as everywhere else. For it was a place where people arrived from all over, to learn to think and where a few came to pass on their original ideas, though they did so in secret, fearful of charges of heresy.

Away from the daily influence of my father, with his rules and regulations, seeing how other people lived, I began seriously to question what I had been brought up to believe. I saw young men panting with pleasure as they thrust themselves into older women in the back closes and the women seemed to enjoy the experience well enough and I wondered how it could be wrong. What would be served if the men waited until they were married? Especially when they had not the means to support a wife? And knew nobody suitable, even if they had them? Taking relief in some way without the use of a woman was, I suspected— for of course such things were never discussed in a manse like ours—as wrong as fornication itself. And fornication was severely punished, as I had often seen in the Kirk where it was the principal entertainment: seeing a hussy and her unmarried mate in hair shirts repenting their congress or in the town stocks being pelted or even the jougs which really hurt and were far worse.

The church services I grew up with, I am very sorry to relate, were boring and repressive. Who could enjoy being abused for his sinfulness for over an hour every Sunday?—a process that continued during the week, before or after meals, as if it were a matter of spiritual digestion. Who could enjoy being reminded that sinfulness—and every kind was carefully made clear—would land us in hell where we would burn till eternity? Faced with an unmarried couple when every detail of where and how and when they did it, was a welcome relief to the whole congregation from the blasting it was every minister's duty to give us. The kingdom of Bute was a hell on earth where you behaved like a human only in peril of perdition. Beside it the Kingdom of Heaven seemed an unattainable paradise—so unattainable that it stretched credulity to believe in its existence.

My doubts about everything I had been taught came upon me gradually, I hardly know how. The first I remember was when a man, an older man, sat down beside me on the bench in the alehouse, one evening. He must have seen my woebegone expression or wanted company and I was the nearest, unattached.

'You're a student,' he announced presently, surveying my dark looks stooped over the tankard on the table.

When I said nothing, he continued: 'I was once your age and once a student. I even got a degree. I am sitting here alone because my wife and childer are dead.'

'I am sorry,' I managed to say, though I was irritated by the intrusion upon my own self examination. 'What did they die of?'

'How should I know? They took to shitting all the time and couldnae keep food down and one after the other— they went.'

It was a sad litany but one that was true of many. People suddenly fall ill and die and the survivors are bereft, inconsolable and completely at a loss to understand the reason for it.

'Life makes no sense,' I said, clapping him comfortingly on the back. 'I wish it did. My own life is a mess. And I told this complete stranger my history. How I grew up on the island and learned my letters and came to Glasgow to study and how my hopes had been dashed by nothing more than my own burgeoning manhood—over which I had no control—and the stupidity of those adults who had condemned me for something that must also afflict them.

The man peered at me out of the matted hair that covered his pock-marked face: 'If the cock didnae crow there would be nae childer to continue the world when we older ones die off.'

I told him my ambition to be a minister like my father, one I now wondered if I had any hope of fulfilment.

'Why do ye want tae be a minister?' he asked me aggressively.

I was taken aback by his tone but I stood my ground. 'I want to be of service. I want to help people, especially people in need of help.'

'But could ye no' do that without becoming a minister?'

'I suppose I could but I don't know what else I would be. A minister is supposed to help people beyond anything else—beyond helping himself. I approve of that.'

The man smiled at me sadly and yet not unkindly.

'I was a minister, though not like your father. I thought the milk of human kindness was what it was all about. I was wrong. There is no kindness, only cruelty. Senseless cruelty. Ye see it even among ministers, them most of all. They're all trying so hard to uphold the commandments: the ones we were given and all the others we have ourselves invented—Jesus Christ wouldnae recognise them as his flock, never mind his disciples. Any deviation is punished far too severely. It is hell on earth, so it is. And there is no escape from the poverty and cruelty, of every man for himself.'

The man took a sough from his pewter and looked around him covertly: 'I have begun to wonder if there is a God at all.'

The idea shocked me. A statement like that in Bute would have got me a week in the jougs. When I gasped, the man explained. 'What is the point of a loving God bringing us all into such a life of bloody misery? What's it all for? It makes no bloody sense, don't ye see?'

And I did see, that was an addition to my troubles. How could I be a minister with doubts like these? What other way was there of making a living? What else was there to do?

It was not something I had ever considered: an alternative career. Had I even mooted the idea, my father would have stopped my allowance and kept me at home rather than see me engage in some occupation in which he did not approve. The ministry was his life and he expected me to follow him. There was status and security and quite a lot of money really—at least if you added it to the rents provided by all the property my father had inherited and acquired by prudent purchase.

When the term ended and I could remain no longer, I made my sorry way back to the Island where I expected to be ridiculed as an exposer, a condition hardly ever known in Bute. Fornication, slander, swearing, failure to observe the Sabbath—those were the crimes that were committed in Bute in a routine and regular way, though there were few enough. The idea that a man would actually choose to reveal his aroused condition to someone unconnected to it, was inconceivable. My crime, I reflected, sounded as if it would even amount to molestation—maybe even of a minor, for I was not quite sure of Jane's age.

But as I got off the small ship that conveyed me across the Firth and began to walk up past the Castle and along the road eastwards towards Roseland Hill, I met several people going about their business and all were welcoming. And by the time I reached our own door I knew that my father had somehow succeeded in covering up my problem with the Jamesons.

Of course I had to make my report as soon as he returned from his own business. He learned of my failure and suspected my doings well enough.

It was a painful interview and it ended with me—the young man returned from university, apparently trailing clouds of glory—so far at least as the town was concerned—bent over the back of a chair with my breeches at my ankles getting my backside whacked with the strap, as if I had come back to the nursery when my miserable life had consciously begun.

I was immediately confined to my room and took no part in the dinner that evening.

Next morning, half starved, I was permitted to attend breakfast at which, after the customary Bible readings and prayers, my father set about the task of recovering my standing in the world: his world at least and perhaps my own. The books I had failed to study were howked out of my satchel and I began the process of acquiring what laziness and debauchery had denied me. And I was grateful for the diversion. In a few days time it was as it had been before, working hard to learn, to understand, to memorise and to translate: hard put to it by my iron-willed parent. My mother took no part in this, but I knew she was sympathetic.

About the problem of the flesh my father said nothing and I knew it was embarrassment. I supposed at one time he must have suffered it himself and knew that there was nothing useful he could have said. I also supposed that I was different: more vigorous and more frequent.

It caused me to take desperate risks.

I remember taking the family dog for a walk, a small copper spaniel we had. Down to the town we went, the dog on a string in case it was set upon by any of the mongrels of the place. I exchanged remarks with everyone I met, all of them eager for news of the world of Glasgow and its university and how I did there. A lying dog I soon thought myself. How could I tell them of my humiliation and failure?

I soon tired of the admiring smiles of people happy to see me returned and believing me improved by my adventures across the sea. So, leaving the environs of the castle, I headed south[65] up the track[66] and past the Kirk until I came to the fork that heads down to the Loch and the steading, Lochly[67], which is about the middle of Loch Fad on the east side. Since we were by now well clear of the town, I soon let the dog off the leash and it bounded on ahead into some furze bushes on the hill to one side, under the croft of Corsmore[68].

As we ambled down the path, I beheld a woman bending down amidst the bushes on the left. I did not know for sure what she was about, though she may have been peeing. The idea lodged in my mind and, far worse, the image of it and in a trice I had one of my moments. The twig became an oak and I ached at the sight of her, imagined how she would be—there! In her secret place. The image took my breath away and I found myself ruddy-faced and panting.

She stood up, turned and saw me and smiled in a distracted way, as if she had been thinking of something else. I went over to her and I am sure she must have been aware of my condition for her eyes seemed to sparkle in the sunshine. I forgot everything-—where I was, what my duty was, the penalty of discovery by the Kirk Session—whose spies were everywhere—and in a halting, stammering, feverish volley of words, I

---

[65] The 2 scenes following have been made from the confession of Margaret McWilliam, burnt as a witch many years later. See p 267. It is in ID p18. [250+18 =268, approx 267]
[66] Editor's note: there were no roads on the island in those days, only bridle tracks, as well as no street names. If you needed to identify a place, invariably you used the name of the person who lived there- except for farms, which sometimes were used instead of the names of their owners. Thus William Stewart of Largizean might be simply, 'Largizean', a farm at the south end of the island., because several shared his name.
[67] Known now as Lochend
[68] This is a deserted settlement which lies between Kerrycresach and Lochend. Time has altered the name to Crossmore. In 1750 all Roy shows is Crossbeg, Crossmore perhaps having been destroyed by then as the home of a witch.

held out my hand and blurted out: 'LLLady, will ye..ye..ye go with me?' She stopped dead still and made no reply. I never saw anyone more astonished in my life.

Desperate now to have her, I promised her anything she wished. 'Just name it, lady, name it: And you shall have it, if only you agree to serve me.'

For an instant I thought she was about to agree and I reached out and grasped her by the thigh, for she was standing on a knoll a little higher than my footing and I slipped and tried to break my fall with my hand upon her and she fell and I. 'It'll not do, It'll not do,' she cried, rolling over in evident pain from my stronger than expected grip upon her leg.

I stood up first and, realising that she would not have me and what peril this immediately put me in, I fled in a flurry of green furze, mindless of the prickles that stabbed me and, leaving her far behind, raced back the way I had come, hidden by the furze and followed by the little brown dog. All the way home, a march made with long strides in a fever of anxiety, I prayed the prayers of the damned and cursed my projecting flesh which, thankfully, soon subsided owing to the terror in the heart of its owner.

All that week, I waited with baited breath for the knock on the door that would preface a visit to my father, the minister, either from the lady herself or from her husband, for I knew she had one. And on Sunday itself, the terror reached its height for that was where, in front of the whole congregation, such matters often first saw the light of day.

God be praised, it did not happen! It was not to be. I heard no more about it.

But I did have the woman. Ten years later, I was walking on the hill on the other side of the loch behind a house called Chapelton[69] and I beheld the woman a second time. I wished her good day and enquired how she was. Alas, her horse had just died and also her cows and she was sore affected with poverty. My heart went out to her and I gave her all the money in my pocket and she asked me what favour she could do for me. At this question, the surge in me which was never far away, asserted itself. And then she remembered our meeting all these years ago and knew what it must be. And so she served me in a byre upon a heap of straw and I was well pleased. But before I was finished for the second time, a boy appeared who berated me savagely and beat me on the back of the head and tried to pull me off his mother. I was very angry and was made worse when, having pulled myself out, he tried to seize me by the instrument

---

[69] Chapelton is shown by Roy 100 yds towards the town on the road from the Loch Fad Causeway after the Dhu Loch road junction; and on the north side of the road.

and would have hacked it off with a knife he carried in the other hand. I slapped his wrist and he cried out in pain. We stood opposing each other, the boy and I, he with the knife threatening to stab, me trying to cover myself, the boy spitting fury and indignation at me. The woman, who had mended her dress, attacked the boy and cuffed him and punched him until he ran off sobbing. Then she turned to me sorrowfully and offered to finish me off, if I wished, but I said I had had enough for one day.

Her apologies came thick and fast. The boy was a trouble to her, she told me. 'In what way?' I enquired.

'He just willnay let go. He's like me, come tae think of it. He's iron-band stubborn. Nothing will shake him. He always thinks he's right and he fights me all the time. I just canny control him at all. When he gets bigger he'll gi'e me a thrashing. I know it. He was a right trial to his faither when he was here.'

She broke down and wept then and I soon understood the full horror of living with a boy who was growing up without a father present to keep him in his place for the father was often away from home, staying in bothies, labouring for others in outlying parts. The way he fought her and pulled her hair and hit her on the breasts with a besom or anything to hand that would serve as a club. She stooped and lifted her sack-like dress and showed me the bruises from one of his beatings, that I might have noticed already had I not been in such a fever of desire. They were black and yellow—and red, even, with the blood—recent hurts, then. Plainly his temper was uncontrollable and worsening all the while. 'What should I do? What should a poor woman do? He eats enough for the pair of us, takes the food off my plate.'

'What would become of him if you gave him the door?'

'He would take the hale hoose! He would throw me out to fend mysel' on the bare moor! That's the way he is.'

'Well, if it ever becomes you or him, you will just have to defend yourself as best you can. There is nothing else can be done.'

'But I do that already, so I do! But he's getting so big and strong. I'll no' manage him much longer!'

'If it becomes impossible, bring him to me and I will see what can be done with him. Will you promise to do that?' And she assented and even went so far as to offer to serve me whenever I needed her, so grateful was she.

I thanked her for her kindness and told her how thankful I was, for I was a very needful man and the need was overmastering and sudden and often there was no answer to it.

But the bruises and other obvious signs of injury she had been taking worried me and I said, finally, 'You need to have a weapon which you carry all the time, something to parry his blows and return the compliment.'

I looked around for something and my eye fell upon a long thin shard of stone, a very hard stone, about a foot and half long. I picked it up and tried it out as a kind of short sword. 'There,' I said, eventually, well pleased with my ingenuity—for of course a woman of that sort had no access to weapons—'this will serve as a defence. Make use of it and do not be afraid to do so. I just hate the thought of you being continually beaten by this young ruffian.'

As I took my leave of her I told her she would want for nothing. If in difficulty, she should come to me and I would help her in any way.

A while later I heard that the child had died. No notice was taken by the officials of the burgh, for it was a commonplace for children to die or adults, come to that, and in a hundred ways, most of them not well understood. But I wondered whether the weapon I had found for her had been the cause.[70]

I survived my father's rough handling and at the start of the new term we travelled to Glasgow together and there he found me accommodation to his liking: in a house with a man and wife who had no children, who were strong in the faith, like most people and under whose supervision I soon began to thrive again.

Some years later I took my degree and even passed out as a minister with a degree in divinity. After that, I again returned to Bute, this time to remain. My father had often wanted an assistant to share the load of all the Sunday services we had to hold because the church did not accommodate more than a quarter of our flock, every one of them counted in every time, each with his appointed place and duties, where appropriate. And I quite liked being a minister, even if only a novice and viewed as such by the locals.

In a few years time I even applied for a sole charge at Knockfergus across the water in Northern Ireland but I was unsuccessful. Since there were few candidates, I am not sure why I failed. Had there been many I might

---

[70] The description you have just read is the ordinary version of events that will appear in Margaret McWilliam's alleged 'confession' where the Minister has put his spin on the record. In that, she makes a covenant with the devil who promises her anything she needs in return for her service which she offers any time in the future. The devil is taken by the 'witches' and the Session, once the witch-hunt begins, to be Robert Stewart.

have expected it. But graduates able to preach in the pulpit were thin on the ground at that time and I am not sure why I lost. I had to preach a sermon and meet the congregation and I thought I did that well enough. Maybe I was trying too hard to ape my father. Maybe they sensed my underlying doubts and confusions which surfaced under the heat of oratory, something nobody can ever quite control. If you are in a pulpit you are there to have an effect upon the people and it had better be a good effect: it should make them feel better about themselves and come out happier than when they went in and more able to cope with the many vicissitudes of life. So at least I think. That may have been my undoing, for that was not the temper of the times. Hellfire and brimstone was what seemed to be called for. And yet it may have been something other: the old problem. I was not aware of having one of my moments during the few days I was in Ireland but someone may have understood my true nature and seen the danger to the womenfolk I represented; though it was no real danger at all, but a blessing. My father was of course well aware of it, having seen it first hand—or at least heard about it on the grapevine.

II   Wanting Widows[71]

While I was an assistant minister I often came into contact with women, especially women who had recently been widowed. Once, a few months into my ministry, I was visiting a house after the death of a man ten years older than myself. I had attended the funeral in my father's place, performed the service and attended the wake. A month or so later, the grief having diminished and knowing the attention of friends, neighbours and kin would have worn off, for such things are tiresome, even to the finest souls, and, being in the district on other business, I decided to call on her and see how she did.

The house was thatched and small and a bit tumble-down but the interior was not displeasing: well furnished and cared for. The woman invited me to sit and to take a dish of her herbal tea.

While she set about the brew, we talked of her loss and what a fine strong man her husband had been. And by the time the tea-cup arrived in my hand, I knew that there were things she missed and that I very much lacked the same things myself.

---

[71] Recall, that Robert is accustomed to meet women at night as the women confess later at their trials.

She was not beautiful and she was several years older than me but she made her need so plain that I lifted my other hand and touched her lightly on the thigh, nervous as a colt and frightened in case I had misunderstood. But no, she made no move to retreat and said nothing; stood quietly beside me. Her face softened, her eyes smiled an invitation and I knew what she wanted. I moved my hand around her thigh over the front of the dress, pressing inwards and she did not complain. I put the cup down and stood up facing her.

'Do you want what I think you want?'

'Yes, I do,' she replied in a hushed voice out of a reddening face. 'I miss it so! Oh, how I miss it.'

'But what about your grief?'

'I miss the man, the use of the man, but not the man himself. He wasn't a very good man and I didn't love him at all.'

I enfolded her in my arms and kissed her and she kissed me back as if she had never kissed for a year and would continue for ever. She felt me with her hand and gasped with surprise at what had happened to me so quickly and then motioned me to the bedroom but I shook my head in silence and pointed to the floor, a position which could not be seen from the windows. We did it there, in silence, twice, and then once again before I managed to drag myself away.

It was a country place, isolated and far from neighbours but I worried all the way home and with reason. The next day my father took me aside after dinner and demanded we walk up to the top of the hill at Roseland.

I knew at once that he had things to say that he did not want my mother to hear. 'You were seen,' he started on me. 'Do you not know better than to visit young widows so soon after the wake? Even if you did nothing—which I doubt—it is something you cannot do. Ever!' Then began a shouting match, with my lying denials and his abuse heaped upon my head.

I never admitted my guilt, if guilt it was—I thought it a service I provided—and what was the harm?—but he knew what was in me. Maybe that was why he was so keen for me to obtain an appointment elsewhere. If I were found out, the damage—the damage to him and the family name—might be better contained.

I resolved never to do it again with that woman. It was too dangerous. Eyes would have followed me any time I approached that house.

Henceforth, if I went to a widow's house to enquire after her welfare, I remained only a few minutes and invariably stayed outside in full view of any observer.

But the urge was there on both sides and, mostly, it was clear enough to both. The solution was for me to begin a practise of taking exercise at night when, under cover of darkness, I could perform the services my body demanded with the utter necessity of a rod of iron. I only had to convey the fact that I expected to be walking at such and such a place and at such and such a time to the woman on her doorstep and that was often enough for us both. I would usually find that she met me on my route. But there were still many dangers. People did not travel much at night for there were no street lights except in the town and only a few put there because of Cromwell's troops—who were sometimes unjustly accused of rape—in an effort to repair their situation. Most people carried a lantern if they ventured out at night and that was a source of difficulty, for if I went out I was expected like everyone else to announce my presence with a light; in which case, if I encountered another light coming from another direction, conclusions could be drawn by an observer even at a great distance who, afterwards, from the directions taken by the parties, might well deduce who the lights belonged to.

The solution to this was to take care to walk in places so well known to me that I could manage in the dark and if questioned about walking abroad without a light to guide me, to say that there was moonlight enough for my good eyesight or that my light had blown out in the wind. And my reason for being there? Exercise. And it was so. My restlessness and frustration were eternal. My body demanded employment.

I met and satisfied a handful of women in this way over a period of a few years but not all were sensible. Some did not have good footing, did not know the paths well enough and forgot about keeping the lights out in their terror of the darkness, when bogles and other strange creatures (including other men) might be at large and in wait.

As time passed, I suppose, word got around that people were moving about at night and up to no good and I overheard my father instruct the officers of the Kirk Session to keep a watch on transgressors, even though he may have known who was involved. He must have been aware, some of the time at least, of my leaving the house, however I might try to conceal it. It was the kind of thing he was expected to take action upon and could not avoid. Of course he said nothing to me. What good would it have done? By then I was full grown and my father over seventy and in decline.

What is so difficult for others not arranged as I am by providence or improvidence— depending upon how you view it— is that to a young and vigorous man his need is vast, occupies every waking moment. Is a momentous thing that stands between him and his life— between him and actual achievement in any form or career. A man like me is consumed by lust— for no particular person— anybody would do. Thus is it that the branch becomes an oak in an instant and the instants multiply during the day and night.

All the imprecations from the pulpit that ever were, all the anticipated horrors of hellfire that were bound to ensue, were as nothing besides this momentous urgency to mate. And taking relief in some form—an action never at any time discussed— because it was so manifestly unnecessary to discuss it— was just as out of the question—for the most part. In this way young men burned. Even St Paul mentioned it. But I, being of the most vigorous stock, burned to ash every day and was ready to burn again the next.— Aye more fiercely!

And so I prowled and very occasionally met someone with the same intent. Mostly, I dreamed in my head and burnt my very soul because of it. I see now, years later, that my vigour, my unusual vigour, affected my life spectacularly and, as will be seen, my view of the world: that oppressive, restricted, drab, cruel and unforgiving world created by the Church.

One aspect of my night wandering that I did not appreciate the value of at that time was that my eyesight, already very good, became very highly developed, especially at night. The least ambient light combined with my acute knowledge of the island and the town enabled me to navigate easily in anything but stygian darkness. This was suddenly to become very important in the future.

The English arrived a couple of years after the battle lost by the Scots at Dunbar. Three large ships anchored in the bay one morning and by noon a handful of cannons had been shipped ashore with their caissons and the horses to draw them and lined up on the beach just under the Castle with a few hundred Ironsides for company. There was little chance of the Castle remaining free against such an armed force but the commander, General Lilburn, wisely decided to avoid any difficulty or delay. To get the matter settled he ordered the battery to fire and the first volley shattered the drawbridge which had been raised. Sir James Stewart, the Sheriff, who was in residence at the time, brave man, appeared on the battlement waving a white sheet and all resistance was at an end. He moved out immediately to a farmhouse[72] and the soldiers took it over and held it for the next decade. Their rule was harsh but fair, the principal trouble being the poverty of the townspeople who could not provide the food

---

[72] Editor's note: Perhaps Ardnahoe, then known as Ardinhoe, where he had relatives with the space to take him and his family; or Ascog where there were others.

requisitioned by the army, still less, the cess, or tax, for their maintenance. Only the gentry and men of property, like my father, were inconvenienced. They had to sell assets to pay the cess. The occupation hardly affected my life at all. Most of the troops moved on with the General in pursuit of Royalist Scotsmen, like the son of the Duke of Argyll, who resisted for a time but was eventually cornered and sent packing like everybody else who fought the Cromwellians. Only a small company remained under Ralph Frewin, visited occasionally by Colonels McNaughton and McVicar. In a few years time, Lilburn was replaced by General Monk who completed the rout of the Scottish resistance, mainly in the north west.

Life on the island hardly changed. Swearing was punished with a fine of three and four pence [a duke paid ten shillings] and that was new, though the Kirk Session could impose a harsher fine. Travel was disallowed altogether as a way of keeping down sedition but as few people travelled anyway it was no hardship. Weapons of any kind were proscribed, but since the island was so poor only the rich ever had weapons. Since there was not even a blacksmith on the island at that time, making our weapons was impossible. Because the English were commanded by a Parliament of Christians there was no looting or theft or even imposition, especially on those unable to afford to bear it. So life went on much as before and I was little affected.

My best chance of a job was over at Cowal on the Argyll mainland, a short voyage from our harbour at Rothesay. A vacancy occurred and I went and preached and, I think, was thought well of. But testimonials had to be written and some had to come from local men other than my father and that, probably, is where my ship foundered. Suspicions would have been voiced. Anyway, I did not get the job.

My father, when he learned this: that I was compelled to remain on the island—when it followed from the kind of euclidean reasoning to which we had both been exposed that I must eventually be exposed in an entirely different and utterly discreditable manner—resolved the problem in the only way available: he decided to marry me off.

In those days, as ever—when has it not?—it was often the custom for the parents to arrange the marriage. The first criterion was the fortune and status of the bride. Was that suitable? What was the financial advantage to the family? Of course there were other considerations: was her family in a state of neutrality, hostility or friendship with our own? Some families one could not conjoin with, as the great playwright of England reminded us in the tale of the Montagues and Capulets. But far down the list of criteria were the feelings of the persons most concerned. Since these were incapable of getting to know one another because of the weight of proscriptions upon their meeting before marriage, it was actually impossible to get to know eligible young women—at least the kind deemed suitable daughters-in-law for a distinguished wealthy member of the community, like my father.

I had of course noticed the lady in the Kirk, surrounded by her family and had judged her handsome but I never at any time before the wedding ceremony was given the opportunity to get to know her in any meaningful sense. We were formally introduced after church one morning and I was invited to her home and when I arrived, spent the evening talking to her parent and cousin, with her as an interested onlooker who said nothing, perhaps because there was nothing much in her head in any case—she never having been educated to any but a severely limited extent like most girls. Most of the work was done by my father and her cousin who acted as her guardian. Between them, they discussed the advantages and no doubt disadvantages from such a connexion. And at last, after a month or two of preparation and without my ever being near enough to the person involved to touch or even sample her body odour still less her preferred perfume, I was asked by my father what I thought about the arrangement; every conclusion he had reached being made clear to me. Finally, he said to me: 'You could not find anyone better in this place. And I do not know what will become of you if you do not take this step.'

'I don't know what you mean,' I said, stupidly.

'There are whispers about you. It has even got to the ears of her cousin.'

'Well? I suppose he does not approve of me, then.'

'He has his reservations. I have persuaded him that you are a proper, upstanding, god-fearing man who only needs a good woman to settle him down and supply his needs at home. And then you will stray no more.'

'You really said that?' I couldn't believe it had gone that far. I was embarrassed to think how much trouble I had caused. Of course I was the last person to learn what the gossip was and only my father could have related it.

'How could I do less?' he replied. 'They wouldn't have you without arguments of that kind. Of course I will settle a good sum on you which, added to her dowry, will set you up comfortably.'

He looked at me at last, having made everything clear, in that stern way of his. 'Well? Will you have the lassie? Yes or no?'

'I need time to think,' I replied. I was deeply shocked by the finality of the decision required, in spite of the discussions that had been taking place behind my back for weeks.

'You don't have any time. The lassie is waiting. She expects an answer. Her guardian demands an answer. They will brook no shilly shallies.'

'And if I refuse?'

'There is nobody else on the island that would suit. And I can't afford to have you here unattached any more for fear of the scandal that could break out at any moment. People will look at you differently if they see you have a wife to keep you at home at night and they will believe that you no longer have to walk among the bogles in the dark, pestering lonely women who should be in their own beds instead of treating with the likes of you. Some of them,' he added, determined to insert his knife into my soul, 'already take you for a bogle.'

'What ever do you mean?'

'I mean that a few men, married men, uncertain of their prowess as men, have begun to wonder if you are not the person making up to their wives when they are absent at work. One elder thinks you may be the devil himself, because, he thinks—though I am damned if I know why or how— that you have power over women.' As I knew the basis of any power I possessed and thought it fairly discreditable, I chose to ignore the remark and, though red-faced, concentrate upon the unwelcome results implied.

'Do you mean I will have to leave the island?'

'Aye. This island cannot absorb the two of us. You are a great danger to everything I am and stand for and have worked so hard for all these years. You could bring it all tumbling down in an instant. In one night of prowling.'

'So where would I go?'

'To Glasgow or Edinburgh. You could take up the law. I would advise that. There is money for it, as you know. It would take a few more years to qualify and set you on your feet. But you will be less trouble away from here. In a town you will not be noticed. Here you are spied upon all the time. My enemies here would love to catch you and your crucifixion would be harsh.'

Since the law held no attraction and there was no merit in trade or financial enterprise—so at least it seemed to my invariably idealistic spirit—my choices were limited. The lassie was bonny enough, though short of the one department I deemed most essential in a female: the breasts. But perhaps she would serve. Maybe it would work out: that we would eventually come to a mutual regard. It seemed to me to be worth a try, though, as soon as I reached the conclusion, I was struck by the finality of it: the commitment was for life. Failure was impossible. Divorce occurred only among queens, often followed by execution. Ordinary people had to drie their weird.

III   Marriage

Since there seemed to be no effective choice, I submitted my assent to the arrangement. And in a month, my hand was joined in marriage to Jean Colquhoun, the only surviving daughter of a man, recently deceased, with a great deal of land, which would soon devolve upon me; the bosom friend of Elizabeth Stewart, daughter of Sir James Stewart, Sheriff of the County of Bute and her husband, Ninian Bannatyne of Kames the biggest men in our island world and her guardian. So my father had succeeded in connecting his family with the highest society of the island when his first concern was to rid himself of an improvident and potentially dangerous son. This was the more remarkable since for a year my father had fought an action in the Court against Sir James, about his stipend, which, for a time, he continued to be paid after retiring as minister. My marriage was then, actually a repair or cement, a redress and re-establishment of relations lost by my father himself!

But my father's ingenuity did not end there. He gave me a property in which to settle and make my home. It was at Scarrell, a steading looking across the narrow channel to the island of Arran, just around the point to the north from Ettrick Bay on the west side of the northern part of the island. This place had one further advantage so far as he was concerned: it was six miles from town, six miles I would have to travel in full darkness, should I ever choose to roam the environs of the town in search of some widow or married woman not being properly served by her husband. It would have been impractical to ride to town and then ride back in the darkness, for the horse might stumble on the potholed bridle paths and then there would be loss, as well as danger if the horse or myself were injured in the fall. Travel at night, especially without a lantern and even with one, was very dangerous and rarely undertaken except in acute emergency and usually, even then, in company with other lanterns lighting the way far better.

Of course the lady was a virgin and of course she was uppish because of her status—presumed—far better than even a graduate of a university with money. Because of her lands and connections, she thought she was the better catch, though I believe, at least in the beginning, she had some feeling for me on account of my looks. Worst of all, like so many, she was a puritan by upbringing and that meant she knew nothing about the things men do with women and even, had no understanding of the means whereby children were begat into the world. Close supervision for the sake of preserving her value as a bride had successfully deprived her of that knowledge.

Much of that first night was spent in efforts towards her education in these elementary matters. Assuming she would know something, I easily stripped off before her astonished gaze only to be surprised by her amazement. Plainly she had never seen a man undress before and the sight was paralysing.

'What are you going to do with that?' said she. 'What is it for?'

'If you take off your clothes I will show you.'

'Take off my clothes? Never! Why would I do such a thing? Ladies never do such things in front of men. It was dinned into me at birth.'

'Are you saying you expect me to perform my function while you remain clothed?'

I fear that as the lady became increasingly embarrassed by the turn of events, none of which had evidently been expected or prepared for in any way—something I could just about imagine given the stubborn mediocrity of her guardian whom I could never imagine addressing either his cousin or his wife on matters of the flesh—I became increasingly overwhelmed with hilarity and my mirth did nothing to diminish and much to increase the discomfiture of my new bride.

A series of mistakes was then made—mostly by me.

'What function?' she speired.

'The one a man performs for a woman.'

'I know nothing of this.'

'Well, if you take your clothes off I will instruct you.'

'But I won't take my clothes off.'

'Then I cannot instruct you.'

'I would like you to leave.'

'And go where? You are in my house. At Scarrell. If you want to leave, go ahead. For myself, I am content to remain here. Indeed, having spent time and money on the house and garden for your comfort, I see no reason to remove myself. If you are not happy here you can return to your own home.'

As it was 3 miles away and pitch dark, she had little inclination for this. However, she overcame the objection: 'Will you please saddle my horse?' she said.

'No, it is too dark for such nonsense.'

And so for a time, there was an impasse. During the exchange just described, the oak mast had become a twig again but the idea that here at last was a vessel in which I had a right to sail gripped my mind and, even though the ship was in no sense ready for the voyage, I felt suddenly as if I should dip the oar anyway. It was, after all, what even society at large expected me—for once—to do. And so the twig became again an oak, or at least an oar—of significant length and width.

Observing me advance upon her with my manhood so prominent made the lady step backwards. She fell on the bed and I reached for her and threw back the long dress she was wearing till the hem covered her head and shoulders revealing a mass of petticoats and under garments.

'What are you doing? Stop this immediately. I..I..I protest.'

'You are my wife, silly. You agreed to serve me and obey me in all things and swore an oath, by God. So that is what you must do.'

'I didn't swear to have my clothing torn off and my person affronted.'

'Well, that's what happens when brides do not do as they are told.'

I grabbed the under garments and heaved them off without any ceremony and much kicking and struggling from the lady and then looked down upon her. There was not much to be excited about. A small triangle of wisps of dark hair between two long thin legs of no particular attractiveness. But I had never been in a position before where I might view the place carefully. Of course, in the past I had worked mainly in the dark and in a hurry, fearful of discovery. So I was surprised to learn that the lady I had consented to wed for so many different reasons—all of them my father's—should be so mediocre in the very properties I judged most important in life.

I stood back, buttoned myself up and decided that there was far better ground than this to explore and, even, God be praised, that I knew where it might be found. For the widow Spence lived only a short distance of two miles away and it was not so late that she would be abed. And even if she were—so much the better!

I would not have to ride to town but to Kilmacolmac[73]. And I need not chance the loss of the horse, I would walk. So that is what I did, telling her: 'Since you despise my company, refuse to obey and will comply in

---

[73] Editor's note: St Colmac's; now known as Crockanraer. 'Kil' means church.

none of the actions which are customary, I will leave you to sleep alone. In the morning, you may return to your home and good riddance. You are no good to me.'

And so I left the house at Scarrell on foot and, knowing the road well enough and my eyes quickly growing accustomed to the dark, I made my way without showing a light all the way to Kilmacolmac where there was still a light on in the cottage. I tapped on the door and when I heard an advance towards it I whispered my name and my need and the lady inside admitted me and answered it in every way, for her own was just as urgent. A few hours later, well before dawn, my business completed, I carefully and silently let myself out and set off home. At Scarrell, still in my clothes, I laid my body down on a long bench that stood upon the stone-slabbed kitchen floor and, exhausted by the events of the day and without even removing my boots, fell instantly asleep.

After cock-crow, I was awakened by the sound of a voice calling from the room under the eaves upstairs. 'I take a glass of hot water and brandy at this hour. Would you please bring it up?'

I was very angry at this suggestion that in marrying me she had acquired a servant. I built up the fire and brewed myself some hot punch, waited until the room was warm and myself too, with the heat of it, and then climbed the narrow stair with a jug of freezing water from the spring outside which I proceeded to pour liberally upon the head of the termagant who had settled in my home. There were shrieks and then tears and she jumped out of bed to evade the freezing wet that was now everywhere, seeping into every nook and cranny of the formerly warm and comfortable blankets—blankets I had myself been unwilling to share. I laughed at her distress, I am ashamed now to admit, as she stood before me, wide awake, but still dishevelled after sleep and far worse because of the dousing.

'Here, take these things off, you're soaking,' I told her, beginning to feel sorry for her. And I began to take them off. 'But it..it..it's freezing,' she complained.

'Come down to the fireside then.' I lifted her up in my arms and marched with her down the stair, until, still weeping and complaining, she stood in front of the blazing hearth where I stripped her of her sodden garments. And she let me.

What a sorry figure she made! But she was a woman and I had never seen one before in broad daylight without a stitch upon her.

The breasts were indeed small, smaller certainly than I preferred, but the nipples responded when I touched them and suddenly they stood out like little buds, three quarters of an inch in length. That was certainly more interesting, I decided. The waist was narrow, the aperture I could not very well see and, there and then, I sat her down on the bench and opened the legs so that I could examine her construction more carefully than I had ever done before in a female, for lack of opportunity.

'Oh, oh, what are you about?' she wailed. 'What are you doing to me? Nobody has ever done that to me before! Nobody has ever seen me before!' she complained, to which I paid not the least attention, after all that had transpired.

'Lies! You were a babe once, were you not? A child after that? Well then, you were seen like this by every adult who took care of you.'

I inserted my finger and moved it around very gently in the way I had learned by experience and a little instruction, it must be said, by women far older than myself who wanted pleasing and knew I knew not how to achieve this.

The lady was certainly very narrow as all such females are, I supposed, never having been with a virgin before. But, by and by, my manipulations manufactured a wetness and I knew she had so far overcome her shyness that something might be managed. Unused to activity, of course, the place was sensitive, far more so than any widow whose married life had been normal.

Finally, I laid her down on the bench and inserted myself a little and gradually eased myself into the tiny space and felt the membrane break and heard her little cry of surprise but not I think of pain.

The deed was soon over and as I put myself to rights I thought it quite unsatisfactory and wondered when it would be safe to return to Kilmacolmac.

The lady was plainly in need of time to adjust to her altered circumstances, as, indeed, I was myself. I went into the garden and busied myself at weeding between rows of vegetables I had planted and then had a useful idea: I would saddle her horse and maybe, if I were very lucky, she would elect to ride to Kames to visit her friends and family and perhaps even decide to remain there for a night or two, when I would get welcome relief from her and seek it elsewhere in more comfortable terrain.

And so it was that an hour later, having dressed and recovered herself to some extent, she appeared at the door and saw the horse waiting.

'Oh, how kind of you! I can go riding.'

'I thought you might like to visit Kames and see how things were.'

'Yes, yes, I would like that.' And so the separation was managed.

THE STORY OF ROBERT STEWART OF SCARRELL 73

In the days that followed an accommodation was made, one that I guess is made in many connections like ours. The lady would lie back and do her duty when duty called her, which it did, even in her case, a couple of times a week but if my needs demanded more frequent service she baulked at it and pleaded infirmity or the time of the month or made some other excuse. Plainly, she just did not like it very much or maybe it was just that she did not like me enough. I know not. The ways of women are most mysterious and, after a lifetime, I am little wiser than I was at the beginning, even though I have had the benefit of a level of experience denied to most men, so at least I am persuaded.

Soon, having needs that were out of the ordinary, I reverted to my previous bachelor life and took to prowling, though the territory was limited to the mile or two around my own demesne which would hardly inconvenience my father.

In this way for several years we lived and then, my mother having died, my father followed her to the grave, having however taken on a serving maid, Nancy Throw, by name, to look after him in my mother's absence. Since the maid arrived before breakfast and left to return to her father's house by dark and because my father was elderly[74] by then, in any case, the arrangement was judged innocent, especially as my father's character, unlike my own, had been exemplary.

The death of such a powerful force in my life as my father was a fairly cataclysmic event, one that I had never anticipated and never even expected. If anything, my future seemed to be doomed, long before his. Yet I felt no grief or even much sense of loss. All my life he had been on my back, beating goodness into me—and mostly failing in the effort. How, then, could I mourn his passing? Of course I recognised his value to me as a parent: educating me as he had done—and peculiarly qualified to provide me with advantages denied most others, but my main feeling was of relief. At least, henceforth, I need not live my life under the imminent disapproval which was his trademark.

When the news came, it was my duty to see to his interment and settle his affairs, in company with the lawyer, McGilchrist, who was also Session Clerk and had been Schoolmaster just before, the job again having fallen vacant. It was probably the meetings held between us that gave him the idea of appointing me to run the school, retaining the post of Town Clerk for himself, as he preferred.

---

[74] Almost eighty

My appointment was not secured without difficulty, as may well be imagined, given my history. However, my father had been well regarded and I may have attracted a modicum of sympathy on that score. Besides, I was a graduate and that should mean that the young would be well cared for, better by far than by some illiterate or semi literate, like McGilchrist, who, I think, had no Greek and little mathematics. Then, as the world knew, I now had a wife and so could be expected to have completed the process of sowing any wild oats I had need to rid myself of.

IV Schoolmastering

Since the school, which had not been built by then, was held in a room in the centre of town near the Castle, it would be necessary for me to live nearby to save the journey from Scarrell. But since my father's demise, that was easily remedied since his house was left to me. Thus, within a few months, my father was buried, I became the schoolmaster—a post for which there were no other applicants, for lack of a university degree, let alone the ambition, for it is known to be a difficult, painful, even thankless and not very remunerative employment—and I removed my home from Scarrell (which I rented to a tenant) to the far larger house of my youth at Roseland with its spectacular view over the town, the castle, the harbour and the bay that stretched right across to the hills of Argyll opposite.

I do believe that the townsfolk also heaved a sigh of relief—that I now had a profession at last and could be expected to be so exhausted in its exercise that I would leave off prowling and be content with flesh nearer at hand—in my own bed, that is. Little did they know! If they knew. I am not sure that any did. Suspicion is not knowledge and I was confident my few ladies would not reveal their own transactions for fear of the appalling consequences to themselves.

What was my own view of this behaviour? Abject terror! I had no control over it. I was condemned to seek the company of women by walking at night—the only time I could reasonably seek them in something like safety. And I rarely succeeded. But the mast was in the ship and so, of course it had to sail, no matter the outcome. And in my case, I knew it would be shipwreck. It was just a matter of time. My father had known it—probably had struggled with the same cross on his back until age crabbed him—and I knew it. Knew that I was worse afflicted.

Indeed, it may be that my father's bad temper—his rages were legendary—lost him his pension for swearing at my grandmother[75]—might have been the outcome.

With my father's house and belongings I inherited his maidservant. She was blonde, unmarried, about twenty years of age and as comely as any female I ever laid eyes upon. Though the question of whether she should remain was raised it was dismissed in an instant by my wife who, accustomed to a maidservant, demanded to have one again now that the offer was at hand.

As soon as I saw her I knew how it would be but, in my defence, I did struggle against the tide of lust that swept over me. I say lust but it may be that I denigrate myself. It may have been love. The distinction has never been exactly clear to me at any time. Unquestionably, I believed myself to be in love with the lady, this woman half my age.

She immediately cured me of night prowling in search of other ground. I was so completely fascinated by hers alone.

I would get in from the school around mid afternoon and dine at four, after which, Nancy—who had done the cooking and preparation—for which my wife had no taste or interest, would wash up and clear everything away. In summer, immediately dinner was over, my wife would often ride to her friends at Kames, returning in the late evening; which left me alone in the house with Nancy who only departed to spend the night at her father's house, after supper.

And so in summer, spring or even autumn, I was often alone with Nancy in the house and of course I soon began to have my moments.

The first time, I beheld her standing at the dresser washing dishes in the bowl. I could see the light in her hair and the lissome shape she had, even under the rather voluminous covering every female wears. My heart raced and like a person possessed by God knows what force, I found myself involuntarily crossing the room to stand behind her and close to, touching her so gently upon the shoulders with my hands. I am sure she felt the flow of life from me to her and soon became aware of the vigour in me which welled-up hugely, even as we stood together.

Calmly, she dried her hands on a clout and then turned to face me, a face enraptured with shining eyes and red lips I could hardly forebear to stoop and kiss. 'Oh, Sir!' she said and my heart sang with the joy of it: she was not offended, she was glad. Oh, how I had worried from the very beginning that she would dislike this far older person! Nay, she was

---

[75] Editor's note: Whyte, p87

overjoyed at my arousal. I clasped her to me and squeezed her tight against me so that she felt the length and breadth and rigidity of the iron that lay between us. And knew what it meant, fully, in a completely adult way. And was grateful, felt blessed by the joy of it. That was the best of it! No hole in the corner lust, this. It was a passion full grown, right from the beginning—for both of us.

Did she actually love me? I have often wondered. I know not. Who ever knows the feeling in another person? But that day I knew she felt ennobled by my love for her, even if it was but desire.

Standing like that with my lips on her hair, inhaling the scent of her was very heaven! And of course my lips soon searched for more sensitive territory: the forehead and nose and pink cheeks and finally her own lips of even lighter pink, into which my tongue—a first for me—naturally found lodging and sucked and explored as never before and enjoyed moving in those silken succulent places. Why? Because for once I had the time and the opportunity. No one could see. No one was expected. No one would come through that door without a great deal of prior preparation and, most of all, noise. And we both knew this. Until then, every adventure in love—so at least I often thought of them— had been furtive and hurried when there was no time for anything but the act quickly performed and then escape before discovery. Here at last there was time and the lingering was ecstasy.

Of course, feeling me against her— fastened to her I was, by God—she knew what I needed and shivered as she said quietly: 'Oh Sir, I want it too.'

And it was this that held me back, for the idea that I was responsible for her reputation as well as my own struck me forcibly like a rope around the neck of a man who has fallen through the hatch of a gibbet. I stepped back and surveyed her through eyes filled with tears: 'But what will become of you?'

'Oh Sir, I know not. But what can be wrong in a feeling like this?'

And then, foolishly, I began to argue my way out of it. 'It would be adultery,' I told her, 'a great sin against my wife.'

'But do you love your wife?'

'No, I love you. I never loved my wife.'

'Why did you marry her?'

'Because my father forced me to it.'

'But you had a choice. You could have waited.—For me.'

'I did not know you then.'

'I knew about you. I saw you from afar. The great scholar, destined to do great things. And heard of other things you could do.'
'What things?'
'Services you could perform for women in need. It was the gossip of a few and I was one of the few.'
'So my doings are known and I am undone, then?'
'Only a fool would think they were bad things. They were surely good since they were what was wanted by those fortunate to receive them.'
'And you think this truly?' I gasped in amazement, for here, for the first time, was one who did not condemn me as my father had so often, but saw good in me and my 'moments', as I called them.
'Yes, truly. You are a good man, a far better man than these sanctimonious fools who preach every kind of abstinence right up to the entry to the grave in order that the spirit will afterwards go to heaven. How can this make sense? Surely we are put on this earth to enjoy its fruits— of the earth and of ourselves.'
'You think like a graduate. How is that?'
'Your father taught me. I was not only his maidservant.'
'But he did not think this.'
'No, but having learned how to manage the matter, I reached my own conclusions.'
Here then was a wonder: a young woman with a mind. And it was my father had put it there. And yet, I expect it was there already. All he would do was encourage and nourish it.
My own schoolmastering was of course founded upon his with me— except I knew what not to do. There were about a couple of dozen scholars most days—foul weather always deterred some and harvest times and other times for other reasons. The room had beginners who could be any age after six or seven, I wasn't particular, and they gave up by fourteen to take employment of some kind. Like my father, I began with the letters, advanced to small words and eventually to sentences. The mathematics started with counting and tables and not until these were known was any effort made with Euclid. Several groups formed quite naturally, the ablest of which engaged with Latin and even, now, Greek. The one thing I learned from my experience of my father's practice was the virtue of kindness and especially praise. I found that children responded best to both and that terror induced confusion, panic and an inability to learn.
All of this took time to become aware of and I made many mistakes before then. One of them was my own frustration.

After a few months of keeping my hands off Nancy, accustomed to self examination, I suddenly realised that I had changed. That the kindness I thought proper had been replaced by a tendency to fly into a temper at the least thing—my father all over again! Not a few scholars slunk away from my desk who, had I been happier in myself, would have been inspired to do better. I resolved that I would myself try to do better.
My wife adjusted well to these changed circumstances. She rode every day, mostly to Kames and rode from Kames to other places. She was fonder of her horse than me. But at Kames were the members of her family and friends and the animals and the vegetable garden there which she cultivated with particular pleasure. If she knew of my feelings for Nancy she did not reveal it and yet performed her own duties, as she understood them, well enough in the circumstances.
But Nancy herself had also changed. One evening, after my wife had gone out, I went into the wash house and found her standing at the window with her head buried in something.
'What is the matter?' I enquired.
She dropped the article and blushed. 'Oh, Sir. I am sorry!'
'What have you to be sorry about?' said I, stooping to pick up the thing she had dropped. It was my own under-drawers. I lifted them with amazement.
'What were you doing with these?'
Nancy blushed even redder. 'I was smelling them.'
'Oh, God!' I replied. 'You were washing them and they stink. How awful that you have to do such menial tasks. You shall do this no more. I will wash my own things in future.'
'No, No, No, Sir!' she protested. 'I like washing your things. I would never let you or anybody wash them when it is for me.'
'I don't understand. How can you like washing my dirty clothing?'
'I can smell you in them.'
'You mean you like the smell of dirt? I don't understand at all.'
She turned on her heel and stared out of the window and then turned back to face me, having, it seemed, determined to tell the truth about what she felt. As I discovered, her courage in such matters, was ever a source of her distinction. 'It is not dirt, Sir. Not at all. It is your seed I smell. I can even see it on them. And it gives me pleasure.'
It was my turn to blush. 'I am sorry, Nancy. Men are very quiet about their emissions. I was not aware that mine were so obvious.'
'It is natural,' I am sure. 'Nothing to be ashamed of. If men did not produce their fluid there would be no children. And if they are strong and

vigorous I suppose they must produce the fluid whether the proper vessel is to hand or not.'

'Nancy, you astonish me!' I turned to leave but as I reached the door, I heard her say. 'I make do with what little offerings are available.'

Of course this event served only to increase my difficulty. She evidently wanted me just as much as I wanted her. My anguish increased, for my sense of responsibility to her was greater than ever. I knew to the very depths of my soul that if I followed my inclination in this matter my world would come crashing down about me. What devils then would be unleashed?

And so I tried. I tried very hard to do what the Minister, Rev Master John Stewart, newly promoted from Kingarth, the parish at the south end of the island, called forth from us all at every meeting. Keep the devil at bay was his message. Fight the good fight. And the reward will be in heaven. Fail: and hell—a horrific eternal burning together with tortures far greater than the human mind could imagine—was the inevitable consequence. According to John Stewart—and most preachers of the time, it must be admitted—the temptations were deliberately put before us to test us; to make us better men by tempting us away from the road of eternal life by the devil and towards his horrible dominion. And yet, the very anguish I now suffered and the continual drain of my resources because of it, seemed to me as like as anything to the hell-fire promised if I gave in to it.

After a month of further internal strife, I was returning from Kames one Saturday, having accompanied my wife for lunch—she to remain until the Monday looking after a new foal to her mare—when my horse stumbled and fell, throwing me from the saddle into a great pool of water in the road which formed during the incessant rain we had been enduring for weeks that winter. I was shaken and soaked and the horse was plainly beyond saving with a broken leg, whinnying and thrashing with the pain of the injury.

I ran to the nearest houses along the shore and explained my plight. 'Have you a musket with which I might put the poor animal out of its misery?'

After some discussion, and messengers were sent to neighbours, a man eventually arrived with a weapon[76]. I thanked him and asked him to go and dispatch the horse which he agreed to do. I gave him a couple of merks for his trouble and he offered to take care of the carcass and return to me the harness and saddle, the next day in daylight, for which I promised him some more.

---

[76] Editor's note: this is in 1660 by which time weapons were allowed to a few, usually for defending the island. The English troops were about gone by then.

There being no horse I could borrow or hire, I had no choice but to walk home to Roseland. The night was foul with dark clouds scudding across the Firth, and sheets of rain beating the island as if it would give no quarter or respite. It took me over an hour to brave the drenching blasts of rain and reach my house at the top of Roseland Hill and I was completely sodden when I reached it. Full dark had fallen by then.

And yet, a light had been left on by Nancy in the hall and kitchen before she departed at the end of her chores. So at least I thought.

As soon as I arrived I entered by the rear door, made for the washroom and began to take off my soaking clothes, depositing them in the basket kept beside the large basin that stood there, after wringing out the worst of them manually.

As there was no dry cloth to hand I went in search of one to the kitchen where, in front of a blazing fire I found Nancy asleep in an armchair.

At that moment she woke up and blinked and then blushed. 'Oh Sir! What a to do! I waited for you in case you needed supper and I worried when you did not come.' She sprang up and seized a cloth out of the linen box which kept them warm beside the fire and began to rub me down.

And so, blushing in return, for my sins, I stood naked before the fire and was rubbed down by Nancy. 'Think nothing of it, Sir, I have brothers at home and know how men look. But you are cold. Let me make you a hot toddy when you are fully dried off.'

Needless to report, once I was dried off and standing there holding the cloth in front of myself with one hand while drinking from a tankard with the other, I began to have one of my moments.

'It's the heat of the fire, Sir. Think nothing of it.'

'We are in a state of sinfulness, Nancy. If anyone looked through that window now and saw us, we would be up before the Kirk Session every Sunday till Lent and lucky to escape the stocks.'

She laughed. 'Well, I wouldn't mind. It would be a small price to pay for this. I have dreamed of such a thing— many times.'

'You dreamed of seeing me like this?' I replied, astonished.

'Aye, and worse. Far worse!' she chuckled. 'I have sinned far worse than this and care nothing.'

'How have you sinned?'

'How could I tell you, Sir?' she said coyly.

'I am a preacher. How could you not? If you tell anyone you should be able to tell me.'

She laughed in that way of hers, a full throated alto that I loved the warm sound of. Like a burn in summer it was, chuckling over the stones.

'If I told you it would be more sin.'
'I think I know what you mean. You need not tell me if you do not wish.'
Then I began to feel unwell and told her: 'You must go home. Immediately. Your father will wonder where you are and may send for news of you. He will be worried by your being out in the storm. Take the lantern by the front door.'
I went to bed and soon fell asleep but when I awoke in the morning it was to find I had the coughing and sneezing sickness as well as remarkable aches and pains. I got up as usual, dressed and hirpled downstairs to have breakfast. Nancy was there as ever with the cutlery out and a plate of steaming porridge on the board. I ate most of it and then took to sneezing and coughing again.
'You are not well, Sir, and must take to your bed. I will go to the school and tell them to return home.' And when I looked daggers at this insult to my vigour, she added: 'Please, Sir. You are not well enough to go.'
I went to find a looking glass and discovered in it a bushy-dark-haired villainous fellow with red-rimmed eyes and grey cheeks bearded with stubble. Months of anguish and frustration had undone my hale complexion and diminished my strength. Every joint seemed to creak and the places where I had fallen on the legs and back were stiff and sore. Nevertheless, I shaved and dressed properly and made my way to the door with Nancy behind me entreating me to remain indoors for that day at least. I would have none of this, took it as an insult to my manhood that I should be unable to perform my duty. But the pain in my hip especially, as soon as I set foot upon the uncertain footing of the path, rutted and pooled with water amid rain and wind, not much abated since the night before, made me halt. I took but two steps further before I tripped and fell down again on the very hip I was anxious to protect. As I lay in the mire and felt the puddle absorbed by my clothing, I realised I could go no further that day.
Nancy took me by the arm and helped me up.
'Go back to bed, Sir,' she begged and aided my progress in to the house and upstairs where, having settled me on the bed, she left to walk down to the town, mindless of the gale of wind and sleet that swirled in every direction firing twigs everywhere and bringing down even great trees.
There was no sign of my wife that day. Nancy was the only person I saw—though the man at the shore cottages brought the saddle and harness and was paid once the matter was explained to Nancy.
Around noon, Nancy reappeared at my bedside with a dish of herbal tea she had brewed and materials for a poultice. 'I got them from Margaret

McWilliam,' she informed me. 'They have been boiled to a stew and are to be packed around the bruise on your hip.'

She threw back the bed clothes and pulled up the nightshirt I had insisted against her stubborn will, in dressing myself in, single-handed and alone, a few hours before. Now—again, by God!— I was exposed, every inch, before the very direct gaze of those fine green eyes she had. 'Never fear, Sir, I have seen it all before and even seen all of this one before. So it is nothing new. It will be hot, Sir, but that's how it's supposed to be. It draws the black blood in the bruise and lets the new blood circulate.'

She plastered the hot stew around my hip on the clout and then bound it to me tightly with strips of cloth, already prepared, one around my waist and the other round the top of the leg at the groin. The heat was painful and I gasped.

'Now drink your tay, Sir, and you'll soon feel better.'

I did as I was bade and then, tired out with it and suffering at the heat in my thigh, I fell back on my bolster. As she took the dish from my hand, Nancy said: 'You'll get better now. Try to sleep.' And she left me.

For a long while I lay thinking of what queer creatures we all were. Full of lusts—at least in my case—and I supposed other men were not much different from me, even though I seemed to be worse off than all those I knew. Even women had them, as I also knew from experience. And yet we were not supposed to have them, or if we had, to ignore them—as if such a thing were possible—for they were ungovernable, at times anyway. How did other men control their lusts, I wondered? Was that why vigorous men[77] chopped down trees whose fuel they did not need and without any intention to plant crops on the ground in which they stood? It was a mystery, like so many others, that education had not diminished by resolution but increased in intensity,

And why, oh why, had our General Assembly taken such a hard line on all forms of deviation from the expected norm? And why was that the norm? Why was fornication so wrong? Because children would be born out of wed-lock? Why was bastardy so wrong? Did it really matter whether a child was born of church-married parents or from a single night of lust? Enjoyed by both? Was that the trouble? That procreation was enjoyable? God, it was enjoyable! I knew that by God! It was the most wonderful feeling on earth—so wonderful I could not imagine heaven without it. The self evident truth, one Euclid would have carved the initials QED after, was that life was hell without it. And all the elders and

---

[77] Editor's note: Two centuries later, W.E. Gladstone, Prime Minister, would be one of this tribe.

clergy seemed to be of one mind that hell in life was the preferred state: the necessary state for an afterlife in paradise. It was, I thought, ridiculous. Outrageous! Why ever did we accept such nonsense?

Of course the Bible was half to blame. Marriage was to be for life. But why? When some of the great men of the Old Testament had many wives? Why should a man have but one wife when his lusts—and I was not quite sure it was not loves—demanded he have several? But it was only half to blame. Many of the rules, I knew, were man-made, almost as if the leaders of men created them as impossible challenges for their inferiors to wrestle with and inevitably be punished by. Or were they different: lacking in the vigour which made the satisfaction of these lusts compelling? Did it not matter to them? And is that why they set these impossible and actually cruel regulations upon our backs? To test our mettle?

So much thought and the heat of the poultice which had abated to a more comfortable heat, sent me to sleep and I awoke with the customary rigidity and immediately began to think of Nancy.

The door opened and I beheld her before me, bearing another dish of her herbal tea.

'Feeling better?'

'Yes, I do believe I am better.'

'Well, drink this up. I put some aquavitae in it. So you have a toddy and tay in the one dish. In an hour or two I'll change the poultice.' The howling wind and rain battering the window made Nancy go and look out. As she stood before me, lightning flashed and, soon after, thunder boomed around the sky, crack followed by crack, echoing around the hills, as if an army were fighting a battle outside for the very health and security of the island and its people. Her face, at an angle to me, seemed lit up and I never thought it so lovely. When she turned to look at me it was very directly, as was her manner when she had important things to say.

'You are a man who is never ill, I think, Sir. Is that not so?'

'Yes, I suppose that might be said. I have at least never been unwell before now.'

'Then, Sir, you are made ill by circumstances.'

'What do you mean?' I enquired, as if the reason for it had not already been in my thoughts.

'You love me, Sir, I think, and would have me, except you will not allow it. That is what has made you ill.'

'You may be right, Nancy, but what of it? Every man wishes things he cannot have.'

'But you are not every man and you can have what you want. So why not take it?'

'Because it would finish us. Once begun I would be unable to stop and I don't think you would be able to make me.'

'I wouldn't want you to stop, Sir. I have known other men— a few only and only once. You are different. I know this.'

'How do you know?'

'I know.'

'But tell me how. Maybe you only lust after me like these others and as soon as the act is over the lust will be over. And no harm done, perhaps, if we are lucky.'

'Not this time, Sir. Not this time. This time it is real and it is, I think, for ever. If there is an ever. I do not think I will ever love again.'

'Pish! Nancy,' I tried deliberately to shock her into a sense of reality. 'Explain yourself.'

But she shook her head. 'I cannot say it.'

'Why can you not say it? It is easy to say, if true.'

Her fine green eyes swam with tears, tears of love, I think, and, saying no more, she crossed the room and took my hand and lifted her dress with the other and pressed my hand to the top of her thigh.

My breath came in gasps. I gripped her gently around the top of the thigh and found it wet. A thin wet stream coming out of her and when I raised the hand to the crotch found its source. She was wet, wet with desire.

'You see, Sir? The depth of my want of you.'

'Oh Nancy! What are we to do? You must go away. To save your life, you must leave this house!'

'I cannot Sir, I cannot. I will not!' And she left the room, slamming the door behind her.

V Nancy

Though I had had perforce to pray whenever I preached, it was not an activity from which I myself ever derived benefit. That afternoon, I prayed as never before, prayed that I would be preserved from this abyss of moral depravity which beckoned and to which I was drawn, moment by moment; prayed to an unseen God in whose existence I had for years been doubtful and yet I prayed, for his followers on the island were harsh in their judgements and in their punishments. The fires of hell were unlikely to be as painful as those devised by my fellow men. It was, I concluded, not depravity which drove me, still less moral depravity. How could it be when it was as natural as breathing that I should come to love this delightful creature?—who also loved me—so much was obvious! That I should be compelled to mate with her? For was I not constructed to do just that—and do it before I did anything else? To mate and mate and maaaaaaaaaaaate! It was what my flesh and blood cried out to do, by God! Lying abed with nothing else to do, in the warmth, and after ministration by the loveliest creature on the planet, I feared I would never again become inert, and would forever be an embarrassment wherever I went.

I did not see her for some time. At length— at what length!— after it had grown dark, she returned to change the poultice which had grown cold and give me some more of her herbal infusion and some meat and bread and a soup she had made of leeks and cabbage and potatoes. All this she did for me and said not a word. I drank in the scent of her, the gentle perfume of her desire floating above me within a hand's touch and I ached and ached and when the bed clothes were removed at last for the renewal of the poultice, her head lifted suddenly and she gasped at the sight and then set to work and rebandaged me and then, in a hushed silence and with bowed head, left me to myself.

I never heard her leave that night. Long after the moon came up I rose with difficulty from the bed to make water and, rather than go downstairs and outside in the cold, I tried to use the chamber pot and could not without soaking myself, for the instrument was vertical and could only be aimed correctly if I were some distance away and on my knees. Even so, I made a mess because of the splashing and gave it up to stand at the window which I opened full length so that the gale which blew unabated in that impressive storm fluttered the very bed clothes as I pished and the stream blew full circle back in my face.

Behind me I heard a voice cry: 'Oh, Sir, Sir, what are you doing? Close the window or we'll freeze.' She pushed past and shut the window with a bang and then saw what I had been doing. 'Tush, Sir, tush, why do you do this?'

I said nothing and hirpled back to the bed, face crimson with embarrassment, hidden, fortunately by the sudden gloom, the candle in her hand having blown out.

'I am sorry, Sir. I see what happened. There, I'll strike a light and clear up the mess.'

'Have you not a home to go to? Won't your father wonder where you are?'

'I have been home, Sir. I told them about your accident and how you needed care and that your lady was at Kames[78], cut off by the storm. That was an hour or two ago. We agreed it would be best if I stayed to look after you.'

I lay watching her in the dim light which cast great shadows around the eaves. She wore a white nightdress and her golden hair was flowing freely around her shoulders in waves I thought might drown me. Clouts were got and the mess soon cleaned up and even sweet smelling scent to mask the acrid taint of pish. When all was finished and cleared away, she came back to the door and stood in front of the light, highlighted by which I could not avoid seeing her crotch and even the light hairs which surrounded it and the mound above.

'Is your thigh feeling better, Sir?' I told her it was, much better.

She watched me for a moment and then turned to blow out the candle, saying as she did so: 'I am going to do something now, Sir, which will make it better for sure by morning. It is the best medicine of all. And it is all my doing.' And then, lifting the blankets, 'It is even the best medicine for me too.' And she joined me in the bed and I felt her warmth against me and cried out with the joy of it.

'But this could cost our lives, Nancy, do you realise that?'

'I know, Sir. But I would far rather know heaven now and be sure of having enjoyed it, than wait for a heaven after death which I may never experience.'

'But what are you saying, Nancy? That there is no heaven?'

'I don't know. But I know this. This is very heaven and I can imagine no other.'

Knowing that I was ready— God knows I had been ready all day, almost without exception—she leaned across me and kissed me and said: 'You are not the one doing this, Sir. It is me and me alone. You are not to blame, then.'

'But I can easily throw you off. It is what I ought to do.'

'How can you? How can you be expected to? Is it not more than flesh and blood could bear? No one will ever expect it. It is my doing.'

---

[78] They called Port Bannatyne, 'Kames' in 1662; often 'The Kames'.

She came over me and I felt her weight and she pressed down gently upon me and it was like a hot knife entering soft butter, also hot, the thing was managed so easily.

How do you describe heaven? It is a place and time of utmost sensation—all of it good, unequalled in intensity, like nothing ever experienced before. Every fibre of our being is engaged, striving to combine fully to raise the heights of feeling in the other. It is a giving and because of it, a receiving and for me, if anything, the giving was the greatest part of it. Nancy's ecstasy enhanced my own.

Yet, though the place and time were heaven, it was a heaven that did not last for long. So wound up by the anticipation—which I did not in truth foresee, yet still anticipation—acts committed in the mind's eye which I never quite expected to be realities—the release was sudden, premature and involuntary in a shuddering burst that left me quivering beneath her. And I knew she was not finished and I nearly wept for sorrow.

'No matter, Sir, no matter,' she murmured in my ear. 'Another time. It is still heaven for me.'

And yet we continued, for the oak remained a branch and one almost as big as an oak, And so it was that Nancy enjoyed her release, except—so she said afterwards—it seemed to come in waves. What bliss was it to feel her breasts upon mine and see her rapture by the light of the candle, that golden haired, green-eyed face transfixed by joy.

Time stood still until at last she sighed and stopped moving and we lay exhausted together. But we never came apart. I suppose that is one of the things that define the intensity, something I never imagined before. That we would not want to separate, would not have to separate, for the energy and vigour were still available and still pressing. I never knew a mating like it before that time.

Eventually, we moved again and, before sleep took us, we reached heaven twice more.

'Next time or the one after,' said Nancy sleepily, as she finally detached herself, 'we'll arrive at the same moment.'

In the morning, when I awoke, I felt like a God—or at least how I imagine a God (one of my Greek ones anyway) might feel. Nancy was gone. I lay wondering at what had become of us and shook my head with the worry of it. Then Nancy arrived with a dish of porridge and bent over the bed to hand it to me. But I had no time for breakfast. The sight of her relighted the fires in my groin and I pushed aside the plate and got up and pressed her to me. 'You'll spill the porridge,' she said with a chuckle.

'Put it down then, for it is not what I need right now.'

Some time passed before I ate my breakfast which was quite cold by then. As we dressed, I said: 'You must call me Robert, for it is my name.'

'No, Sir, I must not. I might forget when your wife is about and then what would she think?'

I conceded the point. 'I am very worried, Nancy. We must use one of the things the French employ. I will have to find out what to do. A thin cloth placed over me beforehand, perhaps.'

'No, Sir.'

'Why ever not? I must withdraw then, in time to avoid soaking you with seed.'

'No, Sir.'

'What do you mean? Do you *want* to have a child?'

'Of course, Sir. It is what I need, what I crave and it must be your child.'

'I don't understand!' I shouted. 'I am a married man. You are unmarried. If you are with child, you will be publicly rebuked by the Session. You could be killed for it. Do you want that?'

'Of course not, Sir.'

'Well then? Explain yourself. We must avoid having children. Maybe we should avoid each other altogether. You could take a position elsewhere. You would be safe there.'

'Safe from whom?'

'From me. Who else? Do you think I could have you around this house every day and not...not.'

'Not what, Sir? It has a word. Don't go all hypocritical on me now, Sir.'

'Fornicate then.'

'It isn't fornication, Sir. That is not the right word for us, Sir.'

'No, Nancy, you're right. But that is the word they will use.'

'We are above them, Sir. You love me and I know it and I love you. It is all that matters.'

'It isn't all, Nancy! It isn't all! Think about it! We can't marry because I already have a wife. Well then, we cannot do...what we do.. and remain respectable. In this community, that means we will be punished. Maybe excommunicated. Possibly killed. How can you view that near certainty with equanimity? I do not understand you.'

'You do love me, do you not, Sir?'

'Of course. Have I not proved it?'

'Yes,'—and she left off the direct look to laugh loudly and with glee—'Oh yes! But don't you see? We have found heaven in each other. We do not need to wait for it to come after we are dead. And we may be dead tomorrow—of ague or the coughing sickness or the pox or the canker or any number of things, including a pure accident brought about by the weather—the kind that happened to you just a few days ago.'

She gripped me by the shoulders and looked directly into my eyes. 'Yes, we must try to deceive your wife. Yes, we must try to deceive all the self righteous religious fanatics around here. But whatever we do, we must not deprive ourselves of our heaven. How could we give this up? And why should we? To please them? Of course not! They will never see heaven. Never in a million years. Most will never see it after death whatever good they do. I do not even believe it exists at all. But we have it! And we must preserve it. And let it be no shoddy, half-hearted thing. Let us keep our faith. In each other.'

'But we can do that and yet take precautions.'

'Nonsense, Sir. That is to play their game, to bow before their stupid rules of conduct. Why should we cheapen what we have?'

She turned to the window and looked out at the effects of the storm which had abated in the night. Trees were down everywhere. Some of them, I reflected, in a rare moment of amusement, were oaks. Then she turned back to face me. 'We have heaven in our hands, Sir. Right now. Never let us lose it or give it away or diminish it. Hold on to it, Sir.'

I protested, laughing: 'But you will not call me Robert. You will not call me by my name.' She grinned. 'Well then, when your wife is out you will be *Robert* and when she is in you will be *Sir*. And if I forget or get mixed up because I am drunk with love for you or she returns unexpectedly and I do not realise it—then, Sir—Robert—she will know and our heaven may be at an end.'

It was my turn to grip her shoulders and stare into the green eyes whose sparkle captivated my heart and soul. 'Depend upon it, Nancy, we are doomed. One way or another this will come out. It cannot be kept secret. I am afraid.'

'I know, Sir—Robert—that is why I made it happen to you and not you to me. You are not to blame.'

'Of course I am to blame. I let it happen when I could have prevented it. God knows I took you and made it happen to you this morning. I rode you like a horse. I was so deep inside you I thought I would burst us both. That makes me fully responsible. The Session will think nothing of your quibbles.' She said nothing and I added: 'I wonder, Nancy, if you will always love me and what you will think then if you do not. You seem very sure that this love of ours is forever. But maybe it is not.'

'Then we must let time be the judge. If there will be other loves I will accept them gladly. But I doubt they could ever be what this one is. I will never be sharper in my love than at this age and at this moment. Everything else, everything that follows of my life, is downhill. This I know.' I often pondered her word 'sharper'. I think she meant that the process of aging must lessen her appreciation and the very intensity of her sensations.

And so, at the beginning of 1660 began the happy time, a time of deception but a time of intense pleasure of a quality difficult to imagine before and impossible to recollect after with anything but nostalgia for wonders now vanished away like our youth.

My wife appeared after noon and, having observed that my hurts had not amounted to much, took up as before, except that the winter being severe, there were few trips to Kames until it improved. As she was neither a housewife nor a reader, time lay heavy upon her hands. Embroidery she resorted to on such occasions. With Nancy's consent I continued to serve her as before for form's sake, except that the frequency gradually diminished which, I suspect, pleased the lady well enough, for it was a duty in which she took little pleasure.

Nancy made a duty of busying herself in the care of our animals in the stable outside and I, having made repairs to an outbuilding, lit a fire there each day and affected a hobby of carpentry, though my projects did not advance very quickly. Every evening before Nancy had to leave and often during the day as well, she would steal into my workshop and we would copulate joyfully.

If my wife ever wanted either of us, it was too cold for her to venture out and she would call from the house. So the deception was arranged to advantage.

But no progress could I make to the problem of childbirth. If I tried to remove myself before I was finished she would tighten her legs and attempt to retain my position despite my efforts, complaining at the loss, so that in the resulting flurry to escape, I would fire my shots into her just the same. Nor, despite many efforts on my part to construct some sort of device such as the French use to contain them and preserve her from their ill effects, as I judged, would she allow any cheapening of the acts she performed with so much relish. 'Why can you not understand that I want your seed? I live for it. The more the merrier. I love it because it is you and you are giving it to me—with such quantity and regularity. It is a blessing! I am blessed by it. And if I am very lucky I will make use of it, bring a new person into the world—this fairly abominable world of fear and poverty and over regulation.' Once, when—so excited was I—I fired prematurely, she wiped up the seed with her hand and swallowed it, joyfully, wiping the residue inside her self.

Mystified by her attitude and under increasing control by her because of it, I enquired about this. She replied: 'I love you to come in the way you do, spurting forth the seed. I just love to see it happen and I try to imagine what it is like when it hits me inside. It is a hit, you know.'

'How do you know?'

'I saw you. I saw it happen to you. It was like a jet of musket shot. It flew into the air at least a foot.'

'When was this?'

'Once, long ago, when you were having one of your moments, as you call them. You were in the house and thought no one was looking. I saw you through a window. It was very arousing. I wanted you very badly after that. I dreamed of you firing your jet into me.' And she smiled, that golden smile of hers and added: 'And now you have. And I love it so! And I love you so!'

How was I, a mere mortal man, to deny the validity of this? To argue that it should not be or was not right between persons like us? I was completely absorbed by her, in her—as often as could be managed, by God—and a happier man could not be imagined, even though I knew it was a happiness with a finite term. Though not unexpected, for mortals.

Nancy's view that this heaven we had must not be given up by us until— if ever—it was taken from us by forces too strong to resist, even to save our lives, was too idealistic for me to argue against, too noble by far for any quibbling by me. I was being treated as a God might be, a God in heaven, and it was entirely proper, it seemed to me, to go along with it without complaint.

All thought of duty to religion or to that Presbyterian God of Bute, a different one, I am now persuaded, than my own, or to the regulations in force—all of this was outside my concern— or so at least it seemed then.

My work at the school became, I think, very good. My heart and mind and spirit were never in such harmony and my face shone with inspiration, so at least Nancy averred happily. I felt like the holy trinity was in me and I was the holy trinity. I taught like a man with a mission: shot messages of love around the drab classroom at every one of the scholars, be he ne'er so dull and ignorant. And I got it back in their progress which went on by leaps and bounds, so that they came to class full of anticipation, clamoured for my attention and left, reluctantly, burbling with joy at what they had learned, so that I had to kick them out to get rid of them in order that I could get home to my golden maiden.

Even the iron men of the Session came to applaud my efforts. Some visited to see what I was about: whether I was worth the salary and left content—better even! The schoolmastering was soon seen as an asset to the town, one that would in time lead to its improvement when its small citizens took up the challenge of enterprise and ideas and made everybody rich. I was talked about as a coming man and spoken of as a future provost and even a possible commissioner to the Parliament in Edinburgh.

VI Dinner with the Devil

It was not long before Sir James Stewart himself, the greatest man of our island world, had us both to dinner: myself and the lady I was presumed to love: my wife. By this time, he had reoccupied the Castle after the departure of the troops of the Westminster Parliament who, before leaving for London with General Monck to try to clarify the succession after the death of the Lord Protector, Oliver Cromwell, had thrown down enough of our castle walls to make a future defence against them impossible. Yet the great hall and other living quarters remained. In these had lived these last ten years, the officers of the occupying army, now recently departed.

In view of the importance of the occasion, we rode[79] to the Castle where the horses were tethered for us outside. We dined before a great blazing fire in the hall, which had been refurbished since the departure of the English, on silver plate served by an array of flunkies, most of whom I recognised from the town. A few were my pupils.

Sir James was a very portly man by this time with a tonsure of white hair, alone of the company in gaudy attire: scarlet coat and grey breeches. Also present were his lady, Grizell, McGilchrist, the Town Clerk, also the Provost that year and, John Glass—another great man of the Town Council— and the Reverend Master John Stewart, recently removed from Kingarth, the Parish at the south of Bute, each with his accompanying wife, all in Sunday best black. Except for the Minister, that is; for his wife had recently died after a long illness and he himself had not preached for

---

[79] According to John Blain who was a fine scholar, there were no wheeled vehicles on the island until after his arrival in the 18th century. If true, even Sir James would not have a carriage on Bute, though he would hire one in London and Edinburgh when visiting on personal or public business. Yet why would Sir James not keep a carriage on Bute? Or Ninian Bannatyne, who also was really rich? Maybe Blain was wrong. Since he was a very good scholar, he will be taken to be correct. There was not enough work, then, to keep a blacksmith on the island to repair axles and wheels, which may be the reason. The 1792 survey confirms this for 1772 with the caveat: except at Mount Stuart.

years because of it and his own. I knew him slightly because he had rented a house from me, the manse at the top of the town being under construction.

Since our host was a wealthy man—who had succeeded against all expectation in buying off the disrepute into which he had fallen with the Cromwellians in being a Royalist by paying a fine of £5,000—the dinner was lavish. The men and some women began with Madeira imported from the island of that name and then sampled several bottles of French origin from his extensive cellar, newly recovered from the depredations imposed by the quartered troops; for Sir James was recently returned from London with a wagon-load of aristocratic comforts.

The food was a fish soup of local varieties such as haddock, herring and pike—the latter, we were informed, taken from Loch Fad, not a mile from where we sat: a strange tasting mixture I thought it, though well enough textured, flavoured and seasoned. There followed a few pheasants which had been roasted on a tureen in the Castle oven. Then a haunch of venison, freshly shot on Sir James's estate and finally a colourful dish of mixed jellies mingled with chopped nuts, the whole sweetened with honey.

After the prayer that was customary, given by the minister, Sir James called for the glasses to be filled and proposed a toast: 'To our absent friends', at which everyone stood and drank solemnly, keenly aware of which particular friends he meant: the English, who had occupied the Castle for nearly a decade, had indeed prohibited toasts, among other things, ruling the island with a rod of iron, though, in truth, it was less severe a rod for our poor who normally had their backs beaten as well as overloaded when left to the devices of their fellow countrymen. Only the gentry—that is ourselves—had suffered under the rule of the Parliamentary troops. A cess or tax had been levied to pay for the maintenance of the army of Ironsides on whose presence our security—from Spanish invasion, as well as our own 'rebels', evidently—depended. So at least we were told. And that is why the battery[80] was constructed and the breakwater built up with stones by the fishermen: so that any Spanish landing there would be cut down with English cannon before they got ashore. What a waste it all was! They could have landed anywhere. Neither the harbour nor the cannon was necessary. But it gave the English soldiery something to do which may have been the real object of so much construction.

---

[80] Editor's note: the battery was placed beyond the end of the breakwater and across the road from the point, the ground presently occupied by the old baths.

'Will the cess be continued?' was the question in every mind. The Scottish nation was originally supposed to contribute £10,000 a month for the army's welfare: pay and provisions. In practice there was not that much money in the country and far smaller amounts had been collected. Nevertheless, every gentleman had been obliged to sell animals or lands as well as crops to pay his share and could not refuse it. The poor alone did well out of this for, having nothing to sell and no money—no food, indeed, even to offer the troops in exchange—nothing could be got from them. And as the English operated, every one of them, under a banner of Christianity, they were compelled to be charitable to those in need.

Having represented the Scottish burghs in Edinburgh and then been in London for several weeks, Sir James would know the answer to the question.

Once the glasses were filled and the meal had begun, Donald McGilchrist, the Provost, raised the matter. 'What news do you bring from London, Sir James?'

'Chaos reigns. Monck's army sits outside and does nothing. Inside, the rule of law is breaking down.'

'What about the cess?'

'Parliament has demanded £6,000 sterling a month from the Scots.'

'But will Parliament continue to govern?'

'Yes, even if the monarchy is reinstated. So much achieved by Cromwell will not now be given up. So it will be a monarchy with clipped wings.'

'What do you know of the new king?' said the Minister.

'He has, we will say, with deference to the ladies present, the custom of distributing his favours widely.'

'But is he a good man?'

'As such men are, he may have his good points. He will have learned something from his father's fate.'

The Minister considered this for a moment and then seemed to decide. 'If he is a licentious king, his reign is likely to bring evil upon us.'

'Why so?' I wondered aloud. 'If he follows his religion in this fashion, perhaps he will allow a relaxing of the proscriptions which govern our conduct.'

'That would be a disaster,' replied the Minister angrily. 'Already we are beset by evil, even on this island, as I have reason to know.'

'You mean the death of your wife?'

'Aye, there is a rumour of witcherie. She was ill for years—and I myself. Only she died of it. And other malefices.'

'Do we know who the perpetrators are?' Sir James asked.

'It is the usual story,' Rev Stewart answered. 'Some women are accused. Sometimes it is slander. Sometimes it is not. Rarely is it proved one way or the other.'

'I do not, for the life of me, see how a woman in our community—or the one at Kingarth—could or even would do anything to cause an illness in anyone, still less an illness that led to death.'

'The devil comes in many forms, Robert. Of course he seeks to injure the good or those working for that good.'

'I wonder why this should be so,' I said. 'Why would the devil want to injure the good? Why would he bother? But who among us has ever seen hide or hair of the devil?'

'How can that be relevant,' said the Provost. 'Who has ever seen God?'

'This is blasphemy!' declared the Minister.

'How so?' I said. 'It is a fair question and if any have done so their answers would be extremely interesting and valuable.'

'Blasphemy just the same.'

Determined to examine this view of the devil, for it was commonplace, I enquired: 'Is there no limit to the form in which the devil may appear?'

'Of course not,' answered the Minister.

'So he could appear as, say, one of those candle flames that now light up this room?'

'Yes, indeed.'

'Or in the form of an animal?'

'Of course.'

'Then the devil might appear in the form of the cat I saw just a moment ago? I think it has gone under the table.' Since I could feel its fur against my leg, I knew where it was.

'The devil could take the form of the cat, assuredly,' declared the Minister.

'But how do we know whether the cat is just a cat or a cat in which the devil has taken root in some way?'

'By its behaviour,' said the Minister.

'Do you mean that if the cat behaves out of character then it has the form of the devil?'

'I suppose so.'

'Then a cat which jumped up on the table would be acting out of character and would be capable of being the form of the devil?'

'Yes.'

I lifted a portion of pike out of the soup tureen and wafted it beneath the table. There was the sound of purring that a gleeful cat might have made and I felt it stealthily climb the side of my leg for a closer acquaintance with the interesting smell. By luck, as I moved the piece of fish back to the table-top, the cat sprang at just that moment and missed. Then, realising the whereabouts of the delicious morsel, the black cat of the house sprang up my leg onto the board, seized it joyfully, and—seeing the various important personages seated around in their finery and frightened by them—continued across, upsetting a dish of sauce, miaowed in terror at its own doings which it knew to be forbidden—only inevitably forgotten in the presence of a tempting tit-bit—and leapt onto the lap of the minister, depositing a layer of yellow sauce there and sped away with a flourish of the tail, in the direction of the kitchen.

Laughter filled the room, all except for the Minister who was appalled at the ruination of his breeches as well as the loss of the argument.

A manservant was delegated to see to the breeches and for this purpose the Minister retired to the kitchen for a time.

When he returned, however, he was in no mood for concession.

'As you are a preacher, I condemn your behaviour. It is unworthy and does not help our cause.'

'Why, what cause is that?'

'The cause of Christianity, what other is there?'

'Well, come to that, even Christianity comes in many forms. Catholicism, for one.'

'Do I understand that you support Papism?'

'You may understand what you wish but if there is to be a new monarch we may all have to embrace Papism in some form. We will certainly have Episcopal bishops again[81] and some men think that is as bad as Papism.'

'Aye,' said Ninian Bannatyne. 'The last king was of that persuasion and the next one will likely turn out the same[82].'

'God save us!' declared the Minister, praying afterwards a silent prayer before entering the battle again: 'If English bishops are laid upon us again, I..I...I'll demit my charge.'

'You'll do no such thing, minister,' said Sir James, 'you couldn't afford it. You will do just as you are told like all the rest of us.'

Rev Stewart fumed in silence for a bit while the conversation moved on. I was not however satisfied with the examination of the idea of the devil.

---

[81] This occurred by decree in 1661. All acts since 1633 were repealed. Whyte, Trans of Bute Nat Hist Soc Vol XIII, 1945, p44

[82] Editor's note: In fact Ninian was right. At the end of his reign, Chas II became a Roman Catholic.

'If I am not mistaken, the facts about the devil are few. He is taken to be a fallen angel, in opposition to God: therefore evil. He can take many forms, which implies that he has no particular form, though some men have suggested—a thing different from a fact, then—that he is a horned creature, perhaps red in colour and sporting a tail of some kind. That is not much. And I have never met anyone who has seen the devil—in any form whatever.'

'You could be the devil!' exploded the Minister to an amazed silence all round.

I replied: 'You mean because I have been behaving uncharacteristically by seeking to investigate him further than is usual?'

McGilchrist and Sir James, having the intelligence, both laughed. The others did not see the connexion with what had been said before.

'You are not behaving like the preacher you are supposed to be!' declared the Minister.

'It is not a condition of being a preacher that I should be debarred from thought. Questioning is what we graduates were taught to do.'

'But some things are beyond question!'

'There we part company. Everything should be questioned because in questioning it we come to a better understanding of it. Even something like God or Jesus Christ or even the devil himself whose existence I may take leave to doubt. We ought to question what we mean by these and what this meaning tells us. It is likely to be instructive. Better by far than a mindless unquestioning absorption of every notion, many of them half-baked—like the devil—that have been passed down the generations.'

'You offend me, Sir,' said the Minister.

'For asking questions? For seeking answers? How can that offend anyone? If anyone should be offended it is me myself. Did you not a moment ago accuse me of being the devil based only upon the fact that I do not believe without examination, every silly idea, however commonplace?'

'How can you doubt the reality of the devil? The devil came to my house and poisoned my wife and killed her and nearly killed me!'

'How do you know this? Why must it have been some mythical being and not an actual person? Why must it have been poison at all? Why not one of these strange ailments that everybody gets from time to time? Rather look at these ailments than seek the devil under every hedgerow.'

As the Minister had nothing to say, I continued: 'You are not telling us that you saw a horned creature with a long tail enter your house and administer poison?'

There was no reply but a sulky silence.

'Well then, what evidence have you that the devil was involved at all?'

Again, no reply but a sullen redfaced expression as if with too much wine.

'This idea that the devil may appear in many forms is outrageous nonsense,' I declared. 'To say that the form has been taken over by the devil is a statement made on no other authority than that, by coincidence, the behaviour of the animal or whatever is not what we ordinarily expect. That, Sir,' I said, standing up to depart, 'is just stupid!'

As we were taking our leave of Sir James, it was clear that Ninian Bannatyne expected me to accompany him, his wife and ward—his cousin, my wife—to Kames and stay the night.

Anxious to return to Roseland and have the advantage of Nancy as soon as possible, I tried to get out of it but none of the others would agree.

'You must come,' said Ninian. 'I have a shooting party tomorrow. It's all arranged. Why is it you never come and stay?'—which was a clear signal that I had better comply with his wishes if only to discourage further enquiry and perhaps discovery of my reasons.

Thus, despite complaining I had no overnight clothes, I mounted and went with them to Kames. Down Tower Lane we rode and along the shore with the sea lapping close by, to the bridge over the Water of Fad and along the Gallowgate past the Gallowscraig. Though the dinner had begun at five of the clock, it was now dark and our progress was lit by a brace of syces who ran a little way ahead with torches. It was, to be frank, all rather grand to be conveyed in this way to the Castle in the company of the laird and his lady.

Even my wife seemed to be in a good humour that evening, probably, it seemed at first, because of my performance at dinner. 'I am very proud of you,' she announced when we were alone in our room in the Castle and preparing for bed.

'My guardian has been asking me when I expect to be with child. He looks for an heir.'

'What did you say?'

'That one would arrive or not, in God's good time.'

Since the frequency of conjunctions had reduced to once a month, I said nothing.

'You used to use me twice a week, Robert. What has changed? Have I grown old prematurely?'

'I expect it is familiarity,' I lied. 'We become less interested in what we already know.'

Jean undressed and then lay down on the bed, quite naked. 'Perhaps we could try again tonight,' she said. And, so, cursing my performance in the investigation of the devil that night at dinner, when I had evidently won a little notoriety, I was forced to comply. And I have to admit that she seemed to have got over her puritanism and set to the activity with a certain amount of relish. Later, before sleep, she admitted that her friend, Elizabeth, had been delegated to advise her on procedures that might advance their cause.

'Is that the reason for your new attitude?' I wondered sleepily.

'Yes, she agreed.'

'And there I was thinking it was my performance in shooting up the devil and the Minister at dinner tonight.'

'Is that what you were doing? I didn't notice.'

'You mean you did not think I won the argument?'

'No, not at all. Everyone knows there is a devil, don't they? Don't we talk about him all the time? And take precautions?'

'What precautions?'

'Well, you know...'—she seemed lost for words, as if the answer were obvious. 'We plant Rowans near the house to ward off evil spirits like that and stay well away from temptation, for that is the devil acting in disguise. Is it not?'

I had nothing to say, so dumbfounded was I.

'No, I did not understand your argument,' she continued. 'In fact, if you really do not think there is a devil, I am surprised. But I did think you looked very fine, just the same. Even handsomer than Sir James, for all his splendour in that scarlet coat and grey breeches. Your black and silver, your dark hair and healthy complexion—the thing about you I value most, I think—were far superior.'

Next morning after a breakfast of porridge, eggs, new made hot breads and salt herring, people began to arrive to shoot and were given drams to ward off the cold. There was Gustavus Browne, a man of thirty, who had courted my wife at one time until put off and Alexander Bannatyne, a young kinsman of Ninian's, and a few others.

Those who had no weapon were loaned muskets by Ninian who had only recently acquired them, weapons of any kind having been forbidden during the English occupation of the island, for insurrection had been rooted out and destroyed wherever found. These troops were so very competent at that sort of activity that only the foolhardy among the islanders retained weapons and then only when well-hidden. The penalty for discovery of these was severe.

After so little practice over the years no one was very successful at first. But there was game in abundance: pheasant, pigeon, rabbit, hare and even roe deer, all to be found within the boundaries of the estate on which there was plenty of cover on the surrounding hillsides especially, but also in the branches and bushes of the park itself.

Luncheon was served under some great trees in the park on trestle tables brought out for the purpose and I was leaning against the trunk of a great oak contentedly munching a hunk of bread and drinking a goblet of wine while ruminating upon my golden darling back at Roseland, when I was approached by Alexander Bannatyne, a large ruddy-faced youth with a fairly innocent demeanour.

'I understand that you employ a maidservant called Nancy Throw?' said he.

I agreed that this was so. 'Perhaps you would send her my regards.'

'Do you know her?'

'Not very well. Not as much as I would like. She used to work here but then went to help your father.' Then, as if struck by an afterthought: 'If you will allow me, perhaps I might call upon her.'

'For what purpose?' I asked, stupidly, and then recovered: 'Do you intend to appropriate her for your own use?'

He blushed. 'You mean as a maidservant? No, but she is very comely.'

'What knowledge of her do you possess?' I enquired, with as little exhibition of jealousy as I could muster.

'I have seen her from afar, mostly. In the Kirk and around the Mercat Cross on market day.'

When I said nothing more for thinking how this would affect my position, he added: 'Maybe—you being such an older person of standing who knows her well—you could put in a good word for me, even advise me how to advance myself with her.' And when I made no response to this overture, he hurried on as the young often do, careless of the feelings of those they address: 'What can you tell me about her way of life? When is she employed? I mean, when might I see her, on her own, meet her by chance, say, and where?' Finally, looking me straight in the eye, he asked: 'What would you advise me to do?'

'I am not sure I know what you intend,' I lied, displeased by the whole tenor of the conversation which so threatened the little heaven I had discovered for myself.

'I..I...I,' he stammered, 'I.I would like to marry her.'

I forbore to advise him, in that case, to seek out her father and make enquiries there, for, assuredly, Alexander would be very well received by

Robert Throw who was a figure of lesser magnitude by far than any Bannatyne.

After a few more hours spent uselessly in the perusal of game—for I myself declined to shoot anything, considering it such a miracle that these species should adorn the earth and this small island, that it were a crime to kill them for sport—I pleaded my departure and was eventually given leave to do so.

'You must come again, Robert,' said Ninian, finally. 'You do not get out enough. Hunting will make a man of you.'

'My preference is to hunt among books,' I lied.

This was greeted with amazement by most of the gentlemen present. Only Gustavus Browne did not laugh. 'What book are you reading just now?'

'Thucydides: The Peloponnesian War.'

'Ah well,' he said, approvingly, 'have you a good translation?'

'No. I am content with the Greek.'

And so I made my escape. In an hour of fast walking, I was back at Roseland, went in the door and through the hall like a wind, to find my beloved Nancy bent over the kitchen table slicing up vegetables for the expected dinner that evening. I raised up her skirt, pulled down her drawers, found her place and rode her without any preparation being necessary, in a hot frenzy of passion during which she ended up flat on the table crushing all her labour with the carefully cut garden produce, yet laughing with the joy of it.

'Oh, God, I needed that, my darling!' I sighed with pleasure afterwards.

'So did I,' said she. 'I heard your step on the gravel and became wet almost immediately.'

'And you never thought to come and meet me, then?' I protested.

'What need? I knew you would be where you now are, directly.'

That, I reflected, is what it is like to be truly in love. Your needs are urgent, cannot be denied or delayed and you are understood and accepted without any preamble or discussion because her needs are the same precisely. Each knows in an instant what are the needs of the other and acts to satisfy them right there and then because the wishes are the same.

It never occurred to me as I came into my house that Nancy would not need me with the same urgency as I needed her. I was proved right. The feeling in me, and I believe, in her too, is impossible to convey adequately. The touch of her body beside mine was ecstasy! We stood, after a separation of merely a single evening, as if we had been parted for a year; and our eyes dissolved into tears at the pleasure of it.

'Oh, Robert,' she said with a warm huskiness of voice that dripped upon my soul like honey, 'no one will ever love me the way you do, if I live for a thousand years. And I will never love anybody else whatever.'

And so our heavenly existence continued without interruption for a while whenever opportunity presented.

Given my manner of life, my first project as a carpenter in the workshop I made for myself, was, unsurprisingly, a bed.

VII   Defences for Deception

I built the bed of stronger than usual timber, ready planed for my use, and cut the joints with care, hammering them together and then fastening them with glue and nails got from the town. When it was finished, I coated it with beeswax and gave it a polish. Anticipating difficulties and anxious to resolve them in advance, I filled up the window in the wall of my workshop and, instead, to give me light there, cut a hole in the sarking which lay under the thatch and put a sheet of glass over it, from the Glass brothers, our glaziers, fastened down with strips of lath. But the work had to be done by me alone. I could not afford questions about my doings. A tradesman might have understood.

The other weakness in the defences of my fortress was the door. What could I do about that? If I locked it every time I was engaged with Nancy, my wife would soon understand the true nature of my hobby. Especially, if she lay in wait to see who emerged. If Nancy did all was lost. The Kirk Session's practises were so well known that a charitable interpretation of such an event was impossible. And yet I had to have a locked door, otherwise my wife might suddenly appear when least desired. The image of her in the doorway, when I was deep within Nancy, was a torment I wrestled with.

Did I wrestle with the moral disgrace in which I had fallen? Try to combat it? Not much. I was, you see, besotted; head over heels in love. I knew I was behaving badly—at least in ways everyone had taught me were wrong—ways, indeed, I had myself taught so many other people were wrong. But I was captured by love, enraptured by the lady. I was possessed, could think only of her; went around the small world of Bute in a smiling stupor of happiness. —And because of this was far better liked than I had ever been before by the community, for whom I had always seemed an introverted silent thinking person, uninterested— apparently— in their private doings; though as an idealist and a minister, instead, I was powerfully concerned for every one of them: they were my flock, after all, at least I used to think so, as an assistant minister.

I was no more capable of moral discussion, self doubt or feelings of guilt than a cock in eternal pursuit of a hen, a favoured hen, certainly, a hen beloved as no hen ever is. Of course the risks, the absolute certainty that my world would suddenly collapse, probably in a phenomenal explosion of gunpowder, were ever at the back of my mind. And maybe the knowledge of the disaster lying in wait just over the hill intensified the experience of love. I believe so and believe it was so for Nancy too.

I knew I was setting out to deceive my wife (as well as the community) for no better reason than to prolong the period in which I might continue to mate, knew it broached every tenet of the marriage contract and it never occurred to me for a moment to do anything else. The attraction was as powerful as that.

So what was I to do about the locked door?

I thought of many solutions to this conundrum, one being that I might dig out a secret passage into my den from elsewhere, from which Nancy might escape. A priest's hole in the den in which she might hide was another. She could always emerge when the coast was clear. Nancy's whereabouts at the time would be accounted for by a white lie, which seemed a trifle in view of the deceptions being practised. And they were carried out with relish, for we believed we were deeply in love—and were surely!—and that it was our right as well as our duty to preserve this above every other thing in our lives.

One feature of my den that helped were the walls which were very thick, meaning that noises of pleasure made within could not be heard outside. This mattered, for Nancy had the habit of encouraging me in the act, saying, quite loudly at times, 'Oh Robert! Oh Robert! Ohhhhhhhhhhh!' and at others: 'Oh, there, there! Dear one, Oh there!'

My first effort to solve this problem, which began to require an answer as soon as the weather moderated, for my wife would no longer be kept in the house due to the cold and might expect to invade my sanctum at any moment, was to make it known that every day I liked to isolate myself there and would not brook disturbance. Thus, for a few days, I worked there alone at my carpentry and my Greek with Nancy in the house with my wife—a matter of serious discipline to overcome the loss of my lover. Once my wife had become used to the idea of 'my private time', I could people it as I wished without interference. I bought a small bell in the town, which some people presumed was for the children in the school, to summon them to class after a break. Not so! I hung it just outside our back door telling my wife she should ring, if she needed to attract my attention. In this way, our arrangements—Nancy's and mine—to meet in secret, were set up.

And they worked very well for a while. My wife, if she were at home and not at Kames or in the town or visiting a friend, kept to her reception room in the front of the house out of earshot of the kitchen which was Nancy's preserve, I being at the rear of the house in a different building not far from the back door. Yet, with the improvement in the weather, my wife was often away on her own business.

The crumbling of our state of heavenly bliss began, so I now realise, with the day I arrived for breakfast to find the back door wide open to the breeze, which had brought in some snowflakes onto the floor, for snow had fallen and lain for several days. I could see my breakfast, steaming on the table, but where was Nancy? I went to the door to close it and heard the sound of retching. Looking outside, I noticed Nancy stooped over, holding onto the kitchen wall. She was being sick. As the process continued morning after morning at roughly the same time, it soon became clear that she was with child.

'I have missed my monthlies,' she admitted, 'and I am usually so regular.' She was in the kitchen, my wife away from home, when she said this, looking at me directly, as was her wont at important times.

'Oh, Nancy, my dearest,' I told her, taking her in my arms. 'What are we to do?'

'Are you not pleased?'

'Pleased? I wish I could be. Of course I want your babe—ours—but the consequences are dire. I am sorry our heaven is ending so soon. I would have put if off, if I could.'

'You're not sorry, then. You don't blame me?'

'How could I blame you? I am the one who put it there. I know it's what you wanted. I knew it might happen. But I want what you want.'

She smiled and lifted up her golden head to kiss me, which I returned in full measure in the passionate way we had discovered, my tongue inside her mouth, rubbing her inside lips into arousal.

'I want to do it now,' she said. 'I need you there right now.'

'Are you sure it would be safe?'

'Of course. It's only a wee mite: it doesn't know anything yet.'

'I thought it might dislike the physical activity.'

She laughed. 'No, and it will do no harm.' She proceeded to divest me of clothing she judged superfluous to requirements and I soon found myself

THE STORY OF ROBERT STEWART OF SCARRELL 105

on the floor underneath her from where I could observe her closely as she rode me until, in a huge sigh of pleasure she announced herself finished.
'But you are not. So will you please move a little for I am tired.'
'I don't need to,' I said. 'I'm too upset.'
In the days that followed we tried to think of solutions: the babe could be presented as someone else's—except that Nancy would show signs of its existence, in a few months time. To cover this, she could go away from the island—to Glasgow or Edinburgh maybe—in which she could easily lose herself and have the baby in secret. I offered to go with her.'
'But your post of schoolmaster? What of that? How could you leave your wife to come with me? That is impossible.'
'Not so. Maybe it is for the best. I do not love my wife.'
'How would we live and where? You could not take your property with you or collect your rents. The Kirk Session would soon track you down.'
In fact, the Kirk Session were very quick to notice for, on the 17th of May 1660, my Nancy was named in the Kirk Session as a witness in a claim brought by Mary McIlchomie against Jonet Moore and Isabell Galie that they had made scandalous speeches against her.
This meant that Nancy had to appear at the next meeting and she had to give evidence. Yes, she had been present when Jonet Moore and Isabell Galie had made their speeches against Mary MacIlhomie and yes they had been scandalous, for they said this and this and this....
Both women were accordingly found guilty of slander and punished according to the act.
However, the worst of this, from our point of view, was that Nancy's condition had been obvious to the men of the Session, always on the lookout for any bulges on a woman. At that time she was as slim as a stick.
But by October she had gained so much weight that on the 11th of that month, the Session minutes recorded: 'Nance Throw delated suspect with child. Apointis her to be warned.'[83] What added to the calamity was that I wrote these words myself.
One of the accompanying duties of the schoolmaster was Session Clerk. So I had to be present at every meeting of the Kirk Session and take the minutes. As one of the few well educated men in the community it made sense to employ the schoolmaster in this task. My terror as I watched the

---

[83] Rothesay Parish Records 1658-1750: edited by Henry Paton for the 4th Marquis of Bute. The Session Book of Rothesay p33. printed 1931 by Morrison and Gibb, Edinburgh and London for private circulation. The full relevant text is printed at the end of this work.

quill scrape across the parchment was as if my body and soul had been marked down in some heavenly office for impending doom. How I managed to control my feelings—if I did control them, for of course I cannot be sure—I do not know. The shock was so overwhelming that as I left the Kirk that day the entire episode completely left my mind and the first thing I did on reaching home was to mate with Nancy, oblivious to everything outside myself but her. —As if there were, in the wide world, only we two mortals. I did not even mention it to her that day, that is a measure of my shock. And it was just as well, for it meant that she was unprepared for the next development.

The very next day, my wife being out riding, the bell at the back door rang when Nancy and I were joyously engaged. I thought it must be my wife who had returned and I took the time to finish. When properly dressed, I left the workshop, leaving the door unlocked so that Nancy could make her escape at some suitable moment. I turned the corner to find two men waiting for me at the back door of the main house: Donald McGilchrist, the provost and John Glass, burgess, the very men who had so recently dined with me at Sir James Stewart's table in the Castle.

'Excuse me, gentlemen, I have been at my carpentry,' I lied, brushing back my hair which wanted a comb after so much thrusting exercise.

'What can I do for you?'

'It's about your maidservant, Nancy Throw.'

'I am not sure where she is,' I lied, 'but come in to the front room,'—where I led them, knowing Nancy would now get out in safety and soon be available.

'I have some very fine aquavitae, I would try out upon you,' I told them and left them to fetch glasses and the bottle from a cupboard, after which I filled three glasses to the brim and proposed a toast: 'Your health, Sirs,' after which we all sat down.

'Are you here in your capacity as officers of the town council or the Kirk Session?' I wondered.

'The Kirk, aye,' replied McGilchrist. 'Nance is delated with child and we need to ken the faither.'

'You are sure it is a child and not just a woman's trouble? You know how they get fat as they get older.'

'No, No, ye ken. It's a child, I'm sure. I saw her— we all saw her— just a few months ago and she was quite different.'

'So you think she is pregnant, then?'

'Aye, aye, we do.'

'Well, that may or may not be so but I'm not sure I can be of much help,' I lied, almost blushing at my own rottenness, feeling like Saint Peter must have felt when denying knowledge of Jesus.

'Have you any idea who the father might be?'

I was in a quandary, stuck for words—I, the great scholar, speechless with embarrassment—and in real danger right there and then as I instantly appreciated, when into the room walked my Nancy, as if she did not have a care in the world; and I knew in a moment that she had been listening outside, had heard everything and wanted nothing so much as to save me from my peril.

'I think I heard my name, Sirs. Was there something you wanted?'

'The name of the faither,' answered McGilchrist. 'Ye'll need to marry of course.'

'What if there is no father? Or I do not know the father?'

'There has to be a faither, lassie, ye ken that right weel.'

'Well, if there is a father—if that is what the matter is and I cannot be sure it is—I do not know who it might be.'

'Are you saying this is a virgin birth, lassie?' said John Glass, smiling.

'Mind yer blasphemies, John,' said McGilchrist. 'Come on, lassie, ye ken the procedure. God didnae manufacture yon lump in yer belly. A mortal man done it. You must tell us what man. And we'll sort out that man. He will marry you, depend upon it.'

'Well, gentlemen, I have nothing to tell you.'

The men arose. 'You must compier at the next meeting of the Session which is 29th November.'

That evening, as Nancy served dinner, my wife said: 'People are saying you are with child, Nancy. I see you so often that I hardly see a difference but, yes'—surveying Nancy's growing abdomen—'I see what they mean. You have put on weight these past few months. Don't you agree, Robert?'

I could hardly lift my eyes from my soup. 'Yes, maybe there is a slight increase thereabouts. But it might just be getting older. Don't women get fatter as they get older? My mother did, I think.'

'Come Nancy, tell us?' said Jean. 'Are you with child or not?'

'How can you know such a thing? Until the child, if it is a child, appears?'

'I hesitate to say, in front of a man—though he be my husband—for what man knows of such things? They are for women alone.'

'Well, I will leave you women to sort it out,' I said and fled to my workshop where I fretted until Nancy arrived, before leaving for home, with a goblet of hot brandy.

'I thought you would need a drink.'

I took it gratefully and drained it in two gulps. 'What did she say?'

'Just what you would expect. I told her I often missed my monthlies and thought nothing of it.'

'But she must have pressed you to say if you had taken a man or not.'

'I told her it was nobody's business but mine.'

'But they think it is their business.'

'Then, I may let them think I have been with half the town. How would that do?'

'They won't believe it. They'll want to know when and where. Most of the men of the town would have alibis.'

'Well, I don't know what else to do.'

Since there was nothing else to be said, we said nothing. Without a word, a question or even a look, we made ourselves available and mated on the new bed. And with the impending end of our heaven which we could so readily see, there was a fresh frenzy of passion. I do not know when Nancy left that night. After she left, I lay exhausted, spent, without a drop of seed. I could not have loved her again if it had meant the difference between life and death. Nor do I know how many times it was. Only that it was ecstasy! A vibrant pulsating susurration of the most intense pleasure available in the world. We were, that night, travellers in heaven and I do not now know how it was that I agreed to part—even if I did— that I let her leave me for the road in the darkness, winding down the brae through the woods. How could I do it? I am still astounded that I let her go at all.

But I have just this moment thought of the answer. She left me because she thought it was the best thing for me. Everything about our love, about these events tells me this is so.

I only know that by the time I came to myself and got up and left the workshop, the lights of our house were extinguished, as if a message were being sent to me by my wife. As if she knew and yet understood for she said nothing; knew that the love between me and Nancy was not of this world, not a coupling for the sake of children to satisfy the ambitions of parents, still less an abrogation of the religious life of Bute at that time.

Two afternoons later, after school, about to retire to my sanctum as usual and enjoy its occupancy, I heard horses. It was my wife's friend, Elizabeth Stewart and her husband, her cousin, Ninian Bannatyne, come to visit. And so it was my duty to welcome them and entertain them in the best room of our house.

At my instruction, Nancy brought them chocolate, a new drink, much the fashion in London, according to Sir James, who had sent me some after our dinner; and—for Ninian—a hefty dram of aquavitae which I knew he liked and— for all—a pie baked by Nancy while I was at school and also little cakes which my wife liked: light and floury they were and sprinkled inside with currants.

Needless to report, every eye was upon Nancy's burgeoning belly while she served these delicacies. When she had returned to the kitchen, Ninian coughed with embarrassment and said:

'Robert, I must ask you, who is the father of yon bairn?'

I must have blushed to the roots of my hair. I know I took my time to reply. Finally, I managed to say: 'How should I know? Can an employer ever be expected to know who has got his servants with child?'

Ninian heaved a sigh of relief: 'Thank heavens! I knew it must be so. Anybody could have put it there. And she might not know exactly who it was. You are quite right.'

The Lady Kames said: 'Well, that is the matter settled, then. The family name is at stake when their friends and relatives are and we must just stand fast to defend both.'

Jean smiled at these gestures of support but said nothing and I knew it meant something.

When they had departed to return to Kames, I was burning for time alone with Nancy but could not get it. Uncharacteristically, Jean was hovering about the kitchen observing Nancy at her preparations for dinner and making offers to assist in small ways, another unusual and ominous development.

Dinner was conducted in silence and afterwards Jean sat for a time, saying little, but, I felt, sensing for the first time the tension between Nancy and me. I fetched some aquavitae and sat over a goblet. Then, suddenly Jean seemed to come to an important decision. 'I think I will go to Kames,' she announced.

'But it is late. Not safe for a horse. Can't you wait till the morrow? It will be dark soon.'

'There is still an hour of light and it is only a few miles, all down hill. I will walk it in no time.'

'I beg you to leave it until tomorrow,' I said, but it was a very gentle protest for above all things I wanted Nancy and the only way to have her was for Jean to go. The workshop could not be risked tonight. I sensed this from Jean's attitude.

And so Jean wrapped up in a cloak with the hood up and left us to spend the night at Kames: there was clearly no point in returning in full dark.
I saw her to the door and walked her down through the woods— the worst part of her journey—which were already gloomy and just above the lights of the town which were beginning to come on. I bade her a safe journey, stood a while, observing her and then turned to march with quicker and quicker steps uphill homeward.
'I'm afraid,' said Nancy, when I met her at the front door, which was wide open. 'I think she knows.'
'How can she know?'
'She is a woman. She knows. Can smell the love between us. God, but I am running with the want of you! Come, Come in, please!' And I knew exactly what she meant. It was not just to enter the house.
'Where?' she said. 'Where?' looking around.
I pointed to a table in the hall and, being utterly alone for the whole night, we stripped off everything and set to in a high tide of passion that seemed to break in waves over us, at different times and then, most gloriously, at the same time. A wild ride of shuddering ecstasy it was! I know not how long it lasted, for time seemed to stand still. But when my mind surfaced from the tide, and I had just pulled out, I looked up and to the side towards a window behind Nancy and saw the tear rent face of Jean framed in the hood of her dark cloak staring at us out of the darkness..
She said nothing; remained outside, waited for us to dress until Nancy, still oblivious, went off to the kitchen to prepare supper, knowing I would be hungry after so much exercise.
Only then did Jean enter the house. 'I changed my mind and decided to take your advice and go tomorrow.'
Nancy, still with the sweat of our love upon her, like me, immediately appeared and looked horror-struck. 'Can I get you anything, madam? Would you like supper?'
'No, Nancy, I am weary. A glass of brandy, Robert, if you please. And I would like to speak to you alone. Bring something for the Master to eat, Nancy, and then go home to your bed.'
We sat on opposite sides of the fire, I with a plate of bread and meat and a goblet of wine, Jean with her brandy. I hardly ate anything for a time: sat staring into the flames, unable to look my wife in the eye.
'I am shocked, Robert. It was something I never expected. I feel such a fool and I suddenly understand many things. What I am not sure about is what to do, even what to say. The thing is so clear all of a sudden. You

are both in the hands of the devil: possessed. I never saw such behaviour in my life and never imagined it.'

'I am sorry, Jean.'

'When did it begin?'

'A few months after we arrived here. I fought the madness as best I could for a while but, you are right: I was possessed. I am possessed.'

'So it is the devil has got to you, then?'

'I am very deeply in love with someone who loves me, if that is what you mean.'

'It is not your fault, Robert. She has bewitched you.'

'You might as well say that I have bewitched her.'

'No, Robert, this is the devil's work. It is what we are warned to expect unless we are very strong and very careful. But I will help you over this calamity. We are husband and wife after all, sworn to uphold the bond in sickness or in health, even unto death, as you know. My father dinned it into me. And it is so. I will stand by you Robert and protect you.'

I was too distraught to protest at my wife's poor reasoning which was the same as the Minister's: since I was behaving uncharacteristically—as no sensible wealthy man of education ever did—of course it must be because the devil had taken command of me.

'Has the devil ever appeared to you, Robert?'

'No, of course not.'

'So you have made no covenant with him, then?'

'Certainly not. There is no devil. It is all nonsense.'

'You are mistaken,' she declared confidently. Then, she rose and took me by the hand. 'Let us to bed. We will speak more about it in the morning.' And, as she led me upstairs, she said: 'I will not expect you to use me tonight for you are tired—exhausted, I'd say. But in the morning when you are rested I want you then. You are my husband and I find I need you very much.'

When she had stripped and stood naked by the bedside, she added: 'When I saw you with her, saw the manhood come and go, it was a revelation to me. And now I want it very badly myself. I want you to possess me in that way.'

I have often reflected upon that moment. How I missed my chance! But I was too tired for further debate, too exhausted by the frights that put my soul and most of all my body in peril—as well as by the frenzied coupling, of a quality that was extraordinary even in my experience.

I should have said, and did not: 'If you are possessed in that way, do you not see that it will be the devil who is possessing you? He will be responsible, just as surely as you say he has possessed me? For your behaviour will be at odds with your character—the sole criterion you have for the influence of the devil. And yet, if such an event were to occur, it would just be—what it seems anyway—that you have at last grown up and realised what men and women are made for, that their actions are not mere trivialities. That grand passion is possible and a kind of summum bonum, not to achieve which in life, is a serious deprivation.

As I lay in the bed, ready for sleep, I said: 'People change. They grow older and wiser and they learn. And when they do, of course they behave differently.' But there was no answer from the other side of the bed. Jean was oblivious.

In the morning, a Saturday, so one without the labour of school, I woke refreshed, despite my prolonged activity on the previous night, in the habitual state of arousal. Jean, who was already up, brought me a glass of mulled wine and a bowl of porridge and as I ate it, she undressed and got back into bed. 'Now I want you to use me,' she said, when I had finished the dish.

We could hear Nancy about her chores down stairs. What would Jean do if I turned her down, I wondered?

But I was in no state of mind to find out. My wife had need of me and that was something new. And it was something I could provide. And she had earned it by all the suffering I had caused her. So I set to and noticed the difference in Jean immediately. She had learned from her observation of Nancy the night before. Jean had learned to abjure puritanism, to throw caution to the winds and take part, no longer to lie back and think of Scotland. It was a duty no longer but a need, an intense pleasure. She used me just as surely as I used her and the sounds of it were louder by far than with Nancy—as if Jean were saying to her at work in the kitchen beneath: 'See, I can do this too! I can please my man! And I am enchanted by him.'

Afterwards, at breakfast, Jean, dressed in her finest, and evidently restored in her self-confidence by our morning exercise, declared: 'Well, Nancy, what are you going to do? You will have to find a husband. Is there anyone you have in mind?'

Without a blush, Nancy replied: 'No, my lady.'

'Then we will have to find one for you, won't we Robert?'

'I do not need a husband,' Nancy replied.

'Yes, you do. Tell her Robert.'

'It might be a solution,' I said. 'But Nancy does not think this way. She thinks it would be a fraud, something counter to love. And will not countenance it.'

'Well, I will find you a husband, Nancy. You are very bonny with many advantages and a good man will be found and he will take care of you and bring up the child with you.'

'And if I don't accept?'

'My dear, you have to accept. The Session will insist upon it. If you don't, you could be put to death.'

'They wouldn't kill the child, would they?'

'Exodus tells us to keep the sabbath or be put to death. What do you think the punishment for adultery—frequent and utterly animal conduct resulting in bastardy—would be? I don't know for sure. They might. They surely might, rather than see it brought up a bastard and alone, if you are dead.'

'Well, I won't stand for it,' said Nancy. 'I won't marry a man I don't love.'

'You will learn to love him. It is what most of us do.'

Jean then rose from the table and announced that she was going out for the morning. She dressed in her cloak and soon left us to walk down to the town leaving us together.

I was astonished: 'What on earth is she about?'

'Did she say anything? I expected to be given my notice to find another position.'

'She saw us together last night, through a window. It has changed her.'

'And you are ordered to have no more to do with me, is that it? On pain of the Kirk Session.'

'Not at all, Nancy.' And I saw her strategy. She meant to woo me away from Nancy, was too proud to forbid what in any case, so plainly could not be forbidden.

'Are you sore from last night?'

'No, I am refreshed.'

'Well, then? Since the opportunity presents. She cannot return before luncheon.'

'Would she bring witnesses? Is that it?'

'No, what need of witnesses? Her own evidence is good enough. No, she will protect the family name. But she means to replace you in my affections.' At noon, Jean returned with a horse belonging to the brothers Glass and gave instructions to the men accompanying for her purchases to be taken upstairs.

When I saw what she had done I was astounded. She had purchased three large polished steel mirrors. 'What are these for?' I enquired of her.

'So that I can see what is happening when you use me, or rather, when we use each other. I find the sight enjoyable. I want you to install them for me, so that I can see us from the bed.'

When I said nothing for sheer astonishment, she continued: 'You have been learning to be a carpenter in that workshop of yours. Well then, you can put your skill to good use for me'.

And so, shamed into compliance, I put up the mirrors that same afternoon. Never at any time did Jean order me to desist from my enjoyment of Nancy. Nor did she seek to open a discussion about the matter. The subject was ignored as irrelevant. She had grown up, become calculating and manipulative but without malice—indeed, with a certain nobility of style that was charming—for that would not have enabled her to achieve her purpose which was to save her marriage. Only once did I ever come across her crying but she wiped the tears away, determined to look her best and my heart went out to her. Yet I still mated with Nancy and was given opportunities to do so, though fewer than before.

Jean was a person who liked riding and was happiest in the field. It kept her healthy, I expect, and she saw no good reason to hang about my coattails in hope of preventing me from exercising my passion. Maybe, she thought it would burn out in time, as such things do.

At the first calling of the Session Nancy declined to appear—as everyone in the town soon learned on the grapevine.

Accordingly, she was warned to compeir at the next meeting and knew that if she refused, she could be hauled up before the whole congregation on Sunday and put in the jougs—and maybe even stripped of her clothing and made to wear sackcloth.

VIII   Nancy and the Kirk Session[84]

That day, then, Nancy went, accompanied by myself and my wife as her employers, friendly supporters of some distinction, then.

The meeting began with prayers said by the ruling elder, Walter Stewart. Ten men, every one in black, sat on chairs arranged in a circle in the body

---

[84] Editor's note: this account is based on the report in the Kirk Session Records. See p290 et sequor especially 292-294. Ninian Bannatyne's is the only extra name that appears and it does so because it should have appeared. It was probably left out deliberately by the recorder, him being such a great man, one of the Session. Omitted by Robert Stewart of Scarrell, at this time for he was still Session Clerk.

of the Kirk under the pulpit, among them Sir James, Ninian Bannatyne, my wife's cousin and guardian, John Glass, Robert Jameson, crowner, and Walter Stewart—the last, having been elected ruling elder of the synod. I made my notes at a table to one side, as usual.

The accused or the delated people, with any permitted supporters, sat in the front pews and awaited their turn to stand up and be questioned.

The first case was that of Donald McIlduy who was alleged to have fornicated with More McIlrevie. Both confessed immediately and were required to satisfy according to the act.

It was then Nancy's turn. She stood up and faced them and I feared my terror must have been observed.

Walter Stewart said: 'You are with child. Who is the father?'

Nancy replied: 'Alexander Bannatyne.'

'So you admit you are with child?'

'Yes.'

'And the father is Alexander Bannatyne?'

'Yes, I just said so.'

This was a surprise to me. I looked at my wife and saw no answering smile of agreement. Yet, I knew that she had been free any day I was at school, to tutor Nancy in her responses. Nancy herself had said nothing of this in advance. I had no idea what she intended to say. She had merely refused to tell me. All I could say for sure was that I believed she would act to protect me and to prolong our temporary heaven of happiness, as she called it.

'Why did you conceal the name? Do you not ken that Baichalgrie, Gustavus Browne, young Sprinkell and Master Robert Stewart have all been accused? Even Ninian Bannatyne of Kames? All these good men defamed? What have you to say for yourself?'

'I left people to say what they pleased. Why should I defend myself? People will say what they please and nothing I say matters to them.'

'Did you ever name Gustavus Browne as the father?'

'No, I did not. Never!'

The other names were also gone over, including my own, without deference to my rank or presence. The Kirk Session was a hard place. All enquiries received negative replies. She had never been responsible for naming any of us.

'Well, gentlemen what do you think?' said Walter Stewart to the others in the circle.

Jameson said: 'There is a rumour that the real faither is no' young Bannatyne but another.'

'Why would she tell a lee?' said John Glass. 'She's tolt us weel enough. Aw we need is Alexander Bannatyne here tae confirm it. Next case.'

'I don't think so,' said Ninian Bannatyne. 'Alexander is just not up to it.'

After some muttering between the men, Walter declared: 'Nance Throw, you are to compeir at the next Session and confirm the father's name. Alexander Bannatyne will be warned to attend and he will declare himself.'

As we left the Kirk, Nancy said to me: 'What will Alexander have to do?'

'Either confirm or deny that he is the father. And if he is, to say when the act took place and where. Having initiated proceedings, they will not stop until they are satisfied they have the truth of it.'

Since the whole island was on watch there was no opportunity for Jean to visit Alexander to see what he would say and try to influence him. And yet, as I was soon to learn he had been got at.

Seven days later, the Session met again, though neither Alexander nor Nancy compeired, the date having been believed to be the usual two or three weeks hence.

'What am I going to do?' said Nancy to me, woefully, later that day.

'Why did you give Alexander's name?'

'Because Jean told me to.'

'When?'

'Some time ago. She told me Alexander wanted to marry me and that he would comply. And I was to give him forty merks.'

'Well, since you have explored the possibility, offer him, in addition, a butt of land at Scarrell—I don't need all of it— and a boll of victual every year for life.'

'So you approve, then?'

'Yes, it might just save us. It will be execution for me and drowning for you if we are found out.'

At that meeting later[85], Nancy was asked by Walter Stewart when it was that Alexander lay with her.

'About 8 days before Whitsuntide in Master Robert Stewart's house at Scarrell, when I was his servant.'

Master John Stewart, Minister, said: 'But you told me on the Monday before you first came to the Session that the bairn was got in Kames after Whitsunday when you were a servant with the Laird of Kames.'

---

[85] Editor's note: the dialogue given follows exactly the description in the Kirk Session Records. These are printed in full later. See p 293,4 herein.

'Come now, Nance!' said Walter Stewart, 'Tell us again: when and where did he lie with you?'
'About three nights after I came to Kames in the byre about the gloaming.'
'And when and where did he first have you?'
'About a year and a half ago in James McNiven's house when I was a servant there.'
'When was the last time Alexander Bannatyne had you?'
'About 8 days before St Bruxday[86] last in Robert Bannatyne's house at Mill of Ettrick.'
'Alexander Bannatyne, are you the father of Nance Throw's bairn?'
'I cannot deny that I lay with her but I do not know if I am the father.'
'When did you lie with her?'
'About a month before Whitsunday at Drumachcloy at a time when she went up to Scarrell to get meal for the English soldiers.'
'Did you have her at any time between then and Whitsunday?'
'Not until she left Master Robert's house and came to Kames.'
'When did you have her after going to Kames?'
'About ten or fourteen days after that at Knockanrioch outside the house.'
'When did you first have her?'
'About a year ago in Master Robert's house.'
'Did you ever have her in James McNiven's house when she was his servant?'
'No. I never had her till she came into Master Robert's service.'
'When did you have her last?'
'On the eve of St Brux in her father's house.'
'Did you ever have her any time but these two occasions since coming to Kames?'
'Once only as we were coming out of town on Kneslag Moor.'
'Did you ever have her at the Mill of Ettrick in Robert Bannatyne's house?'
'Never.'
'Nance Throw, did Alexander have you at Drumachcloy?'
'Yes.'
'Did he ever have you outside?'
'No. Only at Drumachcloy.'

---

[86] This is what this word is taken to mean. It is given as 'Bruixday.' See Stat Surv 1845 p102 where the name is explained: the minister's stipend was ' the vicarage and small *Brokis* of Rothesay'.

After some discussion, Walter Stewart declared: 'The evidence is contradictory and suggests collusion. Alexander is not the father. Both parties will compeir at the next Session when she will confess the true father.'

Nancy did not attend the next meeting, nor did Alexander.

Everything I and Nancy did was to extend our period of happiness and put off the day of retribution when everything must end. Yet I was then unaware of the full part played by my wife to try to keep the scandal at bay. When we mated now, Nancy and I, it was with the increasing awareness of the child between us. Nancy began to complain of the weight and there was a sadness in her eye whenever we met.

I suppose I became distracted by all the trouble, would retire to my sanctuary to read or make bookshelves and other furniture—which at last was actually useful in diverting my mind from worry—only occasionally disturbed there by Nancy, Jean being around so much and being aware. Yet she never interfered and she was wise in this for as Nancy increased in girth my appetite for her declined. Instead, gradually, all my moments were being expended upon my wife. This is simply a fact. I am not proud of it. The desperate passion of my love seemed to decline just as her girth increased. What an ignoble fellow I soon began to feel. But worse was to come, far worse!

IX SUNDAY SERVICE AT THE KIRK

I have often wondered why the sabbath day attendance, mandatory on everyone, is called a service. It is certainly not a service so far as many of the congregation are concerned but an unpleasant duty, though it may be a service to God, assuming there is one and every Kirker believes there is, with a few exceptions.

As time went on, I found it an increasingly onerous duty. I had to sit among the gentry with Jean, my spouse, and listen to a ministry that I gradually learned was very singular in its concern with sin: the identification, the confession, the repentance and the punishment—that most of all. Exodus says the breaker of the sabbath should be put to death? Then so let it be, was John Stewart, the Minister's view. An opinion he was only obstructed from enacting as a fact by the articles of the General Assembly some of which, the moderating ones, he had doubtless voted against.

On a typical Sunday, Jean and I were in the front row of the pews beside the aisle, as I liked, for I prefer to get up and go quickly. On the way in, we had passed, standing among the servants, my Nancy, big now with child and the object of every eye in the place. After sitting for a while waiting for the thing to start, images of Nancy crossed and recrossed my mind: Nancy looking up at me out of a golden face with a golden smile; Nancy in her shift with the light behind her in my bedroom; Nancy open wide on the kitchen table among her new cut vegetables; Nancy naked on the hall table with Jean's tear-stained face in the dark hood peering at us through the window; and, now, Nancy standing behind me with a huge lump in her belly that could mean only one thing.

I had to wipe away a tear and when I had done it, I stood up, went out to the people standing behind the pews, took Nancy by the arm and led her to a seat in the front row beside me. As I was seating Nancy in the space beside me, Jean said: 'Robert, I don't think you should...'

'—Of course I should. She should not be standing at all in this condition.'

So there we were, the three of us, under the eye of everyone able to see us. And on both sides, the choir was particularly well placed to see us, could not avoid staring at us for the entire duration of the service, by heaven. How I regretted my moment of kindness! To sit there, all three of us in a row, under the merciless gaze of that black-garbed group of Kirkers was a penance in itself.

Was it because he had us under his eye? Was that the reason for the sermon that day? I still do not know. The Minister was ever an admirer of the book of Exodus. That day he gave us a particularly lengthy rendition, waving his arms like weapons, the black cassock rippling around him, showering us with texts so that the sayings of Moses rained down upon our heads beneath relentlessly. Some I remember were:

Exodus 22 v16: 'And if a man entice a maid that is not betrothed, and lie with her, he shall surely endow her to be his wife.' I blanched at this and then turned red. My crime was far worse. And I already had a wife.

Exodus 22 v18: 'Thou shalt not suffer a witch to live.'

v19: 'Whosover lieth with a beast shall surely be put to death.' I had thought of this myself, when in extremis and could not see much wrong with it.

v20: 'He that sacrificeth unto any god save unto the Lord only, he shall be utterly destroyed.' A puzzle, that one, for none of my beloved Greeks who had never heard of the Lord were destroyed, at least for that reason.

v22: 'Ye shall not afflict any widow or fatherless child.' I wondered if my actions with widows counted as afflictions and knew that our Minister would think so.

v23: 'If thou afflict them in any wise, and they cry at all unto me, I will surely hear their cry;
v24: 'And my wrath shall wax hot, and I will kill you with the sword; and your wives shall be widows, and your children fatherless.' So, adults were not to be excused the punishment of death using their children as an excuse. Retribution not charity was what this god promised. I decided that I preferred the Greek ones. But I was in such extremity, I was scarcely rational.

On and on it went and it was as if I had never heard it before. The words, had in truth, swept over me before without disturbing my mind very much by their very habit and insistence. On the point of destruction, my soul shivered and my mind looked about for the first time and realised what darkness it had been existing within.
Then he moved onto temptation, another favourite subject of his.
'The devil is in every inanimate thing and every living thing. When you least expect it, he is by your lug whispering defection from the true path. Fear him, lest he tempt you away and send you to eternal damnation in hellfire. Our road is hard. The Lord has willed it so. And the devil has been sent to test each one of us every day, every moment of every day.
'Do you even think of raising a hand to another? That is the devil within you. Do you even think of another glass of aquavitae? That is the devil within you. Do you think of not stepping on a cracked paving stone in the street? That is the devil within you. Do you see a person or an animal behave strangely? That is the devil within them. The devil can possess anyone at any time and often when least expected. Beware of him! For he will make promises and you must resist them. Fail and you go to hellfire and damnation! The joys of this world must be given up for the sake of the next. You will all receive your reward in paradise.'
The voice of the Minister rose to a high pitch and just at that moment—for the noise of it, the sound and the fury of it must have affected the very fabric of the Kirk itself—a large piece of white paint fell from the plastered side of a great window, leaving a strange shape: a round head with two small horns, a broad body and a long snaky tail with an arrowhead at the end and there, at the base, its presence signalled by some darker stone underneath, stood an erect penis. So at least it seemed to my eye and from the position in which I sat. It was the very image of the devil, the devil so beloved, I now saw for the first time, by our Minister. Why else did he speak so often about him? Only the legs were missing.

There was a gasp from some people but no concerted astonishment. Maybe it was my fevered state that made me see it this way, that gave me this interpretation of an accident. But it seemed like an omen of things yet to come; only I, it seemed, had noticed it.

A psalm was then sung by everyone standing and, for once, I revelled in its beauty. Here was something, a human creation, that lifted the spirit out of the dark abyss in which the Minister had thrown it and I looked heavenwards and felt glad. At my side I could feel the gentlest touch of Nancy beside me and I remembered how it had been between us and I rejoiced—in spite of the danger and the impending destruction of my life—I rejoiced. There was goodness in it, there had been and always would be. It could not be taken away, not by all the rantings from the pulpit that ever were.

The service over, I shepherded my women ahead of me, Jean in the lead, and we three left the Kirk, walking between black-garbed people of the island who stared at us like carrion crows waiting to feed.

X Evidence of Lechery

On the 5th of February, Nancy did not appear as usual and enquiry soon revealed that she was having the child that day. As a prospective father, my feelings were far from what they ought to have been. I should have been joyous and was not. Here, soon, would be the evidence of my lechery—at least as it would be seen by the community.

In time, I learned that the child was male and healthy as was the mother herself. Nancy appeared no more in our house and was supported by her father in his own.

Hoping for a miracle of some kind, I did nothing. Sent no message, no presents of any kind nor any money for maintenance. To have done so would have put the issue beyond doubt.

On 23rd May, 1661, at the meeting of the Session, John McKinley of Drumachcloy was compeired and declared that Alexander Bannatyne was not at home when Nance Throw came seeking meal. John McLennan and John McKinlay's wife were wanted to compeir at the next Session.

On 20th June, 1661, the Session decided that—since Alexander Bannatyne was not in Drumachcloy on the 5th May 1660, when the child was conceived—he was not the father.

Somehow the idea that it was myself that was the father began to circulate even more strongly.

Since there was a 'flagrant scandal that Master Robert Stewart is the father of Nance Throw's bairn'[87], the Session summoned me to the next meeting.

These words were the last I wrote as Clerk to the Kirk Session. I announced to the eldership that, in the circumstances, I must demit the office. And as I stood up facing them, quill in hand, I had the presence of mind to add: 'Until the matter be resolved.' There was, even yet, a slender hope that some miracle would save me, not much, but something.

The night before, while I was in my sanctum, Ninian Bannatyne arrived.

The first I knew of it was when I looked up to see him standing just inside the door with a face like thunder.

'So this is where you did it! You will be crucified for this. And the shame will blight our family for all time!' Then he broke down and wept tears of woe such as I had never seen. 'I should have kenned better!' he wailed, 'You were known as a man that went with wanting widows. Why did I pay no heed? Why did we all pay no heed?'

Jean came in: 'Ninian, Robert, come into the house and sit down. We will talk it out and decide what must be done.' And for the first time in his life she led her proud friend away, stooped over as if he had been shot in the stomach. Before, he had always led.

In the house, in the best room at the front, we three sat around the fire until I got up and poured drams of aquavitae and brandy for my wife.

'You must leave him and come back with us to Kames, Jean,' said Ninian. Then, as an afterthought: 'You are not with child, are you?'

'No, Ninian.'

'Well, that's something. You must come tonight. Keep well away from this man and this house or the mud will stick to you. And to the family. Shame is contagious.'

Jean looked very fine that evening. Indeed, I think she never looked so well before or since. 'I am not coming. Not tonight or any night. I will stand by my husband.'

'No! No, you canny do that!'

'He has some chance if we stick together.'

'He has no chance! None at all! There are calls in the town to hang him at the Gallowscraig. Adultery and lying to the Session and putting the charge on Sandy Bannatyne! And him a preacher. A preacher who

---

[87] P293 herein for full text.

preached here in this very Kirk about all the sins of the flesh and what would happen to offenders. THEY WILL CRUCIFY HIM! And they will be right.' Ninian arose and took Jean by the arm. 'Come now, my lass. I am your cousin and I say: come!'

But Jean would have none of this. She threw off his arm and standing back before the blazing fire said: 'I am staying here with my husband and I will be there when the Session meets to support him, any way I can.'

As he was about to leave, Ninian turned to me and said: 'How could you do this to me? To me! For months they thought *I* was the father! You let them think so! It was a smear on the escutcheon! My family name was in jeopardy! And you did nothing!'

On 4th July, 1661, at the Session, Nancy admitted that I was the father and that I had told her she would be drowned and I would be executed if it were discovered because I am a preacher. Thus, she had agreed to ask Alexander Bannatyne to admit to being the father and if he did, that I would give him 40 merks, a boll of victuals every year and a butt of land at Scarrell, just as soon as the child was baptised in his name.

This was the work of Jean: to get Sandy Bannatyne to take the blame and even the bribes. I persuaded Nancy to say that I myself had made these moves. The idea of involving Jean after she had suffered so much by my lust was repugnant to me. Also, she was doing her best to protect me and her family.

At the next meeting of the Session, Alexander and I were called. He broke down in tears and admitted his deception. He loved Nancy, he said and declared that the child was not his for he never had any carnal dealing with her. He denied that anyone but Nancy had approached him on this matter. Put to his oath, Alexander swore that this was so.

I did not appear. Jean went in my stead.

The idea of appearing before the Session was terrifying to me. Does any man go willingly to his crucifixion? Only Jesus Christ. The rest of us have to shiver in our shoes and will put off the vile moment at any cost to reputation or self image. And why not? The utter destruction of both is at hand.

The effect of the situation in which I now found myself made me ill. I fell to sneezing and had sore joints and felt listless. So I took to my bed and Jean let it be known that I was sick. By God was I sick! And no wonder!

A few weeks later, I received visitors, Sir James Stewart and the Minister. Since they would not be put off by Jean they were allowed to interview me at my bedside.

Sir James was rather fat and very kindly, with only half a head of hair that was white with age. He would have been about 60 at the time. After enquiring after my health, he leaned forward and said:

'Robert, you have been proved to be the father of Nance Throw's child. What do you have to say for yourself?'

I wept. The tears fell for a time and then I said: 'I fell in love with the lady. There was nothing I could do to stop it.'

'When are you going to be well enough to compeir at the Session?'

'I don't know.'

'Well, when you do, make no talk of love. Tell them the devil took possession of you. They'll understand that. I'll hold them off as long as I can but you will have to come and submit to their judgement.' That was the last day I went walking in the town. In the street by the Castle I met Ninian Kerr and Walter Stewart, both elders who had been present at the Session meeting when Nancy admitted my crime.

Ninian took me by the collar and pressed his face close to mine. 'Yer a black herted bastard!' he swore, the anger in him actually grating his teeth. 'And you a minister too! You...you...you're the biggest scandal this island ever kenned!' he stammered, spitting foam with the words that hit me in the face.

'Come on, Ninian, ye canny swear,' said Walter, taking him by the shoulder to pull him away. 'I'll have to report ye. Leave him alane. He'll get what's coming to him soon enough. Come away man!'

And they turned away and never addressed me in the street again.

This was the first sign of ostracism. There were many others. Soon, I went no more into the town, would do anything to avoid it and the slights I would receive there.

XI Meetings With Witches

For months, I remained officially ill. I never at any time saw Nancy. It would have been unwise even to attempt to see her. Anyway, she was taken up with the child and rarely left her father's house. Because of my attitude the boy remained unbaptised. Not until the end of November 1661 was I compeired and so from July until then I was in a state of acute distress. If I went out no one would as much as look in my direction. No one would speak to me—they would hardly speak to Jean, even. For the sake of company she would increasingly take herself off to Kames, often spending several nights at a time. I took less and less care of myself— my appearance most of all—and must have looked a rather wild shaggy dark haired person, indeed, before long[88]. Shunned by the townspeople, I would make for the moors and stretch my legs there.

After a few weeks of moor-walking, when I saw few people, my health returned—at least my physical well being. My mental health remained at a low ebb. I knew I would have to appear before the Kirk Session. I knew I would be crucified—or at least would experience a public humiliation of a kind exceptional even in those harsh times, for my offences, as perceived by the community, were heinous. And the fact that I might regard myself as having been in love would do nothing for my case. Sir James was right. I had to blame the matter on the devil—I had to go along with the prevailing view of the Session and of my wife that the devil had taken possession of me, to have any chance of mitigating my punishment—which might well involve my death and would certainly entail the death of my life as it had been. The very shunning which I now experienced told me that I would be shunned forever.—A feature that I had known well enough from the beginning and took no notice of. Here, now, it was a fact. And I could not face it!

Intellectually, the idea that I should have to tell lies and admit to possession by the devil—by unknown dark forces opposed to everything I had been brought up to admire—when the truth was that I had loved passionately and followed my passion to its natural physical consummation—was hard to stomach. Would it not be better, I asked myself, repeatedly, just to tell the truth?

And Nancy, what was her position? I could not tell; but the absence of any contact for almost a year before we faced each other in the Kirk— for I ceased altogether to attend, pleading illness (which would have suited some elders because of the threat I posed) though she did otherwise. Every Sunday, she went as before, with the child in her arms, unbaptised though it remained.

I think what happened to both of us was that we were caught up in the vice-like grip of the feelings against us, so that we gradually ceased to feel anything for each other; were so attacked within ourselves by every look and gesture that came our way, that we could only look outward and away from what had lain within each other, for it was that terrible passion

---

[88] A description of the man, afterwards taken to be the devil, with whom Jonet Morison made her covenant. SeeI D p 21; p269 herein; 'a black (haired) rough fierce man'. He would have seemed black in the twilight.

that had provoked the onslaught of hatred and disapproval. I felt no impulse to visit Nancy and I do not think she had any either to visit me—or she would have, covered by the darkness, at night time, say, when no one could see her.

The effect too upon Jean, of spending so much time at Kames, separated from me, as well as the daily reinforcement of her family and friends' injunctions to make the separation permanent, was to lessen her feeling of obligation to a marriage that could not be sustained under the pressure of the virulent disapproval of the entire community.

However, the whole community did not think this. Walking on the moor[89] south of Kerrycresach one day, I was marching along keeping an eye out for anyone I might avoid when in front of me, a figure straightened up near a clump of gorse that grows there and I beheld, close to, Margaret McWilliam, whose hair had turned grey over the years, as I could see under the kerchief she had partly covered it with. She wore a grey smock with a large pocket in front, from the edges of which peeped a variety of herbs and leaves which she had evidently been collecting.

'A fine day, sir,' she said, looking at me directly, as was her way.

I nearly wept, for here at least was one who was willing to talk to me. I gave her good day and sat down on a tussock, positioning myself to look out across the water to the high mountains with jagged tops covered over with a light covering of snow on the neighbouring island of Arran.

'Aye, it's a braw day no matter the trouble. I heard aboot it. The hale place—toon and country—is burstin' wi' it. What will ye dae?'

'I don't know,' I replied and, suddenly, I burst into tears which fell like lumps of sleet. I got up immediately, embarrassed by my show of feeling and tried to turn away from her. But she would have none of my modesty at my feeling.

'Na, na,' she said, approaching and put a hand around my shoulders. 'Ye loved the woman, did ye no'? That's aw it was. I ken fine. There's nae haudin' back. It takes ye ower, so it does.'

She clasped me to her bosom and I felt blessed by her presence. It was the first human comfort I had received in many weeks and the surge in my body which was instant, as if by a man starved for a year of female company, was sudden and severe and she knew instantly what I needed.

'You were very good tae me, Sir, a long time ago, and I see what you would be at..'

---

[89] Editor's note: Scoulag moor.

THE STORY OF ROBERT STEWART OF SCARRELL 127

So the lady and I made love on the moor among the tussocks; and, for a short time, I left off thinking of my worries because I was lodged so deep and so gratefully within her softness. What a blessed relief it was to me! When I thanked her, she replied:

'Think nothing of it. It was good. I liked it very weel. Ye were aye a muckle man!' and she chuckled happily. 'And a very handsome man, even if ye are in trouble.'

For a little while we sat together in companionable silence looking at the stone gods carved by the elements on the distant mountain until she said:

'Weel, no' everybody is against ye. I remember how good ye were tae me in ither times. Ye still have a friend here. Aye, there's a few like me.'

'Who else?'

'The witch folk. Did ye no' ken I have the name of a witch?'

'I had heard this but discounted it. I know you of old. I don't believe all that claptrap.'

'It's no aw claptrap.'

'You mean you practise witchcraft?'

'Weel atween you and me, I dae a wee bitty.'

'What do you mean? Do you put spells on people?'

'Aye and worse!' she laughed gaily.

Horrified, I demanded to know what she meant.

'I use my knowledge o' plants and sich tae get my ain back on ma persecutors.'

'Who do you mean?'

'Aw weel,' she laughed, 'there wis John McFie's horse[90]. McFie wanted to flit from Kerrycresach tae Lochly and cross my field at Corsmore. I had crops planted and I didnae want his gear on the sleds[91] chawing up my sore won work. There wis three of them. Hector, his faither, and his brother, each wi' a horse drawn sled. They threw doon my slap atween thaim and ma field and as they pulled it doon I built it up again. I even lay doon alang the tap o' the slap tae try and stop them. But it wis nae guid. There wis jist me, ye ken. I fought wi' John but he wis ower strang. So they won through and drew their sleds across my field. But I shoved a pock o' witchcraft intae the mooth of o' one horse and it gat sich a shock

---

[90] Editor's note: The Inverary Document contains this account at greater length. See ID p 15 ie p 264 herein.

[91] Editor's note: no wheeled vehicles, according to John Blain, even by mid 18th century. This means goods were transported by a kind of pallet, most of it off the ground, resting on the rear haunches of the horse or by panniers on either side of it.

it fell doon and widnae draw the sled for haulf an hoor!' She clapped her hands with joy at this.

'So they ruined your crops?'

'Aye, so they did. Some anyway. But McFie came doon wi' a seeckness.'

'But you had no part in that?'

'Naw, no' me. He got his seeckness aw by himsel'. But he blamed me, mind, jist the same.'

'What did you give the horse?'

'Ugh, naething much. Jist some seeds I had about me in my pooch.' The horse was mair afraid a me than onything.'

'And there are others like you, you tell me?'

'Och aye. It's maistly harmless. We meet on the moors on Saturday afternoons when everybody else is in the town. Ye maun join us, ye ken. Ye'll be welcomed there.'

'How can that be? The word will be out to shun me. I know it is out for I have experienced it. I daren't go into town for fear of being pelted by my former scholars. The worst drunken vagrant will think me a fair target. If they set about me I would get no help from anyone.'

'We go to the Kirk because we have tae. But we don't gang wi' their stern and cruel ways. We put in oor appearance on the Sabbath and then go oor ain ways. So on Saturdays we take a wee picnic tae a secret place and we eat and drink a wee bitty and dance thegither and talk a wee bit fun. Life is no sae drab after that. And if we are aw poor folk at least we get a wee bitty guid company fur wanst.'

In this manner, by invitation, I attended my first meeting of the witch folk. It was held on the high ground south of Kingarth, through a wood and up a steep hill which the high minded members of the Kirk there would have no need to ascend— and therefore well out of sight. Everyone went singly and by disparate routes so that no one was followed, and if they had been, no meeting would have been held. And there, after months of terror at what might befall me at the hands of my fellow men, I was treated to scones and honey and ale and bannocks browned over a wood fire and even a stew of rabbit which one of the men had snared that morning with a sprinkling of carrots and kale which one of the women cooked in an iron cauldron over a fire that smelled like heaven. And there was dancing: Katherine, a young lass of 20, Alexander McIlmartin's daughter, from Kelspoke, the croft above the shore, not a mile away, being elected queen of the dance. It was a pleasure and it was relaxing and so very different from the strict censured life demanded by the Presbyterians.

Best of all, no one condemned me for my love and its dire consequences. I was asked about it and answered honestly and was understood. I had loved the lady and there was nothing I could have done to prevent it or the consummation of that love. And once begun... well, everyone understood that kind of thing. The body was ever the master of the soul when it came to romance. The attitude of the Kirk Session to such affairs of the heart was one that astonished and revolted this company who put up with it because there was no alternative; it was a matter of power, ultimately. They—elders and burgesses—were the masters who paid the wages; they had the power to deprive them of work and livelihood and the power of punishment for infringement of the laws which governed everyone, though why these laws were in force and not others more forgiving and loving was a deep mystery no one bothered to consider.

'But I should not have done it,' I said weakly, after some discussion among them.

'How no'?' said Margaret McLevin of Ardroscadale. 'Ye couldnae help yersel''

'I put Nancy in an impossible position. Maybe I should have sent her away to be a servant elsewhere.'

'But ye couldnae dae that. Ye loved her. Any man would love her! How could ye expect tae gi'e her up?'

The talk moved on from me to them and their doings and I gradually began to understand them in a way withheld from me by my wealth, class and education. Here, at last, because I had been, as it were, thrown out of the community—was at least on the way out, only the formalities yet to be performed—I had made contact with the poorest members of it in a fashion impossible before. I had become one of them.

Margaret McWilliam, I soon learned, was the star. Standing on the top of the hill above the bay she and I looked eastwards to the islands and then north west to where, beneath the wood, stood the manse of Kingarth.

'Mind the time ye put witchcraft on the minister?' said Margaret McLevin who joined us.

'Aye, fine,' answered Margaret McWilliam. 'It wis seven year ago.'

'That would be Master John Stewart, then,' I said. 'He was minister here before he moved to Rothesay.' My companion at dinner at Sir James Stewart's hall, then. 'I heard that his wife died and that he was ill for five years and unable to attend his parish.'

The women— all of them, for they had all joined us— laughed. 'It was what he deserved. And it kept him from pestering us. If there was nae minister there was nae Kirk and if there was nae Kirk we had a better chance at life.' There was more laughter.

'But the Kirk Session. Surely that kept things going as usual?'

'Just the formalities,' said Katherine Stewart of Largizean, the farm to the west, below the hill we were standing on. 'It's a wee Kirk and a wee congregation. With the minister in his bed we were left alane for wanst.'

'What did you do? To make him keep to his bed?'

'Naething much. Just put cow shite in his watter.'

'You mean you poisoned his well?'

'No, he used the burn in the gairden tae fill his pails. It wis easy.'

'But didn't he know?'

'Naw. He niver kenned.'

'But his wife died of this!'

'His wifie died, right enough, but wha kens what she died o'?'

Not for the first time I was horror-struck again. 'But this was murder.'

McWilliam stood tall and eyed me. 'It wisnae murder. He wis persecuting me so I got my ain back and persecuted him. Why should I lie doon and take all his calumnies and punishments? A body has tae fight back. Stand up and resist. Whit else could I do? Do ye think I wasnae tired o' being put in the stocks or the jougs? De ye ken how they hurt? And what for? For breaking the Sabbath or getting drunk or telling off some man that wid take advantage of me? The man was murderin' my soul! No' takin' care o' it. The way a minister is supposed.'

Suddenly my horror ceased. I could see her point at last. Putting cow shite in the water was a small enough action and it may have caused some discomfort but it was unlikely to have led to a death—good heavens, cows were forever shitting in burns and nobody knew, so what was the harm?—and even if it had been the cause, at least the offence had serious mitigation: a minister who had treated her with charity—the charity demanded by the Bible, especially in the celebrated epistle of Paul to the Corinthians—would never have provoked such conduct. The fault ultimately, it seemed to me, lay with the minister himself and his unbecoming conduct. The futility of preaching a harsh standard was never so clear as when the preached unto got back at you for it.

That day up the hill in the south of the island, as it grew dark, Katherine McIlmartine began to sing in a voice that rose like a lark above the flames of the fire and all talk ceased. It was a voice that was made to sing and yet its songs were very simple and mostly the tunes of the church. In that society—the community at large— there were no songs that were not sung in church. It was as if the Church had placed a stranglehold on song as well as every kind of entertainment. She sang in the Irish and she sang well, of a fisherman lost at sea and the girl he left behind him.

Then Margaret McWilliam stood up and said: 'It's time. We'll aw pray for the damnation of Walter Stewart—a baillie and treasurer of the Kirk, who had behaved badly towards the old mother of John Galie of Barmore by demanding money for repairs to the Kirk when she had no money to pay and was too weak and ill to argue back.

And so with Margaret standing in the centre by the fire and surrounded by the small group of a dozen or so, everyone bent their heads in prayer.

'Repeat efter me,' said Margaret, raising her hands to the star-encrusted sky. 'I call on aw the powers ae heaven and aw the power ae darkness...' and everyone repeated the words.. 'tae damn Walter Stewart and caw doon on his heid fire and pestilence and ill luck. May his crops fail and his business fail and his bairns fa' ill and his spouse become barren. For he is a bad man and aw the powers in the universe is tae gang up agin him and bring doon his pride.' Everyone followed her. After a pause for reflection I followed her lead and made my plea in no small voice but in a loud one. And I saw that it pleased her. By taking part, I had joined them, given them the visible sign of my allegiance. It was against everything I had been taught and even believed but I did it. And without regret.

I could have refused, could have gone off, away with from such cantraips[92] but had I done so, I would then have been alone. Saying the spell was a harmless enough thing in itself. If it was the price of my initiation, it seemed to me, it was worth it. But as I left the hill in the twilight it occurred to me that I would try to provide a more Christian philosophy of forgiveness in the times that lay ahead.

In the months that followed that bleak July 4th when Nancy gave up my name at the Session, I lived in a state of continual torment, interrupted only briefly but with what real relief, by meetings with the witch folk which took place every week or so and sometimes oftener.

With them I enjoyed my only society. They treated me at first with deference, as someone of standing, with real talents as well as income and a style of life far above their own. And I was so grateful to them and I wished to do everything in my power to befriend them, for, of course, I could very well see that these poor people were the only ones now available to me for fellowship. I knew, even then, you see, that my life therafter—if indeed I had one—would be outside the church and even, that all the church folk I knew and those I did not would never speak to

---

[92] Editor's note: spells, tricks or paraphernalia of witch craft or magic

me again because they would be told not to. Excommunication was—according to the Act of the General Assembly of 1638—inevitable for me, no matter what I contrived, no matter what miracle of mitigation I could conceive. The issue was, in truth: could I survive at all? I suppose, at that difficult time, I felt a bit like Christ who, conscious of the inevitability of his imminent destruction at the hands of the community, is especially eager to use the time remaining for good works.

Thus it was, being a preacher as well as a schoolmaster, that I was naturally led into the practice of the very professions in which I had training and some proficiency. And because of my isolation I soon came to enjoy these meetings as I had never enjoyed—well, anything, except the act of procreation. I would attend, come rain or snow, and that winter there was a deal of both. At first, I was almost alone when the weather was bad but, in time, some people always joined me and I think it was the comfort I gave them that brought this about. Of course I needed the food they brought, for my stores at home had received no replenishment: that was the worst aspect of ostracism: the lack of food or means of acquiring it. Jean had by then disappeared completely from my life, perhaps held captive by her family at Kames, I know not; maybe it was choice, a recognition of simple necessity on her own part. Like Nancy, she seemed to vanish from my world altogether. Of course, I could have gone into town, even then, at least at that stage, to buy the necessaries and would have been sold them but the disapproval and the questions that would be asked by anyone I came across were too much for my sensitive soul. I could not endure what I knew would be the reaction of everyone.

And there was the new thought in me, the new level of being, almost, wherein, freed at last from the manacles of the Kirk, at least in mind, I found myself examining every one of the beliefs demanded by it. Since I was doomed, had little time left for life, the strictures imposed fell away. In this freedom to think, all alone most of the time, but stimulated to do so at the meetings by the ordinary folk themselves, childlike in their questioning—and yet questions of such power—I increasingly felt blessed not just by their society but by the proper exercise of their minds. The phenomenon reminded me of the Platonic dialogue [93] wherein Socrates draws forth knowledge of mathematics from a child and shows that it was always present in him.

It began quickly—almost as if my soul needed employment in good works. We were sitting, Margaret McLevin and I, on a hill near Barmore

---

[93] Editor's note: the author is referring to *Meno*.

overlooking Scalpsie beach and the blue water which stretched as far as the eye could see between the land and islands to the far horizon, away to the south. The weather was fine, a lovely summer day with few clouds and little wind. The rocks on the mountain on the island opposite glinted in the sunlight. 'Sir', she said to me—they all insisted on this old manner of address, out of habit, I suppose, even though I was on the point of social oblivion—'Have I any chance of getting to heaven?'

The question startled me into wondering, as I had rarely done for a long time and I found myself answering not the intellectual question but dealing with the tortured soul instead: 'Why should you not have as much a chance as anyone else?'

'Because I have the name of a witch.'

'And are you a witch?'

'I don't rightly know. But some folk calls me a witch.'

'What do you do, that makes them say this?'

'I try and help them over their troubles with charms and herbs and potions and poultices.'

'And is that all you do?'

'Yes, Sir.'

'So you do not harm and are trying to help people?'

She agreed that this was so.

'And is what you do helpful? Are people made well by it?'

'Sometimes. At least they keep on asking me to help.'

'And why do they ask you?'

'When there is nobody else to ask. Or it costs money they don't have.'

'Well, I don't see how that could count against you.'

Margaret was cheered by this conclusion. 'Thank you sir, Oh thank you.'

After a silence, she tried to return the help: 'What about yourself, Sir? After all your trouble, I mean?'

'I am not sure there is a heaven,' I found myself saying. 'At least, not as we are mostly given to believe by ministers.'

'But you are a minister, Sir?'

'Yes, but I was not appointed. Probably because I did not have the faith expected. And lately I have begun to doubt everything.'

Though, by rights, I should have left it there for the sake of preserving my companion's comforting illusions, my enforced isolation made me continue to ruminate aloud.

'If there is a heaven, it must be a very busy place with all the countless millions who have gone there. And it cannot be a place up there in the sky somewhere, as most men think. There are stars up there, thousands of them and heaven knows what else but there is no heaven there, I feel certain. Heaven is just an idea and I don't think anything corresponds to the idea. It is an idea men have invented.'

'But it's in the Bible, isn't it?'

'Yes, but the Bible was written down by men.'

'What about hell?'

'Another idea invented by men,' I told her, sadly.

Others joined us and it became a habit of our meetings that I would sit on a rock on the moor somewhere out of sight of the Kirk Folk, usually up a hill and in a hollow somewhere either north of Edinbeg, though the walking there was difficult because of the tussocks, or above Scalpsie or on the moor near Ascog called Scoulag. And I would think aloud for the benefit of my new friends. And it was a task I enjoyed as no other, as if I had been born to it.

Mostly I spoke of love, my love for Nancy, of course, but my loves of other women—a kind of confessional it was. And why not? Now that my future was all too clear what was the point of subterfuge? My friends might actually learn something useful from my experience. So at least I thought.

It is easy to see how I got into this. The women especially, all wanted to know how it was I got caught out by Nancy, how I yielded to temptation, for that was the way they saw it at first, just as any of the Kirkers would.

'Was it wrong of me to provide love to wanting widows?' I asked them. And everyone quickly agreed it made sense. Why deprive a woman of what she needed, especially when I needed it too? The only difficulty was not that a child might ensue—a child was probably wanted anyway and might be conceived close enough to the death of the husband to pass as his own. It was just that the community was against it. And there was no good reason for this. Not even the Bible— the best bits of it anyway— was really against it.

'What would Jesus do in a case like that?' I asked them. 'That is always the test.'

'Aye, right, he would a helped the wumman, sure enough,' said Patrick McKaw, a farmer at Garrochty who laughed and added. 'Ah don't suppose he wid say: away an' fuck yersel'. The wumman couldnay dae that.'

'If there is no heaven,' said the young maiden of Kelspoke who was often appointed queen of our gatherings because she was pleasing to look upon, 'does that mean there is no hell either?'

'What we are told about hell is that it is frightening and painful and hot and fiery, and that those who live there are consumed by flames in a kind of eternal agony. What happens when something burns in flames?'
'It becomes ash and then the wind scatters it and it is no more.'
'Well, if hell is really a fiery furnace it means we are consumed by the flames immediately, which means we are turned into ash and no longer feel anything at all.'
'So hell is not so bad, Sir?'
'I don't see how it could be. How could it be worse than what we already have here on earth? Even the witch burned at the stake is consumed by the flames and turned to ash. And the ash is scattered by the wind, as you say. How could the witch go on feeling the pain of the fire when she no longer has any flesh to feel anything?'

'So what happens when ye die?' said Margaret McLevin.
'What do you think happens? What do you know happens?'
'Yer body rots and stinks and in a wee while there's nothing but bones and it disnae even stink.'
'Well, since you know this, that is what happens when you die.'
'But the minister says yer soul gangs tae heaven,' said Margaret.
'—or Hell,' said Miss McIlmartin.
'And if there is no heaven and no hell, what then?'
'Yer soul doesnae go anywhere.'
'Right! It does not go anywhere because there is nowhere to go.'
'So what happens to you then, when you die?' said Margaret, still unsatisfied.
'You know the answer. That is all the answer there is. This is what all our experience tells us. When men and women die they cease to be, their bodies rot and decay and all that remains is old bones. There is nothing else.'
'But what about the afterlife? The life in paradise, heaven, that the Minister teaches in the Kirk?'
'The Bible does not actually say that this is what will happen. Even if it did, it is an invention by some ancient men who were not infallible. Nobody has ever seen this heaven, so we have no good reason to believe it exists, as some men say.'
'Does this mean that there is no reason to be good? If there is no heaven and hell, what is the point of being good?'
'I am sure there are reasons for being good. But it is not a good reason for being good that there is a reward in heaven. If people are only good

because they expect to live hereafter in paradise, that is a pretty selfish reason for being good. The only reasons for being good that are honourable are those that are unselfish: that we do good things because they are right and proper, and we do them even if we get hurt in the process.'

As time went on, I began to realise that what I had been doing was preaching to a congregation of distressed people and soon saw them gradually grow in number. And the success of the meetings was due to the opening up of my own mind under the duress of imminent destruction. Although these days of meeting were the best times, the evenings were miserable. I took again to roaming the edges of the town in the darkness and occasionally came across people like Jonet Morison[94], a comely enough maidservant who was employed at Wester Kames. In the twilight, one evening, she was on her way back to Kilmory where she lived in a tiny settlement not far from the old Castle, home of the Jameson's, the crowners[95] of the island. As I was having one of my moments at the time—God knows I was never free of these!—it was natural to make a request that she serve me, though, in truth, I could not well make out her appearance then. I knew only that the person in front of me on the path was a woman and one with a sweet voice, presumed young, then.

Because of the new predicament—facing destruction by the Kirk Session—I was even less circumspect than before about approaching women. And why not? I could chap every door on the island and ask the good dame and what difference? I would be condemned just the same. Tuition in Euclidean reasoning had its advantages. The conclusion was clear and you went for it immediately in as direct and economical a fashion as could be provided. I do believe that this confidence in logic is the basis of the astounding success of most great men: they see and they act accordingly and they win through because, having the confidence in their conclusions, honed as they are by Euclid's example, they make the move when everyone else is undecided, static and unready. That alone is almost enough to secure its success.

I offered her everything she wanted, as usual, in these cases but she was coy and demurred and it was only on a second occasion at Knockanrioch

---

[94] Like so many scenes, the one that follows is reported in the confessions within the Inverary Document. See p 269 herein.
[95] Coroner is the English equivalent but the Scottish crowner was different: a man who kept an eye out for evil doing and acted to resolve it; sometimes the Sheriff, sometimes not.

at the edge of the woods when I met her again, that this time she agreed. As I was very needful of her services, the full compact was not discussed until afterward and it was only then that I learned of her infatuation for Adam Kerr, the black sheep of the family of Kerrs, one of whom, Ninian, was an enemy of mine on the Kirk Session. Adam Kerr, it turned out, had been banished to the highlands by his family for reasons unclear. Jonet, though married to a Morrison and living at Kilmory, nourished a crush on Adam that time had done nothing to diminish. Would I write to Adam Kerr and encourage him to come home to Bute? Being unable to write and even unaware of the formalities involved in letter writing and delivery, Jonet could not do this herself. So, in return for her service, I was to perform this one for her. I provided the letter that very day, the money to send it and the name of the man who would see it on its way.

And I did eventually succeed. Adam received the letter, returned to the island and came hunting for Jonet to perform the same service as I had myself so recently enjoyed with her; with what eventual result I know not.

XII To Pray or Seek for Prey?

It was only natural that a meeting was eventually held on Hallow day at the ruined church of St Bride, up on Chapel hill a mile north of the Castle. I addressed them there standing, some of them barefoot, on the damp earth of that once hallowed ground among stones centuries old, rhymed in ferns and moss and ivy, on the subject of love. I began by recounting my own experiences in childhood, manhood and even with Nancy, which all knew about.

'This is how I am,' I told them. 'This is who I am. What would be served by my attempting against my nature to be different?'

There was a silence and I allowed it to stand for a time and then I continued: 'Would I be a better man? Would I be better able to perform my duties? As a teacher, say? How, if I am frustrated? How, if my well-being is thrown into confusion? What merit is there in celibacy? Why, even, must I keep to my wife—especially if she does not enjoy to have me? For, I assure you she did not! —for the first years at least of our marriage. Should I have forced myself upon her, just because she is my wife? How could it be right to cause her pain even if she is my wife? Especially because she is my wife. Of all people I should wish her pleasure.'

There were murmurs of agreement; smiles of understanding; it was a common predicament.

'Are not all men and women the same in this regard? We want to love, the act of love and are made, constructed, to engage in it whenever opportunity presents. We are supposed to perform these acts of love or we would not seek them so strenuously! If this be so, why should we fight it? What good is served by self denial? All that happens with self denial is frustration and even, I am persuaded by my own experience, ill health. It is not healthy to forego the acts of love that are natural to us. Of course, if our wishes are not reciprocated, there is nothing to be done. We have no right to proceed. But where the desire is shared, where is the harm? If there is a God he made us in this fashion and no beneficent divinity could make men in this fashion and then order them on pain of hellfire, for eternity, to behave at odds with the nature he gave them.'

And so, you see, under the stress of my extraordinary predicament, I had begun to think with unexpected originality and worth, as everyone present seemed to be aware.

I felt that the whole group had been uplifted by these insights; that the foul oppression of the customs—they were no more than that—of the accursed Kirk Session had an alternative, one far more humane and compassionate. The one that day by day and week by week, I was busily bringing to life in my mind.

As we trekked down the hill afterwards, I sensed a renewed spirit of hope in the people—my people, as I had begun to think of them. But we were observed. As time would show—a relatively short time—my growing success as an original preacher was having the good effect of swelling the ranks of my congregation. However, this made my congregation and our meetings even more obvious to onlookers than before. It was only a matter of time, then, before these new meetings of the folk of the island were brought to the attention of the Minister himself.

As we rounded the corner, close to the shore road, myself in the middle of the leading group, we passed Jonet Morison. At that moment, John Galie, a cottar of Barmore, the settlement on the hill near Scalpsie, said to me loudly: 'Whit huv ye tae say aboot prayer?'

'Pray[96] if you like,' I replied. 'It will do no harm and maybe some good. Seek and ye shall find. And if ye seek through praying, that is as good a way as any.'

---

[96] Editor's note: this passage is very important. Jonet Morison confessed that the company on this very occasion with the devil went to seek 'prey.' See ID p23, p271

THE STORY OF ROBERT STEWART OF SCARRELL 139

'Wull Goad pay attention tae ma prayer, but?'
'That rather depends upon whether there is any God to listen.' Since the obvious question to this reply was thought ridiculous by this man, he said, instead: 'Do you pray, but?'
'I have done, many times. I can't say I have had much success.'
'Ye mean it disnae wark?'
'I think it sometimes helps to concentrate on what you need and what you want. It might actually help you to get it, though I'm not quite sure how.'
I waved to Jonet Morison, as we moved on down the brae, some of the women skipping and singing as they went, for very joy: my questioning, brought upon me by the imminent prospect of doom, had made them happier than they had ever known. But I little understood how my remarks, innocently made about the value of the concept 'pray', would be interpreted by her and others under the duress of trial within a few months. After the meeting, I walked along towards Bute Quay, the peninsula of stones laid down by our fishermen at the order of the English and it was there I met Jonet McNicoll, a comely woman. As we left the harbour and had to cross the Balskyte burn, Jonet missed her footing, slipped on the wet stones and got wet. I reached down and gripped her tightly and lifted her out and she thanked me. Then I sat her down and helped dry her soaking feet using my own broadcloth. The aftermath of the preaching, when I had become fired up by my own thought and talk, had wrought in me one of my moments and Jonet smiled on recognising it. 'Oh, Sir,' she said, 'just look at you.'
'It often happens after preaching. I know not why. Maybe it's meeting someone as pretty as you. I expect that has something to do with it.'
Of course I asked her to go with me and serve me and she agreed[97]. Other people were not far away at the time but I took no notice of them. We soon found a place hard by, in the woods above the harbour.

XIII Disgrace at the Kirk Session

At the end of November, I could stand the hiatus no longer. Indeed, it was my last chance to avoid the extreme ignominy of being hauled physically

---

herein. References here to ID can be got herein by adding about 250 to the page number for ID. the word 'prey' should have been 'pray'.
[97] Editor's note: this passage is also important. Jonet McNicoll later 'confesses' to this on ID p13; p 263 herein but it is written down by someone who adds the diabolic element for his own purpose or because his mental model of evil will allow no other interpretation.

and with violence by the men I knew so well as friends, to the Kirk Session. I had been given every latitude on ground of illness and now must appear voluntarily or my case would be viewed in an even worse light than heretofore. Someone had seen me out at meetings and reported it to the Kirk Session.

And so I agreed to go. The night before, I could not sleep but lay awake constructing speeches: of the love of God and what it means to men and women; of the pressure upon me by my father to marry, even without love; and the effects—the natural effects—when I should eventually come across someone whom I did love truly. Many a bold speech I made for myself and thought myself a brave soul battling against the community and the country, newly entered into a century of oppression and ill treatment of every sin, however, trivial. But when at last I stood there before the dark men of the Session and faced the accusations of adultery and lying to save my skin and the offence to the church in which I had grown up, and even—God forbid!—actually preached on my own account from that very same pulpit. —When I had brought the church and the community into disrepute, for my crimes would be already talked about as far abroad as Edinburgh—Who ever heard of conduct so vile?

The pressure upon me was intense and I remembered what Sir James Stewart had told me: that I must not argue the toss, must admit everything with utmost contriteness, must beg forgiveness and say and do nothing to bring upon me the wrath of the Session.

'What have you to say to the charges against you?' said Ninian Kerr.

'I beg the forgiveness of the Session, the church and the community for the harm I have done. I have been possessed by the devil. That is my fault; that I was not strong enough to resist temptation.'

There was a dead silence while this was considered.

'Are you the father of Nance Throw's child?' said Ninian Kerr. No generalities were wanted now. In the manner of the Session, everything had to be specific.

All the months of heaven now seemed of no account. Retribution was now. I felt as if it were better that the earth swallow me up and take me out of the situation into a far oblivion. If I could have killed myself at that moment, I think I would have done so. I lacked only the means.

'It is true that I have enjoyed carnal relations with Nancy. I have no doubt of it. I am unable to say for sure if I am the father or not. What man can ever be sure of this?'

'When did you first have Nance Throw?'

'After she became my maidservant. That would be about the middle of 1659.'

'Where did this take place?'

'In my house at Roseland. I had moved there from Scarrell after my father's death to make travel to the school every day easier. It is six miles. Roseland is just a mile.'

'How many times did you have her?'

'I do not know. Many times.'

'When did you stop?'

'About January this year of 1661, a month before the birth, when she became too heavy with child to enjoy it.'

'Enjoy, it? Are you saying you did it for her pleasure?' I was stunned by this. Of course an elder would not understand even that much. The outrage in Ninian Kerr that she might enjoy it or that I might do it only for her, was something very strange. How, I wondered in the midst of this catastrophe, could he think such nonsense?

'It was not something I did for my pleasure alone but what we did together for our mutual pleasure. I would not do anything that she was not pleased by and there came a time when it became uncomfortable for her.'

'Yet she would not be pleased by having a bairn!'

'Not so. She was delighted at the idea of it. She wanted it constantly. Even now, I am sure she is glad of it.'

There was a gasp of horror from the entire Session. 'How can that be? It is against God's law? She is a shamed woman. What man would have her now?'

'Alexander Bannatyne would.'

'Hoots man, that's an idiot! Her life is ruined by you! And she will go to hell—like you! Can you not see how she is shamed? It will be in every eye that looks upon her in the street: the fallen woman. All her life she will bear this scar and these looks.—Aye, if she lives! Ye might as well have branded her head with a branding iron!'

Kerr paced about the room like an angry bear, waving his arms and plainly in a fury. Then he turned on me again: 'So between the middle of 1659 and January 1661 you had carnal knowledge of Nance Throw?'

'Yes.'

'How often?'

'Nearly every day. Sometimes twice a day. Sometimes more often.'

There was a shocked silence.

'How can you say this? No man is like this. Why do you condemn yourself in this way? This must be a lie.'

'I tell it how it was.'

'Are you a fornicating machine, then? Had you no work to do? Where did you find time for these...these...misadventures?'

'I had work to do. I taught in the school but when I came home—then—after dinner, it would happen.'

Neil McNeil stood up and called: 'Jean Stewart born Jean Colquhoun, will you come up here and answer?'

And when she had done so, he asked: 'You were here in this man's house all the time. Is what he says about himself true?'

'Yes, I am sure it is. I used to ride out to Kames after dinner and that was when it would happen between them.'

'But can you definitely say that they did? You were not present. Maybe he is protecting someone else, you see. We have seen enough of this already.'

'I saw them together. They were possessed. I never saw anything like it before.'

'You actually saw them... in the act?'

'Yes.'

'That must have been terrible for you.'

'Yes, but not entirely. I have never seen two naked people like that before. It taught me many things, things I never could have known otherwise.'

'What things?'

'That the devil can possess two human beings at the same time.'

A shock wave seemed to ripple throughout the men of the Session, who almost fell back in their chairs as at the effect of a punch that hit everyone of them.

'Would you explain this?'

'Nancy Throw is a fine woman and my husband is a fine man. Yet they both behaved together as if they were animals: copulated worse than animals and at far greater length and with far more...more...—I can't think of the word— relish? enjoyment? It was more than that. Ecstasy, perhaps. Yes, that was what it was. Ecstasy! They were transported! Utterly absorbed in each other. It was as if they had become one. Not only one flesh but one soul.'

'So—it is like what you were saying at the dinner in the Castle—which was reported here—these decent people were taken over. You knew this because their behaviour was so completely changed?'

'That is how we recognise that the devil is involved, yes. When he shows his evil presence. It is what the Minister thinks.'

McNeil seemed to gather himself. 'Thank you Mistress Colquhoun, you may take your seat.' Then he turned his bald head to me, glared out of piercing black eyes, raised a long finger and pointed at me: 'Master Robert Stewart, you are still under the oath you took and you are in the House of God, remember, and what you say will be used against you at the gates of heaven and you may be barred and sent to the infernal regions because you are judged not fit. I have one question for you. Has the devil taken possession of your soul?'

'Definitely not!'

'How do you explain your behaviour then?' I was asked by a man who fell back a step, stunned with surprise.

'I do not know what you mean.'

'You have been doing for two years what no man ever ought to do: commit adultery. Of all men, you are the last man on the planet who should be capable of such conduct. You have been—by your own admission—fornicating as no man ever did—several times a day! How do you account for this unusual behaviour? Does it not seem, even to you, that the devil has you by the throat? That he is in you and he has been driving you all the time?'

'No, I don't accept any of that.' The Session were amazed, absolutely astonished by this, a wave of shock seemed to ripple among them.

'Then what is the reason for your appalling behaviour?'

'It was not appalling. It was wonderful!' I paused to remember it, lifted my eyes heavenwards as images of that time flashed into my mind and it gave the Session men time to absorb the impossible, heaped upon so many other impossibles. 'I was not possessed by the devil. I was in love. And the lady I loved, also loved me.'

Another wave of shock struck the spellbound members of the Session. They gasped and changed position uncomfortably in their seats as if their genitalia shouted: What about me?

'The one who is supposed to rule here is a God of love,' I told them. 'He would understand this. Alas, this house is not in practice a house of love but one dedicated to the discovery and punishment of sin. That is its defect and my misfortune.'

'Why did you put the blame onto Alexander Bannatyne? Offer him money and land and victuals every year? Why did you lie to this Session and everyone who asked you about your part in this? What have you to say about your lies causing so many other men—Sandy Bannatyne, young Sprinkell, your wife's relative and friend, Ninian Bannatyne, and

Gustavus Browne and others—to be hounded as if they were the culprits?'

'The one thing uppermost in my mind and Nancy's was to prolong our time of happiness. Anything that served that seemed necessary and desirable, even if it caused pain to others. I am sorry for their pain.'

McGilchrist stood up, clearly disturbed. 'I don't understand! How could you ignore the wishes and needs of all these others—your own wife, whom you promised yourself to solely?'

'I believe that we are not long in this world. Most people never know true happiness. I was lucky. I did. And even if it meant my death, to have denied the happiness—the heaven-sent bliss!—would have been wrong. It would have meant a life without it—ever! Don't you see? I had to take the chance because it came my way. To have walked away was the wrong thing to do because I would have deprived my life—viewed as a whole—of the greatest richness it was ever likely to know. Nancy felt the same.'

'Then, then, then... you are not sorry about the adultery, are you? You enjoyed it too much, did you not?'

'No, I am not sorry about it. If I had the opportunity again I would do it again.' The members of the Session looked even more shocked than before. McGilchrist shook his head and turned his eyes away as if I had just condemned myself to death.

McNeil said: 'Mibbe when ye see the penalties ye wull think different.'

'I do not think I will, though they be awful.'

'—Aye, right at least in this! They wull be awful!' said Robert Stewart of Mecknoch

The Minister spoke at last. 'What I do not understand is how you— a preacher!— can stand here and act as if you have done nothing wrong. It is a mystery. You know this is wrong, better than anyone, for you have studied the matter and preached upon it. Yet you say you would do it again, are unrepentant. The Session cannot tolerate this. It is impossible.'

The Session to a man, were stupefied by my attitude of unrepentance. It was a complete surprise, a novelty, never seen before in such unequivocal form in centuries of worship in that place.

Kerr said: 'If you do not repent, there is no salvation! You must repent! The Session must act more severely upon you if you do not.'

'I have sworn to tell the truth. What I have said is the truth. Would you now have me tell a lie? I am under oath. I take it seriously.'

'But you began by admitting that the devil had possessed you! What do you mean by changing your story?'

'I was put up to it: saying that the devil was in charge. I don't really believe that. Because of the pressure I am under from every side, the truth has had to come out.'
'Do you say positively that you are not the father of the child?'
'No, how can I?'
'Whom do you suspect then?'
'Alexander Bannatyne or Gustavus Browne could be the father.'
'Yet by your own admission you were never away from the lady?'
'Yes, that is true. But that does not mean I am the father.'
'Nance Throw, will you stand up?' said McNeil.
When she had done so, he continued: 'Will you state the true father of your bairn?'
'I have already done so.'
'Aye, but not before the man. Will you please do so now.' Nancy did not so much as look in my direction and it cut me to the heart. There was no hesitation now. A child had to be baptised and its position in the world made clear. And my name was better by far than many another, despite the disgrace in which I stood.
'It was Master Robert Stewart of Scarrell.'
'And you are sure there was no other involved?'
'Yes, I am sure.'
'And when did this fornication begin?'
'Just before Candlemas in his own house, when his wife was at Kames.'
'And when did it stop?'
'Until I left his service after Whitsunday.'
'And was this frequent?'
'He could not free me for a week.'

I suppose I should have been sick with regret about Nancy's last statement but I saw it differently. She might have said that I could not free her for a day, for that would have been nearer the truth. During her testimony she looked straight ahead at her interlocutor but once, just as she was taking her seat, I saw her looking at me and I knew that not much had changed. There was the hint of a golden smile. She might present a picture of a woman wronged but that was only because it was a course forced upon her by pressures she could never have anticipated.

Usually, in such cases, the condemned person was taken outside while the Session deliberated upon his fate. This case was so extraordinary that no one thought of it. Since, unlike every other person arraigned before the

Session, I had education, ability, the courage to argue back—all of which I had exercised—it may even have seemed a natural continuance to allow the current procedure, with me present, taking part as my nature determined. In addition, I had been the Session Clerk. So they were used to having me present at their meetings.

Robert Stewart of Mecknoch, no relation, a farmer, declared: 'We have been fining folk for not attending the Sabbath, puttin' them in the jougs for wee slanders. Now we have ane meenister who commits adultery, tells us aw lees and willnae even repent! We have tae dae somethin' terrible here or aw the folk wull rebel. If he get's aff, whaur wull we be?'

John Kelburn agreed strongly, as did most of the farmers present. Donald McNeil of Kilmory, another farm near Mecknoch, actually stated what some of them thought: 'Wull hae tae hangit him. We canny lee him live. It wid gi'e everybody the wrang message awthegither.'

McGilchrist alone seemed to take a different tack. 'This is an educated man—a rare man! We need all our educated men. You can count the number of university graduates on this island on one hand.'

'Whit fur?' said McNeil. 'How kin we have a man like this teachin' the scholars at the school?'

'No one else is qualified,' replied McGilchrist. 'He is the best teacher I ever saw, the best we could ever get. Have ye forgotten that?'

John McKirdy said: 'Have ye forgotten that he has demitted the post and we have appointet anither man?'

John Glass, the provost, said quietly: 'I spoke to Sir James who could not be present, as he is a relation of this man. Sir James thinks he should be punished by a very severe fine. One that will require him to sell property to raise the cash.'

'How much?' said McGilchrist.

'His salary as a schoolmaster is £40 a year. A fine of £200 might suffice. It is a heavy penalty.'

'Will that suffice, then?' said McGilchrist.

'How could that be enough? It would mean that ye can buy your way oota hell wi' cash!' said one.

Another added: 'He'll live his ain life in hell. Jist you wait and see— Aye, if he lives!'

'How do we get round the fact that he will be in the Kirk every Sunday, sitting in his pew beside all these decent folks that never did any offence at all?'

'The only way is to deny him the Kirk.'

'Excommunication?'

'Aye, kin we do that, but?'

'We can do anything we like,' said McGilchrist. 'The English Government is in chaos. It will be a while afore they get around to giving orders. We must just do what we think best and they will be satisfied in due time.'

The Minister said: 'But the law. We must stick to the law. Our own safety demands it.'

'We don't know what the law is,' replied McGilchrist. 'When Episcopy was established by decree last year, every Act right back to 1633 was repealed.'[98]

'We must excommunicate this man, aye and publicly humiliate him as an example to all the rest.'

And so a decision was made. The Privy Council was not operational at the time so there was no need to apply to anywhere else but our own Presbytery. But since the Presbytery was represented fully in the current group, no one felt any need to go through forms that would produce the same outcome—delay was anathema to these men. They wanted the matter cleared off the books.

'What does excommunicate mean?' I enquired. 'In this case.'

'It means you stay away from the Kirk. You are denied the Kirk. People will shun you hereafter, as is natural. If they talk to you or help you they will themselves be liable to excommunication.'

'Will I be able to live here? I mean will I be allowed to buy the necessities of life?'

'Yes, Christian Charity requires that you have that much,' said McGilchrist. 'But we canny make missing the Kirk seem a reward. Some folk might think it was if it saved them the trouble of travel and such. No, you can bide here, you can buy and sell and take your rents from your lands and tenements. But you have no friends here from this day forth. If you are in difficulty no one will come to your aid. You are an outsider, because you have denied the authority of the Session and the Session acts to uphold God's ordinances which you have broken very seriously. The best thing you can do is go back to Scarrell and stay there out of the way. If you go swanning around the town we cannot answer for your safety. You are a damned man; you have damned yourself by your actions. By failing to repent, you have put yourself outside this community.'

'Why don't we just kill the bastard?' said Ninian Kerr.

'Mind your language!' said McGilchrist furiously.

---

[98] Whyte, Trans Bute Nat Hist Soc Vol XII 1945, p44

'I am not swearing. I am using the word that fits. He has made a bastard and does nae repent. What else is he himsel'?
Donald McKirdy agreed: 'Aye, whit else dae we ca' a lying piece of shite?'
'What does the Act say?' said McGilchrist.
'It says, this,' Walter Stewart replied.
'Act of Session 24. December 18. 1638
'The Assembly considering the great necessity of purging the land from bygone corruptions, and of preserving her from the like in time coming, ordaineth the Presbyteries to proceed with the censures of the Kirk, to excommunication, against those Ministers who being deposed by this Assembly acquiesces not to their sentences, but exercise some part of their Ministerial function, refuseth themselves, and with-draw others from the obedience of the Assembly.'
'This means we canna excommunicate him, because he's no' been deposed by the Assembly.'
'We can't wait for that. They are bound to excommunicate him.'
'That Act has been repealed, I tell you,' said McGilchrist.
But no one was interested in that. In lieu of anything else they fell back on the laws they knew.
There was soon a split among them: the more educated (except McGilchrist) demanding the letter of the law as promulgated by the General Assembly of the Church, even though it had been repealed; the less educated, the farmers and burgesses, wanting me excommunicated forthwith. A few wanted execution as well. It took a fresh turn when the Minister, John Stewart, said, wearily: 'I am afraid we must excommunicate him for he has been holding meetings, secret meetings outwith the church, when he preaches doctrines which are anathema to this church.'
'What doctrines are these?' I shouted.
'That it is all right to make love to the maidservant and even all right to get her with child. He believes he could not do anything else. That he did the right thing. Don't you see? We cannot leave him within the body of the Kirk. He is a danger to it and he has been excusing his vile behaviour in front of the poorer members of the Parish and they are persuaded by him!'
But McGilchrist, the lawyer and town clerk, was not finished.
'Have you forgotten that he's not a minister? He never got appointed to a charge. He is just a schoolmaster, then. That is the only function he has performed here during his trouble with Nance Throw.'

'But he is a qualified minister. He was even an assistant in this place.'
'But he never became a minister and he is not on the list of ministers of the Kirk in Edinburgh.'

Thus was it that, by a hairsbreadth, I was saved from excommunication: by having become a schoolmaster, if only until I was unmasked as an adulterer and fornicator, when I was compelled to resign.

Soon it was decided. Since the law was evidently in chaos and likely to remain that way for a while, since Sir James would never agree to my execution; and it would not be safe to kill someone of my class without a clear legal title to do so; and since I could not be excommunicated, I was to be fined £1,000: more money than most people ever saw in a lifetime; and to appear at the Kirk to receive my public rebuke. I would be stripped in the vestry and dressed in sackcloth. The fine would be demanded by officers appointed to hound me until it was paid. I would be denounced from the pulpit in my presence, as an adulterer, liar and deceiver, who had no regard to the feelings of other decent God-fearing people, of whom I was evidently not one myself— whatever my training and ordination. I would, in short, be kicked out publicly and officially shunned thereafter but not excommunicated. What other penalties I would suffer, time itself would determine.

Of course I declined to attend. And, after reflection and discussion among themselves, they did not come and force me to do so, as was their wont. They wanted done with the matter. Everyone knew what my punishments were. They were judged sufficient. That was enough.

That night, the night of November 24th 1661 was one of the worst I ever lived through.

I walked home in the rain, Jean beside me, and when we got there she turned and said to me: 'I must leave you now and never return. I'll pack a few things and send a man from Kames to come tomorrow for the rest.'

'I thought you were going to stand by me,' I said, with tears in my eyes.

'How can I do that? You were possessed by the devil and still do not really regret it, after so much heartache. That means that you are still possessed. How can I live with a man who is possessed by the devil? I would condemn my soul and my life. Don't you see? I have to leave you right now because you have left me no choice. Do you think I want to spend eternity in hellfire?'

And she left that same night. Nobody ever came for her clothing. Years passed before I saw her again and then only fleetingly.

To be suddenly so utterly alone was a hateful experience. Yet I could understand her reaction. She viewed me as the devil incarnate. That was the gist of it. How could she willingly allow herself to be penetrated by me? She had no choice but to cease to be my wife and, knowing me and my ways, that required her to distance herself from me.

The next day, after a sleepless night, tossing and turning, I went out and made my way to where the witch people were to meet.

When we had gathered together, I told them what had happened to me in full, sparing no detail. When I had finished there were murmurs of compassion and a few people came to comfort me according to their ways. But Margaret McWilliam was not one of them. She was on her high horse. 'They're rotten men all!' she declared. 'That Walter Stewart'—who, as treasurer, was a collector of money for the Session when she did not often have the amount required. 'And Ninian Kerr, a black hearted man, if ever I kent ane. Ye should kill the pair. And that minister, tae, a damned rotten man he is.' Then she came and tapped me on the shoulder and said: 'Niver you mind, I'll get back at them for ye. I have ways.'

I thought nothing of it at the time, for I was too engrossed in my self pity but I remembered it later. When Margaret had gone off for firewood to heat the cauldron and make stew for everybody with rabbits that had been caught, Patrick McKaw said to me: 'Did Margaret McWilliam serve you? She says she did, twice.'

'Yes, she did.' I admitted.

'Was that no' wrang? She's merrit on Robert McWilliam and has childer by him.'

'It is certainly wrong from the point of view of the Kirk Session and the teachings of the church.'

'How was it right for you, then?'

'I was in difficulty and she helped me out. She was kind to me and I was glad of it—so thankful, that I helped her out in return. I gave her money and advice and other things. I would have helped her at any time and she knew that. All she had to do was come and ask me. And I would have helped her again.'

'But she was an adulterer.'

'Yes, so it seems. I was unaware that she was married the first time. The second time too, until afterwards. I don't think it matters very much that she did it.'

'It wid maybe matter to her husband.'

'Yes, maybe. Maybe he would appreciate the help I gave the family, himself included. They were very poor and I put bread on their table.'

'It jist disnae seem right somehow.'

'It seemed right to me at the time, that's all I can say for sure. If Margaret McWilliam wanted to serve me as a woman serves a man, even though she had a husband, I don't think it matters very much, especially if he never found out.'
'What if he had found out?'
'I would have told him what I needed and why I needed it and what had happened. Maybe he would have understood.'
'Maybe he would a been angry and belted you.'
'Maybe he would.'
'Would you have belted him back?'
'I would have defended myself of course.' The matter of my own adultery was never raised; but the immorality of that was not in question, at least by Patrick. It might be imagined that I would harbour a deep resentment against the Kirk Session for their treatment of me. Not so. I did not have the money to pay the fine but I did not worry very much about it. They could not very well take from me what I did not possess. In time they would come for it and an arrangement would be made whereby money would be advanced to me using some of my parcels of land as security. Ninian Kerr and John Kelburn[99] were both men of substance and willing to put it at my disposal for the advantage it brought them, nor could they make charges against my capital which were unreasonable, given their connexion with the Kirk. For now, I had some money stored away and I lived off this easily enough, even distributing small sums here and there among the poor, as usual.

I was not resentful for another reason: I understood the Session, all the better since I had myself been Session Clerk up until the time my own name began to be mentioned in connexion with the process against Nancy. And I soon saw my disgrace in a new light: it enabled me to think very clearly about the church and the community. Of course, thrown upon the mercy and sympathy of the witch folk and finding kindness and compassion there, they became my main concern.

---

[99] Editor's note: Both men's estates are mentioned in the Town Council Records as having received some of the lands of Robert Stewart of Scarrell eventually by transfer, the latter in 1673. See p301 et seq herein.

XIV Consequences of Disgrace: Original Insights

'Are you not going to get back at them?' said Katherine Moore, one day, as we sat on the hill above Glecknabae looking out across the channel towards Arran and Kintyre. 'That's what my mother[100] always does.'
'You mean she tries to poison their water or leave deadly nightshade in or near their house?'
'Among other things. But that would do.'
'No, I won't be doing any of that. They're only doing what they are supposed too: following the rules of the General Assembly of the Kirk.'
'So you're just going to let them away with it, then?'
'Jesus said we must forgive those who harm us, especially those who are our enemies.'
'Maybe Jesus was wrong.'
'I don't think so. If only the Kirk did follow the teaching of Jesus all the time there would be no difficulty.' People were beginning to gather about us to listen as I started to think about it. 'Would the men of the Session who condemned me be better men if I got back at them in some manner?'
'I don't know,' Katherine replied.
'Well, I think I do. I don't think it would do them any good at all. How could it be right to do them harm, even if they have harmed me?'
'So you think we should just turn the other cheek?'
'I think you should defend yourself as best you can and I have done that. But when that's over, I think you need to forgive and forget, if possible.'
'But how can you forgive that kind of thing? They are ruining your life, taking all that money from you.'
'They are only doing what they are required to do. The money will be put to good use. It's not as if I am being robbed. It will be doled out to the poor and needy. That's what the Kirk always does with any money it gets. You should know that. I don't even mind because of this. I don't even need the money.'
'So you don't think they are wrong, then?'
'I think they are not as compassionate and understanding as they might be but that's all. We are all human. That is the first thing about us. We fall in love and we mate and we should not be punished severely just because we behave like humans. We can be expected to do the things that humans are designed to do and should not be punished for it.'

---

[100] Editor's note: Margaret McWilliam was her mother.

'Doesn't the Bible tell us that we have to obey God's laws?' This, from Jonet McNicoll. 'The ten commandments.'

'These are the laws of Moses. They do say, thou shalt not commit adultery. And I have done that. So I have broken the law. But what should be my penalty? Should I be thrown out of the community for this? Should I be fined more money that some of you will ever earn in a lifetime? Should I be spat upon and sworn at and slandered, for I have experienced this too? Maybe the laws of Moses are not really very good now, though 2,000 years ago in the Sinai Desert they made sense. Why should a man have to commit himself to one wife? Especially when many great men in the Old Testament had several? And it was accounted no sin? And to have to commit myself, as I did, without even knowing very much about the wife or even liking her at all? I was forced into marriage. Most people are. Few marry for love. And even if they do, maybe they fall out of love. And if they come to hate the spouse what is the point of continuing as a couple? Shouldn't they separate? Would it not be better to find somebody different, that you wanted very much to live with? I expect there are even women and men too who have been murdered by their spouse because there was no escape from them. The rules of the Kirk make escape impossible.'

And so it was, that December of 1661, that I met with the witch folk many times; and I thought aloud and they listened and asked questions and I told them what was in my mind. And I do believe that it was the happiest time I ever experienced, in spite of my ostracism, for the sense of impending doom under which my life had always been lived, had ended: the doom was over. The women catered for my needs in every way and I felt useful to them in providing guidance and advice. Even the men followed me and I felt my leadership was worthy, far better than when, as a young man, I had preached at the Kirk as the assistant to my father and under his spell of severity as an omnipresent model. I didn't really miss the contact with the great men of the town where, in the past, I had always to be on my guard to follow the rules of the place, some of them unwritten—and, as we have seen, I could not, having a vigorous nature physically. It seems to me now that freed from all that, I was able to develop into an even more useful and adult person and it was all done by thinking things out for myself.

to be continued....

XV Two scenes from the play: The Witches of Bute

Scene 13: St Bride's Chapel, on a hill near Rothesay, Dec 1662. The Chapel is a ruin. A low wall, ruinous, lies between the audience and Robert. He sits on a stone reading from a Bible. There is the sound of a crowd of people close by, to the right, off stage. In fact the theatre audience is about to act as this audience.
(*Enter Margaret McWilliam from the front right of the stage*)
McWilliam (agitated): Ye must come! They've aw climbed the hill tae see you! There's near a hunner folk.

Robert: Why have they come? Is it to mock a fallen angel?

McWilliam: Naw! Ye seen it yersel'. Every week there's mair. They micht come tae mock but they stay tae pray. The word is spreadin' roon. They say ye're a grand preacher. It's you yersel'. Ye're like a loadstane. When they hear there's a meetin' they aw come. It's a miracle. Ye've bewitched them.

Robert: I don't understand. All I do is try and explain myself. Try to see what it means and what might be done about it to make things better.

McWilliam: Well, they like it. So come alang the noo and get sterted. (*thinks*) We'll never feed this lot. Things is a lot worse since you joined. We used tae huv a feed and a dance. And a bit drink and talk. Noo aw they waant tae do is listen tae you. Come oan, wull ye! And see if ye kin figure oot how tae feed the five thoosand.

(*Robert climbs up onto the low wall, begins speaking to the right and then changes his stance to address the theatre audience. He begins slowly, apologetically, humbly and haltingly. Gradually, the spirit that is within him begins to shine forth. A spotlight comes on gradually, lighting up his shining face as he starts to project the love that Jesus wanted[101]. There is no introduction. He is here to talk and people have come to listen.*)

---

[101] In case the manifestation which follows be thought imagined and impossible, I am bound to point out that this very quality was seen in the Kirk 12 years ago when Gary McIntyre preached. It was the best preaching I ever saw and, during a 17 year religious quest which often took me across country, I never saw it equalled. Sadly, Gary was

Robert: What comes first? Righteousness or forgiveness? What matters most? What did Jesus say? Forgive your enemies. What was the major quality in St Paul's epistle to the Corinthians? Charity. The expression of forgiving love. In short, unconditional love. So righteousness is some way behind. What matters is disinterested love of all, including one's enemies. There was, from Jesus, no talk of an eye for an eye. For punishing people for their sins. That is old Testament stuff. Our Kirk is ruled by this and is out of date. That is why there are fines and jougs and sackcloth humiliations and actual physical punishments.

Voice from the Crowd: Should there be nay fines and punishments? Would folks no jist dae whatever they wanted? Would there no jist be disorder?

Robert: Do you think they only behave well because of the disgrace and fear of punishment? Would they suddenly behave badly if these are withdrawn? Is it worth having rules that can only be enforced by cruelty? How can that be right when Jesus tells us not to be cruel? If love is so important, instead of cruelty there should be forgiveness. That is the key, not cruel punishments. Jesus told us even to forgive our enemies and love them. (*his face shines with love, projecting outwards in every direction*) I love you all! The worst offender, the poorest, the worst sinner, even the person who hates me. I want to show you how to love each other. But this goes beyond my wants. It makes sense, don't you see? That is the message of Jesus. If we love each other, every one of us, then we will have no enemies. There will be no wrongdoing. How can there be if we love each other? I would like everyone to turn to the right hand and say to the person: I love you and say it meaningfully. And then turn to the left and do the same and then behind you. (They do this: some near the front) And when you leave here remember this, that you love everybody here. And I want you to see that this is practical. It works! It will bind us together and will make us brothers and sisters, truly. And every time we come together we will repeat our vows of love.

---

driven off the island by a few Kirk Session men who did not appreciate his unique quality, a common fate of excellence. Note: in no other way does Gary resemble Scarrell. The words and ideas are imagined, of course. Gary is not responsible.

Voice from the crowd: But you loved Nancy Throw and got her with child. That was illicit love.

Robert: Only by the outdated, cruel and unforgiving standards of the Kirk Session. What I felt for her and she for me was natural and good and we both knew that. It would have been a denial of what we are to have remained apart and not expressed our love. What good would have been served by it? The Session would have been happy, I grant you. Is the Session the sole judge of what should be? Why should it? Who said the Session was in charge? Not the Bible. Not Jesus. Why should it, when it is so cruel and unfeeling? And contrary to Jesus's teachings. The hell the Session creates on earth is worse than any hell that is ever likely hereafter.[102]

Voice from the crowd: Do you love the Session?

Robert: I love the men in it, though they be my enemies. For Jesus tells us to love our enemies. To love without exception or conditions.

Voice: What if I cut off your arm?

Robert: You know the answer. I would give you my other arm as well. You would soon grow tired of cutting off arms. You would be deprived of their use. How could I help you if you have cut off my arms?

Voice: You might think differently if I did it.

Robert: Nobody said the way of Jesus is easy. But once you get used to it, it will be easy, for everyone will be doing the same. If you are in any doubt about anything, remember: Just ask what Jesus would do. This is so obviously right! Don't you see? If everybody will love everybody else, there will be no difficulty of any kind! All it takes is the will! (*Robert throws his arms into the air and calls down a*

---

[102] According to the Acts of the General Assembly, he could have been executed for these words. See Acts in the Appendix. But they would have to be proved and for that a verbatim transcript made available by a witness sympathetic to the Session. No one in the Session would have been permitted to attend. Even so, execution was not wanted by the Session. It might have turned Rothesay into another Nazareth. One was enough.

benediction) Dearly beloved, help us to love each other and forgive each other.

CURTAIN

Scene 16: The Manse, January 16th 1662. The Minister is talking to Robert Stewart of Mecknoch, an elder, in the Church Manse. The men are seated in front of a fire of peats and on either side.

Mecknoch (*hat in hand*): I have something serious to report, Minister.

Minister: Well, let's hear it.

Mecknoch: It's my duty as an elder, ye ken? I canny keep silent any langer.

Minister: Out with it, then, man!

Mecknoch: I don't want tae stir up a wasp's nest, ye ken?

Minister: Perform your duty and never mind the wasps. I'll deal with them.

Mecknoch: It's the snaw.

Minister: The snow? What do ye mean? Are ye havering or what?

Mecknoch: It is the snaw, I tell ye! A lot ae fowk are meetin' in secret.

Minister: What do ye mean? How do ye know?

Mecknoch: I seen the tracks in the snaw. There's hunners.

Minister: I don't believe it!

Mecknoch: I kent fine ye'd say that. Weel, ye kin come oot wi' me tae Mecknoch and ye'll see the tracks. Thur aw ower the place, up and doon the brae. Fae every direction. Some fae Kilchattan. Some fae Dunagoil. Some fae the Kames. Some fae Bogany and Ascog. And a hale lot fae the toon. Ah coontet ower a hunner. Mibbe even twa hunner.

Minister: Meeting in secret? For what?

Mecknoch (*hangs his head in shame*): I confess, yer reverence. I went alang and folleyed some ae thaim. I ken I shouldnay. I hope ye dinnae hold it against me? I hid doon ahint a boulder and keeked ower. It wis him. Scarrell. They aw went tae hear him.

Minister(*shocked*): You mean he is preaching?

Mecknoch: I couldnae quite say that. He wis talkin' tae them. It wisnae a service. Mair like a man jist speaking his mind.

Minister(*deeply shocked*): The Devil he is! Who else did you see?

Mecknoch: Marget McWilliam, Marget McLevin, Isobel McNicoll and Jonet. Kirstine Bannatyne and Kath Moore and a lot ae ithers.

Minister: The witch people. It figures. Who else would go and see a disgraced man like him?

Mecknoch: What are we gonny dae?

Minister: He was always such a damn fine speaker. He's taking them away from me! The Devil he is! That's what he's about! He's starting up a rival church.

Mecknoch: But they aw still come tae the Kirk. His meetin's are never on the Sabbath. Merket days and Setterdays, maistly.

Minister: Did ye hear what he said?

Mecknoch: I canny richt mind. But they liked it. Whatever it wis. They came away wi' shinin' faces. I've never seen thaim look sae happy. They were aglow, insteed ae aglum, if ye folly me. (*remembers with awe in his voice*). There wis a kinda halo aboot thaim aw. I felt like joinin' in. A kinda holy glow.

Minister: Well, we must tread carefully. If we draw attention to him he might gain from it. We need to break this up right now. They're mainly witch people, you say? Well, we'll start with them. Witchcraft's an offence ye can be executed for. We'll burn a few of the known witches and that will stop the meetings.

Mecknoch: Should ye no' see Scarrell himsel'? Ask him whit he's aboot?

Minister: Certainly not! He's disgraced! Cast out. If he's taking people away to secret meetings, that's enough. If they are secret there must be devilment afoot.

Mecknoch: Wull we delate him at the Session?

Minister: No! We must not draw attention to him. More might attend his meetings. Leave him out of it. No, we'll have a few trials and that will finish the meetings. Especially if we can get something on one or two. They will all run for cover. No, we must not make a martyr out of Scarrell.

----

continuation:

XVI The Witch Hunt Begins

In January, 1662, then, Robert Stewart of Mecknoch was the first to notice the tracks in the snow of many people meeting in secret in a fold of the hills above Barmore. As his duty demanded, he immediately made a special journey to inform the Minister whose first question was: whom had he seen in the vicinity? The McWilliams, McLevin, Morison, Kirstine Bannatyne, and Patrick McKaw he had all seen, coming or going. These were witch people. But he had also seen me. The Minister knew I must be preaching to them. He had heard I had been doing this before. That was the danger. A lot of people were now flocking to hear me. If more were allowed to join them, perhaps they would cease to come to the Kirk. Maybe they would start up a new Kirk! People plainly liked what I was saying. What could he do about that? Hunt the witches. Hunt the vulnerable members of the group meeting in secret. Robert Stewart of Mecknoch supplied the first testimony that could be investigated. Once that was in, innocent though it was, since it named several people, these could be interrogated and soon other names were thrown up.

By February, a trial had been held and Margaret McLevin was found guilty of witchcraft. The crucial evidence was that she had met the devil at Ardroscadale in a barn and he had asked her to go with him and perform any service for him which he wished. She had agreed and he had rebaptised her Jonat. This much I learned from talking to a few of the women who under cover of darkness came to see me at Roseland. By these admissions, she had, in effect, made a pact with the devil.

The worst of this was that I could remember meeting her at Ardroscadale on a sunny market Thursday, when everyone was in the town, and enjoying her in the barn in just this fashion. It was clear, then, that I was myself now cast as the devil. And it had a certain logic to it. I had confessed to being possessed by the devil, to explain my extraordinary behaviour, put up to it by Sir James, as an utter necessity to ward off the most terrible retribution. Jean, my wife, had described the extent of my possession in graphic terms. And, socially—if not actually—excommunicated, and forced into the company of the witches, I had myself transformed their numbers and even their spirits by what the Minister and others would take to be my preaching. And it was preaching a doctrine different from that acknowledged by the Kirk. Who else would be taken to be the devil? The leader, who had caused the increase in numbers of the meetings held secretly without Kirk sanction.

By this time, all meetings were at an end, lest informers—watchers appointed by the Session—should see who was in attendance and round them all up for trial at one swoop.

Surprisingly, I was not myself called up to the Session to answer any charges, perhaps because I had been so heavily fined and punished already— being officially shunned was a heavy punishment, as all knew. Worse than death, some thought. But I was also considered dangerous: would argue back, effectively; might even turn the Kirk Session into the Sanhedrin.

But when I heard about Margaret McLevin's trial I determined to attend the next one myself.

By then, news of the confessions obtained in the prison at the Tolbooth had spread like wildfire around the island. About a dozen people, half of them children, were said to have been murdered by the witches. The

THE STORY OF ROBERT STEWART OF SCARRELL 161

elders and burgesses had told their wives and they had told their friends. There was soon a widespread hatred of the witch people or anyone associated with them. The fact that the confessions had been witnessed by several worthy men was taken to be conclusive proof that they were correct. In this way, the antipathy to the witch people, who had until then been taken to be harmless folk with some knowledge of herbs and spells, took root in many people's minds.

The Tolbooth is bounded by the Castle on one side and stretches all the way to the Watergate. Downstairs there are three large shops rented out to burgesses. Above, there are cells at the Watergate side and the rest of it— most of it— is the Burgh Court.

Not unexpectedly, my arrival at the front door produced a sensation.

'Ye canny come in here, Master Stewart. Yer no' welcome, ye ken.' This was James Stewart of Kilwhinleck.

'This is not a church service, nor a meeting of the congregation, I replied. 'This is merely a court. The meeting is open to the public and I am one of that public.'

After some discussion with the others, all of them elders too, who were not unmindful of the need to satisfy all proper procedures, I was at last admitted and I immediately elbowed my way through the folk, who were compelled to stand, to the front of the onlookers where someone moved aside to give me one of the seats reserved for the gentry, of whom, I at least, still counted myself a member.

The room was packed with spectators. Even the windows outside revealed more people trying to see inside from the few buildings round about from which a view might be enjoyed. The jury, a dozen, mostly elders, who were also burgesses, the Provost, John Glass, among them, sat on benches to the right. In the centre was a long table set up on a wooden platform a few feet high, specially constructed for the purpose, behind which sat three men: the Earl of Argyll and two others, one on either side: Sir James Stewart and Ninian Bannatyne of Kames. The Prosecutor, John Campbell[103], the fiscal, stood at a small table with a ewer of water and a tankard beside it, along with a sheaf of papers.

The Dempster, Duncan Clerk, seated at another table in the centre, below and in front of the high table, wrote something, probably the date, on a paper, banged the table with a gavel, waited for silence, and then rose to begin the proceedings. 'This is the Justiciary Court of Argyll, with the noble Earl himself in attendance, along with deputes, Sir James Stewart,

---

[103] Rothesay Town Council Records p64, appointed 9 Oct 1661

Sheriff of Bute and Ninian Bannatyne, Laird of Kames. The court has convened to rule upon charges of witchcraft which have been brought against some 24 persons.

We are here, today, to try whether Margaret McWilliam is guilty of witchcraft. Bring in the prisoner.'

From the cells at the side of the court, through a door that was partly ajar, two big men, each with one of her arms, led out the accused.

There was a sudden hush as her appearance struck everyone by its alteration. After a couple of months in the hands of the Session, warded in the Tolbooth, her hair, once grey had become snow white, straggling in long untidy, uncombed tresses down onto her shoulders and down the back of the shapeless brown sack she wore to her ankles, which served as a dress. Her cheeks, once ruddy with health, were shrunken into a face that now looked like someone too often racked with pain and maybe even starvation. As usual, she was barefoot and her feet were none too clean, the soles black as pitch, as could be seen when she walked or rather staggered, held up partly by her warders. The transformation was awful. What had been done to her?

She was led to one side, the left, yet still centre stage and, as she was clearly weak and unsteady on her feet, a chair was got for her to sit on. The two hefty warders sat themselves behind her at each side within easy reach if she tried to move or escape. On the right, in front of the lectern and below the pulpit stood the Prosecutor, who said 'With your lordship's permission, may we begin?' to which the Earl made some barely discernible comment and signalled his approval with his hand.

'Call the Reverend Master John Stewart.'

The minister, who had been sitting in the front row, centre, stood up and went to stand on the right of the court, at another table on which was a Bible, facing the accused,. The oath was administered by Hector Bannatyne.

The Prosecutor said: 'You are Master John Stewart, Minister of this parish, are you not?' And receiving his assent, 'Were you present at the Tolbooth, Rothesay, on February 14th 1662, and then again on 23rd February 1662, when Margaret McWilliam made her confessions of witchcraft.'

'I was.'

'What was the substance of her confession?'

'I have a record [104] I made at the time. Can I read it?'

---

[104] This record is the Inverary Document printed in full in the Appendix: the notes taken during or soon after the confessions. Seen before by the careful reader three times!

'You may.'

'She said this, or words to this effect: The year before the great Snow about 28 years ago, when she was dwelling in Corsmore about Candlemas, at 12 noon, she went out to a field beneath her house called Faldtombuie and out of a furz in the midst of the field appeared a sprite in the likeness of a little brown dog and desired her to go with it which she refused at first. It followed her down to the foot of the field and appeared in the likeness of a well favoured young man and desired her again to go with it and she should want nothing and that time gripped her about the left haunch which pained her sorely and went away as if it were a green smoke.

'That between then and the May thereafter she being in a field above the said house the devill appeared to her first in the likeness of a cat and speired at her: How do ye? Will ye not go with me and serve me? At which time she said she made a covenant with him wherein she promised to be his servant and he said that she should want for nothing and put his mouth upon the sore and healed it. She renounced her baptism and he baptised her and she gave him a gift of a hen or cock.'[105]

—'So,' said the Prosecutor, interrupting, 'She admitted to you that she made a covenant with the devil to be his servant in return for his assurance that she would want for nothing. And she renounced her baptism and he then baptised her by a different name. Is that so?'

'Yes.'

'Was anyone else present when this confession was made?'

'Yes. John Glass, the Provost.'

'And did you receive a further confession on 28th February 1662 from Margaret McWilliam with John Glass again present and John Campbell?'

'I did.'

'And did she repeat her confession of February 14th at that time?'

'She confirmed that it had taken place and was correct.'

'So before three people of stature in the community, this woman has twice confessed to the crime of witchcraft, namely, that she made a pact with the devil and agreed to be his servant and the reason was that the devil would see she would want for nothing?'

'Yes, that is true.'

'What does the Bible say about witches?'

'Thou shalt not suffer a witch to live. Exodus 22 verse 18.'

---

[105] Editor's note: How do you give a hen or cock to a cat? Throw it down to be plucked and eaten raw or was it ready cooked? What has been left out by the recorder is that a well favoured young man was present again and he is the person taken to be the devil.

'What punishment is suitable in that case for this crime?'
'Death.'
At that moment, the minister turned slightly and stared straight at me with a look of sorrow but also of triumph and I saw for the first time the awful dilemma he had set me. If I were to blurt out that I understood the story of her pact and that it was made with me and not the devil and even that it had not been a pact of that kind at all, but an agreement to provide me with sexual favours on a once only basis, I would instantly brand myself as the devil. And having done this, my own death was assured. After all I had been through, I would be lucky to reach the gibbet—lucky to get out of the church—alive! I would be torn to pieces by that vicious community, encouraged and even led by the elders of the Kirk Session themselves. By getting out of the accused a version of this kind—and I could easily see how it had been done—torture would have done it—he made it certain that my silence was assured and therefore my hold over his people—the people he considered his rightful flock—was at an end. I could only save my life by giving up my leadership of them. He must be very much afraid of me!

But a moment's reflection made me realise that he was very much afraid of Margaret herself and her tribe. Had they not the name of people who cast the evil eye? And suddenly I saw something else: Rev John Stewart hated me! Not just for my taking away his flock in numbers and even teaching them a better doctrine, one more in keeping with their lives, but because he had hated my father. For years they had quarrelled over the stipend in and out of the Session and the Synod of the Presbytery. And always my father was in the wrong. His anger and relentless pursuit of anyone who owed him money was a legend, often making the courts. And I had never said anything to reveal my true attitude. No wonder John Stewart hated me. But I did not see it all at that time.

'I know you have further testimony to give, Minister, but I ask you to stand down meantime until we explore in another direction.'
'Call Henry Tavish,' shouted the Dempster.
The man who took the stand was not one of our islanders. He was of middling height and rather rough looking with dark bushy eyebrows and coarse features, so not a member of the gentry. Yet he was well enough dressed in his black broadcloth and wore shoes with bright buckles which looked expensive and new.
'Are you Henry Tavish?'
'Ah am.'
'What is your occupation?'

'Ah been a butcher and an undertaker. Noo Ahm a witch-pricker.'

'And did you prick Margaret McWilliam, for a witch on February 7th this year?'

'Aye, Ah did. Ah fund three merks oan hur. Yin up her left leg. Yin hard be the shin bane. The ither wan wis up her hensh.'

'Would you show the jury where these marks were found?'

'Aye, nae bother.'

'Bring her over here so that the jury can examine here closely,' ordered the Prosecutor.

Margaret was led across the front of the court by the two men, who then stood back, so that she could be seen plainly by everyone assembled.

'Now, Mr Tavish would you stand between her and the gallery so that the jury and the earl can see what you are pointing to. And when you have done this, stand on the other side and show the marks again so that the gallery can see?'

'Aye, Ah wull.'

So Henry Tavish raised the hem of the sacking that covered the body of Margaret McWilliam, white and gaunt as it was, and pointed to a mark on the upper left leg, thereby exposing a fine bush of white pubic hair. There was not a sound in the Kirk. The feeling was like an impending thunder storm, only held in check by some divine force, as if a spark could fly at any moment. Then, still holding the sacking up, he pointed to the shin bone and then turned to the buttocks, pulling the sacking even higher and with the whole of her lower body fully exposed, pointed to a mark there.

'Aye, ye can see it fine. It's still blue, but no as blue as it wis, mind. Mibbe it rubbed aff in time.'

Then to provide a better view to the jury, he said: 'Turn roon lassie, so they can see yer erse.' As she made no move, with the sacking still clasped up, he laid hands upon her buttocks and turned her himself and then stooped for a closer sight. 'De ye see the blue merk?' he called to the jury. 'Its damped near rubbed aff but ye'll kin still see it fine.'

'Would you please repeat the process from the other side.'

When he had finished, the Prosecutor said: 'Now, Mr Tavish would you describe the process of witch-pricking?'

'Aye, ye pit a needle intae the flesh when she canny see ye daeing it and if she disnae cry oot, its because she canny feel it and ye ken it's a witch's merk.'

'Could you explain further, please. What do you mean by a witch's mark?'

'A merk where the witch has been taken hold of by the divil. Efter the covenant is agreed atween the witch and the divil and she's renounced her baptism and been rebaptised, ye ken, and when she's promised tae serve him ony way he wants, the divil tells her tae get doon so she kin start her service and he shags her. Where he taks hold ae her, the merks o' his grip can still be seen efter. And she loses feeling there.'

'How do you know all this?'

'I ken a lot ae weemen that telt me aw aboot it. Ah make a living oota this noo. Ma services is in demand. They aw say that the devil's part is cauld[106]. No like a human man's at aw.'

Suddenly, Margaret, who had been standing still, like a person, not quite dead, half starved, gaunt, and with dark circles around the eyes, edged in red, as well as an unhealthy grey pallor from months spent in the darkness of the jail, came to life.

'His cock wisnae cauld! It wis waarm! We wur in the barn. Ootside it micht hae been cauld, but no' inside!'

The atmosphere—the very air itself, so redolent of stinking, mostly unwashed, humanity, close packed—was so charged a thunderclap seemed imminent.

'They merks wisnae caused wi' nae deevil,' shouted Margaret pointing an outstretched arm at the Minister with a long finger and a dirty, elongated nail curling over the end of it. 'Ah had twa a they merks aw ma life. The ither Ah goat when Ah struggled wi' they twa ruffians ye set on me.'

'Would you return the accused to her place,' replied the Prosecutor. 'And I remind her that this is a court of law and she is supposed to respect the procedure. And if you don't, you will be bound and gagged.' While the men dragged her back her to her place, the Prosecutor said: 'Recall the Minister, Master John Stewart. Please take the stand again, Minister, and continue your testimony. You are still under oath, as you know.'

After consulting his notes, the Prosecutor continued: 'Have there been any cases of malefice associated with the accused?'

'Plenty. Anybody who crossed this woman has reported that things took an unexpected turn for the worse. Crops would fail, animals would die, people would fall sick and even die. She is credited by two other witches as having murdered several persons, namely, William Stephen, Adam Kerr, Alistair McNiven, Donald Moir McKaw's bairn, John Andrew's son and even her own bairn, William McWilliam.'

---

[106] The Witches of Fife, by Stuart Macdonald p110: "Even the sexual act follows a stereotype: his nature (i.e. penis) was cold, and several echoed Janet Hendrie's comment that he used her 'after the manner of a beast'."

Margaret shouted: 'That's a fucken lie! Witch ye may ca' me and witch Ah may be. But Ah niver kilt anybody nor anybody's bairn. And ma ain bairn that wis kilt wis accidental. Aw Ah ever did wis try and help folk that couldnae help theirsels and get ma ain back oan folk that tried tae cock a snook, tak a lend o' me or drag me doon.' Her eyes blazed out of their dark circles and red rims and some people around me shuddered as if she were about to infect them with some malefice, that very instant.

But the general feeling was that here in this shrunken corpse-like frame was an alien being, a being different from everyone else in the room, a being who had sold her soul to the devil and committed murder at his request.

There was no defending counsel and no defence, only this brave woman's defiance. And it was not enough. Everyone thought her guilty as charged. She had even admitted involvement in the death of her own son. No one was interested in the accident, as she called it. But then, everyone knew her reputation, one she had done nothing to refute—used it, even as discouragement to folk who would take advantage of her in future.

The sackcloth cover and the startling nakedness which had been so clearly and deliberately exposed made her into an alien being. And her outburst—that had done nothing to call up sympathy—or the mention of malefice. Instead, they had provoked fear and hostility.

Other witnesses were called to substantiate the charges against Margaret McWilliam and told what they knew or had heard or believed or even wanted to believe, in some cases, and it was mostly nonsense. After another hour, it was growing dark outside which meant it could not continue without the lighting of many candles, an expense not wanted by the town at any time.

The Prosecutor said to the Earl: 'My lord, I believe we could settle this matter right now and that would get it out of the way.'

'What have you in mind?' replied the Earl.

'That the jury be asked if they are able to make a decision on the basis of the evidence given. We have the dittay read out by the Minister, of her confession. She made a covenant with the devil and is evidently notorious for acts of malefice, including murder. Perhaps we have flogged this horse enough.'

'Yes, I think that might be so. Perhaps the jury would confer and see whether a decision is possible without further waste of time.'

It took the jury no more than a few minutes of whispered talk to reach a decision. Finally, Archibald Glass stood up and said: 'We are of one mind, your Lordship. She is guilty as charged.'

'Very well, then. The sentence is clear enough but we will leave it until the other trials are complete.'

The Court then adjourned for another day.

People stood aside when I passed out of the Court and, as I made my way homeward, I wondered what I might do to assist my new friends.

XVII   NIGHTWALKERS IN THE PRISON

A 'woman that was suspected, according to their thoughts, to be a witch, was twenty eight days and nights with bread and water, being stript stark naked, and laid upon a cold stone, with only a hair cloth over her. Others had hair shirts dipp'd in vinegar put on them to fetch off the skin.'[107]

That night there was a new moon and little cloud, and as I stood at my window before turning in, the idea of visiting the prisoners at the Tolbooth where they were warded came to my mind. But how to do this since they would be under guard? Another difficulty was that they were upstairs. The Tolbooth occupied the floor above three shops which were let out by the Town Council to whoever made the highest offer. If I were to present myself at the door of the cells, I would be refused admission. The Minister would have seen to that. No one who was not an elder or burgess would be admitted and I was persona non grata everywhere but in the witch group.

The problem of gaining entry or achieving anything worthwhile seemed intractable until I remembered that at the Bishop's house[108] under the hill, where my father had once lived, was a ladder, held in place at the back wall by a couple of straps. It was useful for replacing the occasional slate that fell—often by a piece of thin wood cut to size, as a temporary measure until a slater arrived, an action both I and my father had both performed as needed at times.

---

[107] Enemies of God, Larner, p75 quoted from Spottiswoode Miscellany Vol 2 p 90,91
[108] He means at the top of Bishop Street which did not exist at that time where the Bishops's house lay near the top also of what is today Castle Street. Most of Bishop Street was included within the Bishop's glebe. See 1780 map. By 1662 a new manse had been made at the top of High Street, as it is today, on the east side of the street and about 50 yds down the street towards the town from Minister's Brae and very close to the street, unlike today, where the Manse, still used in the 1950's, where Dr (later Prof) NHG Robinson lived then, is well up the slope of Minister's Brae and even backs onto the Pleasance.

THE STORY OF ROBERT STEWART OF SCARRELL 169

With this possibility in mind then, I dressed myself again and set off for the Bishop's house in the darkness. Only a few streets had lighting of any kind and it was easy to remain out of sight with the streets empty at such a late hour. I soon discovered that the ladder was still in place. I untied the straps and removed it quietly lest the occupants should hear. I had it on my shoulder in an instant, for it was not twenty feet long and light, and I marched off with it silently in the direction of the Tolbooth which lay only a 100 yards down the street to the Castle. Most of the houses of the town were in darkness at that late hour but there were lights in the Tolbooth and a few street torches were lit to the front which cast an eerie light upon the ruined walls of the Castle just across what had been the moat, now overladen with great stones which had been thrown down by the English troops, just before their departure.

In the Watergate, behind the front of the Tolbooth which overlooked the Castle, I laid the ladder against the rear wall and climbed up quietly. The Watergate was a narrower street, hemmed in on both sides, mainly by workshops, so not occupied at that time of night, and much more gloomy in the darkness in consequence. Yet even here there were some street torches. So the danger of discovery was great. Anyone passing up or down the Watergate would see the ladder. My only hope then would be that they would be too tired or too drunk to do anything about it, a feeble hope, assuredly.

There were, on the other side of the wall, three cells in a line. The walls were wooden mostly, with lath and plaster in places, stone being an expensive luxury not many buildings enjoyed at that time. I found I could hear people talking on the other side. As I had brought a few small tools, I set to work with a sharp-pointed bradawl and looked for places where it might be pushed into the wood. Sure enough, after moving the ladder quietly a few times, I found an area near the edge of the Tolbooth down the street where rain-water had penetrated the roof above my head because it was joined to the gable wall of the next building. The rain-water had been trickling into the timber and that wall, so frequently, that the wall was sodden and rotten. I made a small hole about an inch across and put my eye to it. The bradawl had gone right through and I could see very clearly into the interior and even hear what was said. I saw a bed against the wall and someone lying on it. I saw a figure shaking the person on the bed and when I heard his voice knew it for the Minister. 'Wake up, now, Jonet. Wake up!' he shouted at her. Then, he seemed to turn and speak to another person: 'Willie, will ye get this one up. We'll try her tonight.'

I was aware that another person appeared in the room and he took the one called Jonet by the hair and pulled her upright. 'Come on lassie! It's your turn.'

'But I want to sleep. Please let me sleep.' I could not recognise the voice then because the speech was slurred and weary.

'Ye've tae come oot tae answer yer questions. When ye've told yer tale ye can sleep.'

'I huvenay any sleep for days,' protested Jonet in a voice cracked with fatigue. 'I need to sleep. I'll tell you anything you like if only you'll let me sleep.'

'Get her on the chair, Willie,' I heard the Minister say. Then: 'Are you taking the dittay, John?'

'Aye, fine.' And I heard the scratching of a quill on parchment and the writer said as he wrote: 'Confession Jonet McNicoll, February 24th, saxteen saxty twa. Quhilk day confesses that'—

'Now, Jonet,' said the minister. 'You told us you were at Bute Quay at Hallowday when the devil appeared in the form of a gross copperfaced man but there was a well favoured young man along with him. And you knew the gross copperfaced man was an evil spirit and he asked you to go with him. Is that right?'

'If you say so,' she replied sleepily. 'Can I no' get back tae sleep?'

'Once you tell us what we need to know. Are you quite sure the devil was the gross copper faced man and not the well favoured man?'

Jonet yawned and could hardly stop yawning. 'Gi'e her a cuff on the ear, Wullie,' said John, whom I now identified as the Provost, John Glass, 'tae waken her up.' Having said which, he yawned noisily.

When Willie did this, Jonet moaned: 'Aw gi'e's a rest fae aw this. Am so exhaustet. I canny dae anything because I need tae sleep.'

'I ask you again,' said the Minister. 'Was the devil the well favoured man?'

'How should I ken. I niver saw the divil.'

'But you said you saw the devil!' shouted the Minister, 'in your confession— twice, for you confirmed everything you said.'

'I canny remember anything about a confession. I canny think straight. Ma heid's aw mixed up, fur ye wullnay let me sleep. For God's sake let me sleep!'

'Write that down: blaspheming. Take down the exact words, mind.'

'Whaur she's going it'll likely no' matter,' said the unseen voice of John Glass, making the record.

'Yes,' admitted the Minister, 'I am short of sleep myself. Losing my sharpness. Yes, indeed, she's for the bonfire.'

'Did ye hear that Jonet?' said the man writing out of sight. When there was no response, he added: 'The bitch is asleep again.'

'Wake her up, then, Willie. We'll get this out of her, by and by. It's always worked up to now. It's just a matter of sticking at it. If we don't give up, we'll get the truth out of them.'

The Minister himself took Jonet by the hair and heaved her head upright. 'Did the devil have a cold part when he...he..he took advantage of you?'

'What devil? What do ye mean?' slurred the lady who was on the point of sleep again having just woken up.

'Was his prick cauld or hot?' shouted the man out of sight.

'I don't know. How should I know. I don't know any devil.'

'But ye said ye did.'

'No I niver!'

There was the sound of a blow and a sharp cry and then weeping. 'Don't hit her again. You'll have to watch it, Willie. She is to appear tomorrow— aye today, for it is tomorrow— and we canny have her in the court all black and blue.'

And so for an hour I remained and heard how testimony was got from the witches. In the intervals between interrogations, I could hear many people snoring but they did not sleep for long. Two men were employed all night to keep them awake. One by one they were interrogated by the Minister and some of the elders and burgesses but the Minister was nearly always present, I could see. Around three of the clock, the Minister said: 'I have had enough for tonight. I am going to my bed. Feed them as usual at eight.'

'Wuv nae mair parritch,' said Willie.

'Well, bread and water will have to do. There is little money for this warding of witches.'

'We could let them sterve?' suggested Willie. 'They're jist gonny burn anyway.'

'We need them to appear in court. If they canny stand up because of starvation or they're black and blue, we'll look bad. So keep them free of bruises and make sure their bellies are full. We don't want them calling out for food in the middle of a trial.'

Then Wullie seemed to stop in his tracks. He scratched his head and wondered: 'What are we goin' tae aw this trouble fur?'

'We have to!' said the Minister, with force. 'We could lose the whole congregation if we don't.'

Suddenly fearful that I or my ladder would be seen, perhaps by the Minister on his way home, I quickly descended, lifted it onto my shoulder and set off up the Watergate and then turned left making my way as quickly as possible up the way to the old Bishop's house. Within a few minutes I was at the back of the house where I soon attached the ladder to the straps which kept it in place out of sight of passers by in the street.

At my home later, I immediately fell asleep but when I awoke in the morning it was to images of Jonet and her interrogators. What was I to do about this? The answer was not long in coming.

The next day was a day of trial.

If anything, spurred on by the prospect of seeing women in a near naked state, the crowd was even greater than before. So great that it could not be accommodated within the Court so that it sprawled around it. As before, I had to assert my authority to gain entrance but once inside, I managed to occupy the front row again, admittedly at one side.

After the formalities had been observed the cry went up from the Dempster:

'Bring on the accused, Isobel McNicoll.'

Two burly farm hands led Isobel out from the vestry, one at either arm, and sat her down facing the jury and the Prosecutor. Her black hair, too, had turned grey in a few months. She had dark circles around her eyes, which were red-rimmed. She was barefoot and clad only in the same standard issue of a brown sack with a hole cut in the bottom from which her head and neck appeared.

'Call the Reverend Master John Stewart.'

On this occasion, given his importance to the proceedings, a chair had been made available to him, on stage, as it were, to one side, the same as my own. All the Minister had to do was stand up.

'Minister, since we have been here before on this business and everyone knows the answers, the usual formalities can be dispensed with. So, will you please state the evidence against the accused.'

'May I consult her dittay from my notes, as before?'

'Certainly.'

'On the 21st of February 1662 before myself and Duncan McOnlea late baillie of Rothesay, she confessed as follows:

—'Excuse me, Minister,' called the Prosecutor, 'but when was she apprehended and when did she confess?'

'She was apprehended on the Tuesday and this confession took place on the Friday.' Plenty of time to deprive her of sleep, I thought, and extract whatever confession was wanted.

'Seemingly very remorseful and praying to God to deliver her soul from the power of Satan, she confessed that when she was in her house drawing aquavitae, the devil came to her in the likeness of a young man who desired her to go with him. She confessed that she made a covenant with him in which she promised to be his servant in return for his assurance that she would not want for anything.

'After this was agreed, he baptised her and gave her a new name, Catherine. A month after in the night, as she went out the back door, she met with the devil and spoke with him.

'Another month later the devil came to her again as she was there alone brewing and they had a conversation together.

'She also confessed to being in attendance at the meeting of witches at Bute Quay.'

'So,' concluded the Prosecutor, 'She made a covenant with the devil and she renounced her Christian Baptism and was rebaptised?'

'Yes, that was what she said and Duncan McOnlea will testify that this is correct.'

'Perhaps Duncan will raise his hand if he agrees. It will save time.'

A hand was raised over on my left and the Prosecutor said: 'You are Duncan McOnlea?'

'Aye. Ye ken fine.'

'Do you confirm what the Minister says?'

'Aye.'

Well, that seems clear enough. The charge of witchcraft has already been established beyond doubt.'

From the raised table where he sat in the centre, the young Earl said: 'It would be interesting to know what services she was asked to provide and whether she did provide them.'

The Prosecutor smiled. 'I think we can tell from what has been stated to be the normal practice in a case like this, without embarrassing the ladies present with a detailed description.'

'Nevertheless,' argued the Earl, 'their embarrassment is a lot less important than the life of the woman who is accused.'

'My lord, with the greatest respect, the devil asked her to go with him. She agreed. We all know what that means.'

'Yes, but where did this happen?'

'At the house, twice, and again at Bute Quay—if he had any inclination on that occasion, for there were other women at that meeting whom he might have preferred. *Going with* him immediately is obviously the first service the witch always provides.'

'Very well. Proceed.'

I knew that the young Earl had done quite well but still failed to demand the questions in everybody's mind: Was the devil's instrument hot or cold?—especially in the light of Margaret McWilliam's testimony and Tavish's; and: What acts of malefice had she been guilty of? Had she been tried for the mark? And with what result? Maybe none. Yet if there were no marks, how had she provided the service? How could that kind of service be provided without touching? But no one was making any objections except the Earl and that was because only he could do so without inviting hostility. Of course I knew the answers to all the questions. As may be easily understood by now, I was myself present at all the events described and I knew that the only service Isobel had provided was the one most wanted by an active man like myself. What had happened was that relatively innocent events—at least in my moral code, not the Kirk Session's, for whom all such events were utterly reprehensible—had been given a diabolical interpretation by the Minister, who, of all men, had a vested interest in such a view of them. And yet, I was compelled to recognise that with his view of the world and of the devil, such an interpretation was inevitable—it was the only explanation that could be provided by him for fornication. It was a kind of theorem in his mind, I could see, that to fornicate was to be possessed by the devil. And the man doing the possessing was indeed, the devil, even though the woman was just as guilty, often wanted the event just as much as the man, as I knew from long experience; experience, it must be confessed that the Minister had never enjoyed. So how could he be blamed for failing to understand?

'Since the matter is clear cut and has been confirmed,' said the Prosecutor, 'I suggest we invite the jury to decide the issue.'

A few bowed heads and nods among them were enough to gain their unanimous assent.

The Chancellor then stood and announced: 'We find the accused guilty my lord.'

'Take her down, then.'

XVIII Jonet McNicoll's Trial

'Call Jonet McNicoll.'
Like others, Jonet was just as dishevelled and wearied by sleep deprivation and yet she had been allowed to sleep after I had left, for she was not quite reduced to a state of mental incapacity, which was what I had observed only ten hours before. There were the hostile murmurs which had become usual on the appearance of such a harridan.
The Prosecutor was about to begin as before when the Earl addressed him:
'I do not wish to interfere with your proceedings, but I would like to know what the accused person thinks about this.'
As Jonet said nothing, the Prosecutor said: 'Well, lassie, have you anything to say?'
Again Jonet, who seemed at a loss, terrified by the crowd of people, shamefaced by the flimsiness of the rude garment which alone covered her and then only partly, volunteered no comment.
'You see, my lord, she has nothing to say? People like this are too aware of their own guilt and that all is lost for them, condemned to hellfire, that they are rendered speechless as soon as they enter the Court.'
'Aye right!' I heard a few people in the audience say or words to that effect.
But the Earl was not satisfied. He stood up and went around the table until he stood between Jonet and the Jury where he eyed her for a moment.
Then he passed his hand in front of her face and got little reaction. 'This woman is unwell.'
'Unwell, my lord? How unwell?'
'She does not respond as people do. She seems distant, distracted.'
'Since she is facing her death and hellfire, my lord, that is hardly unexpected.'
The Earl stooped over, looking into her face very directly. 'Come madam,' he said, 'Tell us what you think. Are you guilty of witchcraft or not?'
And suddenly, the lady seemed to wake up. At least she shook her head from side to side.
'Are you saying you are not a witch?'
'No.'
'Does that mean that you admit that you are?'

'No, it doesnay. I am not a witch. Niver! How could I be a witch? It's a damned lie.'

'Then why do these men say that you are?'

'I don't ken.'

'But you confessed. They say that you have confessed. And there were several people present—Or they are about to say this, if I am not mistaken.'

—'Quite right, my lord. The Minister has the confession and other people heard it,' consulting his papers, 'John Glass, Provost, Robert Stewart, leech, and John Campbell.'

'I don't ken what ye mean. I ken they kept me awake for hoors and kept pestering me with questions till I fell asleep and then they hut me till I came awake again and then they pestered me again. I canny hardly mind whit happened. And aw the time I wis sterving and freezing—Have ye ever been in that jile? It's as cauld as a tomb. There's nae fire there. And they don't even feed ye. Breed and watter it is maistly. How kin I mind whit happened?'

'Is this true?' said the Earl to the Minister.

'There is no money to feed them and since they are on the side of Satan it hardly seems necessary to afford them Christian Charity. If they had any money they could buy food. It would be sent for. But they don't.'

'How do you know this woman is guilty?'

'Because I was there. I asked her and she confessed and other good men heard her.'

'Well, you had better proceed with your testimony,' concluded the Earl, taking his seat again. 'But it seems irregular to me. I am not satisfied.'

'There were three meetings with her: once on February 22nd and twice on February 23rd. At the first were myself John Glass, Robert Stewart, the leech, and John Campbell. At the second there were myself, Ninian Bannatyne of Kames, Robert Wallace and Thomas McKinlay. At the third meeting there were myself, Donald McGilchrist and Duncan McNicoll.

'At the first meeting she expressed remorse, prayed to God for forgiveness and admitted that about Hallowday she was in Mary Moore's house when two men appeared to her. One was a gross copper faced man and the other a well favoured young man. The copperfaced man she knew to be an evil spirit and he urged her to go with him. She confessed that she made a covenant with him and that he promised she would never want for anything in return for her serving him. He gave her a new name and baptised her Mary[109]. She also confessed to being at Bute Quay on Hallowday last and she was crossing the burn[110] where there were many people when the young man spoke to her and asked her if she wanted a drink of watter. As she was taking the cog with the watter, her foot slipped and she fell in the burn and the young man lifted her out. The company then went away. The young man stayed with her and escorted her till the foot of the broad waste[111].

'She confirmed these items twice more at the two later meetings and added that Jonet Morison, Elspeth Spence, Patrick Glass's wife, Margaret McWilliam, Christine Bannatyne and John Galie in Barmore were present.'

'So,' said the Prosecutor, 'a covenant with the devil was made, she did go with him, she renounced her Christian baptism and she was rebaptised. Would the elders who were present at these interrogations, please stand up.'

All the men stood up and the Prosecutor asked them one by one if what the Minister had reported was the substance of the confession of the accused. They all agreed that this was so.

'I respectfully submit, my lord, that we now have enough to decide the question.'

'I have one or two questions of my own. Was she tried for the mark?'

The Prosecutor answered: 'I do not know, my lord.'

'Well why not, if it was tried in other cases?'

'It did not seem necessary, my lord,' volunteered the Minister.

'In that case, could we try this right now, here?' said the Earl.

'I don't see why not, my lord. Call Henry Tavish.'

When Tavish arrived at the witness stand, the Prosecutor said:

'Will you try for the mark here and now, as his lordship wishes?'

'Aye, Ah wull. But, ye ken, she'll need tae be strippit. Ah canny dae it withoot that.'

'Go ahead,' said the Earl. 'Since her life is at stake, I don't suppose she'll object.'

But nobody asked for her permission.

---

[109] In the trial in 1673, this name is given as Mary Likeas. See p278. In ID it is Mary.

[110] Editor's note: this will be the Balskyte burn which went down Castle Street, turned down Watergate and entered the harbour at the east side of the breakwater erected in Cromwell's time, a decade before.

[111] Editor's note: this is probably waste ground with whins, seaweed and shingle around the Lade where it enters the sea close to the present Montague St, then..

Tavish left the witness stand, approached the accused, took hold of the sackcloth, lifted it clear of her body and threw it down on the floor, to a strangled gasp from the onlookers. Every eye was immediately arrested by the cupped breasts that stood up off the torso and then fell to the dark triangle of pubic hair which, against the white background of the rest of her, had the prominence of a great treasure—like the one just beneath, I decided. I had not realised how great a treasure she was, despite my prior knowledge, never having seen her in the flesh before.

'Richt, lassie, let's tak a look at ye.' And he proceeded to examine her body minutely for signs of the witch's mark.

'Well, do you see anything?' said the Prosecutor after a while.

'Aye, Ah see a wheen o' merks. There's yin here,' pointing to her thighbone, 'anither oan her erse here. There's a richt guid yin on her shooder and at least fower on her legs.'

'What is the procedure now?' said the Earl.

'Ah tak ma pricker and an see whit happens when Ah stick it intae hur at yin o' they merks.'

'Get on with it then, will you?' said the Prosecutor, distastefully, as if the procedure were now irrelevant because of his earlier demonstrations.

Tavish stooped behind Jonet, aimed carefully and stuck the point of the pin into the mark on her behind. Jonet's head rose suddenly, she jumped forward and at the same time screamed: 'Christ, what are ye doin' tae me! Get away!' And she turned and pushed him with her hand on his chest so that he fell over backwards onto the stage.'

'Mark that for blasphemy,' said the Minister, wearily.

'So what does that prove?' said the Earl, smiling.

Tavish stood up: 'The merk is sensitive. So it's no' a witches merk at aw.'

'So what is the procedure now?'

'I kin try the ither places. But Ah need help tae haud hur. If she sees whaur she's being stuck it's nae guid. She wid ken tae scream. We need tae distract her attention so she disnae ken it's happening.'

But all efforts to achieve a satisfactory pricking by Tavish resulted in every case in a scream.

Eventually, the Earl said: 'Well, that's that. It seems she has no witch's mark.'

'Naw, yer eminence, it jist means she wisnae distractit enough. She kens fine whit we are aboot. If we had her alane and gi'ed her a guid drink or twa or three and kept her occupied in converseetion, she wud soon show a witch's merk.'

'The fact that we have no mark on this occasion is immaterial,' said the Prosecutor. 'There are just too many places to examine.'
'Well, I can think of one,' responded the Earl quickly, 'where a pin could be stuck in an inch or two without producing any sort of screech expect maybe pleasure.'
A few people—a miserably few people—had the presence of mind to laugh.
'Well, my lord, will you permit the jury to determine the charge? The woman has confessed to making a covenant, renouncing her baptismal name and being rebaptised. That is enough surely?'
'And yet there is no witch's mark. And up to now that has been taken as a conclusive proof. Do you see what that means?'
The Prosecutor looked puzzled. 'No, my lord.'
'Well, if there are no marks it means she may have agreed to be his servant but she did not go with him— at least not then and not any time, indeed. How could he enjoy her without touching her somewhere? And if he did touch her, there has to be a mark, so at least you tell me. But you can find no marks. This suggests that she never did go with him.'
Tavish protested: 'But, your eminence, if ye gi'e me a hale nicht wi' her and a quart ae aquavittie, Ah'll guarantee tae produce a merk by the morn.'
The Earl smiled a knowing smile. 'Yes, I do believe you could. If you filled her full of aquavitae I dare say she would become insensible in several places. In fact, now that I consider the matter more deeply, it may well be that after you had spent the whole evening at your business, there might be a few places a lot less sensitive than before which were not caused either by the devil or the drink but by your handling of the matter, if you see what I mean.' Of course hardly anyone did. The levity of the Earl was out of place in that cauldron of hatred of all things alien to the teachings of the Kirk Session. And a woman with beautiful breasts and an arresting genital area was supposed to be anathema to every elder at least, some never having cast their eye upon such a sight before, despite years of the wedded state.
'May we proceed to decide the issue, then, my lord?'
'I think not. It is late. I do believe we should adjourn for the day. Maybe we should all take some aquavitae ourselves and think over what we are about here.'
Thinking it over myself on the way home, that evening, long before I came anywhere near my own aquavitae, I knew that the Earl was not going to have any effect upon the outcome. The confession of the

covenant, confirmed by all these worthy men, no matter how it was obtained, would stand. The jury would see to it. She would be condemned and she would be executed.

I decided that there was but one thing for me to do: try to get them liberated. They had to be got free and given time and the means to get completely free of the island. The question was how?

XIX Planning Escape

How could I free them? The obvious answer was to widen the hole in the wall of the jail. But there were 3 cells and the others might be locked. Then I must just content myself with freeing the ones in that cell. But how to get them away? Should I try and hide them until the hue and cry died down or get them off the island immediately. The latter sounded best but could it be done? Only by stealing a boat and if that were done, the shores around would soon be scoured for signs of them. Boats would set out for every seaport around and questions would be asked and when it was known that escaped witches were sought, every hand would be against them.

Then there was the problem of clothing. They were being kept in sackcloth, so much was clear, and so lightly clad in this wintry weather even in March, they could soon die of cold if asked to fend for themselves. And when should this be done? This was easier: as soon as possible, the sooner the better. Since it was costing money to keep them warded, the burgesses would want the matter closed quickly to keep down the costs. Feeding a couple of dozen witches and many others just to watch over them for months—and paying these!—was a serious drain on the finances of the Town.

At midnight, I set off again for the old Bishop's house, carrying on my back, a large bundle of clothes, mostly left by Elizabeth, wrapped up in a plaid. I soon shouldered the ladder and reached Watergate without incident where I put down the plaid and erected the ladder in the place I knew to be vulnerable to penetration.

Only two torches were burning that night in the Watergate and both were some distance away, yet there was just enough ambient light for me to see what I needed. I felt for the hole I had made the night before in the better conditions of moonlight and then proceeded to make further holes in the wood with my bradawl, an instrument about six inches long which tapered to a sharp point and had a rounded handle at one end which fitted the palm of the hand very well and allowed a lot of force to be exerted.

I made several holes around the hole of the night before and then tried to push out the wood between them. Failing in this, I took a little saw I had brought and gently sawed out the wood between a few of the holes. Then I could push the wood in that place and presently the entire piece came away without so much as a splinter. I found myself staring into the cell through a ragged hole now about a foot across. The first thing I noticed was the smell—the acrid stink of urine and shit and so many unwashed bodies and soon found the reason: my hole, in one corner of the cell, was right beside the chamber pot. And the chamber pot was under a wooden pallet acting as a bed and someone was asleep upon it, lying upon some stinking straw that had not been changed for months. I inserted my hand into the hole and searched around, delicately, until I encountered what could only be human hair. What to do?

There was the sound of talk, but it was far off, outside the cell and snoring in the same cell from other sleepers.

I decided to chance it and tug upon the hair, though fairly gently at first. Presently, the head attached to the hair lifted and murmured: 'Wha's a metter?'

'Sh,' I urged, 'I have come to set you free.'

She lifted her head suddenly and I saw who it was: the lady of the most recent trial: Jonet McNicoll. She wiped her eyes of sleep and said: 'Oh my God be praised! It's yourself, I ken yer voice.'

'Keep quiet,' I instructed.

'They're all in the Council Chamber walking them roon and roon tae keep them awake. It's whit they do every nicht.'

'You must wake the others in the cell and then escape through this hole. I'll make it bigger while you do this.'

Jonet moved to my left and in the space vacated, I could just discern, over the top of the bed pallet, the bars of the door of the cell and beyond them a corridor and beyond it, the Council Chamber within which, lit up by candles, I could dimly make out a partial ring of sack-clad, white faced, barefoot figures, like a treadmill of ghostly slaves, walking around the room, being prodded with sticks by the elders and burgesses and their followers, all in black.

'Wake up, Margret!' cried Jonet, so that I worried she would be overheard. 'Wake up for God's sake!' as she shook the figure out of my sight.

Meantime, I had been pressing my bradawl into the wood and making another ring of small holes around the former. It took longer this time but when at last the piece in the centre came away and fell onto the straw on the floor of the cell, there now was just enough room for a person to squeeze through.

But Jonet's efforts to waken Margaret McWilliam, as I now realised it was, were unavailing. Jonet wept: 'They kept her awake for a hale week, so they did.'

'I thought she had been convicted?'

'Aye, but they're no' done wi' her. They want mair confession about ither fowk. They jist brought her back an hoor ago. She'll no wake up! Ah ken fine! Ah've seen it aw afore.'

'Who else is there?'

'Margret McLevin. But she's the same. Deed tired wi' exhaustion. They been at her tae.'

'Can you move them over to the hole, then? And push them through?'

'No Ah canny. They're too heavy. I couldnay move a moose. Ah kin hardly staun up at aw. We've had naething but breed and watter for months. We're sterving, so we are.'

'Well you must try, Jonet!' and Jonet lay down on her pallet and wept.

'I'm that tired, Sir. I canny.'

'Please try it, Jonet.'

And she tried and got Margaret off her pallet and Margaret hit the floor with a confused thud but failed to stir.

'Push her over to me, now, head first.'

Jonet tried to do this but made little impression. 'Ye'll ha'e tae come in yersel' Sir. Ah jist canny shift her. An if Ah shove her oot tae you she'll jist fa' and break her neck.'

'She'll have worse than a broken neck before long. Come on Jonet, try harder.'

But, just as soon as Jonet had tried and failed again, there was an alteration in the noise from the Council Chamber across the corridor and, soon after, the sound of footsteps.'

'Get back on your pallet, Jonet,' I whispered urgently.

By the time the keys were rattling in the cell door lock, Jonet was lying on the pallet again and by so doing concealed the hole I had made.

Two men entered the cell and, cursing, unceremoniously began to lift and then to drag Margaret back to the Chamber. 'Come oan ya witch, ye!' said one prodding her in the back with a baton with which, on other occasions, I could see, he had beaten her about the head and shoulders.

She was like a great slack doll, white haired and gaunt, in the sackcloth, stained now with shit and piss and even blood, I could see, for there was no reason now to withhold physical torture since her next appearance in public would be at the Gallowscraig. She was no longer considered a human and could have done to her what no elder or burgess would do to a rabid dog.

The cell door was left open and for a few minutes with the blood pounding in my heart, I wondered whether anything could be managed by me entering the cell. Could I lock the door of the Council Chamber? Was there a lock and key for it?

But while I still contemplated this new development, footsteps arrived again and the other sleeper was lifted and dragged away. It was Margaret McLevin, much thinned down due to the starvation rations and much misused though not as badly as Margaret McWilliam. The cell door was locked and the footsteps marched away.

There was nothing else to be done. The hole was made and could not be unmade without discovery which must surely follow in daylight as soon as someone entered the cell, especially if Jonet were not lying upon her pallet to conceal it. I would have to be content to remove Jonet only. But could that be done? I gripped her by the hair and pulled gently. She was falling asleep again! I heaved on her head and pulled it towards me and she woke. 'Come on Jonet, you must get out of the cell through this hole I've made.'

'Ah canny, Sir. Ah'm aw wore oot. Ah kin hardly staun.'

'You don't have to stand. Just put your feet through the hole and I'll pull you through.'

'You'll no' let me fa', wull ye, Sir?'

'No, I'll hold onto you. But be careful. There will be two of us on the ladder.'

I caught hold of the feet and pulled and Jonet began to emerge from the cell, hissing and murmuring curses at scratching herself on the rough edges of the hole in the wood which I had made. Somehow, the sack which covered her came off and she suddenly appeared beside me on the ladder, quite naked, held up by my right arm around her back.

'Now turn round, carefully,' I ordered.

'But Ah hiv nae claes on, Sir,' she protested quietly, shivering.

'Never mind. I have some in a plaid down below. So don't worry about that. You must get down without injury. That is very important. You need to be able to walk. And you must be silent.'

I managed to turn her and I went down a step keeping a firm hold on her with one arm around her breasts now. Then I began the careful descent: myself a step and then her a step, until finally we both stood on the ground in the Watergate where I searched for a dress in the folds of the plaid and she stood shivering in the freezing cold with her hands over her breasts.

'Here put on this dress,' I told her, having found one at last.

'And here are shoes. And stockings too. Put them on and quickly. We must be away.'

My plan had been to lead them to the harbour and set sail in a skiff. Now that there were only the two of us there were not enough hands to launch the boat. Yet, having seen the state of the women so recently, I knew that we would never have managed to launch a boat large enough to take us, even had there been a handful. They had no strength left at all. It had been starved out of them—as well as tortured and frightened.

'You carry the plaid, Jonet, please, and I'll take the ladder.'

'Kin ye no' jist leave it, Sir? We maun get away from here afore they find us.'

'No, we must cover our tracks as best we can. Starting with the ladder.'

And so, in a few minutes I had strapped the ladder back into its place behind the Old Bishop's House at the head of the Castle Street.

'Where do we go now, Sir?'

'To Roseland. I will hide you there for as long as I can.'

'Oh, Sir, thank you! Thank you!'

'Thank me when you are completely free', I said. 'But we must hurry and it is a steep hill.'

Jonet was already done in and had to be half carried up the hill called the Loaning. But well within an hour or so we had made it to my home where I sat her in front of the fire and told her to take any clothes out of the plaid she wished while I fetched aquavitae for us both and brewed some herbal tea.

In an hour we had both eaten some rabbit stew out of a cauldron I had heated and she was feeling much better.

'Now Jonet, there is something I must do and it will take me all the hours of night that remain. I must make you a hiding place for they will come and search this house and all around tomorrow, once they discover you have escaped.'

'I'll help, Sir, let me.'

'You're not fit. You're out on your feet. No, you must sleep in my bed upstairs and leave it to me.'

I took her upstairs with a hot water bottle and settled her between the blankets, kissed her gently on the forehead and then went down to start excavating a small room under the floor of my workshop.

In the next few hours before dawn, I dug out a space four feet deep, three across and four wide under the floor near the door and to the right over which the door would swing if left open or ajar. This I covered over with a piece of wood which had to be cut very exactly to fit into the rebate around the top the of the hole on which the lid would rest. There remained the pile of earth I had excavated. That too had to be shifted and in the dark this was no easy matter. Where to put it? I laid it against the side wall of the workshop outside, spread right across and about a yard wide and a foot deep, as if making a border for flowers.

When I had finished, I fetched a chamber pot and some bread, water and raw vegetables and even some of the stew in a plate and laid them on the floor of my hiding place, beside the seat I had made in it.

Around dawn, I woke Jonet and took her to see my handiwork. 'Do you think you can manage there?' I asked her.

'Aye, Sir, I can sit doon there jist fine. An' I'll no' make a sound if anybody's aboot.'

'Then in you go and I'll make the lid look as if it has been there forever and is part of the floor.'

When she was properly installed and said she was ready, I began to fix the entry and then remembered how cold it would be and went to fetch the plaid and blankets and more clothing. Once I had stuffed this down around her and been thanked for my kindness, I shut the lid again and completed my preparations.

'I'm going to bed myself, now, Jonet. So you must keep still and keep quiet as long as you can, especially if you hear someone coming. If anyone calls your name pay no attention. It might be a trick to discover you. Once they have been and gone and it is safe, I will let you out. I will probably sleep late and when I get up I will go out to the trial without disturbing you. I won't see you again until I return. I must attend and make things look normal. They will come to the house tomorrow and search it—when I am out probably—but maybe before then.'

But Jonet was not happy. From below came a wail: 'Oh Sir, Ah don't mean tae be a trial tae ye, but how dae Ah breathe doon here?'

'I am sorry, Jonet, I forgot about that. Wait a moment and I'll bore some air holes for you.' Once I had done this, a handful of tiny holes started with the bradawl and then hand drilled, spaced out, and near the edge where they would not undermine the wood and cause anyone standing on the lid to fall through, I bade her farewell.

In the event, they did not appear at breakfast, which I took late, having gone to bed after dawn. As soon as I could, still very sleepy, I left the house as if nothing untoward had occurred, leaving the doors unlocked as everyone does here. The Kirk Session has such a powerful hold that theft is practically unknown—the reason, indeed, that people like Margaret McWilliam could so easily put a pock of witchcraft under the bed of the Minister, as admitted by her in her confession.

XX The Trial of Jonet Morison

As the Prosecutor was about to begin the proceedings, after a long delay, an elder strode into the court and spoke to him quietly. Then the Prosecutor, with much surprise, said: 'My lord, I fear there has been a development. The prisoner, Jonet McNicoll, has escaped.'

There were gasps of amazement from most of those present— including myself!—I was more amazed than anyone for different reasons—and then a lot of confused talk among everyone and even angry shouts that the warding of the prisoners could not have been better managed.

'Minister, will you please tell us what you know of this?' said the Earl, having hit the table with the gavel he had asked for and been given, now that he was determined to play a leading role in the Assize.

The Reverend Master John Stewart replied: 'She was at the jail last night, for I saw her there myself—even interviewed her again. There was some tooing and froing of prisoners as we continued to examine them for cross questioning. And you must realise that the jail is not well lit at night—especially the cells. The prisoners don't need lights there anyway. All I can say for sure is that by morning she had disappeared. The warders did not notice her absence until this very morning.'

'But how did she escape?' said the Earl. 'How did she get past all of you?'

'I have been told that she has knocked out a bit of wood that was rotten in the corner of her cell and that she got out that way.' How relieved I was that they had not noticed the holes I made. Probably took the few they did see for woodworm.

'But it is high up, this cell, is it not?'

'Aye my lord.'
'So she must have jumped down, then?'
'Or climbed down, more likely.'
'And what is being done to recover her?'
'Everything possible. The island is being scoured by elders, burgesses and others co-opted for the purpose.'
'Well then, you may proceed.'
'Today we try Jonet Morison, my lord.'
'Call Jonet Morison,' cried the Dempster.
Jonet was very much like the others I had seen. Exhausted by starvation and sleeplessness, partly covered in sack cloth, hair uncombed and sticking out everywhere, including strands of the stinking straw on which she had slept—when allowed to for a few minutes—and altogether looking like a being from another, utterly alien world, someone less than an animal, someone to fear because she was so very different from everyone of us. And what no one seemed to realise was that we ourselves—the Minister and Kirk Session and their minions, at least—had made her into what she was now: that it was not her doing at all. Had she been treated with decency, fed and looked after properly, so that she presented an appearance we could identify with, then I believe her cause might have turned out differently[112]. The Prosecutor turned to John Stewart who had sat down and said: 'Minister, would you please read out the confession of Jonet Morison.'
The Minister stood up: 'On the 15th January[113], 1662, Jonet Morison sent for me to speak with her at her own house and I, accompanied by John Glass, Provost, and John Gray, burgess, heard her confess as follows.
'First, that about a fortnight before Hallowday last, as she was going from the town of Bute to her own house in the twilight she met, on the way at the loaning foot[114], a black, rough, fierce, man who came to her and desired her to go with him. For you are a poor woman, begging amongst harlots and uncharitable people and not better of this. I will make you a Lady and bring home Adam Kerr for you. His people are witch people and will care for you and make you a Lady. He drew near her and would

---

[112] Editor's note: this is not so. The law would have condemned her however she looked.
[113] The date given in the document found at Inverary is 19th January. As the record shows on ID p22, this date is incorrect and should be 15th January. See ID p20-28;268-275, herein, for the full 'confession' of Jonet Morison. Notice that she has invited the inquisition to her home: is anxious to confess: a symptom of psychosis..
[114] This Loaning must be between the town and Kilmory, where she lived; probably around where Barone Road and Columshill Street are today.

have taken her by the hand but she refused, yet arranged to tryst with him that same night eight nights on at Knockanrioch. Asked whether she knew what that man was, she said she knew him to be the devil and at the beginning she was afraid.

'She declared that according to her promise she kept the tryst with him and that when he appeared he had a white middle and he said to her: you are a poor woman and beggar among harlots, goe with me and I'll make you a Lady and put you in a brave castle where you will want for nothing. And I will free you of all poverty and trouble and show you a way to bring home Adam Kerr.'

—'So there is a doubt, then, Minister? She did not say she made a covenant with the devil?'

'She did, but not at that time. On 18th January, before John Glass, myself, Ninian Bannatyne of Kames, Ninian Kerr, bailie, John Kelburn, older and younger, burgesses, Master James Stewart, Robert Beith and Archibald Glass, burgesses, she said this:

'She declared over again all that she had said on the former occasion and further declared that that night she trysted with the devil at Knockanrioch, being the second time of meeting with him, that she made a covenant with the devil wherein the devil promised to give her anything she desired and to teach her how to bring home Adam Kerr and the devil won her so that she promised to be his servant etc. And she asked what was his name? And he replied: my name is Klareanough[115] and he asked what was her name and she answered Jonet Morison, the name God gave me. And he said, believe not in Christ but believe in me. I baptize you Margaret.'

—'So that is the matter made clear, then?'

'Aye, I believe it is.'

'Would the persons who were also present to hear this confession please stand up.'

When they done so, the Prosecutor addressed them one by one and in every case they agreed that the account given by the Minister was correct in all particulars.

'In that case, my lord, I believe we can have a decision.'

'Indeed,' said the Earl, 'she has clearly renounced her Christian religion and joined the devil's battalions. And yet, I am loath to leave it and would

---

[115] This is what this document, written in 1662, actually says. All these trials are reconstructed from the confessions in the document. Of course the scene is imagined. The Prosecutor was the one appointed for that year: John Campbell. All the names of witnesses to the confessions are accurate, for these are listed in the document. They are not stated every time, as it would be a bore.

hear more of this confession. There may be more to this than meets the eye.'

'It is a very long confession, my lord. And it makes painful reading. Many are accused of murder.'

'In that case, I suggest we adjourn until the morrow. We have had quite enough for one day already. And I would rather be fresh to this further inquisition since it is so arduous. It will also give you and your Session more time in daylight to discover the whereabouts of the runaway.'

But, as we were soon to find out, there was another reason for the early adjournment.

Returned home, I looked carefully around outside and inside the house for signs of entry and saw none. But it was still too light to be sure that there would be no search. Inside the workshop, I spoke to Jonet through the lid of the secret place where there was some sign of disturbance.

'How are you? It's me.'

'Ah'm very cramped and a bit cauld but no' too much, ye ken.'

'So no one came, then?'

'Aye, they did awricht. There was twa o' thaim. I heard them fine but they werenae here long.'

'There is no sign anywhere else.'

'Can Ah come oot yet?'

'I think you should remain until it is dark, just in case. If you don't mind, that is.'

'Anything you say, Sir. I am that gled. You've been wonnerful, saving ma life.'

'It's not safe yet.'

As the afternoon wore on to darkness I scanned the environs of the house and saw no sign of any watchers and when night fell I was satisfied that it was safe—especially since the house had already been searched.

I lifted the lid and escorted Jonet into the house, having drawn curtains over the windows first and built up the fire. She nearly wept with the pain of returning circulation to her limbs. 'Ah'm sorry, Sir, that Ah moved the lid. Ah jist couldnae help it, ye ken. But it was after the men were here.'

'Think nothing of it, Jonet. I'll make the space bigger tonight and perhaps it will be more comfortable.'

'What am Ah gonny do, Sir?'

'First we must get you well. Feed you up properly and keep you warm. Then, when you are able to travel we must get you away to the mainland somewhere.'

'What am Ah gonny do there, Sir?'

'I wish I knew. I think I can get you there. I can give you money and clothing and food, even, and the means of catching small game or fish and cooking pots, maybe even seed for growing things on if you can find somewhere to plant them. What I cannot give you is a life there. This you must make for yourself.'

'So, I'll be alone then?'

Unless you meet someone and attach yourself to them in some way, as a servant or a lover or even a husband.'

'But Ah'm married awready, Sir.'

'Yes, I know that now. Your husband wouldn't leave the island would he?'

'Naw, Sir. He'll niver leave. Maist people niver leaves as ye ken fine. What wid he do somewhere else?'

'Will you miss him?'

'No' very much, Naw. He's no' much ae a man. He thinks Ah should be burnt.'

'How could he? He must know you are not guilty of much.'

'He's a dull man, Sir. He believes what the Session tells him. Ah will miss my son, Donald, but. He's ma only living bairn an' he'll miss his ma. He's only twelve, ye ken. But he's better off withoot me now.'

'When you've rested and warmed up and eaten I want you to walk around the house inside and get some exercise,' I told her. 'Then, I think I'll put you to bed until just before dawn. We'll make breakfast together and you must be in the hole by the time the sun comes up.

'When you exercise, you must do so without a candle in case there are watchers. I will set to work excavating more soil to make your place more roomy and comfortable.'

And so the pattern of our lives was set for a few weeks at least. And during that time I began to make preparations to get her off the island in safety.

I had to make a ship of some kind and it had to be transported across the hill to the east and down to the shore, a matter of a few miles through woodland, but difficult walking if I were to steer clear of every habitation. Then I remembered that Jonet would be present to help carry things. But how to make a ship that did not look like a ship? For if I simply set to and built a boat of the traditional shape, what it was for would be obvious and anyone who came to visit or to search my house again, as was likely, would see what I was about. When had I ever taken an interest in sailing the sea? They would immediately know that I had her concealed somewhere and planned to ship her out.

After much reflection I hit upon the idea of a patchwork of saplings in the shape of a rectangle about 6 feet by 4 feet. This would be made with the expressed purpose of tying my tools onto, as it rested upon the inside wall of the workshop: an easy way of having them in sight and at hand when needed. A claw hammer could be hung on it as could anything that could be tied on and untied quickly.

But it would have another purpose. If the long edges were folded together and yet separated in the middle, it would make the framework for a small, light sailing craft. The hull itself would have to be of some fabric already available to me, linen sheets—perhaps two or three—stretched over the frame and painted with tar. Tar barrels were plentiful down at the harbour where the fisher folk used them for caulking the strakes of their much larger vessels. When the time came, I would steal some tar out of a barrel. Almost everything could be done with string and saplings alone. There remained the two middle supports, each a hollow semi-circle of lath with a cross piece on the diameter. The lath had to be strong enough to separate the sides and yet be able to bend into shape. This was achieved by setting the kettle on the fire in the kitchen and directing the steam onto lath of about 2 inches across by a quarter of an inch deep. By making the shape stay in place using strings and weights, the wood soon retained the shape after cooling and the two inner supports were easily fashioned. The lath I made from a branch after splitting and planing. I thought about a sail and decided against it as likely to capsize the boat if the wind gusted, as it might easily do in mid channel. A short oar or paddle—even a pair of paddles, in case of loss—was the best solution for a sailor like Jonet without experience of any kind.

In the days that followed, when not attending to Jonet, my life was entirely taken up with these arrangements. But every day there was a trial, I attended, to keep up the appearance of normality. The first sign of my absence might result in a thoroughgoing search of my household. Since further searches were likely, I was careful every time I left the house to leave no trace of Jonet's presence.

XXI Jonet Morison Exposed

The second day of the trial of Jonet Morison began and I was there in the front row in what had come to be accepted as my seat.

Once Jonet was installed in her place looking pale and wan like her sisters before her, the cry, unnecessary now, went up: 'Call the Reverend Master John Stewart,' who had already taken his place.

The Prosecutor with a look of surprise at the Dempster then said:

'Minister, will you relate the remainder of the confession of the accused? Perhaps to save time you could summarise the main events recorded in the dittay, beginning with the names of the other witnesses.'

'There were two meetings with her in January. On the 18th, beside myself there were John Glass, Ninian Bannatyne of Kames, Walter Stewart, Neill McNeill and Duncan McAlastair.

'At that meeting she stood by all she had said before and added that the devil desired her to take the life of the Provost's dun horse by shooting him which she refused to do and to take the life of Walter Stewart, baillie, by shooting him to put him[116] for a neighbour of his that dwelt in the highlands which also she refused to do.'

—The Earl interjected: 'So she was told to murder an animal and a man, a man present at the confession and the animal belonging to another man at the confession: the Provost, and she refused?'

'Aye, that's what she confessed.'

'Why would she be asked to do this, do you think?'

'Maybe the devil had something against the Provost, John Glass and the Treasurer, Walter Stewart. Who can read the mind of the devil?'

But the Minister was disturbed by these questions from the young Earl who alone had the authority to challenge the proceedings and the testimony.

'Item,' continued the Minister, reading from his notes, 'the accused declares that at the time she met with the devil when he was going by with a great number of men that she asked him what were these men that went by and he answered: They are my company and when she speired where they were going, he answered that they were going to seek a prey.[117]'

'Did it occur to you, Minister, to enquire what the devil looked like? What form did he take? Was it a man? And was it perhaps a man that we would all recognise?'

'I have no memorandum on this, my Lord,' replied the Minister sheepishly.

---

[116] This is exactly what the dittay says. See p273. Perhaps it means: to revenge him.

[117] As the reconstruction says, the word 'prey' may have been confused with the word 'pray'. See p271 Remember that the Minister is reading from the paper which has been handed down and is printed in full herein.

'Well, continue, Minister, I am increasingly surprised.'

'On 21 January 1662, in my presence and with witnesses John Glass, Major William Campbell, Master Archibald Beith, Walter Stewart, Baillie, Peter Gray, Alastair McTyre, James McNiven, James Stewart, William Gillespie and Archibald Stewart, Provost[118], the accused confessed as follows:

'What she had said before, she repeated. She confessed to healing the daughter of McPherson in Keretonle[119] who had a very unnatural disease of paralysis of hand and foot and was speechless. This was blasting by the fairies and she healed her with herbs. She also healed Alistair Bannatyne who had the same disease and also Barbra Glass, the daughter of Patrick Glass. Both had been blasted by the fairies and she healed them with herbs.'

—'What does blasting by the fairies mean?' said the Earl.

The Minister leafed through his papers and said: 'Being inquired what difference there was between shooting and blasting, she said that when they are shot there is no recovery from it and if the shot be in the heart they died presently but if it is not at the heart they will die in a while with it yet will at last die with it and that blasting is a whirlwinde that the fayries raises about that persone which they intend to wrong and that though there were twenty present yet it will harm none but him whom they were set for, which is healed in two ways either by herbs or charming and that all that whirlwind gathers in the body till one place if it be taken in time it is the easier healed and if they get not means they will shirpe[120] away.'

—'That is not exactly crystal clear, Minister, would you agree?'

'Yes, my lord. I am reading from the dittay and the writing was taken down in haste and in some difficulty.'

'And these are your words?'

'Aye, my lord.'

'And were all the dittays written down by yourself?'

'Mostly, my lord.'

'I notice that the devil takes the form of a young well favoured man in at least 4 cases, I think. These are your words then?'

'They must be, my lord.'

---

[118] In fact, John Glass was the Provost. This is a mistake but that is what the dittay says. The Minister would have lost a lot of sleep himself and been liable to error.

[119] A farm in South Bute.

[120] The word actually used in the dittay. It means 'wither away'. This entire speech is a quotation from the confession, as usual.

'Could the form of the devil so described have anything to do with the fact that you wrote down the description?'

The Minister became puce with fury. 'Are you suggesting that I made up these words myself, my lord?'

'I am merely asking a question, Minister.'

There was a pause and then the Earl insisted. 'Would you please reply, Minister.'

'What I wrote down was what they confessed. I used the same words mostly but always I used words to that effect.'

'But did they all, all the 4 witches, agree in that form of words? If they did, it becomes a question: Who fits the description? What I fail to understand is why you did not ask the question yourself—repeatedly!'

The Prosecutor intervened: 'My lord, I think it would be helpful if the men who were witnesses were invited to confirm the confession as related.'

'Have them stand up and declare themselves, then, since that is your practice.'

Of course all did so and all confirmed the Minister's version.

The Earl seemed dissatisfied, however. 'Minister, are there any other references in this confession to the devil?'

The Minister bent over his notes, turning papers and then said: 'Aye, there are. On the 22nd January, Jonet Morison sent for me and before James Stewart, Adam's son and Colin Stewart, burgess, declared as follows: That about three nights before Hallowday last year as she was going out of the town to her home at Bute Quay, she saw the devil and a company with him coming down the side underneath St Bride's Chapel, on the Chapel Hill, and that himself [the devil] was foremost and after him was John Galie in Barmore and his wife Jenat McConochie, Elspat Galie in Ambrisbeg, Margaret McWilliam, Katherine Moore, Margaret McLevin, Kirsten Bannatyne and Jonet McNeil. And when they came to a craft went in a ring with himself [the devil] in the midst of them and that she heard them speaking to him and the devil came out from among them to her and convoyed her to the Loaning foot[121] where he and she set a tryst to meet in eight days time.'

---

[121] The same Loaning as before, as it is near the south west of the town and on her way home to Kilmory and on the same side of town as Knockanrioch and Chapel Hill, both places she would go to naturally, even on her way from Wester Kames if visiting the town for supplies after work before going home.

The Minister clearly wanted to continue, perhaps to increase the confusion but the Earl would not allow this. 'It is perfectly obvious that the devil is in a human form. The question is: who is the human?'
The Minister, flustered, said nothing.
'Minister,' insisted the Earl. 'did it not occur to you to enquire the identity of this person who is being taken by all these women to be the devil?'
'Not always, my lord,' answered the Minister, huffily. 'Sometimes he is in the form of a cat, sometimes a little brown dog, sometimes, even with this witch, as a stalk of heather [122].'
'And yet we have repeated reports of the devil with other identifiable people who all must have seen him. What did he look like?'
There was a dead silence around the court. Then the Earl sprang to his feet and approached the accused. 'Since no one else will do this I must do it myself, I see. Madam, what did the devil look like?'
Jonet, bemused with sleeplessness, starvation, her own relative nakedness among so many men, and the sheer awful indignity of being in that place at that time, like a trapped animal facing a pack of wolves, said nothing, did not seem to hear the question.
The young Earl reached out and took her nose between thumb and forefinger and moved her so that she swayed, to bring her to a more alert and responsive state, and said: 'Madam, will you answer?'
'My lord, Ah canny!'
'You mean you do not know?'
'Ah mean, my lord, I wis telt no' tae say.'
'Who told you this?'
'Ah don't mind, my lord. Yin ae the elders, Ah think. Ah wis near asleep maist ae the time, ye ken. Ah canny remember who it wis. It was dark tae.'
'But you do know who the devil was?'
'Ah dinnay ken, my lord.'

XXII The Devil Exposed

The Earl threw up his hands in exasperation. 'You have confessed to meeting the devil on several occasions! Several worthy men all confirm this is so. Well, then, what did he look like? Did he have a red face and a long tail? Did he have a couple of horns as some say? How was he

---

[122] p21 of the Inverary Document; p270 of the verbatim printing herein.

dressed? Was he dressed at all or was he naked? Was he a well favoured young man as several witches have testified?'

Jonet burst into tears—tears of confusion at not knowing what to say. And I suddenly saw her difficulty: she had for months been encouraged to say what the Minister wanted her to say and now she did not know what answer was wanted.

When she continued to weep but say nothing, the Earl stepped back thoughtfully and said: 'You say, or are supposed to have said, that you met the devil at the foot of Chapelhill 3 nights before Hallowday. Is that correct?'

'Aye, my lord.'

'Was it dark at the time? You said it was 3 nights before Hallowday.'

'It was no' full dark. There was some light.'

'What time would it have been?'

'I dinnae ken, my lord. Mibbee aboot five or sax o' the clock.'

'Then it would not be full dark, as you say. What was the devil wearing?'

'Just a black suit. The kind most men wear.'

'Was it a good suit? Or was it ragged, like the clothes of a beggar?'

'It wis guid broadcloth, Sir.'

'Like mine?'

'Aye, something like.'

'Thank you. We are getting somewhere at last. Now, Jonet, what colour was his hair?'

'Black, Sir, just like yer ain.' The Earl smiled at the suggestion, suddenly looming ahead.

'How tall was he?'

'Taller than you, sir. A big man.'

'So it was not me then?' There was a startled hush at the direction of the questioning: every mind alert. What if she said it was him?

'No, my lord. It wisnae you.'

'I am relieved to hear that,' said the Earl with a smile. 'Well then, to continue: Was this man well favoured?'

'Aye, my lord, he was.'

'Do you consider that I am well favoured?'

'Ah don't ken, my lord.' The Earl and some others laughed. Of course what 'well favoured' could mean was open to interpretation and conceivably, on hers, she might never have been so placed as to be able to judge.

'Come now, Jonet, you are to tell the truth. Am I well favoured or not?'

'Aye, my lord, I expect ye are that!' Seeing that the other one was possible and anxious as ever to give the answer wanted.

'Thank you again.'

'How did this man speak? Did he use English or the Irish[123] or some other language?'

'English, my lord. I widdnay unnerstaun if it wisnae.'

'Did he speak like me or was he rough spoken?'

'Like you, my lord.'

'So we are able to conclude that he was an educated man, then?'

'Aye, my lord. He must be. A richt clever man.'

'Would you expect that he had money?'

'Aye, Ah suppose a man like him wid hae money.'

'What would be the source of this money?'

'Ah dinnae ken, my lord.'

'Well, would it be inherited, like my money? Or would it be money made at business, the wealth of a burgess, say? Or would it be the salary paid to a man like the Town Clerk, Donald McGilchrist?'

'Ah'm no sure, ma lord. But Ah expec' it wis money got oota property and mibbee a salary as weel.'

'But not through trade?'

'Naw, my lord.'

'Thank you, Jonet. You have just excluded all the burgesses, for which I am sure they are grateful. So this man, whoever he is, has education and money and is a tall person with black hair and has good black broadcloth and he is well favoured.'

'Aye, my lord.'

'Are there many people like this on the island?'

'No' many, my lord.'

'How many would you say there were like this?'

'A haundfu', my lord.'

'I agree, Jonet. Well then, who among this handful of men is the one man we have been speaking about?'

There was a sudden silence throughout the court in which one could have heard a goose feather fall.

Jonet turned away from the young Earl, looked straight at me and pointed towards me. 'Master Robert Stewart of Scarrell, my lord.'

The gasp throughout the entire audience was like a wind that threatened to lift off the roof.

---

[123] Editor's note: the Gaelic language was known in Bute at that time as 'the Irish'.

The Earl smiled at me engagingly and said: 'Master Stewart, would you please stand up and take a few steps forward so that we may see you in a clearer light?'

As required, full of anxiety and even blushing at the attention of every eye which I never got used to all my life, I rose and stepped forward.

'Do you see a tail on this man, Jonet?'

'No, my lord.'

'Do you see horns on his head?'

'No, my lord.'

'Is there anything in his appearance to suggest that he is the devil?'

'No, my lord.'

'Then why do you think that he is?'

'Ah dinnae ken, my lord.'

'Do you now think that he is the devil?'

'No, my lord.'

'Well, why have you identified him as the devil?'

'Ah don't ken, my lord.'

The Earl, young, slim and sprightly, turned on his heel, threw up his hands with exasperation again and then walked around the court room as if he were the master of it, which by now he had become. Then, pausing for reflection for a few seconds, he advanced upon the accused again and pointed a long finger at her directly.

'Come now, madam, we shall have the truth of this. Was there a time when you referred to this man only by his name: Master Robert Stewart of Scarrell?'

'Aye my lord.'

'When was this?'

'Before aw this trouble.'

'What trouble? You mean the witch trials or his own trouble?'

'Before the trials and such.'

'So am I right in thinking that for the whole of 1661, you did not think of him as the devil? Is that so?'

'Aye, my lord. Ah think so.'

'Did you think of him as the devil when you saw him at that meeting on Chapelhill 3 days before last Hallowday. That would be in late October, 1661.'

'No, my lord.'

'So when in 1662 did you start to think of him as the devil?'

'When all the questions sterted.'

'And yet you invited the Minister to your house before you were apprehended? To inform him about witchcraft?'
'Aye, my lord.'
'Why did you do that?'
'Ah wanted tae staun in a guid licht with the Minister and the Session. Ah wis telt that nae harm wid come tae me if Ah telt everything Ah kenned.'
'So you wanted to save yourself by delating the other witches?'
Jonet wept. 'Aye, Ah suppose so. I wanted tae be helpful tae the toon and the officers.'
'I see,' said the Earl, motioning me to regain my seat which I did thankfully. Taking from his pocket a sheaf of notes and holding them high he continued. 'I have been reading the dittay written down at the time of your confession which the Minister kindly provided yesterday at my request—my demand, indeed. I spent most of the day studying it carefully and copying parts of it. And I wish to question you about what you said.'
Reading from the papers, the Earl said: "On the 22nd January you claimed that Margaret McLevin, Margaret McWilliam and Katherine Moore 'did by witchcraft shoot to deid'—I quote—'William Stephen and that the cause thereof was because a long space before, John Stephen was blasted with ane evil eye when he dwelt in Balskyte.' Is that correct? Did you confess this?"
'Ah don't ken. Ah canny richt remember, my lord. Ah wis hauf asleep, ye ken.'
'No, you were not, madam, for you invited the Minister and witnesses to your own home to hear what you had to say. That means you were wide awake and in full possession of your senses.'
Jonet blanched and then said: 'If you say so, my lord.'
'I do, oh I do.'
'Do you now remember saying this?'
'Aye, mibbee Ah do, my lord.'
'Yes or no, madam?'
'Aye, my lord.'

'Do McLevin, McWilliam or Katherine Moore possess a firearm?'
'Ah don't ken, my lord.'
'Come on woman! You must know! Do they or do they not?
'Mibbee they do, my lord.'
'Where did they get it?'
'Ah dinnae ken, my lord.'
'But you are sure they have such a weapon?'

Jonet began to weep again and show the same distress as usual at not quite knowing what answer was expected.

'Will you answer, madam!' snarled the young Earl, taking her again by the nose and even lifting her up off her heels.

'Aw don't, Sir, don't!' she bleated. 'Ah'll tell ye onything ye want.'

The Earl dropped her and stepped back suddenly. 'That, madam, is precisely the point.' He walked about the court a bit and then addressed the Jury: 'These people did not shoot anyone because they did not possess a firelock or the powder and shot necessary. There cannot be very many firearms on this island because of the prohibition during the English occupation when to be found with a weapon of any kind was to face punishment by death, as everybody knows. Powder, kept for years in a secret store would be unusable. A weapon stored for these ten years in this wet climate would be rusted beyond belief. So the idea that these women shot anybody is simply outrageous. And no one, certainly not the Minister or the elders'—stunning them all with a look of contempt—'or any educated person, should have believed it.

'So when you use the word 'shot' in your confession, you do not mean shot with a pistol or a weapon of any kind, do you?'

'No, my lord.'

'Heaven be praised!' shouted the Earl. 'At least these other women are not murderers though they be witches. What did you mean by 'shot' madam?'

Jonet knelt down and looked as if she were praying for the earth to swallow her up. 'Ah...Ah...Ah only meant that they gave her a richt dose ae the evil eye.'

"How could that be so? Did you not say—consulting the notes of the dittay—'McLevin offered to heale him of that blasting but he would not, saying that he would have none of the devil's cures which was her quarrel with him and that he was shot underneath the short ribs and that when she found him there was a hole in it that you might put your knife in.' Did you say this?"

'Ah dinnae ken, my lord.'

'Well that is what the dittay says and you confessed to the Minister, he wrote it down and other men were present to hear it. What have you to say to that?'

'Ah didnae write it maself. Ah canny write.'

'Do you admit that you are guilty of misrepresenting the facts about the death of William Stephen?'

'If ye say so, my lord.'

'But what do you say? Was it a weapon or was it the evil eye they gave him?'

'The evil eye.'

'Very well, at last.' Then turning to the Minister and fixing a gimlet eye upon him. 'The confession as reported by this dittay is hopelessly confused! It says that it was William Stephen that was shot by McLevin and the McWilliams because John Stephen had been blasted by the evil eye. It suggests that William Stephen blasted his brother John. If anyone could have blasted John Stephen it is McLevin and the McWilliams. Yet, had they done so, why would McLevin then offer to heal William Stephen if she had been party to the shooting? This dittay, Minister, is worthless!' And the earl threw his copy of the document to the floor where the papers fluttered like fallen leaves in autumn.

'Jonet Morison, is it not the case that on 6th June 1661, you compeired at the Session for slander? Against Elspeth Spence?'

'Aye my lord.'

'And what was the outcome?'

'I was found guilty and fined.'

'So you have a history of slander?'

'Ah don't ken, my lord.'

'Yes you do. You were found guilty. Why did you do it?'

'Ah don't ken, my lord.'

'And yet, let us pursue the case a while more. You say John Stephen lived at Balskyte and he was blasted and died of the shooting? Is that right?'

'Mibbe so, my lord.'

'But I thought it was blasting he died of?'

'Aye, I think so.'

'So there is no difference between blasting and shooting?'

'No' much, my lord.'

'Tell me, did William Stephen also live at Balskyte?'

'Mibbee he did, my lord.'

'That will do well enough. Do you know what will have killed William Stephen, madam, or John Stephen—whoever it was that you say was shot—and, since you cannot remember, it now matters little? Indeed, since one was blasted and the other shot, both have suffered in this way. Not the evil eye but the fact that they lived in Balskyte!'

There was general amazement at this revelation by this obviously very able young nobleman.

'The Balskyte is defined by the burn which comes down the hill to the east of the town from Roseland and goes down to the harbour by the Watergate. Is that not so?'

'Aye, my lord.'

'Have you ever seen so much piss and shit in any street of the town? I have not. All the piss and shit of the town collects in the Balskyte. That is what killed him: the piss and shit. The fools will have drawn their water out of that burn—perhaps when drunk—perhaps when sober, if they were lazy and the fools I imagine them to be. Rather draw that water so close to hand than go to the town well a distance away. That's what killed him and the hole under the ribs will have likely been gnawed out by a hungry rat while he lay there in the Balskyte burn—if there ever was such a hole as you alone describe. So much for the evil eye!—and no matter who it was you claim was murdered—one or other or both.'

'But, my lord, they weemen dae have the evil eye! Ah ken fine they dae.'

'You mean they heal when it suits them and cause ailments to people who rub then up the wrong way?'

'Aye, my lord, that's about it.'

'So we can take it then that all this talk of delating witches for murders by shooting is just you trying to get on the side of the angels? Is that it, Jonet Morison?'

'Aye, Ah suppose so, my lord, if ye have it so.'

'Yes, I will have it so, madam, but I would like you to admit it.'

'Very weel, my lord.'

'You admit it, then?'

'Aye.'

'Were any of the people you claim were murdered shot by anybody?'

'No, my lord.'

'You did not see it, at least?'

'No, my lord.'

'And nobody told you that they had been shot with a firelock?'

'No, my lord.'

'Excellent. Reading this account of your so called confession I had begun to wonder what sort of murdering savages inhabited this island so close to my shire.'

The Prosecutor, confined to his chair for so long, stood up and said: 'My lord, my congratulations upon such a successful cross-examination. May we now have the jury confer?'

The young Earl, well pleased with his performance, returned to his seat and gave his permission with a wave of the hand as he did so.

The Chancellor, Archibald Glass, soon announced that Jonet was guilty of the charge of witchcraft which provoked general sighs of relief throughout the audience.

'My lord, may we proceed to sentence?'

The Earl seemed to consider the matter for a little and then declared: 'Yes, I think that is possible now that things are clearer.'

'Do we have to approach the Privy Council, my lord, for permission to execute? That used to be the procedure under the English Parliamentarians.'

'That will not be necessary. The Government in Edinburgh has yet to organise properly after the restoration of the monarchy. My authority will be sufficient.'

'But, my lord, should we not at least lay the matter in their hands just in case?'

'In case of what? Do you question my judgement? I am, as you know, a Royalist. I have defended the king all the years of my life and, almost alone among the nobility, for the duration of the English occupation, I fought against them— aye, and lost many a good man. Do you think our new King, Charles II, would reverse my decision when I am rightfully in charge of a Justice Ayre in my own territory?'

The Provost, John Glass, spoke up: 'Aye, my lord, we canny delay, for the cost of warding aw they prisoners in the Tolbooth and paying for their warders is a great burden on the hale toon. We need this wrappit up smertly.'

'Well, then, we are agreed.' Placing his hands in the position of prayer, the brilliant young Earl now began to think aloud about the trials so far.

'It is now clear that the person taken after the fact by these women to be the devil has been identified. However, it is equally clear that he is not the devil now nor is he ever likely to have been so. Yet, I am informed, he has himself admitted to having been possessed by the devil, at least for a period of months when obsessed with a young maidservant of his. Maybe at the time mentioned by Jonet Morison he was possessed by the devil. But whether this be so or not, she did confess to having made a covenant with the devil, of renouncing her baptism and promising to do the devil [in whatever form he chose to appear] any service he required of her in return for making sure that she would want for nothing thereafter. That is the gist of the matter. Well, then, she is guilty of witchcraft and the penalty for that is death. She is to be taken to the Gallows Craig and there burnt[124]. So that no man will be stained by the burying of her, or any decent person offended by burials near her in hallowed ground, let the sea wash away the remains. Her goods and chattels are forfeit, as usual in such cases. These may reimburse the town a little.'

'When is this to be done, my lord?'

'As soon as the trials are complete. The convicted witches may yet be needed to substantiate charges against those yet to be tried.'

So the burnings were to be held back until all the small fry like Kirsten Bannatyne, John Galie, Patrick McKaw and others were dealt with. All had already been delated as present at meetings of witches. But did that make them witches? The question was: had they made covenants with the devil? This, the dittays made by the Minister and read by the Earl, did not reveal.

This all took time and I did not attend all of them, like many people who grew tired of the same process repeated over and over. By then, most people were tired of it, especially the Earl himself who was anxious to be away to Inverary to deal with the problems within his own lands. His father having been beheaded just the year before, the Earl was trying hard to assert his authority. His experience in Bute had definitely convinced everyone of his worth as a lawyer. He was quick and able and very discerning, as everyone had seen. But mercurial too. I have wondered whether his mind could have been persuaded to acquit the witches, at least from death. Was it because of the challenge to his authority, as he would see it, that he insisted upon asserting it? Probably not. The law—the law of King James VI[125] who was particularly severe upon witches—demanded the death penalty. No excess of ability or compassion could have ignored the law and the crimes were clear as day.

XXIII Jonet McNicoll's Departure from Bute

While these trials were ongoing, I busied myself in arranging Jonet's departure from the Island. After midnight, a half full cauldron of tar was taken from a barrel on Bute Quay without spilling a drop, either there or on the way home, for that could have spelled disaster if noticed by an

---

[124] Editor's note: as a consequence of the facts of the execution, as they will soon affect him, this sentence will be modified ten years later to 'strangled and then burnt' to avoid abuse from the convicted in public.

[125] Editor's reminder: King James VI was the author of a book on witchcraft.

observant eye. I sensed that the search for Jonet had been largely overtaken by other preparations and events: the executions as well as the trials. Thus, the final touches to the little ship could be completed.

Once the two ends of the trellis of saplings were brought together at each long end and the steamed bracers set in place to keep the centres apart, layers of sheets were fastened around the outside and inside. Of course, at bow and stern, the saplings cracked but did not break altogether when forced to bend back upon themselves. This was resolved by taking them out and replacing them with others specially bent with the steam kettle. An extra bracing support of bent lath here and there was introduced without compromising the weight and both I and Jonet independently could carry the ship with ease. Indeed, before ever beginning to shape the boat, I had asked her to lift the cut saplings to see whether she could manage it; which she did easily. Every gap was stuffed with fabric, mostly cut up bits of cloth, and then soaked through with tar. After drying out we had a narrow boat a bit more than 2 yards long with a wide hole in the top into which one person could admit herself, sit upright and paddle and it was pitch black everywhere, inside and out—even the spars, for, one by one, they were carefully painted and every joint of string soaked in it. And the result was a solid, yet pliable little ship which might take Jonet to safety across the Firth of Clyde to the mainland about five miles from the eastern shore of the island.

But would it support her? There is a loch not a mile away at the edge of Roseland but I judged it dangerous to try it out there first. If we were seen, all was lost.

The route to be taken by us over the hill was carefully trod and studied by me to avoid all contact with another human soul. I provided her with as much coin as I could and advised her to secrete bits of it in different places among her clothes, some of it carefully sewn into the hems and even into her shoes, in case she was robbed. Seeds for planting and snares for catching rabbits and hooks and lines for fishing and a small trowel to dig up worms, and the plaid and lots of string to tie it up and shoulder on her back with all her possessions which now included extra clothing and food: bread, dried meat, salt—and water, even, in case she got stuck out at sea or on a small island without water. I gave her two knives: one small, in a little sheath held on a string close to her body; the other, larger, at hand in her plaid for defence. A pot and a spoon, I gave her and most important of all, a tinder box with extra flints. Making fire would be immediately vital if she were not to perish of cold, especially if she got wet through, as seemed likely. Any increase in the wind would raise the level of the waves and then water would enter the boat and perhaps swamp it altogether. The final item was a linen sheet, also painted with tar and two very light, thin poles to keep it up a yard above the earth. It had strings tied on at the edge in places and could be tied down. Inside this, I hoped she could rest and sleep, even in rain and cold weather. I also made two smaller pieces to stop up the triangular ends.

But what was her story to be? How to avoid the suspicion of having fled a witchcraft trial? 'People will want to know where you come from and what brought you to that place, wherever it is,' I told her. 'You must try to repeat the accent of the talk when you hear it and seem to have come from a place not too far away. You should say that your husband died and that you are alone in the world, seeking a position as a maidservant if one can be found.'

'What place, Sir?'

'Well, some place where there have been no witch trials. What about Arran? Say that you could not bear to remain there after your loved one died and you left, having no one there to keep you.'

'But will they no' write and find out that I am no' from there?'

'The Minister might, if he hears of it. Even so, there will be plenty of women with your description and some may have lost a husband.'

'But no' with ma name, Sir.'

'That is true. But if they come back with another name you must just say that you gave your married name and that the other name they have told you is the name you were baptised with—or vice versa.'

'They'll no believe me, but, Sir.'

'If you become afraid, then you must run away and make it quick. I think you will have time before they move against you. You should be able to move around from place to place keeping a step ahead of anyone who discovers you are not who you claim to be and therefore that you are an escaping witch. Don't be surprised to meet others like yourself on the way. But don't trust them too far. They'll give you up to save themselves. That is what Jonet Morison tried to do.'

'It sounds a damn dreich sorta life, Sir?' she said plaintively.

'I know. It cannot be helped. At least you will be alive and maybe you will meet some kind person who will take you in and give you a comfortable home. It is what we must hope for. Better than burning to death to amuse a few pyromaniacs, eh?'

All we had to do then was wait for a suitable night, one with little wind and a good moon, preferably.

I decided she must go before the executions for they might have a last search more thorough than the rest which must reveal the presence of the boat for, in its completed state, it could not now be hidden.

One night, we set off with the boat between us to walk across the hills to the eastern shore and launch her on her way to a new life elsewhere. We had no light to guide us but the stars and the moon when it was not behind cloud and we stumbled a few times but the boat came to no harm and in an hour or two we were in woods close to the water and the boat was put in. The sea was not quite calm, had a small chop in the waves. Getting Jonet in that first time was not easy but it was eventually managed and her feet were kept dry at the expense of mine.

'Now,' I said, when she was sitting upright with one of the paddles, 'see if you can move it along the shore close to me. You can put the paddle on one side or the other as you desire. You will learn, you'll see.'

And so for an hour or so under my earnest instruction, she practised and I stood by in the water holding the stern to make sure she did not capsize and presently she began to feel more confident.

At last she said: 'Oh, Sir, I don't want tae go.'

'I know. But you have to go. They will murder you if you stay.'

'Whit have I done tae deserve this?'

'Nothing. They have rules that are unnatural and make no sense. At least I transgressed them. You have done nothing ill.'

'Will God look after me, Sir?'

'If there is one. But he is not looking after the others.'

'Do ye mean there isnae a God, Sir?'

'Well, he is not very helpful or loving, is he, if he could stand by and do nothing while some innocent women are burnt to death?'

'Could there be some reason for it, Sir? That's what the Minister always says, Sir. We're no' clever enough tae unnerstaun, that's aw it is.'

'No, how could it be right for these poor women to suffer that sort of torture and humiliation and death? It makes no sense in this world or any world.'

Sitting beneath me in the small boat, Jonet began to weep and I put my hand upon her hair to comfort her.

'Could I not go and see my son before Ah leave, Sir?'

'I am afraid not, Jonet. If you were found out they would kill him too, for aiding and abetting you. If you love him, he is the one person you must not see and he must know nothing of this. He must know by now that you are safe. Let that be enough.'

'Sir, could you do me one last favour before I go?'

'Name it.'

'I would like to get out and come ashore one last time and serve you sir, like Ah did once before.'

In all those weeks the question had never come up, because of the intense fear in which we both lived, I suspect. Of course I continued to have my moments as ever, but it never occurred to me to make use of her in that way. It seemed, somehow, inappropriate, when her life—and even my own too, for helping her against the Session, the town and even the Earl—was at stake. We were constantly on the watch all that time. Indeed, the very involuntary unconsciousness of the act would have made it doubly dangerous. How could we have moved apart if the noise of people approaching were heard? The urge would have made me continue, regardless. I did know myself, after all.

But now, it was a different matter. We were in a very quiet part of the island with no inhabitants within a mile and well hidden by woods. No one could know where we were or what we intended. I judged it safe.

'Of course,' I agreed. I helped her out and we lay down together in the moonlight on the sand and made love for the last time with the wavelets lapping at out feet. And it was so heavenly that after a rest we did it again for the action had relaxed us, and we felt secure in the darkness, knowing we were safe till daylight. After which, having poured out all I had in me, I arose and said: 'You must go now, Jonet, and never return. When you reach land you must sink the boat so that no one ever finds it or they may understand what has happened to you. Put stones in it in deep water and sink it. That would be best. And make for the south of the Cumbrae opposite and then for the south of the other one, staying as close as you can to the shore for safety's sake, and only then direct your course to the mainland. You must try to avoid the villages around here if possible. News of your escape will have reached there and you will be sought for. Go ashore finally at some very deserted spot and choose a small creek or burn where it enters the river. Camp there a wee while if it's safe till you get used to being on your own.'

'You have been wonnerful tae me, Sir. Ye have saved ma life with aw yer aid. Ah canny thank ye enough. Yer the best man Ah ever kenned, Sir.'

I kissed her one last time and then helped her into the boat, turned it and pushed it out to sea in the direction she should take, for the islands could be seen easily in the moonlight. 'And remember when dawn comes you must be ashore, well hidden in some creek or fishermen may see you from afar and come looking.'

THE STORY OF ROBERT STEWART OF SCARRELL   209

The tide, I knew, would soon rise up over the markings in the sand we had made and cover them from any observant eye that chanced upon the spot. I waved one last time at the tiny figure disappearing into the darkness and turned to make my way, soaked to the thigh and squelching sea-water in my boots, back across the hills to Roseland.

Jonet's departure was none too soon, for the very next day I received a visit from Ninian Kerr and John Kelburn. They wanted the money I had been fined by the Kirk Session and had come with documents for me to sign for pieces of my lands as security for the loans they proposed. As the terms were fair, I signed readily enough, though how I would ever be able to pay off the loans I could not foresee. But if I failed, the lands would eventually become forfeit, so much was clear[126].

After they left and I was on my own again I racked my brains to see if I could find a way of rescuing the four remaining women, without success. The hole I had made would have been repaired and a very active guard set on the prison day and night and even outside in case someone tried to free them.

XXIV   The Burning of the Witches

Some time later, the day of executions was upon us, a day of cloud and rain which accentuated the gloom. I was there early but not early enough. A crowd had begun to assemble hours before the time selected. They came from every part of the island and for many reasons, some of them for entertainment, some out of curiosity, some out of malice and yet some out of compassion because they knew the people who were to be publicly murdered.

By the time the condemned women appeared at the foot of the stairs to the Tolbooth, the crowds had swarmed up and down the street outside far above the Mercat Cross and into the vennel south of the Castle. Having disguised myself as best I could in a cloak with a hood and scarves, I stood at the other side of the Castle, near the drawbridge, indistinguishable among many others, close-packed, on such a bad-weather day, and when the women were sighted at last, after a long wait, a cry went up, a cry of exaltation even, from those close to them and I felt

---

[126] Editor's note: In fact, the lands had to be transferred in perpetuity to the lenders as the Town Council Record reveals in 1673. See p 301 et seq.

a deep sadness that my fellow men could exult in so much unnecessary cruelty.

But they were not all like that. As the women were led along the road past me towards the Gallowgate, there were cries of hush, as well as of joy and, in time, everyone, or nearly everyone, had decided upon an interested silence as the only appropriate demeanour at such a terrible moment in the island's history. The plain fact is that so many of the townsfolk believed the women had done what they were accused of, because they believed in the existence of the devil and they believed that because the Minister and the elders had been reinforcing that very belief in their minds every Sunday. It was no wonder then, that so many people wanted the executions. From their point of view, it would make a fresh start possible, free of the malefice they imagined these women guilty of, which in some cases they mistakenly believed they themselves had suffered from.

The crowd surged around the figures so that little could be seen and it swirled along with them like a river, eddying around them, as they were led, roped together on foot, under the towering mass of the Castle; to the bridge across the Water of Fad from the loch of that name, a mile or two southwards, which flowed into the bay. Then, onward the crowd eddied and flowed, still silent, still appalled by its own progress, to the Gallows Craig, a basalt rock beneath St Bride's Chapel, in which holes had been drilled out, four long wooden posts inserted and then wedges driven in with hammers to hold them fast. Beneath the stakes were faggots and on the shore, hard by, more piles of firewood and kindling and barrels of something, tar, oil or spirits, I know not.

In time, I elbowed my way to a position inland, up the hill a little, not far from the rock. There, over the heads of the others, I could easily discern the four women, in their sackclothes, as they were tied to the stakes above a platform of kindling, many feet thick.

They faced the people with their backs to the sea. I could see the stains of shit and piss on their legs and clothing, as well as blood, that too, and tears. Margaret McWilliam, white haired and gaunt with torture, beatings and starvation, stood in the middle with Katherine McIlmartin, whose once lovely face was haggard and dirty. Jonet Morison was at the north side and Margaret McLevin at the south. I learned later that Isobel McNicol had died in the prison because of the cold, starvation and stress of torture. Her old heart, weakened by drink over the years, could not stand it.

Behind them the waves broke upon the rock and the very air seemed charged with a force sufficient to sing a dirge of madness. The hills of Argyll opposite were hidden by dark clouds which presaged a storm and, as we waited, still silent as the grave, the wind, a wind from the north-east, began to increase in force so that the Minister's black cassock swirled about his legs, as he made his final statements to them, which could be heard clearly despite his murmurs, borne by the breeze which blew into our faces. And then there was only the solemn silence apart from it, as every eye studied the four doomed women, all half drunk with the aquavitae which a rare kindly soul had provided the night before.

The Earl was there, high on a white horse, having ridden along the shore, alone of all that crowd, resplendent in the coloured clothing of the old Royalist, newly restored—a pink gambezon striped with yellow, pale blue breeches and a wide-brimmed beige hat which some unfortunate pheasant had been plucked to adorn and which he held fast with a hand to keep it there. A dazzling, brilliant, slim figure he seemed—at least at the beginning. He it was who controlled the final rite. First he dismounted to be addressed by the Minister and as he did so there was a sudden lull in the rising storm of wind and the voices of the central figures carried clear across the silent multitude.

'Good day, your Grace.'

'Is it though? It seems a damnable day to me when I have to pay for my decisions.'

'You have regrets, then?'

'I do.'

'But the law is clear. They confessed to a covenant.'

'But with whom? The devil or Robert Stewart?

'Be assured of one thing, your Grace, Robert Stewart is a devil, was for sure the devil— as far as these women are concerned— and they did make covenants with him. They renounced their baptisms, for heavens sake! That is witchcraft. They have to burn. The Law of King James says so.'

'Well, if he is the devil, why are we not burning him? Rather him than those women he fucked for favours.'

'He would be a martyr then! Don't you see? He has been preaching! Against the Kirk! If he dies, a new religion could start up and then where would we be?'

Argyll laughed, a weary, sad laugh. 'You mean, one Jesus Christ is enough? What was it Scarrell preached?'

'That love is natural and normal— sexual love with anybody! That fornication is all right so long as you are in love. He would destroy the whole fabric of marriage and family to whom loyalty is everything. If he succeeded, every family on this island would be broken up. Every man fornicating with anybody he met. Who would look after his wife and children then?'

'What is a man supposed to do if he falls in love with someone not his wife?'

'Nothing! It is what the Bible tells us. The vows are for life and you go to hellfire if you break them.'

'Does the Bible really say that? I don't believe it. What if he can't help himself? Is it really so bad? To be possessed by the love of someone, like that? Don't we all know people who have done it?'

The Minister was deeply shocked. He spluttered: 'Of course it is bad! What could be worse? To desert your wife and...and...and join with someone else. Uggghh! What about her feelings? The wife's?'

'What about his, if he's possessed by love? And his lover's, if she is? How are they to stay apart? God man, it is more than flesh and blood can bear. I know the feeling myself!'

'We can't give into such feelings. They ruin lives on earth and make an afterlife in heaven impossible.'

But Argyll was unconvinced: 'Maybe heaven doesn't exist at all, Minister. Maybe there is only now and the reward you expect for abstinence is an illusion. If so, it is all for nothing— this unnatural avoidance of anyone not your wife.'

'What are you suggesting? This is blasphemy, your Grace!'

'It's what I heard someone say at St Andrews[127]. They burnt him for it too. But maybe he was ahead of his time. Why must we burn people because they are different? And why must they all be the same? There are savages, I hear, in other parts of the world, who seem to live long and happy lives without our religion— without the jougs and fines and sackcloth and the beatings, for every trifling offence.'

'But afterwards, after death, what then?'

'Maybe there is nothing then. Why must there be something after life? Is not life itself bad enough without a further life dependent on the earthly one? For these women, earthly life is a bloody misery— especially today, by Heaven! If they knew this was going to happen to them, they would

---

[127]Editor's note: The Earl's father attended St Andrews University and probably his son too. People were burnt there for heresy.

rather not have been born! And what evidence is there for this afterlife? Not an iota!'

'You are a freethinker, then, your Grace, like Scarrell.'

'We have a lot in common, certainly. But I must go to Inverary for I have my estates to secure. And you must burn your women, for the law is the law and without it we are undone, you and I. Is everything ready? Have you said your clerical piece?'

'Yes, your Grace.'

'Then since it must be so, get on with it.' The Earl then put his thumb and finger to his nose. 'What is that awful smell?'

The Minister approached the women and sniffed. 'One of them has shit herself, your Grace. Will you say something?'

'Not I. I wish I had never come here. What is there to say? Get on with it.'

'Light it then, Willie,' said the Minister. And Willie set to with tinderbox and began to strike a light but the wind began again to rise in intensity and extinguished his efforts.

Suddenly, the air was torn apart by a scream of awful intensity and anger and Margaret McWilliam shouted: 'Ah see you all, ye fucken bastard Session men and you tae ye black herted Minister. Minister ae what? Yer fucken sinister, is what. Yer a fucken daurk goblin, ya bastard ye! Did Christ die on his cross so you could put innocents like us on oors? Yer a fucken hypocrite tae preach a gospel ae love tae us and then burn us tae deeth! May ye die in shame! A pestilence on aw that's yours! Ah hope ye fucken burn in hell for ye've brocht hell here the day. Whit hell could be as bad as this wan you've created? Eh? Eh? Ye don't fucken ken the answer, dae yes?' She spat with deadly aim at the Minister and he stepped back to avoid the solid-looking missile anger summoned from her interior. Puce with rage, he yelled: 'Get on with it, Willie! For God's sake!' But the wind was not assisting his scratchings at the tinder box. The sparks blew away from the kindling.

MacWilliam laughed, an eldritch screech of a laugh out of a voice cracked and parched for lack of water. 'Swearing, Minister! Fined three and four pence!'

And then, on the point of tears of embarrassment, the Minister clapped his hands over his ears and, more urgent under these public rebukes, cried out: 'Get the thing alight, Willie. Pleeeease!' he beseeched.

Above the hills, the clouds gathered, and out to sea the waves grew larger and the wind close at hand blew Margaret McWilliam's mane of white hair so that it flew like a flag of war above the shore of Bute. 'Yull aw rot in hell fur this day. Nane ae us did anything we shouldnae! We're all innocent as lambs, ye ken!'

McWilliam screeched more laughter, a terrible, defiant screech and shouted words that carried far in the rising wind: 'Ah see you tae ya wee bugger earl, ye, in yer fancy claes. Ye ken whaur your gaun? Like yer faither last year. Thull cut yer fucken heid aff, jist like him.[128]

It was the earl's turn to be humiliated. 'Set it alight, damn you!' he shouted.

But McWilliam was not done. 'Ye ken whaur ye went wrang? Eh? Eh? Ye huv forgot how tae live! Yer that bound up wi' hard rules and harder punishments, ye've forgot tae be human. Christ never meant folk tae live the way youse dae wi' a Bible up yer arse! A Bible ye wrote yer sel's. Dae ye think an animal wid burn ither animals tae deeth? Nae fucken chance! Animals kens better!'

Beneath her Willie had still not got the fire lit after many attempts. 'Kin ye no licht a fucken fire?' she shouted. 'Dae Ah huv tae come doon there masel' and dae it fur ye?' There was a strangled gasp of astonishment from the assembled multitude and the gradual realisation that she hated them far more than they her. So far from trying to save herself, she wanted done with life with them!

'Whit kind a God wid put folks tae deeth for no' keeping the Sabbath? Whit kind a God wid put folks tae deeth fur stealin' breed fur their childer tae survive? Whit kind a God wid burn weemen fur staunin' up for thersel's agin men wha wid fuck them as soon as look at thaim? Yer aw fucken hypocrites, ya bastards! Yer Auld Testament God isnae worth a fuck!'

The silence was broken by a wave of horror which swept across the crowd at such blasphemy so coarsely expressed and any sympathy was extinguished from nearly every heart and mind.

'Dae ye ken wha the deevil is? Eh? Eh?' Margaret McWilliam shouted, pointing a long scrawny arm with an extended forefinger at her persecutor and the words, captured and carried aloft by the wind spread over the entire gathering of black clad humanity so that every ear heard: 'It's yersel' Meenister! Yer ain sel'. That's wha. It wis yersel' put the notion o' the deevil in every heid hereaboot.'

McWilliam gave a great heave of a once powerful torso, broke free of the bonds and stooped as a prelude to getting down and helping the firelighter,

---

[128] She was right. In 1685, the young earl suffered the same fate as his father on the scaffold in Edinburgh.

shouting: 'Ah waant oota here! Away fae youse fucken bastards! Ah canny staun the fucken sight of yes!'

Then, at last, the fire caught and the blaze reached her hair and she straightened up with her white hair, blown by the wind, a searing pennant of bright yellow flame against a sky darkening with black equine clouds leaping across it apocalyptically.

A spectacular whoooooooosh! announced that the flames had taken a ferocious grip on the faggots soaked in pitch or whatever, flame blasted into the sky, screams rent the air and people all around, mindless of the heat that scorched them, clapped hands to their ears in a vain attempt to prohibit sounds that would haunt their dreams until their own days of judgement.

It was the end of speeches—from the damned or anyone else, come to that. Nobody had any taste for more speeches. The blaze seemed to rise upwards to heaven itself as if in protest to convey the souls of the women to paradise. But to every live soul present it was a disaster. There might be arguments for resisting the temptation of the devil, for remaining true to the Church of Scotland but every argument for these went up in smoke that day and no one who saw it doubted the fact.

So at least I thought at first. But, as the crowd began to disperse, with angry looks in my direction from a few who recognised me—as if to say: See what we do with people who follow the devil— I began to see that I was mistaken. The women had been burnt, had they not? Tried and found guilty? Well then they must be guilty. And good riddance to bad rubbish. Far too many thought this. It made me sick at heart that my fellow men could be so lacking in perception. The idea that the women had been found guilty of covenants which had nothing to do with the devil, only with me—fairly innocent arrangements [punishable under the church law, but not diabolical]—or that these had come from the very ministry which had investigated, condemned and punished them and been extracted under duress and reinterpreted to give a satanic dimension in keeping with the concept of wrongdoing of that ministry—this idea was too sophisticated for our ordinary folk.

Not for the first time, as I came away, tearful at the loss of fine people I had known, following the crowd which always, as before, that day, had parted to leave an unnatural space around me, as if to say: you are not one of us, I wondered what I might have done to stop it. And knew that they would not have listened to me. The Minister for sure and some of the elders like McGilchrist, had to know that their interpretation of innocent events was, after the earl's performance, without foundation. They had been present at the interrogations, for God's sake! Of course they knew! But I was an outcast. They would never listen to me. Would squash me like a beetle underfoot. To have done anything else would have condemned them all for their many inhumanities these long months of inquisition and trial.

5. Jonet McNicoll's Story[129]

Leaving the island for the first time was hard, harder still because it was so dark and the water so near and the little waves so threatening to such a small ship. But the slight breeze was at my back and it helped me. I paddled in the direction of the south of the near island and after an hour or so I came to the end of it, close in, and then I made for the next one.

I was half way across the channel between the two islands when I heard a big splash close by. It was a fish, a great fish whose giant head rose above the surface right in front of my eyes and then dived and the tail went down below out of sight again. I shivered and cried out with fear and then I worried that somebody would hear my woes. But none did. Not many people lived on the islands I was approaching and none near the shore.

In another hour I was down by the end of the second island and I decided that the tide or the river must be driving me down away from the places of danger around Bute where people might expect me to arrive.

Just before dawn, I could make out the mainland very easily and I went in closer and closer and when dawn broke I was paddling along the shore line and not a house anywhere could I see. And then I saw the creek, the creek that the good Master Robert had said I should look for, because that was where I should land. There was a hill and a glen down from it right down to the sea and in the glen was a burn, a fine flowing stream from another far higher hill, a long way off.

I paddled into the creek and grounded the ship and then climbed out to stretch my legs on the smooth sand. It felt so good to be free at last of the danger, though, as I looked back at how far I had come in the dark, my heart beat a bit sadly at the thought of leaving. And it was not my son or my husband that I missed most, for both thought me a witch, deserving the punishment of one, but of Master Robert, the finest man I ever knew,

---

[129] Editor's note: the language has been modified, especially the spelling, for modern readers; the story she would tell.

a man I wanted! Wanted right now, again. I was wet with the wanting and I knew, whatever happened, I would never be free of the wanting. He was, I knew, a man much beyond every other man, a man maligned for things most men had not the courage to grasp and do: to live. That he and I were both married to others was nothing. That he did not love me was nothing. I knew he cared for me, had shown how royally he cared by his unstinting help. I nearly turned back there and then just for the sight of him again. I was that much in love with him. But it was more than that. I saw that he loved women and I did not mind. He was a man made for love and he overcame the restrictions of the Kirk and expressed himself as he found most natural. The doctrine of love proclaimed in the Kirk every Sabbath was nothing to this man's own philosophy. The first was repressive and oppressive, meant curbing your natural desires, suffering the pains of self denial— and for what? His was about living through the desires, making the most of opportunities without denying the self.

I looked around and saw that I had landed at the foot of a steep hill, steep in every direction, which meant there would be no houses nearby because of the very difficulty of getting here. Inland, the burnside further up was cloaked with bushes and trees on both sides which looked nice and then behind me was the sea and, far off, the islands I had passed and beyond them another which must be Arran by its mountains which, of course, I had often seen from Bute though never visited.

The first thing I had been told to do was sink the boat and I thought about that and I patted the little ship that had kept me dry and safe and carried me so far in so short a time and I knew I could not sink it. At least I could not leave it to the mercy of the sea and storms. Leaving it resting on the sand, I began to explore my surroundings and walked up the burnside a bit and beheld a fine deep pool above the tide line of sea weed with bushes and plenty of birch trees covering its edges and I saw some fish lying there as if exhausted after a long journey, just like me, and I determined to try my hand at catching one.

I went back for the plaid and looked out line and hook and trowel for worms as I had been taught by my loved one and I started digging in the earth, not far away and quietly so as not to disturb the fish. When I had a worm at last— found under a stone and not in the earth after all— I baited it on the hook and tied on the line and crept up to the bank of the pool and there I waited a wee while till my breath calmed down and then I gently tossed the line across the head of the pool and watched it land like a feather and float a wee bit and then it sank from view and I wondered where it had gone to. All of a sudden the line tightened in my grasp and I knew the hook had been bitten by one of the fish. I held on for a time until the struggles grew less and less and then I drew it in, hand over hand, and before very long on the bank beside me was a wee sea trout of between one and two feet long. I was well pleased. I decided to cook it right away. I went back to the boat, collected most of my gear and took it up to the poolside where I built a fire and that was easy with the materials at hand. I cleaned the fish with my knife and roasted it over the fire on a stick stuck down the middle of it. Afterwards—and what a fine breakfast it was—I put up the cover of the sleeping place and sat down in it on the plaid and fell asleep for a time. When I awoke it was full day, near noon, I think, and I suddenly remembered the ship beached on the sand and sprang up and ran down to the shore. The tide had come in and lifted the ship and I saw it floating out to sea.

I suppose I should have left it but I was that fond of it, made with such loving care and attention for me—me alone!—that I determined to get it back. I waded out after it and soon had water up to my neck and still I could not reach the ship and I stood there in the cool water and wept tears of frustration and then tried again and went right under and I would not give up and thrashed the water onward towards the ship which actually moved it further off to my horror and then I sprang out further towards the deep and—God be praised!—my hand fell upon the bow and I grasped it and pulled it to me and it came and still floated, though taking in water because I pulled it over. But I lifted myself out of the water a bit onto it, spluttering with the sea-water I had drunk and, by kicking my legs, got it back to the sand and I pulled it up and I was glad that I had got it back. It was mine and I would never willingly give it up, except to him that made it.

By evening I had carried the ship to the inland pool above the tide line and put stones in it to keep it still on the bottom and tied the paddles together and hid them under some bushes close by and below an overhanging rock well out of sight and I was glad, for I knew that I could return at any time and reclaim the boat and sail back to Bute if it ever became really necessary. No one would ever notice it, I knew, for it was shrouded in bushes and trees and people never did go there, so much was obvious. The grass and the beach were pristine pure.

Somehow, I knew I had not seen the last of the boat.

After some travel to right and left I soon realised that I was at a part of the coast much strewn with rocks thrown up by storms which made it fairly inaccessible on foot. Inland, the ground rose steeply and when I climbed up I found myself on a kind of cliff top with whins growing nearly to the edge. As there was no easy way through them, I returned to my landing place. I stayed a whole day there, resting up, feasting on some bannocks griddled on a hot flat stone and another trout I caught and I had fine spring water to drink. But by the next morning I had begun to feel lonely and I decided to leave my gear and do some exploring further off.

Once I was through the whins which took a while and left me with a hundred prickles in my clothing I would rather do without, I came onto a cleared section of grass on which sheep grazed and I knew I must be not far from a steading of some kind. Across the next hill I found it soon enough, a poor enough place with thatched roofs falling in and an acre of mud around it which looked a permanent feature, a vegetable garden full of weeds, a few hens and some rather woebegone cows which lowed at me as I approached.

There was no sign of smoke, which was odd and no sign of life, which was stranger still. I walked through the mud to the rough door, scratched by many an animal, and held in place by only one hinge, the other having broken some time in the past. 'Is there anybody home?' I said. Receiving no reply, I repeated my call, more loudly.

It was then that I heard a noise, deep within the house. I opened the door and entered to find myself in a kitchen with a table on an earthen floor, a few chairs and a grate in a broken down chimney without a fire and on the table dirty pewter plates and a tankard or two with ale still in them.

'I'm ben here,' said a voice, a hoarse masculine voice but quiet. Into the next room I went and beheld a man lying on a sack of straw under a blanket which lay on the earthen floor. He had staring eyes shrunk into his face which seemed to invade my soul and he was in evident pain. 'Who are ye?' he asked me.
'Just a widow woman come from Arran to get away from sad memories,' I lied, as I had been told.
'How did ye come?'
'In a wee boat.'
'Where's the boat now?'
'At the bottom of the sea. It sank when it hit a rock.'
'Well, ye can help me, then, since ye've nothing else tae do.'
'That is for me to choose,' I replied. 'But what ails you?'
'I've hurt ma leg and canny walk.'
'Show me it then.'

He moved the blanket tenderly and I saw the leg which was red and sore at the top of the thigh. In the centre, there was a circle of yellow pus under the skin at least three inches across.

'How did ye get that?'

'I got a sharp stick stuck in it and it went bad. It's very sore.'

'Ye'll need it lanced then and a poultice likely enough. Would you like me to do it for you?'

The man nodded and I began to look for things which might help. 'We need a fire first,' I said, 'and boiling water. I'll see to that and then I'll scour about and see what else I can find that is useful.'

I was delighted at my find. Here was a place in which I might be useful. And I know a thing or two about wounds of this kind.

Once the grate was cleared out I lit a fire and collected extra kindling and set a cauldron to boil on a movable angle iron fixed to the chimney. What was I to do for cloths? All I could find were filthy. They would have to do; so I boiled them in the cauldron and let them dry by the fire. When I was ready, I took out my little knife and heated it in the flames and then went through with a basin to the room where the man lay.

'What are ye going tae do?' he said to me worriedly, at the sight of the cloths and the knife and basin.

'I'm going to cut out the pus and the thing that's still stuck in your leg and is causing your pain. The wound is dirty, that's why it won't heal.'

'Ye willnay hurt me, wull ye?'

'I will hurt you—for sure. But I might just save your life. That leg looks as if it might have to come off.'

The man screamed: 'Ye'll no cut my leg off!'

'You might die if I don't. All I mean to do for now is try and save the leg.' So under his protests, I washed the thigh carefully and then took the knife and began to cut. 'This will soon feel a lot better when the pus is out.'

'You'll no' cut my leg off, wull ye?' he repeated with tears in his eyes.

'Not me. At least not until I try and save it first.'

'I've twa sons, ye ken, and they'll soon be here. They're away for help.'

'Well, you won't get any better help than mine,' I told him and he seemed to accept this and lay back but still keeping an eye on me and my knife to make sure that I left his leg on.

I cut through the top of the area of pus and no further and then squeezed out as much as I could, with the man screaming under my hands, as if his life was at stake and I was killing him. But the pressure of the pus soon decreased and he began to feel slightly better. I soon found that there was a small sliver of wood stuck fast in the wound and I scraped it out gently but not gently enough for him. He screamed in agony but I ignored it, knowing what must be done.

I made a poultice of stale bread that I found, soaked in hot water and bound it right around the thigh over the red area. 'There now,' I told him, 'that will do ye for an hour or two and then we'll do it again and maybe the leg will recover.' Of course he screamed when I laid the hot thing upon the wound. But it had to be done. Something in the bread and the heat might draw the pus and clean the wound—that, anyway, is what experience has taught me. Herbs and plants too were useful but I did not have time to go looking for the right ones.

I set to with a scrubber and soap and hot water and tried my best to reduce some of the filth in the kitchen and the room where the man slept but I soon realised that what he needed now was food. I went outside, caught a hen and slaughtered it, plucked it and soon had it cooking in the cauldron. I hunted the garden, found some vegetables among the weeds, chopped them up on the table and added them to the broth.

That night there was no sign of the two sons and I fell asleep in a chair by the fire after I had fed him some of the soup with a healthy amount of meat. Using the basin to heat water, I washed out his poultice last thing, before the light went altogether, and renewed it with more of the stale bread.

In the morning, the man was noticeably better, the leg had cooled down and a further poultice soon had him talking about getting up, though I found that he had already been up in the night to make water.

I had noticed a bee hive in an old tree trunk among the whins near the shore when I first came up. So that morning I went back, took some twigs and dried grasses and lit a fire near it; and then put the smoke inside. In a little while, the bees—preparing for flight—had taken on so much honey they were drunk on it. I was able to get inside and steal a good lump or two of honey, with only a few bees stings for my pains.

Applied to the man's wound directly, it had a marvellous healing effect.

Around mid afternoon two large young men arrived who, when they saw me, were very surprised. 'We couldnay get a leech tae come,' they told their father. 'He wanted twa merks and we widnae gi'e that much.'

'So ye wid a let me dee, wid ye?'

'We huddnae the money.'

'Ye hud so.'

'Aye, but we drank some ale. There wisnae twa merks left, ye ken.'

'Weel, this lassie has fixed me up fine.'

One of them, the younger and larger of the two, named Jock, turned to me and said: 'Yer no a witch wumman, are ye? There's a lot o' thaim aboot.'
'I am not a witch,' I told them.
'How did ye fix the auld man, then?' said the other whose name I learned was Tam. 'Only a witch wumman could dae that.'
'It disnae take a leech to lance a festering sore. A poultice did the rest.'
'Dae ye ken aboot herbs, tae?'
'I know a few things. Some herbs are useful.'
'So ye are a witch, then?'
'No.'
'Where do ye come fae?'
'Arran,' I lied as before.
'Where were ye going?'
'I'm not sure.'
'Ye could stay here, then and look after us.'
Since I had nowhere else to go this seemed a good option at the time but events were to prove it was a mistake. 'Why is there no woman here?' I said.
'Oor mither died and we huvnay merrit yet. But we have hopes.'
'Where would I sleep?'
'Ye kin sleep wi' me,' said the father.
'I will not,' I replied and I should have left there and then but necessity made me careless.
'We'll make ye a place tae yersel' in the stable. How wid that dae?'
'Let me see the stable.'
I was shown a tumble down hovel not fit for a horse. There were three walls and a great hole in the thatch and a pile of very shitty straw on the earthen floor. But I did my best to make it habitable with a brush, hot water and soap. Thatch was fetched for the hole in the roof and the young men went up a ladder and mended it in rudimentary fashion. A door of sorts was got to stand over the open end and keep out most of the draught and some fresh straw was got for me to sleep on. When night fell, I went in and was asleep very quickly after such a tiring day.
The next day they found my belongings at the pool near the shore and stole nearly everything. I complained, in vain. They waited for me to cook and I boiled a haunch of lamb, freshly slaughtered, in the cauldron which, with vegetables from the garden, they ate with relish. 'A peety wuv nae ale,' said the father who had joined us around the table. 'Did ye no' think tae bring some wi' ye?'
'He drank it aw on the way hame,' said Tam, with a laugh.

That night they stole more than my belongings.
By morning they had all enjoyed me and there was nothing I could do about it. 'I'll tell the Minister!' I managed to croak under the large hands that held back my head and my mouth half shut while their relatives set to work upon me.
'Naw ye'll no',' said the old man. 'He wid merk ye for a witch, soon as look at ye! The land is lousy wi' witches aw runnin' fae the fires.'
'Come oan faither, it's ma turn,' said the elder son. 'I've no been twice yet.'
Just before dawn, they had all given me up to return, exhausted, to their own beds in the house. I got up and in the growing light, crept back up the hill towards the bank of whins above the shore, and when I reached the pool down near the beach I walked straight into the freezing water and tried to wash out the stink of them. The tears began and would not be stopped until I had run dry.
The cold eventually brought me to my senses. I stood up suddenly in the pool. They would look for me! I must flee. Now! They would want to keep me prisoner to serve their needs.
There was only one thing to be done; get the boat up. In a flurry of energy I set to, heaving the stones out while shivering in the freezing cold of the dawn before the sun is properly up in the sky, and then pulled on the gunwale and turned the boat on the sandy bed made by the stream and in a little while it was afloat again. I fetched the paddles from their hiding place under the rock and the bushes, threw them in and quickly moved the little ship, none the worse for its submersion, back down to the beach where, without a moment's hesitation, I boarded and set sail. What was there to wait for? Nor was I premature. I was not twenty yards from the sand when I heard a voice calling me. 'Come back! Come back, the noo. We want ye! For God's sake turn roon and come back here!'
I paddled as hard as I could and soon was far out beyond their reach.
I headed straight out into the great firth without any plan but escape and did not stop until I reached the Cumbrae where I beached the boat and stared back the way I had come for the first time. There was no sign of pursuit.
I had made a mistake and it was not the last. I had set off by sea and been seen doing it. These men would tell others and I would be looked for.
But what to do and where to go? I did not know. I lay up on a beach on the Cumbrae and wondered where to head. I could not remain for there was no water and I had lost all my gear for fishing and snaring rabbits; and the plaid and the sleeping place, that too had gone, taken by the men.

All I had were 2 paddles and my little knife which had been no use the night before because I was taken unawares by the three of them at once. I began to fear that I would get too cold, exposed out there on the island without much cover. Of course I wept a lot in my misery. Before long I realised that only one course of action could save me: I must return to Bute at night and hope to find Master Robert and try to enlist his aid again. Without it, I would not survive.

And so I waited for night and prayed that the wind would stay mild and that the weather would not come on to rain. I was cold and had no means of heat or starting a fire and no food and I became very depressed for I could not see how I could survive. If the countryside was full of women like myself trying to escape from the witch hunts, what chance of life had I? Wherever I went I would find the same difficulty. A woman on her own was being taken to be a witch no matter what she was. There seemed no obvious solution and even Master Robert would be unable to resolve this for me. All he could do was resupply my wants and send me on my way. Anything else was dangerous for him. They would kill him for helping me. This I knew.

Thus, when the night fell, I set off again back the way I had come, though I crossed to Bute immediately and sheltered in a bay at the south of the island where I rested for an hour before setting off against the slight wind and force of the current, upstream. Straight across Kilchattan Bay I paddled but it was very dark by then, the moon obscured by clouds and no one would have seen me, so low down upon the water among the small choppy waves. Travelling by night at sea was eerie at first but you get used to it and you can see just about well enough. If you can't see anything at all, which is rare—there is usually some light—you just bang into things, like rocks and in a tiny boat that is no harm in a light wind, or run aground. The shapes of islands are usually very clear and if you know them you always know where you are. Only when you get close to them is there a difficulty at night because then you can't see the outline sometimes. But it doesn't matter by then, when you come aground, usually onto a beach in these parts, you are safe anyway. Of course you have to keep a clear picture in mind of where you were and where you are heading, using landmarks which, even in the dark, are essential.

The going against the elements was harder by far than previously and took twice as long, but before dawn I beached the boat at about the place from which I had left the island so recently. There, I hauled it up and hid it in the woods that grow close to the red sands thereabout.

I was tired by now and afraid of discovery when execution must follow but, driven by fear of meeting someone in daylight, I struggled up the hill through the woods and in an hour I was standing outside Master Robert's house at Roseland. Not a light was showing and I worried that perhaps either he had removed as he had once suggested doing to Scarrell or that his wife Jean had returned to live with him, now that the trouble that had plagued him was largely over.

I decided to wait in the woods and watch and see what happened.

After dawn broke, I realised there was no horse in the paddock and that Jean would not be at home for she never went anywhere without a horse. I decided to chance entering the house and did so by the back door which was never locked.

I immediately felt better for being in the warm, for the fire was still showing dull embers. I poked it, added some peats, sat down in the armchair I had so often occupied and fell asleep.

I awoke to find Master Robert standing above me with a concerned look upon his fine face. 'What has happened to you, Jonet? You look done in.'

I wept and told how I had been raped by the first men I came across after saving one man's leg, cooking for them all and cleaning up their pigsty of a hovel.

'Well you have a few bruises on your cheeks so they didn't do it very gently.'

Master Robert made me a breakfast of porridge and gave me some aquavitae to drink, saying it would warm my stomach, which it did and all the way down my throat as well.

'You still have the boat, at least? Well that's something. The other things we can replace but it is what to do with you, where to send you? That is the trouble. Women on their own are at risk and every man knows it. An accusation of witchcraft now is like a death sentence. It is at least a trial and, as we both know, they get what confessions they look for. It just takes a little torture, starvation and lack of sleep and people agree to anything. But some of them are ill in the head, that is why they invent things that are not so.'

'You mean they're mad?'

'Not exactly. But it is like a hole in your leg made with a stick or a knife. It hurts and can even kill but it can get better. Maybe the mind is the same. It can get affected and then it does strange things.'

'Affected how, but?'

'Well, if everybody keeps talking about the devil and the temptations he puts in people's minds, "he" gets the blame for any temptations that lodge there. And pretty soon they even see people or things like cats and dogs and they think these are the devil just because they are there at the time the temptation comes to mind. Margaret McWilliam, before she died in the fire, said as much. She blamed the Minister for putting the idea of the devil and the covenant with him for services rendered, in the minds of the congregation. And he and the elders spent weeks at the Tolbooth torturing the same idea out of the very people they wanted to believe were witches until they gave it back to them again.'

'So the Minister is to blame?'

'Him and the elders, both. They are the ones fighting a battle against the devil. They are the ones ranting and raving about the dangers of the devil and what he looks like and how he operates. They supply all these ideas to the congregation and it is no wonder that when they torture people they admit to seeing the devil when the devil can appear in any form as a man, an animal, a dog, a cat or even a stalk of heather. And the people will admit to anything the Minister and elders want if the torture is sufficient. So the Minister and elders are never satisfied until they get back from the people in the jail the very ideas they put there in the first place.'

Master Robert was very angry about all this but I didn't fully understand it all. When I asked him, he told me all about the executions.

'What did the people make of it?'

'I don't know, for sure. They don't talk to me. Some of them think I am the devil—despite what the Earl managed to say. I expect they think that the women were witches and deserved to be burnt. Once people get an idea into their heads it becomes very difficult to dislodge. They seem to build upon it and it becomes part of who they are. The very idea that some of what they believe is incorrect or downright wrong and cruel is something they never stop to consider.'

'So they still think they were right?'

'Yes, I am afraid so. Of course they all see it as a disaster for the town but they do not doubt that they have done the right thing.'

'So there is no hope for me? No hope that they would let me off?'

'I don't think so. If you are caught they will treat you the same way as the others.'

'But why? I wasnae convicted.'

'You met the devil, you made a covenant with the devil, you agreed to serve him for the sake of lacking nothing in future. That is all they need. You confessed all this—or at least they say that you did, in front of witnesses.' Then Master Robert looked straight at me very firmly and said: 'Why did you confess this?'

'They wouldnae let me sleep.'
'But you were referring to me, were you not? You met me that day? Did you think I was the devil, that day?'
'No, of course not!'
'When did you think I was the devil?'
'I never thought you were the devil.'
'Did you tell them about meeting me that day?'
'Yes, but I didnae say it was you. I said it was a weel favoured young man and that was you. I could see how well favoured you were. You were showing it.'
'You mean I was aroused?'
'Aye! I kenned fine you wanted me.'
'But what about the covenant? Where did that come from?'
'You wanted me and were prepared to give me anything to have me. But I would have done it for nothing.'
'So that is 'the covenant'. The word is the Minister's of course, not yours. You would never use that word would you?'
'Not me.'
'What would you have said to the Minister, then?'
'Just what I told you. You promised me anything I wanted if I would let you enjoy me. That's what I would have said.'
'So the Minister translated this as making a covenant for services rendered by you hereafter?'
'Aye, that's it. I never wrote that confession. He wrote down what he wanted to write in the words he wanted to use.'
'So he translated words that are quite ordinary about a transaction between a man and a woman into words that meant a woman was undertaking to serve the devil in words that meant to him witchcraft: a witch being recruited by the devil.'
'Does that make a difference?'
'Not to you or me, to our lives, that is. But at least we understand it. That's something at least. But we still have to live with these people and their stupid ideas. And I do not know what to do about you.' Then Master Robert took my hand and said looking directly into my eyes. 'We do have a compact, you know, even if it is not a covenant and I am not the devil—as you are well aware—and it is that I will help you as much as I can.'
'And I will serve you, Sir, as often as I can too,' and I laughed and so did he.
And very soon after I did serve him in the way I most enjoyed and I think that he was the only man I ever really enjoyed. He was a rare loving man

and that was the size of it. He was gentle and he wanted me badly and I knew it and I wanted him too. And he tried to please me and I knew he did and helped him to do so and it always worked with him and I never felt used. I always felt enjoyed and he enjoyed it fine, every time. I always knew that. He was always so grateful. And so was I. In fact, I revelled in his enjoyment of me and I never gave a fig for his wife or my husband. I cared for him and him alone and would have died for him. And maybe, though I am not quite sure, he would have died for me. He certainly did a great deal for me that my husband would never have done. But then Master Robert was an educated man, a man of parts and I liked all of them very much.

'We have one thing that is useful in all this,' he told me as he sat down in the chair opposite after we had lain down by the fireside. 'The boat. The boat has saved you twice and you are now an accomplished sailor. So long as the weather is fine you will be able to travel anywhere around that is not too far off. You could go to Arran. You could even go to Ireland. It is only fifteen miles or so from Kintyre and you can get to Kintyre easily from here in safety by sticking close to the shore. The only time you would be exposed would be crossing the West Kyle. You could set off just up the road from Scarrell.'

'Are there witch hunts in Ireland?' I asked.

'I don't know. I could try to find out. It might be safer there. The Church of Scotland is the trouble here. In Ireland it might be less cruel.'

'I wouldn't want to go so far.'

'But if it was safer?'

'I wouldn't ever see you though, would I?'

'I suppose not. Myself, I would rather see you safe than anything.'

He took my hand and I knew he meant it. 'I should examine the boat to see how it is wearing. Has it been damaged at all?'

'No, it's still fine and dry. The caulking is quite hard all over and the weather being calm it never hit anything except the sand when beached and that's not much.'

'I think you must go to Arran and try and befriend some nice woman there. A man would abuse you as before. Few people stay there because of the mountains and it is further away. You could get fish easily enough with the boat and there are deer you could poach. If you learned to do this you might live there in secret for a while and do quite well, living off the land. And you could return here from time to time to get a few things from me. Once you are there, you can look around and see who might be befriended. You will just tell them you are bereaved and do not like to

stay where you were before which could be anywhere since you have a boat. Cumbrae would do. You will be a person on her own in need of a change of place to live. They might accept that.'
'I could get very lonely there.'
'Then you will just have to come and see me more often.'
And that was how it was. One fine night a little later, Master Robert accompanied me to the woods where the boat was hidden, carrying a bag of essential supplies like the ones I had lost, with a few more he had made for me, and we parted and by morning I had paddled to Arran where for a time I settled. I made a camp out of the pieces of caulked linen in a creek where a burn fell down from the mountains and I managed very well. I caught fish and I put out a couple of lobster pots made of twine and rope which Master Robert gave me and most days I had a crab or a lobster. I even planted a wee vegetable garden and grew kale, turnip and such and there were blaeberries and brambles in season and I brewed elderflower wine and I began to thrive there, except for the loneliness. Even this I conquered. At dead of night on occasion I would sail my boat across to Scarrell and visit Master Robert who took to going there more often. His wife never did return to him after the scandal with Nancy Throw. So we could meet often and we often did so.
I never stayed too long in any one place. The Kirk Session would have found out where I was and come for me. So after a few months, long enough to harvest the vegetables, I would remove all trace of my presence and move on, always to some secret place, off the beaten track and well out of sight of any fishermen, up a hidden creek and always with a burn of fresh spring water. There were plenty of such places around Bute. There are a dozen or so islands, half of them are uninhabited and all within an hour or so of my own island.
To be near Scarrell I stayed one time near the point just across the West Kyle and when that seemed unwise I moved to the wood at the north end of Inchmarnock, on the other side from Bute, which can't be seen, where the trees, though small, grow thick and I could hide myself and all my belongings from the few farmers who lived there on the upland grass. I even stayed on the Cumbrae once, the smaller, always keeping myself behind rocks to avoid being seen by boatmen or folk on other islands and never travelling except by night at which I became adept. A few times, greatly daring, I stayed on Bute itself. Once in the woods by the red sands from which I had first sailed to the mainland. There I stayed for a fortnight and no one saw hide nor hair of me or my boat and possessions. A fine time then, did I have with Master Robert Stewart. We mated very

often but, alas, he became worried for me and made me leave for some place off the island. So I had to go. And to spite him—for I am a contrary creature like all my tribe—I stayed far up the West Kyle near the island with the castle and told Master Robert where I was headed. A few days later he visited me there, crossing the hills from Scarrell on foot and we had another fine meeting.

In winter it was harder, of course. But I had learned to sleep on a raft of branches, covered over with heather. So I was clear of the cold ground. I also learned to make a wind break of branches between me and the sea and about a couple of yards from my front door. Between the two I would light my fire at night and the windbreak carried the heat to me. Nor could the fire be seen because of the windbreak. In the daytime I was chary of lighting a fire unless it was cloudy when the smoke would not be seen very easily. If I did, I soon moved on in case anyone did see it. But the places I stayed in were far from other humans so I was in little danger of being disturbed.

Another thing that helped were the furs I got from captured rabbits. After the usual stew was consumed, I would stretch the skin and cure it. Sewn together, rabbit furs were very warm. Carrying everything aboard the boat while travelling at night became a matter of careful preparation: everything had a place in such a small vessel. I sometimes had to tie things on.

When snow fell and ice formed which happened for two or three weeks at a time every winter, usually in January or February, my situation worsened. However, I would take to a cave and there are plenty around these islands. In a cave, out of the wind, I would light the fire during the day because the smoke spreads out better and is less noticeable. Experience showed me that my own body heat, the furs and the plaid and remains of a night fire were sufficient to keep me warm in my snug little sleeping place.

Even so, a few times it became really cold and then there was but one thing to do: I would pack up and sail to Scarrell at night. Since I was only an hour or two away this was no hardship so long as the weather was not too windy. I had become a very capable seaman and could manage the ship in everything but a half gale when the waves were over 2 feet high.

I would hide the boat under the trees just round the point from Scarrell and cross the track quickly, run up the hill and then walk down the ridge to Scarrell a few hundred yards southward and enter his back door. Master Stewart might even be expecting me and meet me among the trees on the beach. And there with him I would stay for the duration of the snowfall or the ice until the weather improved. Because of his ostracism no one ever visited him.

In time, it seemed only natural that Master Robert, who had nothing much to occupy his mind but the old Latin and Greek stories he loved and his inventions, should take to the water himself. He built a stout wooden boat three times the size of mine with a keel and a mast and it was half decked which meant two people could sleep inside under cover and be nice and snug. We often lay ahull in five feet of water for the hours of darkness until it would be time to separate an hour before the light came up.

He was a very busy man always inventing a new tool or device to achieve something which is why he was so good at repairing my boat and my gear and supplying me with useful things. I expect the isolation made him this way. He had nothing else to distract him.

He once told me that he had not set eyes on Nancy since that last time in the Kirk and I don't think he wanted to. It was soon in the past and if he had seen her it would be like opening an old wound. The wound was his own, of course. He felt he had let her down, though, by the sound of things, she let him down just as much. Since he never went to church now, with the full approval of the Kirk Session, he never saw her there. But he said he sometimes crept up to her house at dead of night, just like in the old days, and left money for her and the boy on a window sill or pushed under the back door. Of course the fairies got the credit for it. The boy did not thrive. In that community it was impossible. Nor did she. But I am not sure Robert was always this way. I felt that some day he must try and see her, even if it was just one last time. He must have loved her very much and she him. You never forget that kind of thing, even if it is the killing of your life.

I know the Session fined him a lot of money and that he had to sell lands all the time to make ends meet. I often wondered at the punishment. It could have been far worse. I expect it was his class; they couldn't bring themselves to execute a gentleman like themselves. If the folk of the island came across him he could come in for a few dunts—except if they were the poor folk that kenned him. He thought the Minister was afraid that if he was put to death a new cult might grow up like the one Jesus started. That was not wanted.

I relied upon him for everything: flour to make my bannocks—on a hot stone or griddle and with a few currants in them, they taste fine—and ale and even aquavitae of a cold night, for which I gradually acquired a taste and butter and milk and salt and clothing, that too. He was always giving me clothes: new woollen stockings and woollen skirts and shoes when I wore them out and scarves and even hats for my head—a fine waterproof one and a coat which he waterproofed specially for me with tar stolen again from the pier, or maybe paid for since he had plenty money. The rest I could find for myself. I even gave him fish to take home to Scarrell at times. Crab and lobster and herrings and cod and haddock and mackerel I used to catch very easily when I learned the art, which I mainly taught myself: feathers on a hook did very well. I even took to salting the herring which meant I had plenty of food when the weather was too bad to venture out in search of it. And I made jerky: a kind of cured meat from rabbits and deer which would last a long while.

Of course it was his company I needed most of all. I came to love his loving of me more than my very life. I never ever got used to it, never tired of it. Every time it was like a fresh experience, a new adventure in feeling. And he would recite poems to me. And sometimes they were in Latin or Greek or the Irish or some other language he had been learning and I wouldnae understand any of it. But I always understood the feeling, for that was in his voice and in his body and his heart and his soul, there most of all. Of course he needed my company too. He had been ostracised and he never got over this. It was a waste of a very fine man, a man who could have been anything and achieved great personal success. But maybe I was his success. I think he thought so. Perhaps just because we were forced to separate so much because of the danger—and even the danger itself—made us enjoy our meetings together far more.

How did it all end? This wonderful life I had? They said at the trial that I had lived at Kilmarnock, for God's sake. Kilmarnock? What's in Kilmarnock? I've never been near Kilmarnock! Two nights on the mainland with three men was enough for me. I was far safer on the islands around Bute: the two Cumbraes and Arran and Pladda and Inchmarnock. I was even safer on Bute—so long as I was at one end or the other and behind rocks or under the trees away from prying eyes. They wanted to believe it was Kilmarnock I went to and I let them. It was better than the truth. That might have got Master Robert into trouble! I would have defended that good man with my life!—would have turned myself in for him, by God! There, you see, I even learned to speak like him. That is what love does to you.

No, I spent 12 years on the islands around and on Bute, always supplied by my good man with every last thing I needed. There never had been a covenant but he acted as if there was. And he was no devil but the best man I ever kenned. I will love him till the fires of hell get hold of me.

What ended it, then?

JONET McNICOLL'S STORY

Well it was a woman's thing really, a right wee stupid thing....
I was camped over on the west side of Loch Striven, a good place with nobody about at all, lying on the shore behind a rock under my tarry roof and walls, with all the fish in the sea to feed me.—Aye and deer too, if I had a mind to them, for Master Robert even got me a musket with shot and powder, meant to be for men that might stumble into my camp and get the wrong idea in their heads.
He met me there and we snuggled down as usual and made our love once or twice—he was still very young-looking and active even at his age, though his hair turned grey after the burnings—and he was telling me the news of the island, my own home, such as he knew it, for he was still outside most of it but he would get scraps here and there from the survivors among the witch folk. And he told me about a new wee shop in Kames where a wife had started selling clothes—good clothes she made herself specially for women— and who understood what women wanted—not just the home made kind or those made by a tailor-man. It entered my head that I might pay a visit to this shop and acquire for myself a new coat and such. I had plenty money, for Master Robert made sure of that just in case I needed to bribe somebody. I even persuaded myself that it would be safe, since I had never lived at Kames and nobody would know me there. But reason asserted itself, of course, and I determined not to take the risk.
Then, two days later, I found myself standing above a pool of water and I could see very clearly because of the direction of the light. I was horrorstruck. My hair had turned white and the face beneath was reddened by wind and weather and wrinkled all over. As I looked, tears fell down my cheeks and I rued my departing life. I had become an old woman.
I soon turned away and looked no more in pools of water. For the rest of that day I was miserable, sick to my soul at what had become of me. And then the next morning the sun was high in the sky, the world looked a fine place again and I looked about me and my life did not seem quite so bad. But the notion of visiting the clothes shop still possessed me. I could not get it out of my head. I suppose my head has become stupid with age, stupider, if there is such a word, as I live so much alone. Anyway, I told myself, I would be in and out of the shop in no time and get back to my boat and set sail again before anyone knew anything. And who would recognise me when I hardly recognised myself? I fought it for a wee while but, by and by, the attraction of the shop was too great to resist.

So one fine morning, I took my boat and crossed over to the Ardmaleish side and hid it in a bush just above the beach and I walked in to Kames, just like one of the locals. And there was hardly anyone about. It was Thursday, market day and most people were in the town.

It was a nice wee shop with a counter and clothes hanging from the low roof and since I had not been in one for so many years I was desperate to buy many things. I suppose I attracted a bit of attention in the shop. When I came out an hour later dressed in a fine new coat with a new pouch full of purchases, I saw someone eyeing me.

It was on the hill above Ardmaleish that I heard the horsemen and I knew what it must be to have them galloping. I began to run for the boat and nearly reached it when they caught me up and held me. In an hour I was warded in the Tolbooth in Rothesay town.

Since they caught me running towards the shore they never saw the boat which was well hidden in bushes at the point, a distance off. They just thought I was running from them. It never occurred to them that I might be running to something. If they had found the boat, they would have found my gear, understood my manner of life these dozen years, realised that I had enjoyed the advantage of a supporter and even who it must be.

In the few weeks I have left I have often wondered about my boat. I was that proud of it. Master Robert had made it for me—specially—and repaired it often over the years, even adding another layer of fabric painted with tar on both sides which made it stronger than before. By then, I was stronger myself and could move it very easily. All you needed was a sense of balance and you could manage it fine with a paddle. In time, I could get in and out very easily and with hardly a ripple, I rarely got my feet wet and it was fast, faster than walking, and very quiet which was just what my predicament needed.

It was simple in design and yet ingenious, very light and stable in most weather. Being around islands all the time, with hills for shelter, I could always lie up in bad weather and, travelling only at night, I was never spotted. So close to the surface, I would be taken for a seal but nobody else went out at night, especially at sea, because big boats would get wrecked. Mine was too light to suffer if I bumped into a rock. It would take a real gale of wind to wreck my little ship and I was always beached out of sight in bad weather.

The boat will still be where I left it and as good as new until the sun's rays dry it out altogether and the hardened tar splits, one of the things I always had to guard against. But then, being out in the boat every day and

JONET McNICOLL'S STORY

maintaining it as if it were my life, of course that was never an issue so long as I was at large. How I miss my boat!

On 15th October 1673, at a Justice Ayre at Rothesay, before the Earl of Argyll and Sir Colin Campbell of Aberuchill and Ninian Bannatyne of Kames, deputes, the following jury was chosen: Archibald Bannatyne of Lubas, Mr. Robert Stewart in Kilchattan[130], Donald McNeill of Kilmorie, Robert Stewart of Mecknoch, James Stewart in Largiend, Donald More McKaw of North Garrochty, John McKaw in South Garrochty, James Crawford in Drumachcloy, Donald Hyndman at mill of Ettrick, Ninian Stewart, late baillie of Rothesay, Robert Stewart of Lochlie. Adam Stewart in Rothesay, John Kelburn elder there, Colin Stewart, there, Ninian Stewart of Largiend.

On 16th October 1673, at the instance of Henry Melis, Prosecutor Fiscal, Jonet[131] McNicoll was stated to be 'apprehended anno 1662 foresaid and imprisoned within the Tolbooth of Rothesay and fearing to be put to death with the rest who suffered at that time. [sic] It is true and of a veritie that she brake ward and escaped out of the said Tolbooth and fled to the Lowlands where she remained in Kilmarnock and other places[132] there

---

[130] A different person to Mr. Robert Stewart of Scarrell, who is mentioned many times in the records and even in this same year as such, 1673. He was still known as Mr Robert Stewart of Scarrell when he lived in Rothesay at Roseland. This will be a relative. Master Patrick Stewart, the schoolmaster in 1673, might be one of his kinsmen.

[131] In this document alone is she called 'Jannet'; in all the others, especially the dittay found at Inverary, she is known as 'Jonet.' Since there are others called 'Jonet' this is the more common form of this name. She is even called 'Jonet' within the same document, the actual original handwriting: see left hand side under 16th Oct 1673

[132] To reach Kilmarnock she had to have access to a boat. Yet she could not manage a boat of the conventional type by herself: it would have been wooden and would have taken men to launch it from the beach. Both her husband and son, Donald, continued to live at Rothesay, where the son complained that he was suffering taunts because of his mother being a witch [See footnote next page and p300]. If she had a boat she could manage she was far safer living around Bute on the islands than inland at Kilmarnock. Melis's statement is unlikely to be accurate. It suggests that he or others wrote to the authorities at Kilmarnock to ascertain her doings. Yet had she been there, she would have used an assumed name. Without identification nothing could have been learned about her stay in the Kilmarnock area and there is no suggestion of evidence from there. A dittay referring to Kilmarnock by her, of course, means nothing, given how these were created. It only had to occur to her inquisitors that she lived around Kilmarnock for that to be a 'fact' she could readily admit to under torture, which ended up in the dittay then. It is quite unlikely that she wandered around Kilmarnock unmolested for 12 years performing acts of malefice without being apprehended there and executed. They did not

about these twelve years by gone always under an evil fame both at home and abroad. And where she committed several malefices notorious to all the country. As at more length is contained in her said dittay for the which crime of witchcraft she was put to the trial and... fyled culpable and convict of the crime aforesaid contained in her dittay in respect of her own confession...And therefore the said Justice and his deputes be the mouth of Duncan Clerk dempster of Court decerned and ordained the said Jannet McNicoll to be taken and strangled to the death and her body to be burnt at the gallows of Rothesay upon Friday the 24th October instant by two hours in the afternoon and her goods and gear to be escheat.'[133]

Also killed that day at the Gallowscraig 'betuixt twa and thrie hours eftirnoon', but by hanging, was Mary McThomas. Her crime was incest and charming. She had 'fallen in fornicatione' with John Campbell of Otterferry uncle of John McKennan with whom she lived for six years, twenty years later, even having a male child between them. So they killed the mother because she had fornicated with the uncle twenty years before! And her goods and gear likewise, were escheat

---

know where she had been and made this up. She kept to herself where she had been, probably to save the person or persons who helped her. She has told us in her story where she spent the 12 years. Had she really been in Kilmarnock, why would she have returned to Bute of all places after 12 years away? Why not go somewhere else? Anywhere else was safer. The answer is that she never really left Bute and its environs. That is why she was apprehended in Bute 12 years later. It was bound to happen sometime. Only this version of events makes sense.

[133] Editor's note: Some spellings have been modernised for the sake of the reader.

6. Aftermath

Master Robert Stewart of Scarrell seems to make no appearance in public life after his trial by the Kirk Session, though his name is mentioned several times when lands belonging either to him or his spouse are sold, probably in settlement of money borrowed using land as security. Though mentioned in court, he is never present. He may have lived at Scarrell, at Roseland or elsewhere, though Scarrell is likely, being out of the way. He probably had no job—would have been unemployable—and relied upon rents and sales of land and property for his income, though even here he could not do well being outside the community and not therefore privy to its news of possible deals. It is likely that at Scarrell or anywhere else he chose to live, he would take up fishing as a way of providing food for himself. In 1662, if born in 1620, he had to be around 42, but still young-looking and vigorous because of his natural advantages. To the witches, who would mostly have been older, he was, indeed, a young and well favoured man, especially so, because of his class and superiority in every way. By 1673 he would have been 53. Given that his father lived into his eighties, his life might have been long also, except for the stigma under which he lived which must have had an adverse effect upon him.

7. Questions

1. Who laid the charges against the witches? No record of this has been found. On the explanation given it should have been the Minister or someone designated by the Minister, probably on the Kirk Session. The Crowner or Crownaer, Jamieson, is the most likely person, since that was his job. The Minister had most to gain from the witch hunt but he may have chosen to remain as much as possible in the background after the pre trial inquisition in which he played a leading role..

2. How was the Earl of Argyll involved in this? Since his father had just been beheaded for treason the year before, and his son had been an active Royalist supporter who had fought against and been defeated by the occupying Parliamentarian troops, after the news of the Restoration he would have been anxious to establish his authority and would have quickly travelled to the area from where he had been exiled. Once present, he would have taken an interest in all the doings of the territory and he

would have been approached during the chaos of the change of government, to oversee the trials. It is certain that he did oversee the trials in 1673 for the records say so. It is therefore likely that he presided over the Justice Ayre of 1662 in addition.

3. Was the conduct of the trials as the reconstruction supposes? Very little is known about these trials except that the accused had no defence, were even unable to defend themselves because they were not allowed to; and, being for the most part poor and ill educated, would have been unable to mount a worthwhile defence in any case. So much would have been assumed by the prosecutors. The behaviour of the Earl in the reconstruction is of course remarkable. Whether it was like this it is impossible to say. However, it has been written this way because he is the only person with the authority and ability to have exposed some of the deeper aspects of this matter, as we have seen him do. No other person had the clout to stand up against the might of the Kirk Session and the burgesses, which is the same thing, in effect. As an outsider and superior, eager to impose himself, he is an obvious candidate for the moves that he is taken to have made. Since Master Robert Stewart of Scarrell was effectively allowed to go on living on the island, though ostracised and effectively excommunicated and with enough money to live comfortably off sales of lands and rents of property, it can be inferred that the Session did not want to make a martyr of him. That could have been even more dangerous to the preservation of the status quo in religious matters. This very fact— when his punishment could have been as severe as he thought it would be: with his execution— suggests that they were afraid of what he had started. And what he is likely to have started is an investigation of the moral values assumed and demanded on pain of many punishments from everyone. His very disgrace was the catalyst to his questioning the mores of the society and community. In a highly educated man who has sinned in this way and done so knowing the consequences, it can be expected that he would examine his conduct very carefully and try to understand it and justify it. When he looked for reasons— real reasons, not the laws and commandments invented by men down the ages—of course he began to find a better way of life.

4. What about witch trials at other times? Robert Stewart of Scarrell was not old enough to be involved in 1630. But there was no trial then: the

QUESTIONS

accused persons were forgotten about and died in the Castle Dungeon[134]. And in the other investigations, such as they were, there would be no talk of covenants with the devil. Even in 1661, when Jeane Campbell was accused of going with the fairies, there was no trial, as far as is known, other than an inquisition before the Kirk Session. In 1673 there were two trials of women accused of witchcraft or charming, one of them Jonet McNicol. Even then, there is no need to speak of covenants with the devil for that had already been established in 1662.

5. What about witchcraft in other places like Forfar and Haddington where there were more executions in 1662? If there was a man involved, as there was in many cases, that man could have been named as the devil and the covenants confessed by torture could have been reinterpreted by the Minister and elders, just as in Bute, to put a satanic spin on otherwise quite ordinary arrangements for sexual favours in exchange for presents of money among other things. Given the nature of the torture and the method of recording confessions, virtually anything could have been 'confessed', including covenants without sexual favours or the involvement of a man.

6. Why was Robert Stewart of Scarrell not executed, as he expected? Because he had been leading secret meetings, because he was a qualified minister and schoolmaster. It follows that he would have been both justifying his own conduct to the people and, in so doing, suggesting not only that a more liberal and more forgiving attitude to what the Church of Scotland regarded as sin, was desirable, but that it was a better response to the teachings of Jesus in the Gospel where forgiveness of sins is paramount. He was, in effect, starting up an alternative church, the same thing Jesus of Nazareth had done and been killed for. One of the outcomes of his martyrdom was the very Church of Scotland with complete power in Bute. If they killed Robert Stewart, the fear might be that he would be such a martyr, that the established church would be overthrown by a philosophy which was different: liberal, forgiving, caring and even loving.

---

[134] ID p14. See 'Proces Margaret McWilliam' note 2 in ID printed herein. p 264

8. Cause of the Witch Hunt

(i) General

1662 was the time when Newton was already at Cambridge beginning to put the whole of knowledge on a scientific footing, a process already begun by Galileo, Copernicus, Nicholas of Cusa, Johannes Kepler and others. All over Scotland the educated men, seeing everywhere the oppression of the Church of Scotland and the misery in which many people, especially the poor, were condemned to live, would be wondering if a better—more compassionate, forgiving and humane— way could not be found. That precisely is the spirit of The Sermon on the Mount in the Gospels. The contradiction between that and the current, unforgiving and harsh reality of Bute would have been noticed because so many minds, like Newton's, would be waking up from their sleep. They would be wondering if the hell of eternal damnation really was so very much worse than the hell of real life— at least for the poor and disadvantaged. And if they were like our Robert Stewart they might be performing the kinds of experiments of life (unavoidable for some of them) which would bring about their disgrace and then threaten the established values once they started dealing, intellectually, with their predicament.

At one level, the level of the whole of Scotland, the salient facts are that there had been a period of acute social, psychological and moral repression under the Church of Scotland, followed by a period of occupation for a decade by the English army which must have been seen as a worse calamity, especially by the gentry, who were expected to pay large sums for its maintenance. Those of the gentry who opposed the English, such as Sir James Stewart, were treated far worse. He was fined £5,000, a huge sum. The Duke of Argyll, who had tried to sit on the fence while his son fought against the English, actually lost his head. But even the poor and the tradesmen would have felt cast down by the occupation, for it was the first time the country had lost its independence in 3 centuries. Then, after a hiatus following the death of Cromwell, there was a restoration. Charles II was known to be both licentious and pro catholic. To the stolid, rigid men of the Kirk Session and the Town Council and those who followed them, it must have seemed that their values were endangered. In Bute in 1755, Webster tells us[135], there was not a single

---

[135] Scottish Population Statistics, p32 op cit.

QUESTIONS

Catholic on the island. It would be the same in 1662. So there was no fear of conflict. The absence of any Catholic presence simply fortified the opposition to the possibility of the monarch becoming a Catholic and to the reimposition of Catholic-style bishops. It was a time too when the hierarchy of the island, the gentry and the Kirk and Council, would try to reimpose themselves upon the community, after so many years under martial law, ruled by alien Ironsides. When the English left, the twin aims of the gentry to make the place secure for themselves over their social inferiors and the protection of the values they held dear would make them more inclined to act against any resistance or defection from these values. And so what was being attempted by the leaders of the island was a reinforcement of the status quo, more action against sin, against dissent, against all the things disapproved of by the Church.

And then there is another strand, a movement throughout the country that wanted the fetters of oppression, the demand for assiduously Christian living and the punishments for failure, lifted and removed, at least to some extent. People had had enough of the hell on earth made by their own leaders. The arrival of Charles II on the throne, and to a power now curtailed by events, suggested that there would be a relaxing of all the harsh penalties for trivial offences. From the Inverary document it seems clear that throughout there had been meetings of a few very poor people who met in secret to get away from the prying Session men and their strictures. There to dance[136] and make merry and carouse and tell stories and sing—all of which had been prohibited. Maybe these meetings did not begin until the English left. But by 1661 they would be happening. The Inverary document tells us they were happening[137]. And the gentry would hate it when they learned about it. Would definitely act to put them down and stop them. If they were held in secret, of course— would go the thinking—they are against the teachings and requirements of the Church.

This is likely to have been a phenomenon that was widespread in Scotland. And there is the intellectual strand. Some of the educated and ablest people had begin to think for themselves and question what the Church was demanding. Isaac Newton was one: a secret unitarian which, had it been known, would have brought about his dismissal from Cambridge and the world would have been a very different place for he altered it as it had never been altered before in intellectual terms, in a period of 35 years residence at Trinity. But Scotland too would have had its share of thinking men who would question the church's ideas of how

---

[136] ID p19, McWilliam herein p268; ID p8, McLevin herein p259, ID p10, p260 here.
[137] ID p24, Jonet Morison; herein p272; ID p7,8, McLevin; herein p258-259

men should live and begin to formulate their own. It must be very likely that Robert Stewart of Scarrell was a man of this stamp. He had been well educated for the time and, freed from his father's influence after 1658 he would have had the stimulus for such thinking. But in his case, there was a further dimension. He was humiliated and disgraced for having fallen in love and got with a child a woman half his age not his wife. He was driven into the hands of the poorest of the community and soon would become its leader. He would both examine the values of the community that condemned him and question them and convey his ideas to that initially small group of the poor. When he was successful in attracting others to himself, it was eventually noticed and the idea that he was unwittingly starting up a rival church would have provoked a reaction from the Session and the Council and the gentry proper. How did you break up these meetings? Not by making a martyr out of Robert Stewart but by hunting some witches. And it would begin with a request for information about these meetings. The first confessions are innocent enough. It is only when they come across a psychotic, Margaret McLevin with an urge to confess and invent things that never happened, that the trouble really begins. For then the men of the Session believe that there is in their midst a group of murderers and that that is what these secret meetings are for. Their method of extracting information was primitive and unfair to the accused, the idea of fairness in this being some distance in the future. The mental model of the law and the devil and the acquisition of evidence and the idea of a defence were all at that time seriously defective.

(ii) Particular [The main argument]

What might be said in opposition to this theory[138], for that is what it is? It cannot be anything else. If Robert Stewart was not in the witches group in 1661, he could not have been its leader. He might simply have been ostracised from all society. If so, someone else was the leader. That person was the devil. As the various dittays mentioning the devil all tell us, the devil was a living, breathing man— a white man with dark hair[139] and one who was young and well favoured[140], at least in appearance (and

---

[138] Like Newton's, Darwin's, Einstein's Special and General Theories of Relativity etc; hardly any worthy knowledge is not a theory.

[139] According to Jonet Morison ID p 20, 21, herein p 269-270

[140] As several witches agree.ID p12, herein p262 Isobel McNicol, ID p13, herein p263, Jonet McNicoll, ID p18, herein p267, Margaret McWilliam:

QUESTIONS

in comparison to the witches who were mostly middle-aged or old) and a man with 'a white middle' i.e. not a copper faced or leper faced man but a well favoured Caucasian. Could a man not of the gentry, not with Robert Stewart's advantages of education, wealth, connections and status, have led this group and enlarged its numbers so that it suddenly became 'a great company of people'? No. Patrick McKaw or John Galie were uneducated farming folk, not even elders, but toilers in the fields, who could not have brought about this sudden transformation because it was beyond them. There is no mention of any other man in that group who might fit.

Because of his recent history, Robert Stewart of Scarrell is uniquely qualified for the job of leader, the one wealthy, educated person with leadership skills already developed, as a minister and schoolmaster, who could have brought about this transformation. And the only person on the island who could have joined this group on the periphery of the community. No other person of his class would have considered such an action. Joining this group was his only hope of society, having been ostracised for his sinful behaviour. Once in that group, they would have quizzed him about his doings and he would have wanted to examine them publicly among them. That was the start of his questioning the values and practices of that unforgiving community. And it would be this questioning which enabled him to find a more compassionate answer to the problem of living. Of course, as his ideas developed, people flocked to hear them and we know that they did flock to these meetings from ID. When the Kirk Session heard of these, the threat they presented was clear. These ideas were contrary to the beliefs of the established church. These meetings and the ideas discovered during them and promoted by them had to be investigated and destroyed.

Who, but a schoolmaster, would expect people to arrive at such a meeting on time? This happened when Elspeth Spence was not present[141]. Asked if Jonet Morison 'saw Elspa Spence at the meeting', she answered, 'No but that she heard one of the witches say to the devil: we want one of our Cummers yet viz. Elspa Spence, Patrick Glas his wife. **He [the devil] answered: 'That is a great fault**.' No other person would have expected them to be on time for a private meeting out of doors but a minister and schoolmaster. Who but Robert Stewart, one of the handful of educated men on the island, would have been capable of language like that? And it does not sound like the minister's words either. No farmer or burgess or

---

[141] ID p26; herein p274, Jonet Morison

servant would have said this. Who but Robert Stewart, minister and schoolmaster, would have come down the brae from St Bride's Chapel (in the ruins)—where he had been preaching—with his congregation—and when they reached the shore, had them come around him to convey further insights made on the way down from his earlier 'Sermon on the Mount'?[142]. This is what Morison says of him. Who but a qualified minister (but not an ordained one) would think of holding a secret meeting within the walls of a ruined chapel? And why this one? Because in 1662 it was out of town, out of sight up a steep hill. Who but our Master Robert Stewart of Scarrell, university graduate, preacher and schoolmaster, member of the gentry, moneyed and a star— a fallen star— in the community, could have suddenly attracted 'a great company'[143] coming from Ardbeg, 'a great number'[144] from Kilmory to his outdoor meetings, in the autumn and winter of 1661, as McLevin says? Who but he was 'The devil and a company with him coming down the hill side from St Bride's Chapel'[145] as Morison saw as she was coming from Bute Quay? Few people were capable of that kind of thing. It was quite exceptional for someone to hold secret meetings outside the Church. It took ability and motive. He is the only man with both; the only man with either! And remember that he had failed to be appointed to a charge as minister, not only in Ireland but, nearer hand, in Cowal and, most of all, in Bute itself, where, in ordinary circumstances, he should have followed his father in the job. Half a dozen vacancies on the island were filled, over the years, by others that he might have received.

Who but our Robert Stewart would have needed women so much, after his wife left him (as well as before), that he offered any suitable candidate money for sexual favours 'to go with him' and 'to want for nothing' thereafter? And who but him would have been believed to have that money? Klareanough![146] The name he gave Jonet Morison when she asked his name. And who but him, with his status and advantages of all kinds, being of the gentry, would have been successful? No ordinary man could have bought women in this way. It had to be some exceptional man. Would Ninian Bannatyne of Kames or Sir James Stewart have been capable of this? No! The only man capable among the gentry is the one man who had already shown he was capable of it, by the abuse of his

---

[142] ID p24; herein p272/3, Morison
[143] ID p7, herein p258, McLevin
[144] ID p8, herein p271, McLevin
[145] ID p23, herein Morison p272
[146] ID p22, herein p270

position and getting with child the maidservant half his age. For these other men that would have been inconceivable. Their grandsons would never have become earls. When were the records doctored? When the possibility that they might be ennobled was mooted. Imagine if the records had been scrutinised. The escutcheons might have been seen not to be without blemish..

How could any other man have offered money to any woman in that community? He risked execution! He believed he might be executed[147] and we can see why when minor offences were so humiliatingly punished. But our Robert had already taken that risk! And for the whole of 1661 he knew he was doomed. He was the one person— the only man in that entire community— who could have done that and he did it all the more easily after 4th July 1661 when he was admitted to be the father of the child by Nancy Throw. Knowing he was doomed, he could ask any woman for sex for money with impunity. What had he to lose?

Who was the man who met Jonet Morison in the twilight and then eight nights later at Knockanrioch?[148] Who was the man, later called the devil by Issobell McNicol[149], who met her at night outside her back door and spoke with her? What man would have been accustomed to go out at night, of necessity in the dark without a light, or risk being seen, to meet with women not his wife? Robert Stewart of Scarrell. The man already shown to have taken extraordinary risks in pursuit of women. Why else did Master Robert Stewart of Scarrell, wealthy, well-connected, well-educated and well-qualified, fail to be appointed to a charge as a minister, the profession he had trained for? Because he was perceived to be, long before his fall from grace, the kind of man that we see him to have been: an extraordinarily highly sexed, risk taker, the kind that—no matter how qualified and connected—would not do in the post.

---

[147] Kirk Session Records p45, 4th July 1661; herein p293
[148] ID p20. Herein p269
[149] ID p12, herein p263

9. APPENDICES

(i) Inventory of Persons accused of Witchcraft in Bute County with charges

[99% of this is original. The Inverary Document so often referred to herein is printed verbatim after this inventory. Since this begins on p254 the actual reference can be read on the appropriate page herein with 254 added, at least roughly. E.g. Margaret McWilliam's actual recorded confession should be found herein on p254 +18 because it is on ID p18. In fact her confession appears herein from p267-268 ie approx 272. ID ranges from p3 to p30. IDp3=p254; IDp10=p257; IDp15=p263; IDp18=p267; IDp20= p269; IDp23= p272; IDp25=p274; ID p27=p275; ID p30=p277; and proportionally]

The Edinburgh University data base survey, an alphabetical list of names of persons mentioned in a criminal trial and dates, was the starting point. It has been modified because some are mentioned twice with different spelling and greatly amplified and extended; ID {Inverary Document} is identical to Highland Papers Vol III where ID also appears. Essentially, what follows, far more than a mere list of names, is a summary of the Inverary Document in a different form: reordered under names of accused rather than accusers and confessors with dates. All but 3 place names can be found on the Roy map of Bute. Persons mentioned in a witch trial is not what is wanted; the accused rather and who accused them and of what they were accused.

1.**Ballantyne**, Kirstine, 1662: wronged by witchcraft Peter Gray; bewitched the Lady Kames which was the cause of her sickness ID p26,27, HP3 p26,27 delated by Jonet Morisone. Delated witch by McLevin ID p8. Delated (probably) by McLevin ID p8 as maiden at a meeting on Scoulag side when a child of McCurdie was killed

2. **Boyd**, Jonet 1662 ID p20. Delated by McCarthur for stealing his wife's milk.

3. **Campbell**, Jean, 1660 going with the fairies; Ambrismore farm, Kingarth Parish

4. **Cristell**, Katherine, 1662, delated by McLevin ID p9

5. **Frissell**, eldest son of Katharine Moore, 1662 [? database only]

6. **Frissell**, Geillis 1649

7. **Frissell**, Katherine, 1662, ID p28 delated by Jonet McIlmertine and ID p8 McLevin as witch attending meetings

8. **Frissell**, Marione 1662 ID p28 [delated by Jonet McIlmertine]

9. **Frissell**, Mary,1662 ID p28 [delated by Jonet McIlmertine] may be same as above.

10. **Galie**, Elspat, 1662 [Ambrisbeg] delated by Jonet Morisone ID p25 wronged by witchcraft Hew Boyd in Kilwinning whose 4 wives died and a child 'never lived' and lies sick. Delated ID p19 as present with witches Oct 1661 at meeting with McWilliam at Kilmory. [born Elspeth Gray]

11. **Galie**, John, 1662   [Barmore] delated as witch by Jonet Morisone ID p24. Delated as a witch who attended meetings ID p8 by McLevin.

12. **Heyman**, Annie, 1662, delated by McLevin ID p8; maiden at bay head meetings [Kilchattan Bay, probably] where she often danced in the midst of them.

13. **Hyndman**, Amy [elder], 1662 ID p28 [delated by Jonet McIlmertine and Issobell More McKaw]

14. **Hyndman**, Amy [younger] 1662 ID p28 [ditto; unsure which one McKaw meant]

15. **Hyndman**, Finwell, 1650 [disappearing for 24 hours]

16. **McAllan**, 1662, delated a witch by McLevin ID p9

APPENDICES

17. **McAllester**, mid most son of Soirle, 1662 Delated by McLevin ID p10 as present when McKeraish shot Robt McKomash
[Katherine Stewart of Largizean is noted later, she appeared twice on the list]
18. **McAllexande**r, wife of Soirle, 1662 [?data base only]
19. **McCan,** Issobell, 1662 [?data base only]
20. **McCartour**, Donald, 1662 ID P20 delated by Jonet Boyd for seeking the milk of his wife which had been lost. He swore she had stolen it and would suffer before that day month; within 3 months her husband died suddenly. Delated by McLevin for carrying flesh on his back after the death of a child ID p8
21. **McConachie**, Jonat, 1662 ID p29 [Barmore, wife of John Galie; physik and charmes] delated by Jonet Morisone ID p25 wronged by witchcraft Hew Boyd in Kilwinning whose 4 wives died and a child 'never lived' and lies sick; took the life of Neil McNeill's horse; delated as with the devil at Bute Quay by Jonet Morisone ID p24. Delated by McLevin as a witch who attended meetings ID p8.
22. **McCuill**, Marie More, 1662 Delated as present at meeting by McLevin ID p10
23 **McIlduy**, Margaret, 1662, ID p27 [This is Donald McConochie's wife in Ardroskadill] speaking to the devil after the meeting on Bute Quay delated by Jonet Morisone.
24. **McIlmartin**, daughter of Alexander, 1662 [Kelspoke] delated by McLevin ID p8 often maiden at meetings, black haired, broad faced and jolly.
25. **McIlmertine**, Jonet, 1662 confessed covenant and baptism. ID p28, herein p263 [should have been executed or died in prison] Delated by McWilliam as present at Kilmory meeting in Oct 1661 ID p19. This may be the same person as listed above. Described as Patrick Muck's wife. Delated by McLevin ID p8 as a witch attending meetings.
26. **McIllvein**, Margret, 1662 [may be McLevin] ignore in accounting
27. **McIntyre**, Jonet, 1662 ID p28 [McNivan's wife 'in Keighs', delated by Jonet McIlmertine]
28. **McKaw**, Issobell More McKaw, 1662 [probably Dunagoil, wife of Patrick McKaw] Delated by McWilliam ID p19 as attending meeting Kilmory Oct 1661.
29. **McKaw**, Marie, 1662 [Garrochty?] Delated by McWilliam ID p19 as attending meeting Kilmory Oct 1661.
30. **McKaw**, Patrick, 1662, [Dunagoil] shot a bairn of Donald Roy McKerdie at Elanshemaroke [probably Inchmarnock]
31. **McKerraish**, Unknown, 1662 [Argyll, Glendaruel] delated as shooting Robt McKomash ID p10 by McLevin
32. **McKirdy**, Lachlan, 1649
33. **McKirdy**, Marget, 1649
34.**McLevin**, Margaret, 1662, [seems to be wife of McVicar] confession and baptism [therefore executed or died in prison] in a small room at Ballichtarach [place unknown] about 1658, where the devil came to her in the lykeness of a man and asked her to go with him ID p6. The devil injured her hand and her leg. She refused him. But he came a second time in the barn at Ardroscadale where he healed her hurts and she made a covenant then and was baptised. In 1659 employed in a service for the devil to destroy John McFerson, Wm Gillespie and two others. The devil carried her under his armpit to the back of Inchmarnock where she was supposed to pull the mast out of their boat. But God prevented this by turning the boat on another course. At the devil's command she was to sink John Moore's boat en route for Lochfyne. She went to the shore side and cast

a stone into the sea. The devil brought her back from Inchmarnock under his armpit. [Inchmarnock is half a mile from Bute with a deep channel between] and let her fall in the sea, but it was on a rock. Confirms Jonet Morison's statements about meeting the devil with a great company 3 nights before Hallowday; says they intended to harm Mr. John Stewart Minister and John Glass, Provost. Says John Gely [Galie] and his wife Jonat McConachie were are witches meetings and were witches. Confessed to having a charm for wristing or brising ID p5 in Irish, that she laid the charm in tallow or herbs and applied it. She charmed John McTyre the tailor who had a sore shoulder; applied charm of the evil eye to some fishermen especially McIntaggart of Ballycurry. Has another charm good for preserving in Irish. ID p5 Delated by John McFerson who had trouble at sea in a storm. McLevin told him he was in her debt for she had helped him and without it he would have been food for crabs. Says she has several charms effective with men and animals; charmed Allan McConnachie in Ballenlay[Ballanly], in Irish, put it in water or a curchief (sic) ID p4/5. delated by Jonet Morisone ID p25 put a pock of witchcraft on Finley McConochie and told the devil that what he got would be better doubled; ID 24 offered to cure John Stephen. ID p19 delated by McWilliam as attending the meeting at Kilmory in Oct 1661 c Hallowday [31st]

35. **McMaister** in Barone, 1662, female, a charmer ID p30, delated by Sara Stewart

36. **McNeill**, Issobell, 1662 [may be the McNeill on ID p19 who attended the meeting at Kilmory in Oct 1661 delated by McWilliam; if not it is the one above probably]

37. **McNeill**, Jonat, 1662 ID p27 [daughter of Kirstine Bannatyne] delated by Jonet Morisone for healing a bairn by binding with string and knots, the binding a cat with it; the cat died immediately; delated at Bute Quay with the devil 3 nights before Hallowday: 31st Oct. Delated by McLevin ID p8 as witch who attended meetings. All her bairns also delated witches by McLevin ID p8. Delated by Jonat Man ID p4 for charming her bairn

38, **McNeill**, Margaret, 1662, ID 19, delated by McWilliam for attending a meeting.

39. **McNickell**, Margret, 1662 delated witch by McLevin ID p8

40. **McNicoll**, Jonet, 1673 also called Jannet for the first time at her trial but also Jonet there and Jonet in 1662, confession and baptism in Mary Moore's house, was executed after escape and return in 1673; met copper faced man and a young well favoured man; the former stated to be the evil spirit who asked her 'to go with him'; this may be a transposition by the recorder, since 3 others refer to the latter as the devil; mentions the devil 'conveyed her be the left arm' ID p13 and that the young man lifted her out of the burn (Balskyte burn which enters the harbour beside the Quay) and conveyed her to the foot of the broad wasst (probably the shore around the Lade where it enters the Bay). Attended meeting at Bute Quay on Hallowday. Delated by Jonet Hugin, Robt Walleis' wife who said Prestoun the slater told her she had damned those who wronged her.

41. **McNicoll**, Issobell, confession and baptism in her own house, the devil came to her as a young man who 'desired her to go with him'. ID p12. A month later she met the devil at night outside her back door and spoke with him. A month later there was a further meeting with the devil and conversation. Attended meeting at Bute Quay or Craigandow on Hallowday with the devil. ID p28 delated by Jonet Glas, Margaret Glas and Margaret Galy; child died; delated ID p26 by Jonet Morisone for having red clay said to be witchcraft. Delated by McLevin ID p8 as witch (different spelling). Spouse of John McKirdy [RothesayKSRecords p42]

42. **McNive**n, Alester, 1662 ID p28 [delated by Issobell More McKaw]

43. **McNiven**, Mary, 1662, [daughter of Marione Frissell ID p28, delated by Jonet McIlmertine]

44. **McPhee**, James, 1670 [Kerrycresach, father of John and Hector]
45. **McThomas**, Mary, 1673 charming and incest, executed with Jonet McNicoll. Justiciary Record of Argyll and the Isles 12a 16.10.1673
46. **McWilliam**, Margaret, 1662 [of Chapelton and Corsmore, aka McCuilem]; should have been executed or died in prison, given her confession of covenant and baptism ID p18 dated 1635 between Jan and May; she is taken to be the worst offender in other people's confessions, according to the Inverary Document[150], at least; delated by Jonet Morisone, ID p26 wronged by witchcraft Donald McGilchrist, laid a pock of witchcraft in his house, nothing went well for him; ID p25 killed by witchcraft a cow of Neil McNeill's; took or meant to take the milk of a cow of Mr John Stewart; took by witchcraft Alister McNiven's life; ID p24; took by witchcraft Adam Kerr's life by laying cantraips in the burn when the millstone was to be drawn; shot to death William Stephen. First met the devil in the winter of 1634 at Corsmore, covenant in 1635 at Corsmore, met devil in 1644 at Chapelton, who gave her an elf arrow stone with which she shot her son William 10 days later. Attended a meeting at Kilmory for dancing in October 1661 ID p19, Also present John Galy, and wife, Elspeth Gray, Agnes [blank] in Gortans, and McNeill her daughter in law, M. McLevin, Jonet [blank] Issobell {?} Margrat and Jonet McNeill's {?} Elspeth Spence and her own daughter, McIlmertine, Patrick Muck's wife and Issobell and Marie McKaw; and McIlduy Donald McKeresches wife [blank] McLevin, McVicar's wife. Elspeth Stewart and [probably] (Jonet) McNicoll 'fell at the flash' i.e. fell at a burn (probably the Balskyte near the harbour at Bute Quay). McWilliam was tried for the mark and 3 marks were found ID 17. ID 18: said of her that she never fought or fell out with someone but that person came to harm. Delated by Jonet Stewart [Ambrisbeg] ID p17 that she and her two daughters were shearing rushes in Ambrisbeg Bog [The Quien Loch probably] when Jonet and her husband hindered them from taking rushes. Revenge promised. Jonet, being with child, was upset for a while, took her pains and was 20 days in labour. All their cows died suddenly and nothing went well for them. ID p16 Major Ramsay delated McWilliam for taking his cows milk and when he complained giving it back again. Delated by Jonet Stewart ID p16 when Alester McNiven was lying sick lifting her curchief and saying 'devil never let him rise.' He died. Delated by Agnes McGilchrist wife of Alester McNiven ID p15 who threatened to poynd Katherine Moore, McWilliam's daughter, for malt silver owed him, he took an unnatural disease on the way home which lasted 3 days in agony. She asked McWilliam to take off the witchcraft. When she got home he was well. Two years later, when McNiven was poynding for the common maills, McWilliam and Katherine tied him to a post ID p15 till John Moore released him. McWilliam said she would kill his wife. When he got home he took sick and eventually died. His wife Agnes was also sick. When she asked McWilliam to see her husband she refused. John McFie ID p14 said that McWilliam denied his family passage across her fields when he was moving from Kerrycresach to Lochly. McWilliam fought him and his family, the horse fell down and would not move and John took an unnatural sickness which lasted 3 months. Also against her ID p14: Always known as a witch; delated in 1631 by witches who died in the Castle dungeon at Rothesay; 1645 delated, nothing proved. But the evils she threatens come to pass, the crimes delated and ill repute among neighbours. Tried for the mark in 1649 and several found but no action taken due to the confusion of the times. Delated by McLevin for witching Donald McGilchrist ID p8 with Katherine; that they

---

[150] Printed in Highland Papers volume III

bound Alexander McNiven to a post and witched him till he died.; that they put witchcraft under Mr John Stewart, minister's bed about Hallowday 1661. Delated by Major Ramsay ID p1, reported by Robt Stewart [probably of Mecknoch, an elder]: when his cows gave no milk he threatened to burn her and she told him to go home and he would find his cows milk restored. On his return he found this was so. Also, in 1660, Jonet Morisone came to Robt Stewart's house to get some gear promised her by his wife. When refused some of this, Jonet Morison threatened his wife and within 3 months she felt something strike her when she was in the byre and still complains of this. She blames Jonet Morisone.

47. **McWilliam**, Elspeth, 1662 [2nd daughter of Margaret] took (with others) by witchcraft Adam Kerr's life.

48. **Moore**, Katherine, 1662, daughter of Margaret McWilliam [witch's mark found, probably died in prison: would have been executed for sure otherwise; delated by Jonet Morisone ID p26 for speaking to the devil who asked why her husband was absent: he was child minding; member of company who set out to kill John Glas the provost; delated by Jonet Morisone, ID p26 wronged by witchcraft Donald McGilchrist, laid a pock of witchcraft in his house, nothing went well for him; ID p25 killed by witchcraft a cow of Neil McNeill's; took or meant to take the milk of a cow of Mr John Stewart; took by witchcraft Alister McNiven's life; Took by witchcraft Adam Kerr's life by laying cantraips in the burn when the millstone was to be drawn ID p24; shot to death William Stephen. Aug 1661 delated by Jonet Boyd ID p19 who, being with child, dreamed that Kath Moore took a nip out of her breast and her milk was gone and the place of the nip was blue. Told Kath Moore and asked to give it back. It soon returned. Delated by Jonet Stewart, Ambrisbeg for malefice ID p17: caused a 20 day birth labour and all their cows died for hindering the cutting of rushes. Delated ID p16 by Donald McGilchrist, Town Clerk, for unfairly unlawing McCartur for the theft of a coat and burning his house in revenge with her mother. Delated by McLevin ID p8 for putting witchcraft in Mr John Stewart's house at Kingarth ie pre 1659 which caused the death of his wife.

49. **Moore**, Elspeth, 1662. ID P18. [McWilliam's daughter] Delated by McConnochie, Neil McNeill and John Allane who refused to plough land of McWilliam's. They saw Elspeth Moore on the ground going several times about.

50. **Moore**, William ID p16. Delated by Donald McGilchrist, Town Clerk, for burning his house and that nothing thrived for him after Moore complained with McWilliam that McCartur was unlawed for theft.

51. **Moore**, Margaret, 1649

52. **Morison(e),** Jonet, 1662, definitely executed or died in prison, given confession: covenant and baptism, first met the devil on 17.10.1661 ID p21 and made covenant 25.10.1661 ID p22; confessed healing with herbs the daughter of McPerson, Keretonle and Patrick Glass; and Alester Bannatyne; the last pair had been blasted by the fairies. First service for the devil stated to be to bring home Adam Kerr and replace Ninian Kerr by him by shooting the latter ID p22; gathered herbs to heal Patrick Glass's daughter !! ID p23 devil desired her to take the life of John Glass provost's dun horse and 'put him' for Wm Stephen which she refused. Devil desired her to shoot Walter Stewart, Baillie; confessed that the fairies took the life of John Glass's child. Asked devil ID p23 where he was going with a great company who replied; to seek a prey. Heard voices ID p21: at the Lochtie, voice forbade her to go home but drown herself; and then it said do not go home; then near the deck of the Gortans a stalk of heather told her not to go home but believe in me; heard voice of Adam Kerr ID p21 asking to be let into her house; seeing a

great number of people come from Kilmory a naked man with a great black head bid her go with him to the Knockane; met the devil at the Knockanrioch (may be same place, abbreviated). Delated by Jonet McNicoll ID 13 for attending meeting at Bute Quay. Delated by Nans Mitchell reported by Robert Stewart [probably of Kilwhinleck, near Kilmory who was an elder] ID p1who dreamt of Jonet Morison and within half an hour her child took an unnatural disease of which he died. Jonet Morison said it was twice shot and could not be healed.

53. **Nicoll**, Jonet, 1662, [might be Jonet McNicol; assume different] ID p4, delated by Janet Huggin who says Preston [slater] told her that she (JM) had wronged her (JH) children

54. **Spence**, Elspeth, 1662 ID p26 delated by Jonet Morisone for being late for a witches meeting, as one witch said to the devil; also put a pock of witchcraft in the back room of Patrick Glas. Delated by Jonet McNicoll IDp13 for attending the meeting at Bute Quay on Hallowday who also describes her as Patrick Glass's wife. **Contradiction**: why would she put witchcraft in her husband's house? ie her own house? Not impossible, alas: maybe she wanted rid of him or to get back at him.

55. **Spence**, daughter of Elspeth, delated ID p19 by McWilliam.

56. **Stewart**, daughter of black Heu, 1662

57. **Stewart**, Katherine, 1662 [Largizean] incorrectly listed earlier in the data base. Delated by McLevin ID p8 as 'a great witch' attended all meetings who at Corsmore carrying a corpse on a beirtree 'lifted a young man who fell under the beirtree and there was nothing but the stock of the tree.'

58. **Stewart**, Jeane, 1662 ID p30 [sent to charm a cow; delated by John Allane; refused by Kat McPhune; a cow of hers died immediately after]

59. **Stewart**, Marie, 1662 [mother of Neil McLachlan in Kilbride] ID p10, delated by McLevin as a great witch who attended nearly every meeting..

60. **Unknown**, Agnes, 1662 [Gortans farm] McNeill her daughter in law, delated by McWilliam ID p19.

In addition in ID there is mention of others unnamed, some of whom would already be on this list.

Of these, Only 5 are delated at times different from 1662. Jonet McNicol should count for 1662 also, having escaped before conviction. This list excludes the persons imprisoned in the Castle dungeon in 1630 or thereby, as recorded, without names. Another five or six are likely, then. And these are believed to have died there without trial. Two of those listed should not be counted. Note: of the 51 accused in 1662, one [McKeraish] lived outside Bute in Argyll. It follows that about 10 witches were accused in years other than 1662, of whom about half died in prison. 49 were accused in 1662, of whom 4 were executed then and 2 others in 1673. Though only 6 are known to have been executed, half a dozen in 1630 and an unknown number in 1662 died in prison. Given the very serious charges against many of them—being party to murders— it is likely that confessions were tortured out of far more of them, the records having been lost. Since in ID 6 are listed as confessing covenant and baptism with the devil, at least one other must have died in prison for sure. Once a confession had been recorded it could never be taken back or disbelieved by the Session men. If the murders were believed then anyone associated was likely to be executed. Since about 24 people are mentioned as present and therefore involved, this suggests that up to 18 might have died in prison since they are not listed as having been executed. In the reconstruction it is taken that the charges of murder were made by two psychotic women who were exposed as slanderers, one of whom, Jonet Morison, had indeed, already recently been found guilty of slander. If this be so, these 18 may have walked free. Yet even so, some may still have died in prison during the many months there on starvation rations, insanitary conditions of distress and torture.

(ii) Witches 'confessions': The Document in Inverary [151] with commentary and analysis

What follows is the full text of a document 'preserved in the Charter Room at Inverary: a thin unbound quarto volume which has been used for the purpose of informally recording matters connected with certain charges of witchcraft in Rothesay in 1662. It bears no title and there is nothing by which the writer can be identified. Many words have become illegible, but otherwise the MS. has been transcribed verbatim, and the transcript has most kindly been placed at the disposal of the [History] Society by his Grace the Duke of Argyll.'

Thus says the introductory note. In fact, more can be said about the provenance of the document. It has been written by more than one writer, almost certainly one of those stated to be present, and most often the minister, Rev Master John Stewart ['Mr.' is short for Master and only graduates are allowed this style then]. Many of the names mentioned are names of people living in Bute in 1662, as the Parish records confirm. The places mentioned can also be identified. E.g. Major Ramsey lived at Roseland, a hill to the east of Rothesay. Margaret McWilliam, one of the witches who must have been executed, lived at Corsmore, a place close to Little Grenach farm and Lochly [Lochend], which eventually became Crossmore, with application of metathesis: 'unchristened bairn' becoming in burns poem Tam o'Shanter: 'unchirstened bairn' in some versions, at least; as well as Chapelton.

How did this document get into the Charter Room at Inverary? The Duke of Argyll was executed for treason in Edinburgh in 1661. His heir, who had been an active supporter of the royalists against the ruling Parliamentarians in Westminster, after the success of Cromwell's troops against the Scots at Dunbar and thereafter, never did assume the title 'Duke' and was himself executed in 1685 after a further rebellion. That man, the Earl of Argyll, presided over a court in Rothesay in 1673 at which Jonet McNicol, who had escaped from the Tolbooth in Rothesay in 1662, just before her proposed execution, and had been apprehended on her return to Bute 12 years later, was again tried for witchcraft and finally executed. At that trial, in 1673, the notes made for the trial of 1662 would have been made available to the prosecution and would have found their way to the Chief Magistrate: the Earl of Argyll, who, after the trial, would have taken them back to Inverary where he would have deposited them in the Charter Room.

What we have in this document are the notes made in January to March 1662, the dittays, as they are called: statements written down by an observer to the investigation, maybe by the investigator himself, as being what the person investigated is taken to have said or otherwise assented to, not quite the same thing.

---

[151] Published 1920 by the Scottish History Society, Second Series Volume XX; Highland Papers III

Were these made under duress? Almost certainly [yet one interview was at the woman's house and at her request: Jonet Morrison]. The fact that one of the accused women, Margaret McWilliam is reported as having been examined for the witches mark— which was found: a blue mark on her thigh— tells us that the same level of sophistication was probably engaged here in the interrogations in Bute as is found in other places like Forfar and Haddington. If so, it is likely that accused persons were subjected to torture in some form: ducking in the lade or a pond: if the accused floated she was deemed guilty, being held up by the devil; if she sank, as was expected, she was innocent and could be pulled out and revived— at least in theory! The general principle employed was: if something unexpected happens it is because the devil has taken a hand in the matter to defend his subject. Another form of torture was applying thumbscrews or other painful instruments to extract confessions. A further torture, the most insidious of all, was sleep deprivation: deprived of sleep, an accused person could be got to agree to almost anything suggested—if only she were allowed to get back to sleep. What was suggested, therefore, by the interrogator could easily be assented to by the accused, which means that the events described in the dittays could be, at least to some extent, dependent upon the imagination of the interrogator.

That then, is the main difficulty: what is correct in the dittays and what is false; what is assented to only because otherwise the torture will continue and what is the fact of the matter?

At this distance of 4 centuries we are unlikely to be able to estimate every paragraph of 'evidence' accurately. Yet, the task of sifting the truth from the invention (if any) is not quite impossible. There are other documents such as the Town Council Records and the Kirk Session Records which are revealing about the persons mentioned, some of them. There are descriptions of events occurring in places that can be determined very exactly as occurring in particular parts of the island.

In a previous work, Bannockburn Revealed, the idea of a 'close analysis' was invoked: the full text plus commentary, internal cross referencing and, where suitable, an inventory of statements pro and con an issue. This procedure was found to be invaluable: it made it possible to disprove several mistaken notions about the battle believed for centuries as well as to expose some very remarkable errors of an elementary kind made by some of our most eminent historians.

This, or more probably, an advance upon this, will be tried here.

The text will be in standard print, the commentary, full of insights, it is hoped, will be in italics. Everything not italic will be the document and it will be here in full. That is, remove the commentary which is in italics and you have the original document, verbatim. Observe that a few notes are included by the then Duke of Argyll and these are included carefully but not italicised. Anything in italics is a comment made by the present writer; anything else is part of the document as given by the Duke of Argyll. Spellings by the authors of the document are not consistent, so care has to be exercised in making inferences therefrom. At this period, there was no standard spelling and the same author might well use different spellings of the same word. As far as possible, given the limits of printing, every space and character has been preserved carefully.

There might be other documents than this one which have not survived, just as the Kirk Session Records for 1662 have not survived: been destroyed most probably by people who stood to lose by their preservation. Both the heads of the house of Bannatyne and Stewart at this period might have suffered loss had these records been preserved. Only 40 years later, both were elevated to the peerage— events that might have been impossible had there been evidence of involvement in witchcraft by any members of the families or, just as bad, in their prosecution, especially as by 1700 doubts were being expressed about the validity of the witch hunts. Peers of the realm probably had to come from families which had no stain upon the escutcheon.

In this case, there are blanks in the text due to the faded handwriting which are shown by dots or blanks. The hope is that analysis will tell us important facts about these trials. The reconstruction here too, by providing an imagined account of the events, might also add to our understanding, which is why, unusually, both have been combined here in a single work.

As we will see, this documents covers the period January 16th 1662 up to March 26th 1662 and maybe beyond. The executions seem to have taken place on 5th May 1662.

THE INVERARY DOCUMENT [as in Highlands Papers Vol 3]
I

WITCHCRAFT IN BUTE, 1662[152]

DECLARATION Robert Stewart the 16 January 1662. [*Had this been Robert Stewart of Scarrell it would have been addressed; Master Robert Stewart of Scarrell, or merely, Master Robert Stewart. Master meant having a university degree: Master of Arts. The form Mr. is a development of this. Those without a degree were addressed without this title. Therefore this Robert Stewart is not a graduate but probably the farmer of Mecknoch, for he is one of the elders of the Kirk in Rothesay, as the parish records tell us. It may even be his own writing.*]

of Jonet Morisone.

Declares that about twa yeirs sine ther fell a contest betwixt..... and Jonat Morisoun who came to his spouse to seek some quhat geir she aleged she promised her. [*This is not the style of the minister, also a graduate, as will be seen. This writing is by an elder, probably, who has far less education: the first name is changed and he does not see the difference, for example*] Quhen his wife said to her that she would get a peek [*peck*] or two, if she serve not some as she desyred, the said Jonet said I garne to have it and I will garr yow rue it or it be longer; and within a quarter of ane yeir ther after the said Glen's wife [*which fills in the blanks above: someone named Glen*] as she was going in the byre felt something strik her there; the whole house darkened which continued a long space with her, she still compleins that is was Jonet Morison that did it. [*Here we have a typical response by a credulous person: there is an argument, people get angry; one of them later suffers a mild stroke or even just a momentary disfunction due to being upset by the conflict and because the experience is unusual, it is a taken to be related to witch-like action by the other party. Indeed, it may just be that Jonat Morison came by months later and threw a stone at the back of Mrs Glen and struck her. If so, it is hardly witchcraft; merely an aggressive response to conflict.*]

---

[152] Copied from the original in the Argyll Charter Chest. Many words have become faded away, otherwise verbatim.—ARGYLL.[Note: The Duke's remark cannot be taken for granted. There are likely to be a few errors in transcription. The document could be examined by experts with modern techniques.]

of Jonet Morisone.

Nans. Mitchell declares that <u>about two years syne</u> she took a dreaming of <u>Jonet Morisone</u> in her bed in the night, and was afrighted therewith and, within half ane hour after wakning, her young child took a trembling a very unnaturall lyke disease quhair of he died and Jonet Morisone being desyred to heal the said child said <u>it was twice shot</u> and could not be healed. [*What does the word 'shot' mean? This is going to prove important. It appears elsewhere spoken by others. It can mean shot with a weapon as will be seen. But it may just be an act of malefice: a cursing, a pointing of the finger with dire predictions of doom upon the recipient, for it was taken, at that time, that some people had the power to bring about appalling consequences to others without any other occurrence than the application of the will to do so. To say: 'You will suffer pain, or die soon' was taken to be a sentence, at least when some people uttered it. They seemed to have earned a track record of success brought about by mere coincidence but not always, as we will discover: the desired outcome could be arranged by subtle means.*]

Notice that there is nothing very remarkable in these accusations. They seem innocent enough. But these are merely the beginning. They become increasingly disastrous. Why were such statements taken down at all? What we have just seen is the first visible sign of the witch hunt to follow. What prompted them? It may be that the recent effects of Robert Stewart of Scarrell's disgrace, humiliation and subsequent ostracism where, perhaps, he is taken up by the witches and others on the fringes of the community and the increase in witch activity arising because they now have a powerful leader, one at least with money and education and standing— that this alone prompts Robert Stewart of Mecknoch's testimony. As an elder, he is worried about the effect on the community. He has a duty to watch out for any form of deviation from what the Kirk Session demands in the congregation. All it would take is for him to see people meeting on the moor above Kilmory [Mecknoch is the farm next to Kilmory to the south] where indeed, we are told they do meet, to wonder if it was for a bad purpose. He might have recognised people like Margaret McWilliam as a witch, which she was already by reputation. Enough that she was present. He would conclude that the meeting was for no good purpose and, outside the auspices of the Kirk, that was inevitable. And yet his 'evidence' is about Jonet Morison so far. Maybe he saw her first. His next remarks are about McWilliam]

About McWilliam[153]

Major Ramsey declares [*This is still Robert Stewart giving evidence, maybe writing: heresay evidence, then*] that upon a tyme quhen he duelt [*dwelled*] in the Rosland that his ky [*cows*] gert no milk and suspecting that it was McWilliam, who was bruted for a witch and being his neighbour, he cam to her and upbradded her and said to her give my ky ther milk agane or Ill burn thee myselfe and she said to him goe your wayis home and if ye wait Ill be giffened yow, and upon his returne the ky gave their milk.

---

[153] In the document the 'Mc' appears as 'Nc', the custom of the time; the only change made in transcription to avoid confusion.

[typical: what could she do to give the cows their milk? Nothing. Presuming that he is going home straight away which may not be so. That they are found to have milk again is coincidence, then. Why did she say this? Because she believed that she could have an effect. It is not absolutely impossible that she did not. She may even have known enough to realise that the effects upon the cows which she had provoked with a herb were due to cease]

Of Katherin Moore.

[This is still Robert Stewart reporting hearsay evidence. Katherine Moore is Margaret McWilliam's daughter. Katherine has a son, John Moore, and a sister, Elspeth.]

Memorandum. Mclevin sayes that Finley Gelie and Donald Gelie in *[blank]* saw Katherine Moore and her sone feiding twa halked ky at Glenbeg and that immediately they vanished out of sight. [*Maybe they had stolen them and did not want to be seen and moved out of sight rapidly to avoid being seen. Several explanations of this are possible.*]

That is is the end of Robert Stewart's hearsay evidence, which, as an elder, he has a duty to lay before the minister, if it is deemed to contravene the norms as understood by the Kirk Session. He takes all that as indication of witchcraft. What we have next is a series of interrogations by members of the Session, one accused person at a time being questioned.

Declaration Margaret Mclevin the 20th January 1662, immediately after she was apprehended, before Mr. Johne Stewart minister, John Glasse provost, Ninian Banatyne of Kames, Mr James Stewart. *[the latter is probably Sir James Stewart, for he is also probably a graduate and he appears frequently. Conceivably the writer thought his degree more important than his title, hence the mistake; yet it might be another James Stewart altogether, a graduate without a title. Sir James's eldest son was Dougall. An advocate called James Stewart lived at Ascog, probably related to Sir James.]*

<u>Quhilk day</u> [*which day*] she confessed that she had the charme for an evill eye and that she did severall tymes charme both men and Beasts therewith and that it proved effectuall and did good to any she applyed it. Item that she charmt therewith about midsummer last a calfe of Allan McConaghyes in Ballenlay which charme shee repeited in Yrish [*Gaelic*] and that she put it in watter or in a curchif [*kerchief*] or some such lyke.

[This would be about enough to see her burnt at the stake in those times of vicious punishment for trifles. People were put to death for charming.]

Johne McFersoune[154] declares that about three yeires since [he] went in a good day In Robert Clerks boat In Company with James Cuninghame. Johne McKinlay and William

---

[154] This is an exception: McFersoune and not NcFersoune as most mac names are. Mc is the male equivalent of Nc for women.

APPENDICES

Gillespie out of the toune of Boot to Rownieheirine at the back of Arran and there haveing cast out thair anker waiting their opportunitie to makcoast of Ireland there arose sudenly a mightie great storme quhich continued the mater of three or four hours ther after it calmed and they went for Ireland. At the said John McFerson's returne from Ireland within seven or eight weeks therafter being sitting at John McIntalar's fire side besid Margrat McLevin the said Margrat did say unto him, give me some thing Johne for ye are in my common [*obliged to me*], who said how or quhat way am I in your common? She said remember in the night ye redde [*rowed,, sailed*] at the back of Arran ye may acknowledge your self in my common. I remember of that said John and will alse long as I live bot how am I in your common for that? She answered I helped you that night quhich if I had not done ye had gone to parteins [*pieces? the ship broken to bits*] and become lost[155].

Declaration Margaret McLevin 27 January 1662 before James Stewart of Auchinlick and Mr. John Stewart minister.

Quhilk day she confessed that she had ane charme for wristing or brising quhilk she repeitted in the yrish language begineing Obi er bhrachaadh etc. Quhilk proved effectuall to all such as she applyed it to and that she layd the charme in tallow or herbs and applyed it. Item that she charmed John Mctyre the taylor therewith that hade ane sore shoulder. Item confesses that she applyed the said charme of ane evill ey to some fishermen and particularly to one.....Mcintaggart that came home sick to Ballicurrye. Item confesses that she he's another charme which is good for preserveing from mischance quhilk she repeited in the yrish language. [*What we have here is more good witch practice; but wait.*]

January 28, 1662.

Confessed Margret McLevine befor thir witnesses John Glasse provest, Niniane Ballantyne of Kames, Major David Ramsay, Walter Stewart bailie.

That being in a litle chamber in Balichtarach the devill came to her **in the lyknes of a man [*Dm1*]** and deseired hir to goe with him and that she refusing he said I will not.....and she gave him.... she never saw afterward and that she knew it was the devill and after he went that he came bak and asked hir to give him hir hand quhich she refusing to doe he took hir by the midle finger of the rycht hand quhich he had almost cutt off hir and therewith left hir. Her finger was so sorely pained for the space of a month ther after that ther was no paine comparable to it, as also took her by the right leg quhich was sorly pained likewayes as also be the devill. Item he came to her againe as she was shaking straw in the barne of Ardroscidell in a very ugly shape [*he made here be so described because he is now taken to be the devil*] and that there he desired hir to goe with him and she refusing he said to her I will either have thy self or then thy heart. Item that he healed her sore foot and finger quhich finger is yet be nummed. Item that befor he haled her that she made a covenant with him and promised to doe him any service that he would imploy her in. Item that he asked quhat was her name. She answered him Margret the name that God gave me, and he said to her I baptise the Jonat. [*These admissions should certainly have brought about her execution*]. Item that she met

---

[155] I.e. have become food for crabs. [Argyll's footnote: he should have known]

with him a third tyme. Item that he imployed hir in a piece of service about three yeirs since quhen Robert Clarks boat was going to Irland quhair in was John McFerson and William Gillespie and other two quhom she remembered not of and the devill haveing a desing [*design*] to destroy them and the boat did cary hir under his auxter unto the bake of Inchmernoch[156] quhair the said boat was sailing to Arran to the end that she might droun the said boat by putting in hir hand betwine the two boards of the boat and by pulling the mast out of the root and flinging it over, but the same was prevenied by God who turned the boat upon another course, yet albeit the same did not harme there was a storme raised quhich followed the said boat a space. Item confesses that its foure yeirs since she entered in his service [*1658: which implies that Robert Stewart of Scarrell, if he was the person, afterwards taken to be the devil, was up to no good before his disgrace with Nancy Throws which occurs in 1661*] Item at the dival's command she had a purpose to droun the boat that John Moore went in to Lochfine with and quhen the boat loused from Illa McNeill she went to the shore side and raised a storme by casting a stane in the sea. [*coincidence again*] Item that quhen the devill broucht hir bake from InchMernoch she being disapointed of drouning the boat that John McFerson was in he did let her fall out of his auxter (as she thought) in the midst of the sea yet it was not so but upon a rocke beside the seashore under Balicharach and that she was so creesd [*sic*] that she was not able to stir till another woman whose name she cannot remember drew her off the rocke it being about 12 hours of the day. Item confesses that at that tyme quhich Jonet Morisone mentioned[157] she met the divell and **a great company** with him about three nights before hallow day,[158] that she saw the samine also as she was coming from Ardbeg to the toun and that they stood in a knot at the foot of the fauld they went away very swiftly. Item declairs that ther irrand was to doe harme to Mr. John Stewart minister and to John Glasse proveist and that they have a great pick at them, also declairs that the very last meiting that ever she was at that Margret McCuillem [*McWilliam*] and her daughter Ket [*Katherine Moore*] said that they wold be about with the saids persons. Item confesses that McCuillem and her daughter did vitch [*witch*] Donald McGilchrist that nothing did thrive with him and that they put a pock of witchcraft under his bed and a catt to effectuat the samine and that their quarrell against him was that the said Kathrine stole a bairns coat from Donald McGilchrist which was fund with hir.

Item that the saids persons wronged Jonat McConachie his wife, Cirstine Ballantyne, Margaret McNickell, Jonat McNickell, Jonat McNeill and hir goodams bairnes were witches and that she saw them at meitings.

Item that Margaret McCuillem [*McWilliam*} and hir daughter Kathrine did witch Alexander McNeiven and bind him to a post till he died.

Item that Margaret McCuillem and hir daughter Kathrine did put witchcraft about hallowday last under Mr. John Stewart minister his bed.

Item that about a yeir or two since whe (sic) was at a meeting at Corsmore quhair there was a great number and that they were carrying a corps on a beirtreee and that a young man fell under the beirtree and that Katherine Largizean lifted him and there was nothing but the stock of a tree. Item that the said Katherine was a great witch and was at all meitings.

---

[156] A small island off Bute: Inchmarnock
[157] Clear evidence that the witches can hear each other's stories, as expected in a small wooden jail with a few cells. Morison's statement is in ID p24
[158] All Saint's Day

APPENDICES 259

Item that Annie Heyman at the bay head on hir ordinarily to be their maiden and that **she danced ordinarily in the midst of them**.

Item Mcillmartine Patrick Na Muck's wife and Kathrine frissell (sic) were witches and at meitings.

Item a daughter of Alexander McillMartins in Kelspoge being a young lasse blake haired broad faced mirry disposed was maiden at a meitings.

Item that at a voyage they went to Scoulag side and took the life of a child of [blank] McCurdie and that their maiden there was [blank] Ballantyne (*probably Kirstine*) with the one hand and that at that meiting she saw Donald McCartour in the rer of the company carrying flesh on his bak. Item that Kathrine Moore and [blank] did put witchcraft in Mr. John Stewart's house quhen he dwelt in Kingarth quhich occasioned the sickness and death of his wife and was set for himself also but God gave them not the liberty.

Item declares that Mcallen is a witch and elspeth....[illegible]

Declaration McLevine the 28 day of January 1662 before Mr. John Stewart and Alexander Mcintyre (sic).

That she used the charme quhich keeps fcrom mischance quhich sche repeited in Irish to severals and that they were not the worse of it quhich charme begineth thus er brid na bachil duin etc. Item that she hath a receipt for the disease in childrine called the Glaick quhich she heiles by a herbe called achluiuisge after this manner she takes the child with hir in hir armes to the part quhair the herbe groweth eschewing meiting or speiking with anybody by the way and eshewing (sic) also all high wayes and quhen she comes to the place quhair the herbe is she takes a broch and layes upon the herbe and plucks up the samin throw the broch in the childs name and then brings it home eshewing speiking or meiting with any by the way and seiths it upon the fire without suffering either a dog or a catt or anything to passe betwixt hir and the fire till it be boiled quhair of she administers drink to the child three severall tymes and heales it.

Confession Margret McLevin the 29 January 1662 before Mr. John Stewart minister and John glas [*sic*] Proveist,

Item that she was at a meiting with severall other witches betwixt Kilmacholmac and Edinmore [*on the road west from Wester Kames, on the side of the hill above or thereby*] and in the said meiting Patrick McKaw in Tonaghuil [*Dunagoil farm*] was there and that he and all of them went up through the moores to Elanshemaroke and there the said Patrick McKaw **shot** [S2] a bearne of Donald roie McKerdie who dwelt there. Item she declared that she was at another meiting at Crosmore [*Margaret McWilliam's home*] about this time twel month at quhich meiting Kathrine Stewart good wife of Largizean was Annie heyman, Kathrine Cristell, Mcillmartine, Patrick McKawes wife, Isobell More McKaw; James Frissells wife, Katharine Moore [*Margaret McWilliam's daughter*] and her eldest sonne and Margaret McWilliam and that they went to Birgidale broch and in a window Margaret McWilliam **shot** [S3] James Androws son and that Marie More McCuill was appointed by them to take away the body and leave the stoke of a tree [*It is already clear from the word 'body' that really these two cases are shooting, probably by a musket*] in his place quhich she gat nocht done, she not being so skilful as she sould have been. Item she declared that she was with another meiting with Margrat

McWilliam, Kathrine Moore and Donald Mccartour with several others and that Donald Mccartour had a piece of the several bits of flesh upon his shoulder quhich they were to put in the place of Elspa Kelso sister to Donald Kelso who was then servant to Kathrine Mcillmoon and declared that she not being so able to hold fit with them, they went away and she knew not how they lost their prey. [*The child was the prey, he has been dismembered*] Item she declared that she was at another meiting at Hallowday last betwixt Mikell Kilmorie and Killeferne and at that meiting Margret McWilliam Kathrine Moore, John **Gely in Barmore and his wife and severall others were at a dance there** and was purposed to **shoot** [S4] one of Robert More McKemies bearnis (haveing taken two of them before) [*!!*] [S5, S6] but was disappointed that night and then came down to the tounward be Ardbeg and that Margret McWilliam and Kathrine Moore had a purpose to put a pock of witchcraft [*this could be almost any small collection of simple articles like rabbit bones, frogs, twigs etc over which a spell, perhaps, had been said*] under Mr John Stewart minister his bed and another pock with witchcraftis in John Glasses stable quhich she knew was done. Item she declared that in hervest last she was at a meiting in Lochfine with Donald Mccartour Kathrine Moore and a wife out of Kildavanane and Soirle Mcallesters midmost sone and severall other heiland people there (quhich she knew not) and one McKeraish out of Glendaroil [*Glendaruel*] (as she thought) quho was on a fisher boat and that the said McKeraish **shot** [S7] Robert McKomash after dinner being sitting on the craft.

Item she declars that Marie Stewart mother to Neil McLachlane in Kilbride [blank] Stewart daughter to black Heug are great witches and was at severall meitings and that John Gely in Barmore and Patrick McKaw in Tongaheill [*Dunagoil: spelling was not an exact science: one could experiment*] and their wifes are for the most part at every meitings.

Item she declard all her former declarations to be of truth.

Item she declard farder that Kirstine Ballantyne and Jonat McNeill her good daughter and all the saidis Jonats gooddam bearns were all witches and particularly Soirle Mcallexanders wife.

Confession Margrat Mclevin february 2 [1662] before John Glas proveist Mr. John Stewart minister and Ninian Allane.

Quhilk day declared that Margrat McWilliam [blank] Stewart in Arran [blank] McKaw More his wife the witch and [blank] her dochter with diverse others went on a woyag from Corsmore overseas to Kerriemorrie in Kingarth and ther killed a bairne of Donald Moir McKawes and laid by witchcraft a disease upon Donald Mores wife and that for effectuating heirof they took a boy out of Patrick Glas house being a coosine of his and that it was the said boy that shot the child And after they came home to Corsmore to William Moores house that they got to their supper eggs. Item that it was McWilliam and John Mcfie falling at variance for breaking the slap of a dyk at Corsmorre and fighting together the said McWilliam did by witchcraft lay a heivy disease on the said John about the midle of hervest and that John McPhee's wife came to the said Margrat Mclevin who then dualt [*dwelt*] at Knokankamis and desyred her to com sie her husband and help him if she could doe him any good and that as she was goeing in at the dore she mett McCullem [*McWilliam*] beg the witch, comeing out after the aplyeing of some herbs to him and that she herself came home again but that it was McCullem beg [*the larger McWilliam*] the witch that hailed [*healed*] him. Declares that the said McWilliam

APPENDICES 261

went three [*there*] 9 tymes about the house and barne that Neill McNeill dwells in quhen McNilas duelt ther and laid witchcraft in the said house then and that some of the vinume [*venom*] sticks to that house yet. [*'The pock of witchcraft' would be an assemblage of such useful materials as could be found to hand, some of which may have been injurious to health, even without being consumed: we recall that Napoleon died not because his food was deliberately poisoned but because his wallpaper contained large quantities of arsenic. Leaving a lump of such stuff or its equivalent anywhere around the interior of a house would cause trouble to the inhabitants, especially those already old or infirm, like perhaps John Stewart, the minister's wife. Knowledge of plants etc which the witches were famous for, would be the reason for their ability to put down pocks of witchctaft which were effective. Leaving some belladonna (deadly nightshade) around would do a lot of damage if it remained unnoticed*]

John roy Hyndman declares that being at Kilkatten in Johne Hyndmans house before he went to the herring fishing that the said John confessed to him that he hade received a charme and something in a clout to weare about him quhairby she said that he wold further the better with as they were both goeing up to Kilkatten quhich the said John took out of his pouch and cuist [*cast*] from him. Item that she offered the said Johne roy a charme quhilk he refused. Memo. speik to John roy about this.

As we have seen, Margaret McLevin has condemned herself to death by confessing that she made a covenant with the devil in which she promised to do him any service he required. The fresh baptism is a sign of the covenant. Though she may have committed no acts of shooting herself, this is enough. But she has done her share of charming. She has also condemned Jonet Morison for meeting the devil, both Margaret McWilliam and her daughter Katherine Moore for the murder of Alexander McNiven, Patrick McKaw for shooting a child of Donald roie McKerdie, Margaret McWilliam for the murder of James Andrews' son, the attempted murder of another child by several witches already mentioned together with John Gely and his wife, the murder, perhaps by accident, of Robert McKomaish by McKeraish.

According to McLevin, Margaret McWilliam, Katherine Moore, Patrick McKaw, and McKeraish are murderers. And all those who attended the witches meetings such as the Gelys of Barmor— John and his wife Jonat McConachie— Katherine Stewart of Largizean, Annie Heyman, Kirstine Ballantyne, Margaret McNicoll, Jonat McNicoll, Jonat McNeill. McIllmartine and Katherine Frissell are all guilty by association and agreement, some of whom actually assisted such as Donald McArthur, involved in carrying pieces of the flesh.15 persons! Probably, Jonet Morison should be added. Actually, as we shall soon see, she too was at meetings of witches.

By the standards of the time, every one of these deserved to be executed- if this is all true. But is it? Notice that the statement about Jonet Morison tells us that the witches were not all separated all the time and they must have overheard each other's inquisition some times. They would have been held and quizzed and maybe tortured in the Tolbooth of Rothesay and maybe also in the steeple of the Kirk, though all the dittays we possess here suggest interrogation took place only in the Tolbooth. Separating so many would have been difficult. So would feeding so many. That is why, perhaps, having been first apprehended on 18th January 1662, Jonet Morison is able to call the minister to her house on 22nd January 1662 for further disclosures. The construction of the Tolbooth, as with so many houses of the period, is likely to have been wood which means that no matter how incarcerated, the evidence of one person could be overheard by another prisoner.

It is difficult to imagine why children should have been killed by women who themselves had children. Or why so many people went along with this. Our modern value system is revolted by it. Perhaps there was something of value to a witch in the life of a child, for sacrifice, say. These killings of children seem to have this character.

It is also difficult to imagine a set of questions which would produce such a littany of horror. Even a question like: 'Do you know of any witch who took part in the killing of anyone?'

Why would McLevin volunteer all these murders and their victims? Even under torture it seems hard to get these answers. Unless they were correct and volunteered. Moreover, why was there no outcry when these children were found to be shot? Because the bodies were usually taken away for use in ceremonies of some kind? The child reported missing ie disappeared? In 1662, it is likely that people died all the time for every sort of reason and that children did disappear regularly, especially if left alone while their parents foraged for the necessities of life elsewhere. Notice further that since only 5 were executed, some of these statements could not have been believed! Unless every single one of these people not executed, died in prison. What would have happened if one or two had died in prison? Probably better care would be taken of the rest: meaning that no more would die there; but this cannot be guaranteed. Hysteria would have gripped this town and callous things might be done to the aliens in the prison.

Confession Issobell McNicoll upon the 21 februar [1662] before Mr. John Stewart minister, Duncan Mconlea late bayly of Rothesay. She was apprehended upon Tysday (sic) at even and this was upon the friday (sic).

Quhilk day Issobell McNicoll with a great deale of seeming remorse and praying to God to deliver her soule from the power of Satan confessed that as she was in her owne house alone drawing acquavittie [*whisky*] the devill [**Dym2**] came to her in **the lyknes of a young man** and desyred her to goe with him and confesses that she made a covenant with him quhairin he promised that she should not want meanes enough and she promised to be his servand.

[*This is the typical response to meeting the devil.*]

Item that he baptised her and gave her a new name and called her Caterine. [Ther*e are no blanks here. Yet it does seem likely that the services to the devil started immediately with the provision of sex, for this is a feature of similar cases in Fife, for example, where the penis of the devil is usually described as cold as if the devil were different from men in having a penis of this type. In fact, the action is usually performed outside, so of course the penis seems cold. It is very clear that there is no devil as such. If there is any truth whatever in this admission it is that a man did these things and that he was afterwards called by the name 'the devil,' simply because his behaviour was contrary to what was expected and did in some ways conform to that expected of this mythical creature: the devil.*]

APPENDICES 263

Item that <u>about a month therafter **in the night** as she went out at her own back dore she met with the devill and spok with him.</u>
Item that about a moneth therafter the devill came to her againe as she was ther alone brewing with quhom she hade speiches and conference. Item confesses that she was at a meeting with the devill and severall associats about Hallowday last at Cregandow [*At the top of Loch Fyne, maybe*] or Butt key [*Bute Quay, which was then almost immediately opposite the Watergate*]

Confession Jonet McNicoll february 22, 1662, present John Glas proweist, Mr. John Stewart, Robert Stewart leiche [*meaning is unclear: maybe, small stream or mire; may refer to Robert Stewart of Mecknoch, a known elder but may be a different Robert Stewart, distinguished by this word. 'Leech' suggests a surgeon, a man who bled people by applying leeches*], John Campbell being the morne after her taking.

Confesses with remorse praying to God to forgive her sins that about hallowday as she was in Mary Moores house that there appeared to her two men the on(e) a gross copperfaced man and the other **a wele favored young man** [**Dm3**] and that the copperfaced man quhom she knew to be ane evil spirit bade her goe with him. Item confesses that she made a covenant with him and that he promised she wold not want meines eneugh and she promised to serve him and that he gave her a new name saying I baptise the Mary. Item that she confesses that she was at that meitting with the devill at Butt Key [*Bute quay*] about hallowday last (which the other witches makes mention off) quhair ther was a company with hir and as she was comeing over the burne that **the yong man** quhilk spok to her before reached her a cog with watter to drink which as she was taking out of his hand her foot slipped and she fell in the burne and that the said young man lifted her and as she rose the company left her and only **the yong man** abode with her and convoyed her till the foot of the broad waast [*probably waste land near the entry of the water of Fad to the Bay*]

By making a covenant with the devil she had condemned herself to death. Here we have 2 men, one copper faced, the other young and well favoured and she takes the former to be the devil. This contradicts the idea that the devil means: an actual well favoured young man, afterwards taken to be the devil. However, the two may have been transposed in the recording or even by the distressed teller— an important factor in serial transmission of stories as Bartlett's work at Cambridge[159] in the 1930's showed. There is no mention elsewhere of a copper faced man nor is there much likelihood of a coloured man, though, perhaps there was a trade such as dyeing or fish smoking, or tanning which coloured the face. The fact that the confession occurs the morning after her taking tells us that sleep deprivation is not probably a factor. She would be unlikely to say such damning things about herself so quickly without a lot of torture of this or another kind. Recognise that the mindset of the recorder, already in place, after McLevin's confession, puts a spin on what he records.

Confession Jonat McNicoll february 23, 1662. Present Mr. John Stewart minister, Ninian Banatyne of Kames, Robert Wallace and Thomas McKinlay.

---

[159] Bartlett tested undergraduates' ability to report stories. After very few transmissions, transposition of events, dates etc, omissions and inventions to make sense of these was normal, even in very able people. See Ch 6 *Bannockburn Revealed*. The seminal work is 'Remembering' by FC Bartlett, CUP 1932.

Quhilk day she confessed her former declaration in the whole susbstance and tenor thereof viz. her speiches with these 2 men that apeired to her, her covenant with him and her recieving a new name from him and her being at the meitting about Hallowday and further added that she saw at the said meiting Jonet Morisone and Elspeth Spence spouse to Patrick glass. Item that the devil coneyed her be the left arm. [*The significance of which is that there should be a mark on her arm there which could be looked for. Witchprickers were employed to look for the devil's marks on witches with a long needle. If the needle went in without complaint, that meant the devil had marked her in that place. Some people had lumps and marks of several kinds, innocently achieved, some of them birthmarks. The skin was sometimes insensitive there: hence no reaction to the insertion of the needle.*]

Jonet Hugin Robert Walleis wife declares that Prestoun the slater told her that she sedd at her fyresyd (meaning Jonet McNicoll)......those that wronged her gedem [*god damn them*]

23 Feb. 1662. Present Mr.John Stewart, Donald McGilchrist, Duncan McNicoll.

Quhilk day she confessed her former declarations and added further that she saw at that meiting about Hallowday Margrat McWilliam, Christin Banatyne and John Galie in Barmoire.

Proces Margrat McWilliam

1. Since memory of any alive that knew the said Margret she went under the name of a witch.
2. Anno 1631. She was delated be confessing witches who dyed in prison in the Castell of Rothesay.
3. Anno 1645, July 13. Ther was a clame given in against her to the Session of Rothesay accusing her of witchcraft quhairanent the Session concluded nothing but took the same to ther advisment.
4. Anno 1645, January 16. The Session of Rothesay ordained that ane accusation should have beine drawne up against her upon these grundis 1° The evills quhilk she threatened to doe and came to pas. 2° the crimes that were delated and made out against her in the sessions book quhen Mr. John boyle and Mr. John Auld wer clerks to the Session. 3° the ill report and brute she has amongst her nichbouris.
5. Anno 1649. The said Margrat was apprehended for a witch and imprisoned and being tryed the devills merk was found upon her in severall pairts of her body. But throw the confusion of the tymes then she was lett out upon bands.

Presumptions against her.

John Mcfie declares that quhen his father flitted out of Kerecresoch to Lochly [*at the Causeway in Loch Fad, crossing the main road of today, probably along the line of the hedge which ends at Lochly or Lochend*] that his father and Hector his brother and the said John was comeing with three horse load of flittings throw a fald [*field*] of the said Margarets and, comeing to the slap [*field boundary of stones etc or opening made in it*] which they hade casten down before, they found the said slap bigged up [*built up*] and McWilliam lyeing thairupon and his father preasseing to cast downe the slap she resisted him and bigged up as he cast downe and that he and she strugled till they fell and after ryseing the said McWilliam flett [*fought*] with him and came to Hector and pulled the helter [*halter*] out of his hand and turned the horse back from the slap. Item quhen his father brocht his horse over the slap the horse fell doune and lay fro halfe ane hour and could not stir. Item after that within a short space the said John Mcfie took a sudden sicknes quhich keeped him neire a quarter of a yeire which was very unnaturall, <u>lyk a weeman travelling with sicknes</u>, he suspected the said McWilliam to have laid on him. Memo to speek Hector about this. Item a child of his dyed suddenly in 3 or 4 hours space.

Agnes McGilchrist declares that her husband Alester McNevan threatening to poynd Kate Moore McWilliam's dochter fer some malt silver she owed him the said McWilliam said that she would gar him repent it if he wold not tak so much as she hade to give him and mediately as he went home to his owne house that <u>he took a very unnaturall disease lyk a weeman travelling</u> [*notice the same phrase from two different speakers; this means the recorder is responsible*] which agonie he continued three dayes and that her said husband suspecting it was the said McWilliam that laid it on him desyred her to goe to McWilliam and desyre her to come sie him which she did and told McWilliam how her husband was and that he was sorely tormented ever since he threatened to poynd her dochter. The said McWilliam answered ye neid not feare nothing will aile him he will be wele enough and she goeing imediately home she found her husband seased of his sicknes quhom she left in great agonie. [*This is possibly coincidence; yet, maybe McWilliam had given up poisoning him just before; she would want to have them think she was responsible, for having that kind of power was a defence against abuse: you were less likely to be troubled by people who believed you had a talent for vengeance*] Item as she went hom from McWilliams house she imagined she fell in a dub [*a muddy pool*] and was all wett nothwithstanding ther was no watter where she was [*maybe she and her clothing had absorbed all of it*]. Item that about 2 yeires therafter her husband went into her house to poynd for the common maills as he was taking away a seck the said McWilliam and Katt her dochter did tye him fast to a post with the said seck untill John Moore her sone loused him. [*Recall McLevin's statement that these two McWilliam women tied Alester McNiven to a post and killed him thereby; this is an important contradiction in evidence given previously*] Item McWilliam said to him she would gar him repent quhat he hade done and he saying to her quhat can ye doe to me she said Ile slay your wife. Item shortly after his homecoming he took a sicknes quhairby he was pitifully tormented most unnatually till he dyed. [*Evidently she killed the wrong one, if this be true*] and the said Agnes took a very unnaturall sicknes lykwise for a quarter of a yeire and suspected her. Item quhen her husband was lying sick still crying that it was McWilliam that hade witched him the said Agnes his wife came to McWilliam and desyred her to come see him and that now being at poynt of death he might forgive her and she...is he hade wronged her. The said McWilliam said the devill one bit she would goe see him.

Jonet Stewart declares that quhen Alester McNivan was lying sick that Jonet Morisone and McWilliam being in her house the said Jonet desyred McWilliam to goe see the said Allester the said McWilliam lifting up her curcheffe said 'devill let him never be seene till I see him and the devill let him never ryse.'

Major David Ramsay declares that a strik of McWilliams eating corne severall tymes, he bound the said strik and the said McWilliam loused it agane and that therafter his kowes lost ther milk and gave nothing but blood and the said Ramsay haveing fletten [*fought*] with her and saying if she wold not give his kowes thair milk he wold cause burne her [*as a witch*]. She bade him goe home and if he wanted his milk could send him it. Item imediatly his kowes gott ther milk. [*Coincidence? trickery?*]

Item that quhen his kowes came out of thair land and Elspeth McLene keping them she came to the said ky [*cows*] and went severall tymes about the said ky suspitious lyk and at every tyme wold sit downe with the las and then ryse agane and goe about them. This she did [blank] tymes. Interrogate Mclen and Major's wife.

Donald Mcgilchrist causing ryve [*unclear*] McCartur's house for a childs coat that was stoline and the said coat being gotten in that house the said McCarturs was unlawed and imediatly thereafter William Moore and McWilliam came to the said Donald Mcgilchrist and said to him why reckis ye ane unlaw upone McCarthur and shamed us they will not be the worse of it and ye will not be the better and within a fortnight his chamber was brunt and sen thence nothing threave with him quhairof he suspected McWilliam and her dochter Kat.

Item ther being a controversie in the toune court betwixt her and her dochter and the said McWilliam challenging Donald Mcgilchrist that he hade wryten her dochters clame before hers said if he knew quhat all that good bird did yow wold not pitie her.

Jonet Stewart Ambrisbegs wife declares that McWilliam her two dochters and another man haveing shorn some rushes in the bog of Ambrisbeg that she and her husband came to them and hindered them to tak the said rushes being shorne away. The said McWilliam said it were alse [*always*] good to yow to let the rushes gang as to hinder them and her dochter said that she wold repent the hindring them and shortly therafter the said Jonet turned distracted a while and being with child took her panes and was sorely handled being 20 dayes in labour. Item that sensyne [*since then*] she nether bade her haily wele [*wholely well*] and that nothing thrave with them but all ther kowes dyed suddenly.

Margaret McWilliam was tryed for the merk february 7 there was 3 merks fund [*found*], one up her left leg, next hard be the shin bone, another betwixt her shoulders a 3° ane uthyr up her hensh [*haunch, thigh*]. [*These are marks presumed to have been made when the devil handled her.*] Present young Kames John Glas Robert McWilliam [*maybe her husband*] Niniane Allane Quhilk day Kat Moore was tryed,[160] and it was found underenethe her richt shoulder a little whyt unsensible spott. Item being pressed whether she went afield the day that Adam Ker dyed answered that she was at her owne house and went not from home. Item being pressed if she said to Donald Mcgilchrist if she knew quhat her dochter hade done to him he wold not pitie her so much as he did, she denyed that ever she spok such words. Item being posed if she lifted up her curcheffe quhen Jonet Morisone desyred her to goe see Alester McNivan, saying 'god let him never ryse till I goe see him.' The said McWilliam denyed the samen that she nether lifted up her curcheffe nor spok the words. Jonet Stewart Donald Bannatynes wife testifies this part hereof.

Memorandum there it is remarked that she never flett [*fought*] or cast out with other but some harme came to the partie sik as contended with her.

---

[160] For the mark.

APPENDICES

Of Elspeth Moore

Memorandum that Mcconachie, Neill McNeill and John Allane refusing to plew a litle peice land of McWilliams they saw Elspeth Moore her dochter sitting upon the grund and goeing severall tymes about. [*Katherine Moore is definitely a daughter of Margaret McWilliam. We now see that Elspeth Moore is also a daughter of hers, meaning that both she and Katherine have by chance married men called Moore, possibly brothers. There is no more here about this woman who was possibly casting a spell upon the—the implication of the statement. One wonders at the fate of any relatives of a witch burned at the stake as Margaret McWilliam surely was. We have now seen that she is unlikely to have murdered Alister McNiven as stated by McLevin, for his death took place long after his being strapped to a post by the McWilliams. Given that her son William might have been killed in anger or by accident, no matter the description she is alleged to confess to, it may be that she killed nobody. If so, she was just the kind of powerful fiesty woman who would not back down in front of men who expected to impose their will upon her, partly because of her poverty. Her agreement at her being a witch and even flaunting it, arose from a calculation that if this were believed her life would be easier; people would not cross her if they feared reprisals. Many of the witches, so called, would have been in the same category*].

Confession Margrat McWilliam february 14, 1662, before John Glas Proveist and Mr. John Stewart minister.

Item that the yeire before the great Snaw about 28 yeires syne quhen she was duelling [*dwelling*] in Corsmoire [*now called Crossmore in a recent survey of deserted sites*] about Candlemes about 12 hours of the day she went owt to a fald beneath her hous called Faldtombuie[161] and went out of a furz in the mids of the fald ther apeared a a spreit in the lyknes of a litle browne dog and desyred her to goe with it which she refused at first, it followed her downe to the fitt of the fald [*the fields fall towards Loch Fad hereabouts: Corsmore is between Kerrycresach and Lochly, given the tale of the flitting that resulted in the upsetting of McFee's horse etc*] and **apeared in the lyknes of a wele favored yong man** [*Dm4*] and desyred her agane to goe with it and she should want nothing and tyme griped her about the left hench [*haunch; thigh, recall the mark there on her!*] quhich pained her sorely and went away as if it [*the young man*] were a green smoak [*smoke*].

(2) That betwixt and the May therafter she being in a fald above the said house the devill apeired to her first in the lyknes of a catt and speired at her How do ye? will ye not now goe with me and serve me? at which tyme she said she made a covenant with him quhairin she promised to be his servand and he said that she should want for nothing and put his mouth upon the sore and hailled it [*healed it*]. Item that she renounced her baptisme and he baptised her and she gave him a gift of a hen or cock.

(3) That about 18 yeires syne being in a duelling in Chapeltoune [*a deserted settlement on the other side of Loch Fad from Corsmore within the trees: there is little sign of it today; probably it was utterly devastated after the burning of McWilliam; for who would have wanted to live there?*] the devill apeired to her at the back of the Caleyaird and she haveing sustained losse by the death of horse and kye [*evidently she is believed to have*

---

[161] Field of the tombs, perhaps: field with standing stones or gravestones

supernatural control over other people's animals— to take or restore their milk— but cannot save her own] was turneing to great poverty he said unto her [*the young man, we presume]* be not affrayed fro yow shall get ringes eneugh and requiring... he sought her sone William a child of 7 yeires old which she promised to him and he gave her ane elf errow stone to shott him which she did ten dayes therafter that the child dyed imediately therafter which grieved her most of anything that she ever did.

[*These scenes are described in the reconstruction wherein the devil is a young man who, only after a time, is known as the devil, not at the time of the events she describes.]*

(4) That about Hallowday last she was at a Meiting and **danseing upon the hill of Kilmory** with severall other witches and came doune under Broadsyde amongst quhom was John Galy in Barmoire and his wife Elspeth Gray Agnes [blank] in Gortenis [*Gortans*] and McNeill her dochter in law Margrat Mclevin Jonet..... Issobell Margrat and Jonet McNeills Elspeth Spense and her own dochter... Mcilmertine Patrick Mucks wife and Issobell and Marie McKaw. She confesses haveing the charme for ane ill ey quhilk she repeited over in the yrish language but that she made no use thair of but to her selfe only.

February 28, 1662, before Mr. John Stewart, John Glas, John Campbell.

Confesses Margaret McWilliam her former declaratione over againe and added farther that at the meitting about hallowday last she saw ther Mcilduy Donald McKersches wife [blank] Mclevine Mcvicars wife. Item that Elspeth Stewart fell at the neirrest stony slap above Restyouel and that   Nicoll fell at the flash [*might refer to Jonat McNicoll's fall into the burn*]   and that Jean grey being..... reached the blude to her and lifted her haveing the blude lyk the......of a most upon a atstack[?].

Jonet Boyd declares that about six quarters of a yeire syne haveing a child upon her breist and abundance of milk did upon a night dreame that Kat. Moore came violently upon her and took a great nipp out of her pape and said help me quhat yow doe with milk and mediately as she wakened that her milk was gone out of her brest and hade not a drop, and that the place quhair she dreamed that the said Kat. nipped her was blue [*the colour of the witches mark, often*]. Item the said Katherine being bruted for a witch she came to her to her owne house and told her how she had dreamed of her and lost her milk and that she suspected it was she that did it desyring her for God sak to give her her owne milk and that within 2 or 3 dayes therafter she hade her milk as formerlie. [*Coincidence as usual: the milk stopped naturally and restarted again normally, as it sometimes does*]. Item Jonet Boyd declares that after this McCarthur came to her house [Kat Moore's house] and challenged her for seeking her milk of his wife and said to her that he should mak her repent it before that day month and within a quarter of yeire her husband dyed suddenlie.

The declaration of Jonet [Morison] haveing sent out for Mr. John Stewart to speik with her at her own house the 19 Januar 1662 before John Glas proveist of Rothesay, Mr. John Stewart minister there and Johne Gray burgess in the said Burgh. [*Notice: this person has an urge to confess, unlike the others. This is characteristic of a mental disorder of a particular type. Other symptoms we will soon observe are hearing voices and imagining things happen that do not.]*

First that, about a fourtnight afore halountayd last [*Oct 16 1661*], <u>as shee was going from the toune of Boot till her own house **in the tweilight**</u> (sic) she forgathered on the way at a loaning [*grassy track used by animals*] foot [*could be the foot of the Serpentine, still known as the Loaning in 1780*] with a black rough fierce man [**DM5**]who cam to her and desired her till goe with him fer that thou art a poor womune and are begging amongst harlots and uncharitable people and notheing the better of them and I will make the [*thee*] a Lady for thow mayst gett Adam Ker brought home for his father and mother sister and wife are witch people and will give the a Kayre [*care*] and make the a Lady. Item he drew near her and wald have taken her be the hand bot she refused bot traysted to meet him that **same night eight** nights at **Knockanrioch** [*the hill from Rothesay to Gortans across the moor; ie the place now occupied by a farm of that name and the old Primary school and including Larkhall and much of Skeoch Woods*] and being enquiered be us if shee knew quhat that man was shee said she knew him to be the divill and at the the first she grew eyry. [*Since it is twilight her description of the man who is taken to be the devil is suspect except that he is rough and fierce. Note: by this time, 3 months after Nancy's denunciation of him, Robert Stewart of Scarrell would be well ostracised, deserted by his wife, not looking after himself and half mad*]

2. Item.....she declared that according to her promise shee keeped the trayst with him and meet in that place appointed and that he appeared clad with a wheit midell and that he said to her thow art a poor woman and beggar among a cumpanie of harlots, goe with me and I'll make the a Lady and put the in a brave castall quhair thou shalt want nothing and I will free the of all the poverties and troubles thou art in and learn the [*thee*] a way how to bring home Adam Ker. [*This makes sense, if she is known to the man, the devil, as he will here be called, after the fact, to have a crush on Adam Ker for whom she is pining, despite, as we will soon see, having a husband. It is perfectly obvious that this is an offer for sexual services. It has to be a human being and this is the only human action that makes sense given the rewards promised*]

3. Shee declared that on a tyme heirefter being cuming from Kilmorie in the evening there appeared as it were **a great number of people** and there cam ane from them to her **in wheit or as a man naked with a great black head**, and bid her goe with him *[Dm6]*. She asked quhair? it said into the Knockane [*a hillock*]. [*We can guess for what purpose, especially with our man who really is a devil of a very particular kind.*]

4. Shee declared that therafter she and her husband being laying in bed there cam one to the window and said Robert rise and goe to the toune and ile give you a penny (worth) of ale for its long since yow wer in the toune and far longer (since) I was in it. Shee hearing the voice did put upon her husband to waken bot could not gett it done bot spake herself and asked who was there. The voice answered and said I am Adam Kerr; rayse and let me in. her answer was and thois were a good Spirit Ile let the in bot and thou be ane evill spirit God be between me and the. With that it ged [*went*] mourning and greeting from the window. [*This man is either our devil looking for a quick fix or he has persuaded Adam Kerr to return, perhaps having written to him, which Jonet Morison would be unable to do. We are not done with this character yet.*]

5. Shee declared (after being challenged at the Session) one frayday thereafter being the liventh [11th] of January 1662. She was cuming home from the Waster Kams and at the

Lochtie shee grew faint and satt doune and a voice spake to her and forbad her to goe hom bot goe in a hole and droune herselfe. She raise and cam forward the voice spake to her againe and said goe not hom. I am not scorning the for thow will be bot troubled and vexed Shee came forward neare the deck of the gortans. [*She is on the road from Wester Kames to the old Primary School at the flat part of Gortans; it looks as if there must have been a pond thereabouts known as the Lochtie, since drained*] She grew faint and satt doune and, as shee thought, **the stalk of heather** that was at her foot said to her belive not, you goe hom for they will be bot troubled seeking the [*thee*]. Shee raise and as she was cuming to the deck the voice spake to her and said belive [*believe*] in me and goe with me and I's warrand the. [*Notice: hearing voices, a basic symptom of mental disorder*]

The Declaratione of Jonet Morisoune in the Tolboothe of Rothesay imediately after she was apprehended, the 18 of January 1662 in presence of Johne Glas proveist, Mr. John Stewart minister, Niniane Ballantyne of Kaims, Ninian Ker baylie, Johne and Johne Kelburnes elder and younger burgesses of Rothesay, Mr. James Stewart, Robert Beith, Archibald Glas burgesses of Rothesay. [*If the date is correct and the previous, she must have been released after first apprehension*]

1. Shee declared over againe her declaratione made at her own house 15 Januar 1662 [*sic*] word be word and farder declared that that night shee traysted with the divill at the Kockanrioch, being the secound tyme of her meeting with him, **that shee made a covenant with the devill** *[Dm7]* quhairin the divill promised to give her any thing she desyred and to teach her how to bring home Adam Ker [*Notice that if anybody would be qualified to teach it would be the ex schoolmaster, now disgraced.*] and woon her hayre quhairin she promised to be his servant etc. that shee asked quhat was his name his answer was my name is **Klareanough** and he asked quhat was her name and she answered Jonet Morisoun, the name that God gave me, and he said belive in not in Christ bot belive in me. I baptize the Margarat and also declared the first service he imployed her in was to bring home Adam Ker and to put Niniane Ker baylie in his stead by shooting of the said Niniane. [*But was it really the first service? Is this the recorder's spin?*]
2. Shee declared that in Summer last being gathering hearbs to heall Patrick Glas daughter who was laying seick of a very unnaturall disease that she got a sore strok upon the hafet the paine quhairof continued for the space of moneth thereafter [*Notice the different spelling of words like 'daughter' instead of 'dochter' and 'thereafter' not 'therafter.' This suggests a different hand.*]

Declaratione Jonet Morisone the said day being the 18 day of January 1662 in the afternoone before John Glas proveist, Mr. John Stewart minister, Ninian Bannatyne of Kames, Walter Stewart, Neill McNeill, Duncan McAllester.

Quhilk day the said Jonet Morisoune did declare and stand by her former declarationes and repeitted the most part of the particulars formerly confessed and said she would not deny anything that she had spoken. As also added further that the devill desyred her to tak the lyfe of John Glas proveists dun horse by shooting him and to put him for William Stephen who was lying sick sore payned which she refused to do. [*'to put him for' meaning, perhaps, 'revenge for' Notice the spelling of 'she' before it was consistently 'shee'.*]

Item that the devill desyred her to tak Walter Stewart, bayly, his lyfe by shooting him to put him for ane neighbour of his that dwelt in the highlands which she refused to do. [*'to revenge the man in the highlands'? Notice that she may herself have wished these things upon these men and the very fact that this is so is attributed to the devil, as the only possible explanation for such unchristian behaviour.*]

Item declares the devill told her that it was the fayries that took John Glas child's lyfe, and that the Spirit which spok to her told her the same that they were minded to tak his lyfe as they did. [*Since there is no devil (though there are living men who might qualify as him in every community and age) and no fairies, what is happening here seems to be that these ideas came into this woman's mind. Ideas of this kind occur to everyone, probably, from time to time. Presented with the balustrade of a high bridge we may consider throwing ourselves off, especially if depressed [why? because some people are so depressed that they throw themselves off bridges, hence the association in our mind]; the image of machine-gunning people that we know because of what we perceive to be their stupidity or moral deficiency may come to mind; or of taking action to revenge ourselves against people who have offended or humiliated us: even so far as to plan their destruction. And yet we do nothing about them; reject them out of hand. Everybody is liable to have his mind overtaken in this way. If this be so, the presence of such ideas is easily attributed to the devil since he is the fallen angel whose stock in trade is such things; a concept reinforced by the community and its way of speaking and thinking and especially by the minister and the elders every Sunday. If this is correct the problem with this community is a deficient psychology: a failure to realise what the mind, any mind, is capable of. Why, however, would she have the idea of murdering the life of a child? It is a particular child: the provost's. Is he so hated by her that this seems a worthy outcome? Has he done something to take the life of her child? Or omitted to provide alms without which it could not survive, because it starved, she being unable to feed it? Maybe, even, the provost is the kind of powerful figure who is expected to solve these kinds of problems. If he fails, no wonder ideas of this kind arise in the mind of suffering women like Jonet. And yet, recognise again that we have here a woman with an urge to confess, and who has confessed the pact with the devil before everything else, despite the inevitability that she herself will be condemned, as she must realise. Further, she has heard voices, the one thing that distinguishes the psychotic and gets them locked up in our society with its far better understanding of mental illness. The final symptom is imagining that events happened which did not. This woman would be locked up— sectioned under the mental health act— were she to exhibit these symptoms today— at least if she were a danger to others*] Item declares that at the time she met with the devil [***Dm8***] **quhen he was goeing by with a great number of men** that she asked at him quhat were these that went by who answered they are my company and quhen she speired where they were going he answered that **they were going to seek prey**. [*This is very important if accurate; it means that the meetings were for the purpose of ganging up on individuals to cause them harm. If some member of the community's heirarchy, of the Kirk Session or Town Council or the landowners were perceived to have behaved badly to some of the group they could be expected to be the target of revenge. Who was chosen* *would depend upon chance: who they met first, who they thought they could injure most easily, or even, through whom: injuring a person's child could be equivalent to injuring them. Was the prey likely to be just anyone? No, though some people seem designed to be the prey of others who seek to vent their wrath or mischief upon others: the swot at school who won't defend himself because he cannot, but attracts attention because he is different. The well dressed, well behaved, boy who meets others in the street and is picked upon just because he is different from them— any difference will do: that is the trigger. Anyone you didn't like or had no reason to love and admire could be the target for you, as a member of the group seeking prey and if enough others agreed with your view of it, the victim had been found. However, in the story the word 'prey' is taken to be a confusion with the word 'pray' which a minister/schoolmaster might have been saying instead]*

Declaration Jonet Morisone the 21 January 1662 [*note the difference in the date and spelling of the first word*] before John Glas proveist, Mr. John Stewart Minister, Major William Campbell [*probably the owner of the Ardbeg estate*], Mr. Archibald Beith, Walter Stewart bayley, Peter Gray, Alester Mctyre, James McNivane, James Stewart, William Gillespie, Archibald Steuart Provost. [*We seem to have two provosts, maybe an ingoing and outgoing one, though the date seems to exclude this possibility: why then? An ex provost or one from elsewhere? Unclear. Not listed as a provost at this period*]

Quhilk day she repeitted severall particulars of her former declarationes viz her meiting with the devill severall tymes and her trysting with him, her covenant with him and that the devill bade her tak Walter Stewart bayly and put him for a nighbour of his in the highlands quhilk she knew not and that he told her that he was intended to tak John Glas his barne [*bairn*] and to tak John Glas dun horse and put for William Stephen. And being questioned anent her heiling of Mcfersoune in Keretoule his dochter who lay sick of a very unnaturall disease without power of hand or foot both speichles and kenured [?] [*unconscious*]. She answered The disease quhilk ailed her was blasting with the faryes and that she healed her with herbes. Item being questioned about her heiling of Alester Bannatyne who was sick of the lyk disease answred that he was blasted with the fairyes also and that she heiled him thereof with herbs and being questioned anent the heileing of Patrick Glas dochter Barbra Glas answred that she was blasted with the faryes also.

Upon the 22 of January 1662 Jonet Morisoune sent for Mr. John Stewart minister [*urge to confess things deeply damaging to her personally*] and before James Stewart, Adams sone and Coline Stewart burges of Rothesay declared to him as followes That about three nights before Hallowday last as she was goeing out of the towne home at But Kyie [*Bute Quay*] **She saw the devill [*Dm8*] and a company with him comeing downe the hill syde underneath Brod cheppell** [*St Bride's Chapel at the top of Chapel Hill*] and that himself was foremost [*It is immediately clear that the devil, the person afterwards taken to be the devil, is an actual person. The only question is: who? Who would qualify as leader— as plainly the leader. Who but an educated man of wealth and social standing, recently joined because disgraced and ostracised by the usual puritanical society of the Kirk. If the devil is not an actual person this makes no sense. Nor is this an invention. St Bride's Chapel really did exist and it was at the top of a brae, Chapelhill, and it is near the town — as it would have been in 1662.*] and after him was

APPENDICES

John Galie in Barmore [*having been mentioned by more than one witch as a man in attendance to the devil, this statement should have earned John Galie the chop.*] and his wife Jenat McConachie, Elspat Galie in Ambrisbeg Margaret McWilliam Katrine Moore [blank] McLevin [*the blank is Margaret obviously*] Cristen Banantyne Jonet McNeil her good daughter who came all orderly doune the brae [*picture it on our brae!*] and quhen they came to the craft [*ship, beached; we reach the shore at the foot of the brae in 1662*] went in a ring and himself in the midst of them [*where else would the schoolmaster position himself?*] and that she hearkened and heard them speiking to him and that the devill came out from among them to her and convoyed her to the Loaning fitt [*foot of the path for animals: the Serpentine, probably*] quhair he and she sett a tryst to meit against that day 8 dayes. Item that all these were witches and that McLevin Margaret McWilliam and Katharin Moore her dochter did by witchcraft shoot to deid William Stephen and that the cause thereof was because a long space before John Stephen was blasted with ane evill ey quhen he dwelt in Balskye [*probably east of Castle Street, for the Balskyte burn went down Watergate. This is evidently a revenge killing for the use of the evil eye.*] McLevine offered to heale him of that blasting bot he would not, saying till her that he would have none of the devils cures which was her quarrell with him and that he was shott underneath the short ribs and that quhen she found him there was a hole in it that ye might put your neive [*knife*] in.

Item it was Margaret McWilliam and her dochters Katharine and Elspeth that took Adame Kerr's lyfe and that they had contrived it the night before and that they laid the cantrapes or witchrie in the burne quhilk the milstane was to come throw and the maire for taken that the said Margrat McWilliam fled and went away to Kingarth or some other quhair from home upon the morne in the morneing that the milstane was drawne that she might not be suspected. [*Typical of this woman: a man is killed in an accident and the McWilliams get the blame*] And that before that tyme they hade taken the power of his syde from him making two onsets on him for he was a man litle worth and as he hade litle ill in him so he had also litle good that therefor they got overtane of him. [*Adam Ker does not seem much of a man. How then could Jonet have a crush on him? Impossible. Contradiction: maybe another sign of psychosis*] Item that Margaret McWilliam and her dochter Katharine took by witchcraft the lyfe of a cow of Neill McNeills quhen they wes bigging the stuid falds [*building the stud fields; at which time he would not be paying attention to his cows which were elsewhere, perhaps*]

Item that the said Margaret and Kate took or was intended to tak the milk of a cow of Mr. John Stewarts.

Item that the said McWilliam and her dochters took be witchcraft the lyfe of Alester McNiven and that they keeped him long in truble but at last got his lyfe; the quarrell was that becaus he craved sorely some malt silver that Katrine Moore was owing him. [*either silver owed for malt or silver dishes which would hold malt; recall that they are supposed to have tied him to a post but he was released by John Moore. This is typical: they harm a man, he is released, afterwards, maybe long afterwards, dies and they get the blame*]

Item that McLevin did put a pock of Witchcraft in the east roof of Finley Mcconochie in Ballicailes stable above the horse on the north side of the house and that she said to the devill [***Dm9***] at that meiting that quhilk finley Mcconochie got he is litle the worse of it, it wold be the better to be doubled. [*The devil is a person you can talk to*]

Item that McConochie in Barmoire and Elspath Galie was at a meitting in the lowlands with one Jonet Isack in Kilwineing and Margaret Smith ther, dochter to [blank] Smeth at the Crosse [*Kilwinning Cross, where the smith would ply his trade*], and they wronged by witchcraft Hew Boyd in Kilwinning quho had four wives and they lived no longer nor they bore a child and that the child never lived and lyes sick himself.

Item that the said McConochie took by witchcraft the lyfe of a horse of Neill McNeills.

Item that the said McConoche and Elspath Galie hade almost taken the lyfe of Jonet Stewart wife to Donald Mcconochie in Ambrisbeg quhen she was lighter of her first bairne and that they laid some pocks of witchcraft under the threshold of his dore but whether it be ther yet or not she knew not but she suspects it be and though the pock or the clout it was in may be rotten yet the the thing itselfe and vertue might remaine. Item that the thing they put in the pocks is the mooles of ane unchristened bairnes threid nailes [*fragments of a baby's thread nails*] and was resolved to shoot a cow of his at that same time.

Item that McWiliame and hir daughter Katherine wrongd by witchcraft Donald McGilchrist and that nothing threave with him since they did medle with him and that they did lay a Pocke with witchcraft in the eising [*eaves?*] of the east side of the house without, betuix the window and Doore. Quhether it be ther yet or not she knowes not bot that Mary Moore hir daughter [*Katherine's*] who duelt ther afterhinde quhen hir child died left that house upon that occasion. Also declares that Isobell McNicoll and Elspa Spence and Margrat McWilliam said[162] a pocke of witchcraft in Patrick Glas his back chamber In the eising thereof in the east side fore against the doore.

Being asked if she saw Elspa Spence at the meeting answered No but that she heard one of the witches say to the divell [*Dm10*] We want one of our Cummers [*members who come usually*] **yet** viz. Elspa Spence Patrick Glas his wife. He answered **that is a great fault**. [*the devil is a man! even an educated man, for the language is of such a man*]

Item declares that she saw with Isobell McNicoll, at a time that she was in her house opened her Kist [*chest*] a clout she took in hir hand and found in it a thing likke ridd clay, quhich she said she had gotten from an other woman quhich she supposed to be witchcraft.

Item that the devill asked at Katherine Moore quhair hir Husband was that he came not she answered there was a young bairne at home and that they could not both come. [*The perils of leaving a bairn at home unattended were self evident to her!*] Also declared that the errand quhich that Companie was about was to take Johne Glas the Provist his lyfe. [*No wonder there were executions. How could such people be left alive? They could get you next time. But is it true?*]

Item that Christen Ballantyne did wrong by witchcraft Peter Gray.

Also declares that at that tyme quhairin she spoke with the devil in the Ferme quhen the great army went by she knew none of the companie bot only Jonet McNicoll. In the great armie that was goeing away more swiftly nor herself. Item that at that meeting with the devil at But Kyie [*Bute Quay*] she hard [*heard*] one speake to him [*Dm11*] like Donald McConochies wife in Ardroskadill, Margaret McIlduy, She saw hir bot she wold not know her wele bot she knew that it was hir voice. Againe being inquired quhat difference was betwix shooting and blasting sayes that quhen they are shott ther is no recoverie for it and if the shott be in the heart they will died presently bot if it be not in the at the heart they will die in a while with it yet will at last die with it and that blasting is a whirlwinde that the fayries raises about that persone quhich they intend to wrong and

---

[162] *Quare* set.

that tho ther were tuentie present yet it will harme none bot him quhom they were set for, quhich may be healed two wayes ether by herbs or by charming and that all that whirlwind gathers in the body till one place if it be taken in time it is the easier healed and if they gett not meanes they will shirpe [*wither*] away.

Declares that day quhich she was challenged at the Sessione, that Jenet McNicoll came to hir in Patrick Rowans house and said Jenat. Look that the fyle none bot yourself. [*See that you defile none but yourself*]

Item she declared that McWilliame had Alexander Woods milk all the summer over.

Item Cristen Banantyne betwitched the Ladie Kames quhich was the cause of her sicknes.

Declaration Jonet Morisone January 22, 1662, afternoon before John Glas proveist, James Stewart adamsone and Coline Stewart.

Quhilk day she repeited her foresaid declaration made the forenoone in all the particulars thereof and declared the same to be of truth adding further that Margaret McWilliam and her dochter Katherine notwithstanding of quhat witchrie they hade put formerly in Donald McGilchrist's house did after his comeing out of Cumray put a pock under the bed that stands in the insett of the house. Item that Jonet McNeill did heale a bairne of Jonet Mans by putting a string with Knots and beids about the bairne which the said McNeill desyred the said Jonet Man to let it byde about the bairne 48 hours and therafter to tak it off and bind it about the catt quhich the said Jonet Mann did and imediately the Catt dyed. [*Asphyxiated due to being bound so tightly that it could not breathe?*]

Declaration Jonet Morisone the 28 January 1662 before Mr. John Stewart Minister, John Glas proveist and Ninian Bannatyne of Kames.

Quhilk day she declared the foresaid declaratione made the 22 in the whole particulars therof about the samen to be of truth.

Item upon the said day afternoone she declared the samen to William Glas and added that john Glas his bairne quhilk he hade in fostering was shot at the window.

Declaration Jonet Morisone the 29 January 1662 to Mr. John Stewart Minister.

That it was Donald Mccartour his wife and goodmother who did drinke out his aile and camped about it. [*complained about it?*]

Sara Stewart declares that she haveing a Kow sick and Jonet Morisone comeing into her house she told her therof and desyred her to goe see the kow if she could doe her any good the said Jonet went into the byre and took off her curcheffe and Strek [*struck*] thrie straiks of her curcheffe upon the kow and that therafter the kow grew wele. Item that the said kow therafter had neither milk nor calfe. [*The fact that this is actually written down, such an innocent testimony, shows just how credulous are the Kirk Session of any behaviour out of the ordinary: clearly this is taken to be evidence of witchcraft.*]

March 26, 1662 [*On the same sheet! So it seems. Meaning that there was no intervening note taken of further investigations. This is very surprising! At the very least there should have been a concerted attempt to identify the devil! This suggests that the identity was inconvenient to everybody, especially the Kirk Session and the noble families of the island; the Stewarts and the Bannatynes! This is very revealing then in telling us the identity that has remained hidden for so long.*] Issobell More McKaw haveing confessed about 20 yeires sine did delate Amy Hindman, Alester McNiven and Mary Frissell his wife, Jonet Mctyre McNivans wife in Keighs [*Inexplicable that a man should have two wives, except that we have already seen a man in Kilwinning with four! Unless one wife has died before the other was married*]

Item Jonet Mcilmertine haveing confessed covenant and baptisme delated Amy Hyndman elder and younger, Katrine Frissell, Marione Frissell and Mary McNivan her dochter, Jonet Mcintyre McNivans wife.

[*Jonet Mcilmartine has just signed her death warrant and maybe for those she delated also. There would not be a more sure criterion for witchcraft than the covenant and baptism. And yet, already, there is a contradiction: at least six women have covenanted with the devil, yet only five were executed. Why? Perhaps because one of them died in prison of disease, starvation, or torture*]

Dittay Issobell McNicoll.

Upon the 21 of Februar 1662 deponed Jonet Glas that Issobell McNicoll comeing into her house said to her that she was in Walter Stewarts house seeing his bairne and that Walters wife seemed to be displeased with her but [,] sayes she [,] Walter put a paper on my face and therafter he or his will rew it within 5 yeiris and les and that it might be best it were long, that he wold have also few children as she hade. [*Suggests that she could kill his children more easily the more there were. Threats then: the usual response of the witch: the defense mechanism is to promise dire consequences.*]

Margrat Glas deponed that she heard Issobell McNicoll say I had a whyt face and its gods will that she (meaneing Walters child) should have a black face and its not come in yet quhat was done to me. [*Suggests fornication with a black man*].

Margrat Galy deponed that She heard Isobel say Walter Stewart put a paper on hir face, God let him nor his never prosper and god tak a revenge of quhat he did to me. Item Walters child David took a sudden disease with cryeing and dyed within 8 days that day that he was buryed his dochter took ane very unnaturall disease her face dying and growing black quhair of she dyed in short space.

McWilliam

Memo. The first yeire that Jonet Stewart Ambrisbeg's wife was mayed big with child that McWilliam and Kat her dochter came to the bog of Ambrisbeg to sheir bent and the said Jonet comeing to her reproved her for shiering therof and hindered her from taking it with her. She said McWilliam said to her that she wold as good let it goe and shortly therafter the said Jonet distracted and took paines and was sorely handled.

Memo about Donald Mcgilichrist.
Memo about Margarat Mcilchrist McNivans wife.
Memo that Jonet Morisone and Margarat McLevin confronted Margaret McWilliam upone the 5 day february 1662 before Mr. John Stewart minister, Ninian Banatyne of Kames, Major David Ramsay and Kilchunlik [*Robert Stewart of Kilwhinleck, probably,*

an elder]. Quhilk day alsoe the said McLevin confronted Ceatherin Moore. Major Ramsay and his wife will be spoken to.

Memo that McConaghy Barmoire [*ie McConachie Barmore: there were 2 Barmores; one at the farm still extant today; the other a deserted settlement 400 yds west up the hill, where remains can be seen. John Gely also lived there*] uses physik asnd charmes. [*A serious offence or it would not be here! Imagine what they would think of covenanting with the devil, baptism and murder even of animals let alone humans*]

Item that McKinley the miller of Scapsys [*Scalpsie: if there was a mill there it would have to make use of the burn that comes out of the Quien Loch*] wife said to James Crafurd that upon a tyme quhen the said Jonet was travelling she had a string and 9 poks [*pocks*] bound about her at quhich tyme Robert Warkes doughter was in the house.

Memo that bothe her daughters are charmers and that Neall McKenans wife recovered by charming a meere [*mare*] of yong Kirilamonts and that John Bannatyne and the said Kirilamonts knowes. Item Alexander McCurdyes wyfe in Baron [*Barone farm*] charmed a Bairne of William Glasses. Item to trye if McWilliam was at home the day Adam Ker dyed Alester Mcconochie they say will prove this.

Memorandum that McMaister in Barone is a charmer Sara Stewart can prove this.

Memorandum that John Allane haveing a cow that was crooked he told his father thereof who sent up to him Jeane Stewart, Thomas dochter to charme the said kow but Kat Mcphune wold not suffer the samen to be done.

Item that imediately therafter a kow of hers dyed suddenly in the byre.

Now that we have a copy of the paper, answers to questions can be attempted and if the deductions made are not agreed, the reader can decide for himself what the evidence means.

An obvious place to start is:

(iii) What was the outcome of the investigations in the document?

As will be seen when we move on to other evidence, at least one of these women was executed: Jonet McNicoll in 1673. She had escaped from the Tolbooth at Rothesay before execution in 1662 only to return and be tried again in 1673. The next document tells us 4 were executed in 1662.

From the Justiciary Records of Argyll number 12:

(iv) Justiciary Record of Justice Ayre at Rothesay

'Justiciary Record of 15 Oct 1673, [Justice Ayer at Rothesay: before Argyll, with Sir Colin Campbell of Aberuchill and Ninian Bannatyne younger of Kames, deputes]

    The Sute Roll called for the first and second tyme and the absents unlawit.

    The assise called and absents unlawit. The assise chosen are :-

Archibald Bannatyne of Lubas, Mr. Robert Stewart in Kilcatten[163], Donald McNeill of Kilmorie, Robert Stewart of Merknoch [*Mecknoch*], James Stewart in Largieend, Donald More McKaw of North Garachtie, John McKaw in South Garachtie, James Crawfurd in Drumchloy [*Drumachcloy, the farm at Ettrick Bay*], Donald Hyndman at miln of Ettrick [*the ruins of which can still be seen by the side of the stream*], Ninian Stewart, late balzie of Rothesay, Robert Stewart of [28] [*meaning of this number unknown*] Lochlie [*the farm at the causeway in Loch Fad*], Adam Stewart in Rothesay, John Kelburn elder ther, Colein Stewart ther, Ninian Stewart of Largiend.

16 of October 1673

The quhilk day entired on pannell Jannet McNicoll in Rothesay being accused and persewed at the instance of Hendrie Melis Prosecutor fiscall for his majestie's interest of the abominable cryme of witchcraft followeing contained in her dittay quherof the tennor followes That quher the said pannell [*McNicoll*] haveing shaken off all fear of god reverance and respect to his majesie's lawes and acts of parliament is guiltie and culpable of the foresaid vile and abominable crime of witchcraft in sua far as she did about hallowday 1661 or thereby meitt with the devill appearing to her in the lykenes of ane gross lepper faced man quhom she knew to be ane evill spirit And made ane compact covenant with him to serve him wpon his promiseing to her that she should not want gear [*goods all kinds*] enough quherwpon she Renunced her baptisme And he gave her a new name saying I Baptize the [thee] **Mary Lykeas** the said pannell keiped meitting and consultatione with the devill the tyme foresaid at the place called Butekey wpon the shoar of Rothesay where **severall other persons witches of whom four were sentanced and executed to the death anno 1662** or therby who likewayes dilated her guiltie of the said crime of witchcraft quhilk she her self confest and could not denny Lykeas for further evidence of the said pannell her guilt she being apprehended anno 1662 foresaid and imprisoned within the tolbuith of Rothesay and fearing to be putt to death with the rest who suffered at that tyme It is true and of a veritie that she brake ward and escaped out of the said tolbuith and fled to the Lowlands quher she remained in Kilmernock and other places ther about these twelf yeers by gone always wndir [*under*] ane evill fame both at home and abroad [*This is unlikely to be true since she would have been locked up by the Kilmarnock Session and burnt there*] And quher she comitted

---

[163] This is a university graduate but not Mr Robert Stewart of Scarrell for, on p251 of Rothesay Town Council Records on line 13, we find: 'The quhilk day in presence of Niniane Stewart baillie compeirit Jeane Colquhoune spous to Mr Robert Stewart of Scarrell outwith the presence of the said Mr Robert hir husban, and ratifiet and approvit ane heretabill Dispositioune grantit be the said Mr Robert with hir consent of the lands callit Laiche Relivoill to wit his pairt thairof lyand within this brughe rigdaill with Donald McGilchrist belonging to Robert McGilchrist on the southe part, the said Roberts lands callit Skioche on the northe part, John Kelburne his lands on the wast part and the commoun gait neir the sie schore on the eist part in favours of Niniane Kelburne burges of Rothesay his airis....' That is to say: Robert Stewart of Scarrell was still alive and living there in June 1673. Thus, unless he removed to Kilchattan during the next three months, this Robert Stewart of Kilchattan is a different person. Indeed, having for fifty years been known as Robert Stewart of Scarrell, he would not suddenly be known as of Kilchattan, especially with many other Robert Stewarts living on the island..

severall malefices notorious and knowne to all the cuntrey As at mair lenth is contained in her said dittay for the quhilk crime of witchcraft above written [*we do not possess this*] the said pannell wes putt to the tryall of the [foresaid] persons of assise [29] ......[who by the mouth of Archibald Bannatine] [*Chairman of the Assize*] found pronunced and declared the said pannell to be fyled [*found to be*] culpable and convict of the crime foresaid contained in her dittay in respect of her owne confession of the samen in judgement And therefore the said Justice and his deputes be the mouth of Duncan Clerk dempster of court decerned and ordained the said Jannet McNicoll to be taken and strangled to the death and her bodie to be brunt at the gallows of Rothesay wpon fryday the twentie fourt of october instant be twa hours in the eftirnoon and her goods and gear to be escheat.

It follows that 4 witches were sentenced in 1662, and that Jonet McNicoll who would have been, escaped at that time.

Q1 Who else was convicted?

The principal criteria for conviction seem to be:
1. Covenanting with the devil.
2. Promising to be his servant
3. Renouncing Christian baptism
4. Being rebaptised [*which, on its own, would assume the former*]
5. Acts of malefice [*evil doing, usually harming people or their animals*]

Notice that there is no better evidence that what we already have. The Kirk Session's records have been lost or tampered with for the months at issue. There is nothing in the Town Council Records about this. Many people from Bute are recorded in the Privy Council Records in Edinburgh as having been investigated and tried, all or almost all of them mentioned here. There are however no records among these of the outcome of the trials. This may be due to the confusion of the times when the Protectorate of Oliver Cromwell was being replaced by the government of Charles II. Because there are no records of what happened to these many people from Bute [given hereafter] at the Privy Council, it can be taken that no decisions were made at that level. Positioned on the periphery of the country, far from Edinburgh, it is likely that the locals took the law into their own hands. The Duke of Argyll had just been beheaded a year before, so he had no part to play in the trials of 1662 nor was his son likely to be involved so soon after the death of his father, being so much persona non grata that he never was elevated to the Dukedom and was himself beheaded in 1685, also for treason. It is possible that the decision about the witches was left to the Presbytery. Yet since that body would be comprised mainly of people from Bute, the outcome is not likely to be very different. There was, throughout Scotland at this time, an appetite for witch burning and the Presbyterians of Cowal and Dunoon are unlikely to have taken an opposing view. In fact, in the reconstruction it is taken that the young Earl of Argyll, anxious to impose his will upon the territory, in accordance with his hereditary right, did preside at the trials in 1662 just as he did in 1673, as the documents show.

(v) Who were executed in 1662?

Who, in the Document in Inverary, satisfy the criteria?
1. Margaret McLevin.
2. Margaret McWilliam
3. Jonet Morisone.
4. Isobell McNicoll

5. Jonet McNicol (escaped)

These are the chief witches: those who confessed to the criteria themselves, in detail, if the Document held in Inverary is to be believed.

Yet Jonet Mcilmartine confessed to covenant and baptism, ID p28 Who else did? The plain fact is that any of these 24 people if subjected to the same conditions of questioning would very probably 'confess' in the same fashion. 6 should have been convicted in 1662 based on the dittays we have records of. And yet only five were which means one, at least died in prison.

In fact, many more should have been convicted if only by association. To be present at a meeting and to know that a murder was to be committed and go along with it without complaint was guilt by association.

A more important question is: were the women guilty of actions deserving of death?

In every case when the devil is said to have made himself known it is, by now, very likely that this was an actual person, a member of the community, perhaps Robert Stewart of Scarrell, but a human for sure. It is perfectly possible that this person, whoever he was, simply wanted these women for sex— like so many other manifestations over in Fife[164] at the same time and that he promised them they would want for nothing if they would agree. What was the point of rebaptism? It may have been a quirk of his to require of them, much as some men have pet names for their spouses[165] and vice versa, to be a different name to him. This part, rebaptism, is of no significance if it was a real living person, as it must have been for there was no other. Had they refused to be known by his chosen name, it is unlikely to have made much difference to him. Sexual and other services were what he sought, not a change of name. And yet what Jonet Morison is alleged to have said is: 'belive not in Christ but in me,' p22 of I.D. Instead, the idea of rebaptism may have been the idea of the minister as an aspect of the covenant made with the devil that would make sense to him and to whom that may have seemed to be an important matter involving as it seems the renunciation of the Christian name. If so, this idea could easily have been got out of all the women, by questioning after sleep deprivation and that is likely to have been a factor here in some cases at least, though not all. The calculation: if you tell the minister that you were rebaptised, he will let you back to sleep, could have been made by all the women waiting their turn in the Tolbooth.

The minister has an idea of what the devil concept involves and can easily obtain the assent he wishes from women anxious to get back to sleep. All the minister or the interrogator had to do by the conditions of writing the dittay was to get an affirmative answer to a question: 'Did the devil demand you change your name? What was the new one?' Almost any name would do to get back to sleep, so long as the interrogator was satisfied. Demands by the devil for this or that maleficent act are less easy to explain. However, it may just be that the human taken afterwards to be the devil because of his influence or effect, wished their help in revenging himself upon people in the community. And in Robert Stewart of Scarrell's case, after his various humiliations, he is likely to have hated some of the Kirk Session and to have wanted revenge: to do them actual harm. A constant factor is the difference between what the author of the document

---

[164] The Witches of Fife, by Stuart Macdonald p110: "Even the sexual act follows a stereotype: his nature (i.e. penis) was cold, and several echoed Janet Hendrie's comment that he used her 'after the manner of a beast'."

[165] Sir WS Churchill and his wife, for example, had pet names for each other.

believes the women have said they have done and what the women have assented to freely, as well as some actual confusion at times as shown in the writing.

There are particular questions such as: 'Who killed Adam Kerr and what do the various references mean? If, as reported by Jonet Morison, she wanted to bring Adam Kerr back from that other place where he was and a spirit calling himself Adam Kerr appeared outside her house one night asking for her husband to go to town and promising him money to do so, it may be that the human taken to be the devil wrote [which, if it was Robert Stewart of Scarrell, as a schoolmaster he would be well able to do— unlike the ordinary male riff raff of the witch people who would be unable to write or know the procedure for sending a letter] and induced him to return (to aid his new recruit in her crush upon him) and that having done so, he went to Jonet's window with the express intention of having her sexually for which purpose it would be necessary to get rid of the husband. Later, as we see, Adam Kerr is killed in an event involving the mill stone. It might be that the husband of Jonet, angry at Adam Kerr's interest in his wife and aware of hers in him, wanted him dead and did the deed himself. If the McWilliams had any quarrel with Adam Kerr it would be natural to blame them for the death and their track-record of revenge would convict them. 1662 is likely to be a time when murders, especially crimes of passion and after sudden rages during fights, were common and unpunished lacking the means to investigate.

That only 4 other women, apart from Jonet McNicoll, were executed at this time is surprising. Katherine Moore took part in most of the malefices which would have got her mother into trouble. By the standards of the time she should have been burnt. The same for Patrick McKaw and others like McKeraish[166] mentioned as having killed people, even Donald McCartour for carrying flesh [probably human, after dismemberment] on his back.

By contrast Jonet McNicoll did nothing at all, at least in the confessions we have seen.

Two disturbing aspects are the killing of children and the army of witches going to seek prey. The latter may only mean: we are going after someone particular with whom we have a quarrel. The arrival of a disaffected minister in the group who has been excluded from his class and his natural place in society because of his fornication might have meant a more organised group of witches which even grew in number because of the status accorded by his presence. If the minister became aware of this counter group to the Christian community this alone could have triggered the witch hunt. Making an example of people would have seemed necessary. And an example could be made by torturing women into admissions which, in some cases at least, they had never made, **these statements were made over them by the interrogators and their assent obtained by torture**. That is, you as interrogator make the accusation and you keep making it until the tortured accused person assents that it is true. There may even have been an interrogator employed specially, who is not mentioned on the ditty. Someone had to look after these women in prison and keep them deprived of sleep if that took place. Someone did do his share of witch-pricking, seeking the witches mark. On Margaret McWilliam it was successful: produced 3 marks, one blue one white. It was also tried on Katherine Moore, her daughter, successfully. [In which case she too may have died in Prison, for it is hard to see how she could survive being an accomplice of her mother on nearly every occasion]. That was a specialised job and someone may have

---

[166] He does not appear on the Privy Council Rolls from Argyll as an accused. He might have been killed in revenge by a relative by May 1662.

been called to do it from the mainland. Someone may indeed have arrived from the mainland who thought himself an expert in this very matter having 'succeeded in identifying witches in other places' by this means. He would charge good money for his services. He may have been the trigger for the entire witch hunt: a man seeking a job!

As for the child shooting: that women who had borne children themselves and brought them up should engage in this is difficult to take. Nor does it seem as if they were taking revenge on the fathers. It might be that the malefice towards the child was presented, was a fact, but coincidence took care of the murder as an accident of some kind. And yet, Margaret McWilliam did say that she killed her own son William, aged 7 and in circumstances which are hard to imagine were invented for her by the interrogator. She does of course regret this 'more than anything else she has ever done'. Does it means that she had a down on children? Male children, say? No, for she has another grandson, John Moore, also tried at some stage for witchcraft. It may be significant that when Katherine Moore is quizzed about her husband's whereabouts he is stated to be at home and that 'they could not both come' probably because of the need for one to look after the children. Perhaps children were believed to be at risk from being stolen by fairies or killed by other adults.

What these women are guilty of, mainly, is ill feeling towards some people whom they are aggressive towards and may engage in putting pocks of witchcraft in their houses under their beds etc. In those days people died suddenly from many diverse causes; a cut that goes septic, a cough that goes consumptive, of pneumonia, of food poisoning which must have been common, of helicobacter and any number of bacteria and viruses whose effects were exacerbated by the dirty conditions which were normal in a society where few people could afford shoes, cleanliness practically unknown and impossible to achieve had its benefits been understood.

(vi) Did the accused commit murder?

Adam Kerr by M. McWilliam and her daughters said by Jonet Morison
Alester McNiven by McWilliam and her daughter said by Jonet Morison
John Glass's child by unclear [shot at window] said by Jonet Morison
Jonet Stewart (almost) by McConochie and Elsp. Galy said Jonet Morison
John Glass (planned) by company of witches said by Jonet Morison
Wm. Stewart (requested) by Jonet Morison(refused)said byJonet Morison
Wm McWilliam by M. McWilliam said by Margaret McWilliam
Bairn of Donald Moir McKaw by McWill, Stewart, McKaw etc dr sai by McLevin
Rbt McKomaish by McKeraish said by McLevin
Wm Stephen by McWilliam and Kat Moore said by Jonet Morison
Son of James Andrew by McWilliam said by McLevin
Bairn of Donald Roy McKerdie by Patrick McKaw said by McLevin
Child of McCurdie said by various.
Alexander McNiven by McWilliam and Katherine Moore said by McLevin.

Shooting might mean a few things, in spite of the distinction made by Jonet Morison between shooting and blasting, that shooting at the heart kills immediately and that shooting elsewhere means death eventually. We also have the case of shooting when a hole is created under the ribs wide enough to insert a knife. The word must refer to the use of a firearm for only a firearm could guarantee to kill with a heart shot. The reason why a shot directed elsewhere always results in death is due, presumably, to the infection for which, in 1662, there is no effective answer. And yet, almost certainly, the fact given

APPENDICES

is not all inclusive; there would be exceptions, depending on where the bullet hit. This description is not covered by a sling, which would be easily made with, say, deer tendon as a strong elastic and a forked stick or even the kind of sling which uses no forked stick. these may have been common weapons at that time. The 'elf errow stone' mentioned by Margaret McWilliam might have been a small stone with a point, in the shape of an arrow, which was fired from a sling. The other possibility is that 'shooting' may just mean, at least some of the time, directing a curse or malefice upon a person. The meaning of a word in 1662 when firearms are not in common use by the poor might be different from what it is now.

If shooting does mean the use of a firearm, where was the firearm obtained? Where did the powder come from? And the bullets?

In years of the English occupation [c 1650 – 1661] weapons of any kind in the hands of locals were banned, a sensible procedure in case the natives revolted. The Cromwellian forces were very effective. Even so, any weapons which had been in the hands of natives of the island would be concealed if that was possible and not handed in when demanded. Thus, when the English left, these weapons would be taken out again and were available for use— if not rusted. Another possible source of the odd weapon during this period was the 'runaways' whom we read of in the Records. These would be deserters from the English army, the Scottish army having been soundly defeated at Dunbar at the start. An English trooper would desert with his musket and it could easily be sold off for food to sustain him and aid in moving to a safer place.

Because there was some difficulty in obtaining and retaining a smith on the island at this time it is unlikely that there was any scope for private industry in gun making. Bullet and powder could be got from Glasgow and might have begun to be available in the shops of Rothesay after 1660 when the troops were having far less effect and everything was unclear. Almost certainly a short barrelled gun, a pistol which used powder and ball. It could easily be concealed.

The likeliest way a musket or firearm of some kind would find its way into the hands of someone like Margaret McWilliam is by theft and it probably is a late development in her life— after 1660. Why would she go to all that trouble to erect a slap to protect her field against the McFees if she already possessed a firearm? A woman with that much smeddum would have shot one of them in preference to lying across the slap while they took it down. Plainly she had no access to weapons whatever, then at least.

One of the puzzles here is why the parents of children or the relatives of adults who were shot, as described above, did not effectively protest. During the occupation, the officer commanding would definitely have taken action: not only to find the culprit, but most of all the weapon for that could be used against him and his troops at some later time. This means that there probably were no shootings during the occupation which means they all took place after 1660 i.e. 1660-1661, during these two years. Why is it possible then for the first time?

Because some people on the island, at least, were given the right to bear arms again in case of invasion or other trouble. This means the gentry would have access to weapons again. But it also means that any weapons which had been concealed could be brought forth. And the most significant point is that, now that the soldiery were either gone from the island or an ineffective unit because of many being taken elsewhere to London, say, where General Monk sat with an army after 1658, there was no local police force of any kind. The weapon might have been a pistol bought from or swapped from a passing ship, fishing boat, or rowing boat. Ships of all kinds passed the island all the time and would seek shelter and food and water at all times and in every place.

Before the arrival of the English, the duty of rooting out wrongdoers was in the hands of the crowner, the Jamesons of Kilmory Castle, an office that was abolished only a decade or two later, perhaps because it was now seen to be ineffective.

So who could you go to if you found your child had been shot? Your elder in the Kirk Session. There was no one else except Jamieson. He might try and find the culprit but he had not the means to enjoy any sort of advantage. People would travel about the island all the time on foot, they would not be recognisable unless very close to, because of the simplicity of clothing, especially for the poor. In addition, neighbours of the person who had lost a child in this way, even if they knew the culprit, might choose to keep quiet in case of reprisals (a serious matter if McWilliam was involved) and more so if she were known to have a gun or, indeed, because, as members of the witch community, they were party to the attack or to other attacks news of which would come out if this one did).

In the years 1660-1662, therefore, there was no law in the island worthy of the name. Only the Kirk Session—but that, as we have repeatedly seen, was formidable and had eyes everywhere. Even the lairds and gentry were still finding their feet after the occupation. This is why shooting of children and adults could occur and why there is no mention of it anywhere until the witch hunt when everything comes out. And yet, one feels, that the parents of the children of McKirdy and James Andrew must have sent up such a wail of lamentation that something would emerge in the Kirk Session records. Not so! What does that mean? That their children just died? or were not noticed to have been shot? No. The accusations of shooting and of murder may be correct but they are more likely to be the presumptions of a couple of women used to the idea that some witches like McWilliam are capable of this. Morison was found guilty of slander just before this so it must be likely that her accusations are just further examples. The fact that McLevin might have confirmed some of these does not in the circumstances add credence to the claim, for the prison walls would be of wood and everything one witch said could be heard by another. Collusion was inevitable under the circumstances, the more especially given the system of extracting confessions which can be imagined to follow the pattern in other places at the same time: sleep deprivation etc.

(vii) Robert Stewart of Scarrell is the person taken by the witches to be the devil. Why?

Good reasons have already been given on p241. There is no mention of his name in ID and yet the notes cover the period from 15th January to March 26th. And yet the devil is mentioned as a person in a group seen in Bute on several occasions and his name has been raised as a question. Who was the person who was called: 'Klareanough'? Any other person would have been identified by now. This one has not been because he is special: a son of the manse, a university graduate, a person of the highest class in the island: the moneyed, propertied set who hold the most important offices like Commissary of the Isles [grandfather] and member of the Commissariat Group which includes Sir James Stewart and his father as extras. This man has been an assistant minister in Rothesay. He is a qualified minister. For him to be delated as the devil would be a catastrophe for his class of educated, wealthy members of the gentry, who are his friends. That is why his name does not appear in 1662.

It has already appeared in 1661 and that was catastrophe enough: adulterer and defiler of his teaching as a minister.

Worse still, he tried to hide his crime by passing the child onto other innocent people. Tried to bribe them and even marry off the lady, Nancy Throw, to a man she did not want, to conceal his offences.

His behaviour was so far different from what was expected of gentlemen that it threatened the very fabric of society which existed on the principle that the rulers were examples other men should follow. It cast doubt upon the behaviour of every other person of that class.

In addition, there has to be a person to whom the appellation 'the devil' applies, even if it applies only after the fact when the witches are compelled to recount details of their lives. For he is mentioned as a person, defined as a well favoured young man, mostly, and a member of a group some of the time. He asks, we are told repeatedly, for the woman 'to goe with him', What else could this mean but have sex somewhere? No particular place is mentioned to which they are to go. It is not going to a particular place but going to any convenient place for the purpose of the only act that makes sense and the kind of act that repeatedly in Fife and other places occurs soon after the covenant is made. As a kind of seal on the bargain. Since she has agreed to serve him in any way he wishes, of course the best way to establish this is for her to supply this service immediately, before she changes her mind.

Both McLevin and McWilliam report suffering injury at the hands of the well-favoured young man who is the devil, at his first manifestation, the former by suffering a sore finger, the latter a sore thigh (hensh). It would be easy to explain away these by referring to the circumstances of the confession: mistakes made by the recorder and inquisitor. This may be valid. Indeed, the injuries may have been manufactured to make the covenant seem one agreed under duress. But, given the character of Robert Stewart it is at least as likely that he was so set upon sex, so aroused, that he seized the women and caused the injuries when they attempted to draw away. That is possible. On neither occasion with these women is he successful at the first meeting. As a member of the ruling power in the island, the gentry, he can be expected to be, at least initially, high handed and even heavy handed. It may not have occurred to him that they would refuse him.

That no effort was made to identify RSS in ID shows that his identity was known from the beginning. And that it had been decided to ignore him, as a danger they could not handle. It is amazing that no effort is made in ID to name him other than as Klareanough. But the earl, as an able outsider with the necessary authority to intervene, would have noticed the discrepancy and, perhaps, saved the day, at least to some extent.

(viii) Why is the devil taken to appear in the form of a cat, a dog or a stalk of heather at other times?

Because at the moment they are thinking about the offer they have received from the devil {Robert Stewart}, still having not agreed, this is the object nearest to hand that they notice. Since they have the idea of the devil in their minds, they associate that idea with whatever apparently live entity is close by. That, for Morison, a message came from a stalk of heather is simply a symptom of her psychosis. it is the modern equivalent of receiving a message though the radio or television— a personal message. This is what happens to psychotics: they hear voices in exactly this fashion. The voices tell them to do things, odd things. In the case of McWilliam, the well favoured young man clearly is accompanied by a little brown dog and she sees it first.

(ix) Why were McLevin and Morison psychotic?

It is impossible to say for certain; but it is almost certain that they suffered in this way. What might have caused them to have a psychosis? The very repressive community in which they lived! That could be enough. It would be very disturbing to be under the eye of everyone on the island and be severely punished for every trifling fault. Not everyone is affected this way but some sensitive souls might be and they might be more prone to this because of particular deficiencies of vitamins, predispositions and even diseases. But it is possible, more likely, that an individual provoked the psychosis by an assault upon their characters. The Minister, if he attacked them strongly, one by one, as witches, as people who harmed others, people who deserved to burn in hell and moreover, soon to be sent there by being burnt on earth— he could himself have induced the psychosis which they exhibit in his record of confessions. The effect of living in a religious cult in modern times can be to so disturb the mind of the person dominated by the leader of it that they become psychotic.

(x) What does Robert Stewart of Scarrell do about his situation?

Ostracised, denied human contact with those he knows in the Kirk and maybe even his wife, he seeks consolation elsewhere: finds some women friends to help him out of his trouble. Since there are people, mostly women, living on the fringes of the community because they seek to live a life that is not devoid of fun, one where there are dances and picnics and mischief, they already meet in secret and he is allowed to join them and he adds status to the group and the group even enlarges and becomes more obvious in the community. Robert Stewart of Mecknoch sees this group, identifies a few because he sees them meeting above his steading on the hilly moor there and lays evidence before the minister who realises that there is a group outside the normal auspice of the church, yet of churchgoers, but outwith his control and he determines to investigate. And he is right to do so, for Robert Stewart of Scarrell will influence them with his different views of what is allowable and decent and Christian, as distinct from what the church and the Kirk Session preach and punish.

The threat presented to the established church and the authority of the island by RSS is removed only by his submission to them.

(xi) The Character of Master Robert Stewart and Nancy Throw.

RSS must have been a vigorous manly man, like Caesar, Burns, Kennedy and Clinton, to take the risks he did in making love to Nancy Throw. He could not stop himself, that is the essence of it. He knew disaster was inevitable and how!: with a child arriving. And it made no difference. He must have loved her desperately to do it so often: for Nancy's admitted 'never freed for week' we can say 'never free whenever opportunity presented.' She must have loved him or she would not have taken the risk and she could have called it off any time she chose by speaking to an elder. The Kirk Session would have believed her immediately and she would know that. The Session existed to discover and punish sinful acts. Even Ninian Bannatyne of Kames was accused of fornication with Nancy and he was one of the two greatest men on the island. Nancy must have been besotted with our Master Robert to have agreed to put the blame for the child on other men and actually to have connived with one of them, Alexander Bannatyne, to that effect—

fruitlessly, as it turned out, for she was not believed, or he. She must have been beautiful and she may have been intelligent and educated beyond her years because of her association with the great men of the place, even if only as a servant.
Right after the first time of lovemaking she could have stopped it. But love is fickle and when a child came and all the hullabaloo about the father and the uncertainty of her position, now a fallen woman, and, above all, the social disapproval, which would be very severe, she changed. Sought escape routes for herself. But she was willing to go along with the idea of blaming someone else and that was because of love for RSS not out of fear for herself. Even were it fear for him, a man in his position, it was still love. What happened was inevitable and she knew it at every moment. She wanted the man and the child too. The one without the other was impossible. She gloried in the man's status, education, presence, money, power, sexual vigour and looks too, probably. He was the catch of the place: the best man around. Well then, what woman would not have fallen in love with him, especially when he approached her in such a rampant fashion? Nancy must have been dazzled by Master Robert Stewart of Scarrell and soon besotted with him. She was bewitched and beguiled by him and he with her.

The Witches: questions.

(xii) Did they kill the children?
No. If they had actually shot them there would have been a loud lamentation from the parents that would have gone on and on and never stopped. There had to be a bullet hole. There had to be signs of shooting. There had to be a visit not only to the elders but the minister too. And it had to be in the Kirk Session and in the minutes by January 1662. There is no mention of any such thing in any of the years from 1654. The lives of the people of Bute are limited to fornication, drunkenness, sabbath breaking and mild slanders, for the most part. Murder of anyone, especially a child, would have been accompanied by an immediate hunting down of the culprits. There could not have been any murder of children by shooting, as described. The questions to Jonet Morison would have been. Did you see this? When and where did it happen? Who fired the weapon and who else was present? And where did the shot hit? None of them she could have answered. It is just a further case of slander. What Jonet means is that the child in question died and she attributed its death, without any kind of proof, to McWilliam et al. And McWilliam, at the time, may actually had failed to deny this, content to make use of her daring and apparent willingness to murder for the sake of reinforcing a reputation for aggressive response if troubled by anyone. The fact that there was a hole in one man, McNiven, under the short ribs that you could put a knife in does not show that he died of a bullet. He could have been injured in some other way. Shooting, even in his case, may be no more than a willing that he suffer some form of malefice: ill will by McWilliam.

(xiii) Why did the two women say that murder had occurred?
Because they thought McWilliam (and others) did have magic powers to injure in this way, the people in question did die suddenly and, just because McWilliam might have wanted them dead, it was assumed that she was responsible. Shooting means: willed them to die.
They thought McWilliam was responsible and were happy to reveal this because they thought it would help their own cause. That is why Morison called the minister to her house to tell them what she had decided to say. It is noteworthy, however, that she does

not tell the tale about the child murders at the beginning, only after she herself has been apprehended and after two other interviews does she reveal this. She was also a convicted slanderer : see p43 Kirk Session Records below for 6th June 1661. Why is it so likely that these murders are fictions? Because no one except McLevin and Morison admitted them in over 2 months of questioning. Why did none of the other named persons present at the meetings when the murders are alleged to have taken place or were mooted, have anything to say about them? The first thing that the Minister should have done after hearing McLevin's confession was examine all the people mentioned in ID 9 and 10 who were involved. He did not do this or, at least there is no sign that he did. The same for Morison: these people should have been examined and should be on the document by the time it ended in March 26 1662. Morison confessed in January 1662. Why is there no mention of this? Because there was no useful evidence. These others had told him nothing of value. Why then is the document left in this form? Because he already has two witnesses who have confirmed murders by some of the witches. That is all he needs. The Kirk Session will confirm the confessions. The Minister knew these allegations of murder were untrue but left them in the document without rebuttal because they were good evidence of malefice, if needed. Remember that this document was still being presented at the court in 1673. This is what Melis the Prosecutor is referring to and why it has ended up in Inverary. The young earl took it there afterwards.

(xiv) Were the four burnt those said in the reconstruction to have been burnt?

This is not quite certain, though nearly so. Margaret McLevin, Margaret McWilliam and Isobel McNicoll should have been burnt because of their confessions. But so, according to the note near the end of the Document, should Jonet McIlmartin[167]. Yet, since there is no record of the confession by that time, she may have got off. Not likely! Not given what we have seen in the method of obtaining confessions: it was just a matter of time.

In fact, so also should Katherine Moore an accomplice of her mother, Margaret McWilliam, on nearly every occasion. That Christine Bannatyne should have been accused of attending witches meetings and poisoning the Lady of Kames should have earned her death also. For, of course, an admission to that effect could have been easily tortured out of her. We just do not know about the other two dozen people delated as witches, some of them men.

And yet the records are clear that only 4 were burnt. What does this mean? That only four of those convicted or about to be convicted were left to burn. The others who would have burnt died in prison— of starvation, disease, ill treatment, lack of sleep, heart attacks (some would have been old and infirm) and just shock and ignominy— and even while trying to escape.

(xv) Records about Robert Stewart of Scarrell.

"On 3rd November 1658, the Council appointed Mr Robert Stewart of Skarrell, son of Mr Patrick Stewart, former Parish Minister, to be Schoolmaster. He was, of course, also appointed Session Clerk. [*This means he wrote the Session book quoted below! Yet his name is not in the sederunt. Does that mean it is taken for granted? His duty to attend and write down what occurred but take no further part? Why then is there no change*

---

[167] p28 Document, p231 herein

of style after July 4*th* 1661? Maybe that is the style approved as standard, easily copied then. After 18 July the Session Clerk is Mr. James Stewart p47 Notice that on 13*th* January 1659 his name appears in those present as 'Mr. Robert Stewart of Skarvell', a misspelling, yet he was the Session Clerk at that time; had been Session Clerk for 2 months.] He was a considerable landowner in Rothesay. He was educated at Glasgow University, of which he was a graduate, and was assistant to his father in 1641. He was recommended to the Presbytery of Knockfergus, in Ireland, in 1645, and to the Presbytery of Cowal[168] for testimonials in 1657, but he was apparently unsuccessful in obtaining a charge. His career as a teacher was short— three years— owing to misconduct with his servant he resigned, and glad to get off so easy, as he had been afraid that 'she would be drowned and he execute (sic) because he was a preacher." R.D.Whyte's Lectures p92 pub Buteshire Natural History Society 1999 ed IJ Gibbs ISBN 0905812131

"During the Civil War there was interference with the Burghs and suspension of the Annual Elections, and so we find that in 1653 and 1654 (the first of the minutes) no election had taken place. Indeed, in 1654 and ordnance {sic} had been passed at the insistence of that section of the clergy called the 'Protesters, giving power to Commissioners to appoint Magistrates and Councillors in the Burghs. The purpose of the 'Protesters' was to gain control of the civil power, and especially to secure a change in the Magistrates of Glasgow. [Consultations of the Ministers of Edinburgh, Scottish History Society, II p xiv]. An Election was, however, held here on 24*th* September, 1655[169]. The Council consisted of 27 members, and included Sir James Stewart and Mr Patrick Stewart, who were marked 'extra'. Mr Patrick Stewart, of Roseland, was the son of John Stewart, Commissary of the Isles. He was one of the largest proprietors in Rothesay, and the senior Parish Minister of Rothesay. He demitted office in 1650 on account of old age, but enjoyed the fruits of the benefice till 25*th* August, 1657, when he was deposed for swearing at his mother-in-law! Now, no order had apparently been secured for holding this election, and on 17*th* October, Duncan Kerr who had been a Bailie demitted his office 'in regard thair was no new ordour granted for a new electione'. But next year Kerr presided at the Burgh Court without any re-election, so his resignation cannot have been taken seriously. In 1657 Cromwell, against the advice of Monk, suspended the municipal elections, and it was not till 24*th* February, 1658, that the ban was removed by the Council of State. The election was held in April, 1658. [See Glasgow Records, 1630-62, p391]" RD Whyte's Lectures, p87.

(xvi) Statements From the Session Book of Rothesay 1658-1750
(a) Going with the fairies.
p23 8*th* March 1660
'The Session finding that ther is a report throw the contrie that Jeane Campbell, wife to Robert McConochie, gangs with the faryes, apointis the elders to tak tryell heireof and how the scandall raise and to mak report to the next Session.
'Delated Robert McConochie in Dunalunt suspect of adulterie with Mary Campbell, his servant. Apointis to be warned to the next Session.'

---

[168] This means that in those days, there was a single all inclusive presbytery on the island of Bute, the Presbytery of Bute consisting of Kingarth and Rothesay.
[169] This is the correct date: the published records quote the date mistakenly.

290 THE BUTE WITCHES

p24 22nd March 1660

'Quhilk day Patrick Campbell in Ardbeg gave in a clame to the Session shewing that he heard the Session was informed that his dochter, Jeane Campbell, went with the faries, desyreing the Session ernestlie to tak tryall of the said scandall and not to let the samen pas vntill his dochter were declared ether free or guiltie.

'The Session finding that the said report was comone and that nether the least presumption of the thing could be found nor a particular author thocht best for the removeall of the scandall to appoint the said Jeane Campbell, Robert McConochie, her husband, to be warned to the next Session, because it was aledged that the said Robert did vent the scandall.

'Compeired Robert McConochie in Dunalunt suspect of adulterie with Marie Campbell, his servant, who denied the same lykwise. The Session finding no presumptions but report that the scandall was raised throw evil will referr the purgeing of the scandall to the said Roberts oath who willingly gave the same and thereby purged the scandall.' [A different Robert McConochie, then, or he would have been compeired for the above also.]

(b) The Process against Nance Throw.

p33 11th October 1660

'Nance Throw delated suspect of being with child. Apointis to be warned.'

p33 25th October 1660[170]
'Nance Throw who formerly was delated with child in fornicatioune and concealeing to quhom was sumonded to the Session but compeired not. Apointis to be warned to the next.'

p 35 6th November 1660.
'Apointis Elspeth Campbell who reported that Nance Throw gave vp Gustavus Browne to be the father of her child to be warned to the next Session.
'Apointis Nance Throw and Alexander Bannatyne to be warned to the next Session.'

p34[171] 29th November
'Compeired Nance Throw and being demanded who was the father of the child he went with answered one Alexander Bannatyne. Being demanded why she concealed the father of the child quhen she heard that Baichalgrie, Gustavus Browne, Yong Sprinkell and Mr. Robert Stewart were named, answered, Never. The Session considering that ther is a privat whispering throw the parish that the said Alexander Banatyne is not the father but some vther delyed her for the present, desyreing that she should be at the next Session and to tell ingenously the true father; also apointis the said Alexander Bannatyne to be warned to the next Session.'

p35 20th December 1660.

---

[170] The date given is 1661, but this is an error as the editor of the Record is aware.
[171] The transcription is accurate: the records are printed out of order.

APPENDICES 291

'Compeired Nance Throw who hade formerlie given vp Alexander Bannatyne to be the father of her child and ther being a constant surmise throw the parish and suspition that ther was some collusion in the matter and that the said Alexander was not the richt father the Session thought fitt to examine her vpon circumstances. And being interrogate quhen and quher the said Alexander lay with her answered about 8 dayes before Witsunday last in Mr. Robert Stewarts house ther, butt quhen she was his servant and that the bairne was gotten then. (It is to be remembered that the said Nance declared to Mr. John Stewart, minister, vpon the Mononday before she came to the Session that the bairne was gotten in Kames after Witsunday quhen she was servant with the Laird of Kames.) Being demanded quhen and quher he lay with her answered about three nights after her comeing to Kames in the byre of Kames about the glomeing. Being demanded quhen and quher he first hade her answered about a yeire and ane halfe since in James McNivan's house quhen she was servant there. Being demanded quhilk was the last tyme he hade her answered about 8 dayes before St Braksday last in Robert Bannatyne's house at Mylne of Atrick.

'Compeired Alexander Banatyne and being inquired if he was the father of Nance Throws bairne answered that he could not deny but he lay with her but that he knew not if the bairne was his, and if it came to his tyme he could not deny it. Being inquired quhen and quher he lay with her answered about a month before Witsunday ar Drumchly vpon a tyme that she went vp to Scarrell to get meale to sojors. Being inquired if he hade her at any tyme betuix that tyme and Witsunday answered, Not vntill she left Mr. Roberts house and came to Kames. Being demanded quhen he hade her after comeing to Kames answered about ten or 14 dayes at Kockingray without house. Being demanded quhen and quher he first hade her answered about a yeire since in Mr. Roberts house. Being demanded if he hade her in James McNivan's house quhen she was his servant answered that he never hade her till she came to Mr. Roberts service. Being demanded quhilk was the last tyme he hade her answered vpon St Brakseven in her fathers house. Being demanded if he hade her at any other tyme but thir twice since her comeing to Kames answered that he hade her ane other tyme as they were comeing out of the towne in the moore of Kneslag. Being demanded if ever he hade her at the Mylne of Atrick in Robert Bannatynes house, answered, Never.
'Nance Throw being called in and enquired whether the said Alexander hade her at Drumchly answered, Yes. Being inquired if ever he hade her without house answered, Never, and yet that he hade without house at Drumchly.
'The Session finding severall contradictiones was the more suspitious of collusion between them and that the said Alexander was not the father of her bairne desyred her to confesse the true father of the child, and in the meane tyme did judiciallie sumond both parties to be at the next Session.'

p37 3rd January 1661

'Quhilk day Nance Throw being judiciallie sumonded at the last dyet to this Session did not compeire. Apointis to warne her to the next Session. Also Alexander Banatyne sumonded compeired not. Apointis to warne him.

'Mr. Robert Stewart gave in his complaint anent the maill of the house that he wantes dureing the tyme Mr. John Stewart dwelt there. The Session promises to tak a course therewith and lay downe a way for his payment quhen the report of the comprisers of the rood comes in quhilk they appoint to be against the next Session.' [*Robert Stewart of Scarrell rented a house to the minister while the manse, at the top of High St. east side, set back about 20 ft, was being refurbished. This manse was about 50 yds down the street towards the harbour from the present Minister's Brae, then non existent. He wanted the rent. The Session were expected to pay it.*]

p37 17th January 1661

'Compeired Elspeth Campbell who declared that heireing of Nance Throw's being with bairne said to her Is, Gustavus Browne the father of that bairne thow he's? The said Nance answered, If I were free of him I cared les for any other; and heireing therafter that she fathered her bairne vpon Alexander Banatyne the said Elspeth said to her, I thocht that Gustavus Browne was the father of thy bairne. Nance Throw answered that she thought shame that Alexander Bannatyne should be eivened to her.

'Quhilk day the Laird of Kames complained that his name was slandered about that bairne of Nance Throws and that it was reported that he promised Alexander Bannatyne a hyre for taking with the bairne in the behalfe of Mr. Robert Stewart to put it off him, and desyred the minister and elders to declare quhat they hade heard of the said scandall and to bring it to tryell. Wherefor Mr. John Stewart, minister, declared that it was told him that Robert Throw, the said Nance Throw's father came to Jeane Boyd, Robert Beithes wife, and asked her advyce how he should cary himselfe anent his dochter who was with bairne and that the said Jeane replyed, I heard first many fathers named to that bairne such as Gustavus Browne, Mr. William Maxwell, James McNivan, and Mr. Robert Stewart, and now I hearr she layes it vpon Alexander Bannatyne. To which the said Robert answered, They would mak it so but Mr. Robert was not the father. Replyed Jeane, If Sandy Bannayne tak with ane other man's bairne I am sure he must gett a good hyre. To which the said Robert answered, He getts her selfe, and Kames is dealing hard to mary her on the said Alexander, but its sore against her will that she had consented. At last the said Jeane said, Ye shall never get my advice till her to doe such a thing and he and she will never doe good if they doe sik a thing. The Session appoints Robert Throw and Jeane Boyd to be warned to the next Session.'

p38 24th January 1661

'Jeane Boyd being sumonded compeired not. The Session heireing that she was sick sent Mr. Alexander McLaine and Neill McNeill to speik to her and to report her declaratioune to the Session.

'Mr. John Stewart, minister, declared that quhen he heard this scandall of Mr. Robert he sent for Robert Throw and spok to him in private to know quhat ground it hade and that the said Roberts declaratioune to him was litle different fra quhat he heard was spoken to Jeane Boyd.

'Compeired Robert Throw and confessed that the conference betuix Mr. John Stewart and him was as followes. Quhen Mr. John told him that he heard his doughter was to mary Sandy Banatyne he answered that she might be some put of [*off*] of the same and that it was sore against her will. That quhen the said Mr. John said ther is a great report that Mr. Robert Stewart is the father of that bairne he answered that albeit he be yet he will never tak with it. And quhen Mr. John said, God can soone bring him to confession if he be guiltie, he answered, I know he will never tak with it for quhen God hardens a mans hert in his sine he will never confess, and that it was a sore thing that he who should be a good example to others should fall in the lyk of that sine. And quhen Mr. John desyred him to tell him how things were brocht about he answered, Ye neid no more of me and ye know the lyk of me is loath to be seene in it and that he would have told it to Mr. John first but that he kent it would grieve him. Being demanded if ther was anything promised answered, Ther was more promised than wold be payd. The said Robert being demanded if he sought Jeane Boyds advyce anent his daughters mariage answered that he did. Being demanded if he told her that Mr. Robert was the father of his dochters bairn answered that he did not pitch vpon Mr. Robert in particular, but that Gustavus Browne, Mr. William Maxwell, James McNivan and Mr. Robert was throw hand.

'The Session continues this proces till Jeane Boyd compeire who is apointed to be warned against the next.'

p39 7th February 1661

'Nance Throw compiered and being desyred to declare the richt father of her bairne declared she would give vp no other than Alexander Bannatyne. Apointis her to be warned *pro 30*[172].

p40 21 February 1661

'Quhilk day compeired Nance Throw and stood stiffe be her former declaratioune that Alexander Bannatyne was the father of her bairne.'

p43 6th June 1661

'Compeired Jonet Morisowne and denyed that ever shed spok the former wordis or heard Elspeth Spence[173] speak them. The Session considering that the witnesses hade deponed against her decerned her a slanderer of Elspeth Spence and apointed her to satisfie according to order and to pay of penultie 40s. As also considering that the said Jonet goes vnder the name of a witch or deceaver by vndertaking to haill desperat diseases by herbs and such lyk the Session did discharge the said Jonet Morisowne in tyme comeing to vse the giveing of any phisick or herbs to any body vnder the certificatioune that she shall be esteemed a witch if she so doe. And that the people may not heireafter employ her apointis intimatioune heirof to be made out of pulpit the next Sabaoth.'

p44 20th June 1661

---

[172] Probably an article in The Act of the General Assembly of 1596.
[173] Elspeth Spence lived at Edinmore, the hill above Wester Kames, where Jonet Morison worked.

'Ther being a flagrant scandall that Mr. Robert Stewart is the father of Nance Throwes child the Session appointis the said Mr. Robert to be sumonded to the next Session[174].'

p45 4th July 1661

'Quhilk day compiered Nance Throw and confessed that Mr. Robert Stewart was the father of her bairne. And being demanded why she fathered the bairne vpon Alexander Bannatyne answered that Mr. Robert had persuaded her that if she would confes the bairne to be his she would be drowned and he execute (sic) because he was a preacher. Being enquired how it came to pas that Alexander Bannatyne took with the child or if he hade any carnall dealeing with her but that she knew he was very desyrous to have her in mariag and that Mr. Robert bade her deale with him to tak with the bairne and promise to mary him which she did, but whether Mr. Robert spok or any other spok to him theranent she knowes not. *Item* also declares that Mr. Robert promised her for maryeing of Alexander Bannatyne and fathering the bairne on him fourtie merks so soone as the bairne were baptised in his name, and after mariage a boll of vituellis so long as they leived yeirely together with ane butt of land in Scarrell.
'The Session apointis to warne Alexander Bannatyne to the next Session, as also to warne Mr. Robert Stewart.'

p46 11th July 1661

'Compeired Alexander Bannatyne and with heavy sorrow and teares confessed his great guiltynes before the Lord in taking with ane other mans bairne and declared that that child was not his and that he hade never hade any carnall dealeing with the said Nance. Being inquired what made him take with the child answered that he was greatumly in love with the said Nance and very desyreous to mary her but she refused still and then quhen she came to him and pressed vpon himto mary her that he willinglie yeilded not knowing that she was with child, and after that he heard of her being with child he was so far ingaged in love to her that for to gett her to mary he was content to tak the child vpon him. Denyes that ever Mr. Robert or any other desyred him to tak with the bairne but only the said Nance who dayly prest him and persuaded him thereto. The Session suspecting that the said Alexander hade carnall dealeing with the said Nance thocht fitt [to] put him to his oath who freely deponed that he hade never any carnall dealeing [with] her.'

p46 18th July 1661

'Quhilk day the proveist and baylyes declared that Mr. Robert Stewart, late scholemaster, hade demitted his place and they haveing the offer of Mr. James Stewart and Mr. Robert Patoune to be scholemaster did mak choise of Mr. James Stewart and desyred him to be present at the Session to know ther mynd of his election. The Session vnanimously did elect the said Mr. James and embraced him to be ther scholemaster for a yeire, his beginneing to be at Lambas next, appointing him for a fyell as was formerly enjoyed by other scholemasters according to the act made theranent; together with the

---

[174] This suggests that he has already given up being Session Clerk. Why would they summon him for the next diet if he was present at that one, writing the minutes? They would quiz him there and then.

mariage and baptisme moneyes according to vse and wont and all other casualities belonging to the said schole; he serveing the offices of keepeing the said schole and **being clerk to the Session.....'** [For the three years he was schoolmaster, Robert Stewart of Scarrell was also Session Clerk, probably until just before or just after 4th July 1661, when his crime was made clear by Nancy Throw]

(xvii) Would the Session have allowed Mr RSS to retain the post of Session Clerk while Nancy's Process was going on and he was mentioned?

He would have had to remain as long as possible in the position. Resigning before he was exposed by Nancy would have sent a signal that he was guilty. So long as there was any chance that the guilt would either fall elsewhere or never fall, for some reason, he would choose to remain in the post.

p50 14th November 1661
'Quhilk day Mr. Robert Stewart heaving recovered of his seiknesse which hade deteiened him this long tyme and occasioned the halting of his processe thir severall Sessions bygone and decIaired that he hade confessed his guiltinesse in adulterie with Agnes Throw to Mr. John Stewart minister, and Sir James Stewart shireff of Bute a qwarter of a yeare since, but because of some consideratiouns moveing him thereto desired them to conceall the samene for a space and that now he did acknowledge his guiltinesse before them, desiring yet (the former consideratiouns moveing him) that the Sessione would be pleased to delay their injunctions for the space of a moneth, which the Session did condescend to do.'

p51 28th November 1661

'Quhilk day compeirt Nanc Throw desiring the Session that they would receave her to her repentance and determine the busness anent Mr. Robert Stewarts being the father of her cheild to the end that shoe might gett the cheild baptised. The Session considering that the said cheild had been unbaptized now thir three qwarters of a yeare and that the said Nance had suffered great miserie therby judged it fitt to call the said Mr. Robert before them, who compeiring and being enqweired if he was the father of his guiltinesse with the womane, and that the cheild was twentie days short of his tyme; as also decIaired that quhen the said Nance told him of her being with cheild that he desired her to enduce Alexander Ballantyne to take with the bairne by promiseing to marie him and to pitch upon a particulare tyme, viz. 8 days before Wheitsunday or 8 days after when the cheild was gotten and condescended upon that tyme before the Session. And being demanded how he could cause ane other to take with his cheild answered that the divill who hade enduced him to sinn had enduced him to that also, and that he had desired them to condescend upon that tyme in als mutch as it was about that tyme only that he had carnall dealing with her himselfe. Being enqweired (that seeing he had confessed carnall dealing with the womane the cheild will be declared his) if he knew any others that he suspected with the womane answered that he suspected the said Alexander Ballantyne and Gustavus Broune. The Session answered that for Alexander Ballantyne he could not suspect him because first the said Mr. Robert had enduced the said Nanc to entise the said Alexander to take with the bairne; 2dly because that the said Alexander had purged himselfe by his oath of the woman before the Session and with remorse declaired how he was entized and draven upon that bussines; and as for Gustavus Broune, if it were his desire the Session wold wreit to the ministers of Edinburgh,

'The said Nance Throw compeirand and being desired to give up the trew father of the bairne declared that shoe had no other bot Mr. Robert Stewart and that the first tyme he had carnall dealing with her was a litle afore Kandlemes in his oune house quhen his wife was at the Kams and that from that tyme untill her leaving of his service, which was after Whitsounday, he could not freeth her a week.'

(xviii) Inferences

There is no more here! [In the KS records for Rothesay] Except for 3 undated baptisms, there is a hiatus until 1673. This is deeply significant. We have the process against Robert Stewart of Scarrell and when it ends— the bit recorded— on 28th November 1661, the witch hunt begins on 16th January 1662! There are no records in between and nothing at all with a date until 1673. Thus, the connexion between Robert Stewart of Scarrell and the witch hunt is immediately clear and not likely to be accidental. Why? What could he have had to do with this witch hunt?

He could be the man taken afterwards in 1662, to have been described as the devil in events of 1661.

Between July 4th 1661 and 28th November 1661 when he compeired before the Kirk Session and confessed his guilt—adultery, fathering a child on a servant, trying to bribe another man to take the child as his responsibility, willing even at the very end, to have other men share the responsibility, when he knew that they were guiltless; and bringing the ministry into disrepute— all the worse since he had himself been assistant minister in the place and was at the time the Session Clerk, had himself been a leading figure in the community with education, money and connexions at the highest level; and having confessed privately to the minister and the Sheriff at an early stage— his humiliation must have been extreme. He would have experienced ostracism from every one of the community — except perhaps from the people on the fringes of it: the really poor, the lame and blind and the witches: poor women dabbling in spells and herbal remedies because they lacked education, any other kind of mental model to deal with life and who had found that the model presented by the Kirk and its vicious requirements which were necessary to secure a place in heaven were impractical and unworkable, at least as far as they were concerned, for it did not stop them dying of disease or starvation or in childbirth—events avoidable only if you had the advantage of money, food and good housing.

RSS had to join them! Without any sort of society he would have gone mad. The community would want him to go mad. It would save them the trouble of dealing with crimes they would all regard as phenomenal. He had to come across the witches on his lonely tramps across the island and he had to join them and the question then is: what effect had he upon them? And them upon him?

He would be a voice for them. A fallen angel now among them who could speak for them against the awful repression of that community imposed by the Kirk Session.

This very able man, very brave man to have courted disaster with a woman in this way, knowing the outcome in advance, would have led them all in his direction: more compassionate, more loving and more forgiving of sins, than the Session. He would have been their preacher! For that is what he had tried to do and been refused. And why was he refused? Because he was highly sexed. Was that his fault? Why should it be construed as a cross he had to bear? He wanted to enjoy women and had the ability to do it often. He was a benefit to them. That is what 'will you goe with me and be my servand' means. The same as it meant in Fife and elsewhere. This is the immediate action following the making of the covenant and we can see why: it confirms the avowal of service in an action.

In those appalling psychological conditions, he may have been slightly mad. He would have resented to the bottom of his soul, the men of the Session like, perhaps, Ninian Kerr and Walter Stewart, who were most antagonistic to his conduct. Men who, like Holy Willie, would have their own share of transgressions— which he may have known about!— and yet who condemned him and wanted him executed for his crimes! And what crimes were they? Falling in love! Behaving as men are programmed to do so at such times— mindless of anything else. He might easily have suggested that these men be killed. 'I wish they were dead!' might be all it took for Jonet et al to say: he ordered them killed. But Ninian Kerr survived for we see him in the Records years later but not so many years that it is his son.

(xix) What triggers the witch hunt?

1. We have more meetings of the witch folk, the folk on the periphery of the community with more attenders. Because RSS is in charge the meetings have point. There are sermons: by him and he preaches a doctrine far more forgiving than the Church of Scotland code. He allows dancing and feasting—except there is little for the poor to feast with—and even fun!
2. Would they gang up on others not of the group? Some of the Session and even not of it would be hated and detested by the witch group and would be fair game. Revenge could be taken against them. They might go looking for prey. But there would be no intent to commit greater cruelties than the witches had been subjected to. The misunderstanding in the use of the word 'prey' instead of 'pray' as in the reconstruction is likely. People will have died in the past from just such misunderstandings.
3. RSS would dampen such revenges (because he is a minister and a Christian) but would fail at times. However, it is just possible that the immense stress upon RSS caused him to be irrationally antagonistic to the leaders of the community who acted against him.
4. The trigger is when the Kirk Session, members of it, becomes aware of this counter movement within the church, within the island community. They are threatened by it, some of its less repressive ideas especially. That is why they start taking evidence. Why they use the old concepts of witchcraft to interrogate the suspected witches and, under sleep deprivation, they make statements that are not true. At an early stage an 'expert' is called in to prick for the mark and apply the torture.
5. The result is a foregone conclusion: any witch who admits to a covenant is doomed. Then the group can be outlawed and disbanded. The community cleansed.
6. But afterwards, all those or most, will still think the women did what they were tortured into saying they did.
7. Because of his actual love of Nancy and her subsequent losing love for him, because of the pressure of the community, he comes to examine this and the very nature of love in life and finds it different— very different— from what the church demands be the standard.

8. The conflict, ultimately, is one of ideas. RSS has one view and the community and the Kirk another. The Kirk had to act to put down his meetings and his influence. He spoke to the people of the true nature of love; and because it did not accord with received wisdom, it had to be defeated. That is the real reason behind the witch hunt.
9. How do we know RSS would have a different view from the Session and that this is what it would have been? Because his experience would have shown him the difference and he would try to justify it, being well educated, probably looking down on everyone else, in this respect. We have to accept that he was in the company of witch people. He had no other company. He had to turn to them. The description of the leader fits him. Also, someone had to be responsible for the increase in the number attending meetings. He, alone, could have achieved this. He alone could be the leader who caused this. Given that he is the leader of that company, it is inevitable that he would preach and inevitable that he would preach a more forgiving doctrine. But whatever he was preaching, he was labelled the devil and that was enough to execute the witches. As soon as the devil was involved, the outcome—death— was certain for those who had made a covenant with him, though it had been a fairly innocent arrangement for sexual favours.

(xx) Robert Stewart of Scarrell's possible excommunication.
(a)Acts of the General Assembly
From The General Assembly of the Church of Scotland, 1638;

p37 ARTICLE XVI 'Anent *frequenting with excommunicat persons*: The Assembly ordaineth that the act at *Edinburgh March 5*. 1569. Sefs. 10. to wit, *That these who will not forbear the companie of excommunicat persons after due admonition, be excommunicat themselves, except they forbear*, to be put in execution.

The Assembly alloweth this Article.

[Note: the italics here are precisely as given in the Act itself]

p37 ARTICLE XVII 'Whereas *the confession of the* Faith of this Kirk, concerning both Doctrine and Discipline, so often called in question by the corrupt judgement and tyrannous authoritie of the pretended Prelats, is now clearly explained, and by this whole Kirk represented by this generall Assembly concluded, ordained also to bee subscribed by all sorts of persons within the said Kirk and Kingdome: The Assembly constitutes, and ordaines, that from henceforth no sort of person, of whatever quality and degree, be permitted to speak, or write against the said Confession, this Assembly, or any act of this Assembly, and that under the paine of incurring censures of this Kirk.'

The Assembly alloweth this Article.

p41 'Act. Sefs. 24. December 18.1638.

The Assembly considering the great necessity of purging this land from bygone corruptions, and of preserving her from the like in time coming, ordaineth the Presbyteries ro proceed with the censures of the Kirk, to excommunication, against those Ministers who being deposed by this Assembly acquiesces not to their sentences, but exercise some part of the their Ministeriallfunction, refuseth themselves, and with-draw others from the obedience of the acts of the Assembly.'

(b) Inferences. The likelihood that for his sins, Mr. Robert Stewart of Scarrell was excommunicated is revealed by the above articles in the act of the General Assembly. In addition, on a few occasions, we find in Rothesay Town Council Records p304 for 16th March 1671:-

'Compeirit befoir Archibald Glas baillie of Rothesay Jeane Colquhoun wyff of Mr Robert Stewart of Scarrell and raifiet and approvit ane heretabill dispositioune granted be hir said husband with hir consent, of a tenement of land callit Butglais lyand on the eist syde of the gait of the kirk of Rothesay in favours of John Mure burges of Rothesay and Katherin Spence his spous thair aires and assigneys heretablie and maid faith that scho was not coactit or compellit thairto, quherupone the said John Mwir askit instruments befoir thir witnesses James Stewart merchant, John Gray smithe burgesses of Rothesay.'

This ground was across the road from the High Kirk. The important fact is that Mr. Robert Stewart of Scarrell is not present, though he is the seller of the land. He is represented by his wife: then Jean Colquhoun. If he had by then been excommunicated this is understandable. Other people were supposed to have no dealings of any kind with him, on pain of excommunication themselves. There are other cases like this of Mr. Robert Stewart of Scarrell selling off land and being represented by his wife. He would be reluctant to appear in a court in person, for fear of causing difficulties for others present; had he done so, the court might have refused to hear the case. Being represented by his spouse was the only way the case could go forward. And yet, we are forced to wonder his spouse? Was she not excommunicate just because he was?

With crimes as serious as his, it is difficult to see how the Kirk could have permitted RSS to continue as a member. Excommunication was inevitable, even had he accepted his sentence, whatever it was and made a remarkable plea and repentance. How would the congregation have felt worshipping with him in their midst? He had admitted to being possessed by the devil and several witches had, probably, identified him as the devil incarnate in their cases of making covenants with the devil.

And yet excommunication did not occur for he was not a listed minister of the Kirk and at the time in question he had been a schoolmaster. In addition, and very significant: he is listed in 1673 as married to Jean Colquhoun as well as in 1655 which means that his wife remained true to him after these events, a thing impossible had he been excommunicated. Nobody could marry an excommunicated person or continue to live with him without being excommunicated herself. Since he was in every other way ostracised it is unlikely that she continued to live with him. Everyone would have understood her separation, if she did so, given his crimes, against her as well as the community and Nancy Throw.

(xxi) Was Argyll at the trials? His father had been beheaded the year before. He never did take the dukedom because it was never offered. Earl was all he could be. He should have been in Argyll in 1662 trying to look after his lands after the disaster to his father just before. In that case he was available and a court would have been convened as soon as he was free to attend. John Blain, a very good author, says that it was an Argyll

Judiciary Assize [Blain p219]. Probably he was present, then, in person. No one else had the requisite authority to go ahead with such a matter: with executions to be held.

Blain, same ref, definitely suggests that Jonet McNicoll was not actually convicted in 1662 but escaped beforehand, knowing she would be, having both confessed and been delated by other witches.

(xxii) The age of Ninian Bannatyne younger in 1673?

Elizabeth Stewart, 1st daughter of Sir James Stewart, Sheriff of Bute[c1615- 1672, according to Blain] married Ninian Bannatyne of Kames. Young Ninian Bannatyne of Kames was a depute at the Assize of 1673 when Jonet McNicoll was tried and convicted to be executed. Is this possible? If Sir James married Grizell Campbell in 1636 when he was 21, and Elizabeth was born that year, she would be 18 in 1654 and if she married Ninian then in 1673, young Ninian would be no more than 19. So no contradiction: he was, however, very young for the job of depute justice.

(xxiii) The relationship between Rev Master Patrick Stewart and Rev Master John Stewart

By the rules of the time, a retiring minister was entitled to retain the stipend when he retired from a church. Patrick had been minister at Kingarth before Rothesay. When he demitted his charge at Rothesay in 1650[175] he continued to receive the stipend until 1658 when he was deposed for swearing at his mother-in-law etc. Since he was appointed to Kingarth in 1597, assuming he was at least 20 then, he was born before 1577, which makes him in 1650, 73 years old and 81 when he died. No wonder he felt it time to retire. On agreeing to give up Kingarth in 1632, he agreed to give up half the stipend to the new incumbent, the Parish having then been divided but failed to keep the agreement on the grounds that the new man, Master James Johnston was not fully qualified. Master Patrick Stewart was minister for both Kingarth and Rothesay till 1640.

In 1654, the Synod wrote to Patrick 'to desist from purshewing wrongfullie the said Rev Master John Stewart' for the Kingarth stipend which he claimed in spite of having given up that part of the island in 1640[176]. In 1658, Patrick was found guilty by the Synod of 'his purshew of Mr. Jon {sic} Stewart, Minister at Kingarth, very violently and unjustlie,' and of 'scandalous and deteastable covetousness.'

Rev John Stewart had good reason to detest Rev Patrick Stewart and maybe also the son, by association.

(xxiv) Was the spouse involved at the trial and confession?

Notice that during one of the later confessions of Jonet McNicoll, Duncan McNicoll (23 Feb 1662, p14) was present. This may be her husband. He may also have been the same Duncan McNicol present in 1673 in the jury at the Assize. His presence may have been considered to lend credence to the conviction. He may have been perceived as the kind of man able to be controlled by more powerful ones, to one of whom he owed his livelihood.

(xxv) What became of Jonet McNicol's child?

---

[175] Whyte p 96, 97
[176] Whyte, p100

From the Session Book of Rothesay 1658-1750 p62:
28 January 1686
'This day Donald McNicoll in Rothesay presented to the Session a lybell against John Ochaltry complaining that the said John had sadly abused himself and his parents calling him the child of a witch and severall other uncharatable and scandalous names. The said Donald intreating his lybell might be examined and consigning an half crown (as is the custom to be lost if he did not instruct his charge against Ochaltry) it is appointed that John Ochaltrie and the witnesses be summoned to the next day.'
17 February 1686
'John Ochaltrie being summoned and cited according to the appointment of the last Session compeired this day and confessed quhat Donald McNicol had lybelled against him, whereupon the Session finding that in the time of Master John Stewart, late minister of Rothesay, there was an act concluded and published before the congregation against this way of scandalizing as occasioning much tumult and malice among the people, fyning and mulcting the contraveeners of the act in ten pounds Scotts, and appointing them publickly before the congregation to acknowledge their sin, theirfore the Session determines about John Ochaltrie accordingly.'
2nd March 1686, p63
'John Ochaltrie is absolved and his penalty given to Patrick Stewart, schoolmaster.'

(xxvi) Records of Robert Stewart of Scarrell and his wife Jeane Colquhoun

From Rothesay Town Council Records 1653-1688 :
18th April 1655, p5
'The quhilk day in presence of Niniane Ker baillie of Rothesay compeirit <u>Jeane Calquhoune spous to Mr Robert Stewart of Scarrell</u> outwith the presence of hir said husband and ratifiet and approvit ane Dispositioune and Renunciatioune maid be the said Mr Robert with hir consent in favours of Allexander Wode burges of Rothesay of the croft of land callit Croftfaik lyand within the said brughe betwuix the said Allexanders lands and kill on the northe part and the Croft of land perteining to John Bannatyne of Cleckinbey on the southe part and maid faithe that scho was nowayis coactit or compellit thairto bot that the samyn proceidit vountarlie of hir awin frie motive will upone proffitabill and foirsein causes tending to my weill and utilitie.'
25 December 1657, p7
'Donald McKinley younger is actit cautioner for louseing of the areistment layd in Patrk Glass handis in Roisland at the instance of David Boyll of Kelburne of all the cornes crope cattell guids and geir belonging to the deceist Mr Patrick Stewart of Roisland that the samyn salbe maid furthcumand to the said David Boyll of Kelburne as lawe will and <u>Jeane Calquhoune spous to Mr Robert Stewart of Skarrell</u> her actit and obleist hirselffe for relieff of the said Donald and all dampnadge he sall incure be reasone thairof. Daniel McKaniely; Jane Collquhoun, Car.'
16th January 1674 p 323
'Item a Band made and granted be <u>Mr. Robert Stewart..[of Scarrell] and Jeane Colquhoune his spouse</u> to the said wmquhill John Ker and they are obledged to make payment to the said wmquhill John Ker his aires and assignays of the sume of   (sic) and for his securities therof of tghe yearly annualrent of the said principall sume they dispone in favour of the said wmquhill belonging to them lying within the said burgh called....'

18th April 1656, p10

'The quhilk day in presence of Niniane Ker baillie personaly compeirit Jeane Colquhoun spous to Mr Robert Steuart of Skarrell and ratefiet and approvet outwith the presence of the said Mr Robert hir husband ane Dispositioune maid be the said Mr Robert with hir consent to Charlis McKeachen and Marioun NcVrarthie his spous of the said Mr Robert his landis callit Fairfaddis laynd within the brughe of Rothesay betuixt the lands callit Aithanes land quhilkis belongit to unquhile Donald McVrarthie and now possessit be Donald McGilchrist notar on the southe part and Hew Allanes land on the northe part thairof togidder also with that part of land callit Fauldtarsin belonging to the said Mr Robert betuixt the landis possessit and wodset heretably be the said Donald McGilchrist on the eist part and the landis perteining to Charlis McKeachen and John McGilchrist proveist on the west the commoun loneing on the south part and the lands perteining to Hew Allane on the northe part thairof and declairit upone hir great oathe outwith the presence of hir husband in a fensit court that scho was not coactit or compellit thairto ne hir husband but that the samyn proceidet of hir awin frie motive will upone profitabill and foirseine causes tending to hir weill and proffeit and not only renuncet hir lyfrent of the foirsaid lands but alswa of all uther lands formarly disponet be hir said husband to the said Charles McKeachen quherinto sche was infeft quherupon the said Charles tuik instruments and requyret ane act of court to be maid.'

Rothesay Town Council Records p16. Top of page worn away. This is almost certainly about Master Robert Stewart of Skarrell.

'....band of wodsett be maid be the said Mr Robert with hir [*Jeane Colquhoun's*] consent to Johne Glase baillie of Rothesay of the fauld of land callit Gallowisfade lyand within the brughe of Rothesay [*perhaps between Gallows Craig and the water of Loch Fad: ie a field left or right of the present day Chapelhill, perhaps*] and renunceit hir lyferent of the said fauld of land in a fenssit court ay and quhill the soume of tua hundredth and ten merks money scotts borrouit be the said Mr Robert fra the said Johne Glase are compleitly payit to him untill the reall payment of the samyn conforme to the said heretabill securety grantit thairupone in all pointes and outwithe hir said husbands presence declairet upon hir great oathe that she was not coactit nor compellit thairto ne hir said husband but that the samyn proceidet of hir awin fre motive will upone profitable and foirseane causes tending to hir weill and proffeit quherupone the said Johne Glase tuik instruments in the hands of me Donald McGilchrist toun clerk of Rothesay and desyret ane act to be maid thairupone quhilk band is of the dait at Rothesay the   day of October 1657.'

(xxvii) They had tar in Bute.
13th March 1656 Rothesay Town Council Records p10

'Quhilk day anent the actioune persewit be Duncan McOnlea contra Hew Waiche for the sowme of thri s. sterling awand him for pick and tar compeirit the defendar and confest the debt justly awand thairfor decernit with vi s. of expenses of pley to be payit within terme of law and give neid beis to caus poynd thairfoir.'

(xxviii) Were the witch trials held in the Kirk or in the Tolbooth? The

latter was usual. However in a series of trials of this kind, the Kirk might have been used because it might accommodate more people some of them on seats. The witch trials of two dozen people were extraordinary events. It makes little difference, either way. The Church was small and maybe smaller than the Tolbooth.

(xxix) Would Jean Colquhoun, Robert Stewart of Scarrell's wife have lived with him after the trials?
Probably not. She risked ostracism herself, a difficult thing for a woman with friends and family. Besides, she may have come to dislike him intensely for his adultery and the problems he had caused her and may even have taken the view, as given, that he was or had been the devil, over and above having been possessed by the devil, which she would take to be a fact. If she did continue to live with him then it is very unlikely, but not impossible, that Jonet McNicol ever stayed overnight with him during her 12 year disappearance. Nevertheless, even so, he could have spent many an evening in darkness with Jonet, while on the pretext of fishing, for example, and would have been able to supply her from his own supplies which were guaranteed by the Kirk Session, which was bound to be charitable to anyone not excommunicated and even then, perhaps. The fact that Jean Colquhoun appeared in the Town Court a few times to perform transfers of lands without him appearing does not mean that they were living together, only that, for their mutual financial advantage, lands had to be sold to pay off loans and creditors. The fact that Robert Stewart's name continues to appear in the Town Records is itself a kind of confirmation that he was not excommunicated. Had he been, it would have been an excommunicable offence to have any dealings of any kind with him.

(xxx) The Status of the Conclusions Reached
It is not impossible that Robert Stewart of Scarrell played no role in the witch hunt in Bute in 1662. If so, the mystery remains: what was its origin? However, for the whole of 1661 and even before, his conduct was the chief topic of the island for it was exceptionally scandalous. For a married man, son of the Minister, trained as a minister, who had acted as assistant minister in Rothesay, as well as the schoolmaster and Session Clerk—clerk of the Kirk Session, the ruling religious power in the place— to father a child, in adultery, by a person half his age and then to try to put the blame onto others would have had the effect of an earthquake upon the social fabric of the island.

Since for the whole of that year, the year before the witch hunt began in January 1662, he was in a state of increasing disgrace and after 4th July, actual disgrace and humiliation given his naming as the father by Nancy Throw, the effects of that disgrace are likely to be a factor in the origin of the witch hunt. And since, from the confessed testimony in the document found at Inverary, a man was involved in nearly every case of meetings with the devil, that man is very likely to be this particular man. Ostracised by everyone else, he had to seek society somewhere and the periphery of it, among the witch people, is the obvious place. The effects of shunning, of this level of social isolation, are very severe and the urge for him to seek succour elsewhere— anywhere he could receive a welcome— would be strong. Once admitted to that group of the poor outsiders, as an educated, wealthy person of considerable gifts and former standing, of course he would quickly become its leader. What kind of leader? As a Christian and a Schoolmaster, it is likely to have been a leadership founded upon love— and his own situation would enable him to make perceptions about it that did go beyond the current teachings of the Kirk, with all its prohibitions and concern for sin. Since he had sinned so royally— knowing that he would be found out!—there would be a reason for it and Master Robert is likely to have seen the folly of these current teachings all too clearly, and not only as a way of excusing himself.

It was these perceptions of his, made after his sins, and related to the witch folk that are likely to have incited a response from the minister and the eldership. Imagine if he had been left to continue to attract people to his meetings? The consequences to the Kirk would have been disastrous. The congregation would have shrunk. The people suffering under the repressive regime of the Church of Scotland would have fled to this far easier and more sensible alternative. That is why the witch hunt was necessary.

If the devil as described was a man and it clearly must be, then there is no better candidate than this man. No other comes within a hundred miles of him.

The very fact that no effort is made according to the Inverary Document to identify the man taken to be the devil is very significant. They may have been afraid to do this, in case they drew attention to this fledgling church, as they would view his activities.

Would the Earl of Argyll have taken the action of identifying the man? He is the only person without a vested interest in concealing him. Indeed, had this particular man been identified by the church as the devil—and not just the form in which he appeared—the idea that the devil could appear in many alternative forms would have been lost and that was a very useful concept in explaining sin and even a centrepiece of the concept promulgated at that time by the Church of Scotland. The very fact that no effort within the Inverary Document, with all its many pages of interrogations and confessions, is made to identify the human taken to be devil, means that the Kirk Session feared to have him identified and did not pursue this line deliberately.

Robert Stewart of Scarrell could not have played the role given to the Earl in the reconstruction for he would not have been allowed to, so recently disgraced as he was. The prosecutor himself would have had no interest in doing so: he was being employed by the town in a criminal trial. And there was no defence at a witch trial. The idea that any person accused of a crime deserved a defender was some distance in the future. In addition, the people accused were all poor which made the fees for a defence impossible to find. However, a defence of the modern kind was not allowed in 1662.

Yet would not something else have been gained by his death? As an educated and strong minded person, like his father, he is unlikely to have given in and confessed to anything, though it may have been tried. But since there is no mention of him as such, distinct from his persona, presumed, of the devil, in the 28 pages of the dittays there is just no sign that he was apprehended, warded and tortured. Because he came from the class of the gentry it would have been very difficult to prosecute him in this way. Indeed, since he is left alive at all, and not even excommunicated, it is clear that he has received favoured treatment and that is the reason: he is in the class that does not receive such treatment, for whom it is unthinkable. A huge fine and ostracism are the only punishments that make sense— though he may have been beaten up a few times by individuals, such as Alexander Bannatyne who loved Nancy Throw and wished to marry her—assuming he was up to it, which he might not have been. Robert Stewart may have been a formidable fellow, probably was, like his father.

Would the Earl have been clever enough to do what he is taken in the reconstruction to have done? He might have gone to a really good university like Oxford or Cambridge, must have gone to some university. He may have gone to Eton (which was founded over a century before) like his descendants. His father went to St Andrews where he fell foul of Montrose, a contemporary. So his son may have gone there. Going to Oxbridge, then as now, was no guarantee of anything. He may have been as able as he is portrayed.

APPENDICES 305

Was the escape of Jonet McNicol as described? Here are least is a solution: why did only one escape? A reason like that given in the reconstruction; the others were under examination at the time of escape. And was she held in Bute until later, just before the trials were over? Probably.

Did she spend 12 years in the Lowlands around Kilmarnock? If she escaped, she had to manage a boat. It had to be a boat she could manage. She would quickly find in 1662 that the mainland was full of escaping witches [most of the witches ever killed (up to 4,000) were killed in that one year—another sign that the mood of the times was changing in reaction to decades of repression] and was not an easy place to survive in without a husband or protector. In that case, having a small boat which she could manage herself would have enabled her to live close to Bute for all of that time, in secret, providing she travelled only at night[177] and with the added advantage of receiving regular supplies from the person who helped her to escape. That was plainly the wisest course to take in these circumstances: better than wandering the Lowlands to be robbed and raped as well as burnt, just the same—like so many hundreds of others. The boat, and she must have used one, would have enabled her to remain free for many years because there were so many islands around in which to seek a temporary residence, half of them uninhabited, most having very few people, always moving before her presence became clear and always travelling at night.

It is quite unlikely that any effort at all was made to ascertain whether she had been anywhere near Kilmarnock or if she had the name of a witch there. She would scarcely have used the same name and the difficulties in investigating from Bute were too great for that period. Melis's statement, then, about her living in Kilmarnock and being guilty of malefices there is probably false, therefore.

Who presented the charges against the witches? Probably, the crowner or coroner Jamieson, for that was his job—a job that was discontinued two decades later—with the Minister at his back pushing.

In brief, the cause of the witch-hunt in Bute seems to be, very probably, that someone, Master Robert Stewart of Scarrell, because he had special experiences of love and disgrace, someone of ability, was locked out of normal society and this encouraged him to question the accepted beliefs of how people should live and to convey his ideas to others. This was perceived as dangerous by the Church Authorities and they started the witch hunt as a way of nipping these unwelcome ideas in the bud by making an example of some of the people at these meetings, who, having also been ostracised already, had

---

[177] As a youth growing up in Bute in the 1950's, the author often sailed a canoe at night owned by the Richardson brothers of the Grand Marine Hotel. Their canoes were launched at the Gallowscraig, mostly ie the Children's Corner, because the basalt had been removed by then. The possibilities of night travel in a canoe barely six feet long were obvious. The possible speed was very fast. In a double canoe, the author aged nearly 15 and Grant Richardson, 17, crossed to Cowal in 15 minutes from a point about 200 yds out from the May Queen Slip where we had spent a fine afternoon adrift, reading Russian novels, instead of Latin at the Academy. This was about 8 miles in an hour. It is about 8 miles to Wemyss Bay from Rothesay Pier and 5 miles to Arran from Bute. Bute to the Cumbraes is 2 miles or less. In fine weather and even in a breeze an experienced canoeist who needed to could reach safety from Bute in half an hour and would, because able to travel in a straight line, even evade a pursuing sailing vessel of the time.

the name of witches, though their crimes were relatively innocent and related to charming, herbal healing and trying to get their own back on men who would take advantage of them. Until Master Robert Stewart of Scarrell's appearance among them, the witch people would have met in secret in small numbers for the purpose of jollification, dancing and even communal feasting— actions the Kirk Session would have condemned— but actions which were natural and a relief from the oppressive lives most of them, as poor people, had to suffer.

How strong is this conclusion of Robert being the cause? Very strong. There is no obvious alternative. This conclusion, though not certain, is very likely. It would be very surprising if no man living at the time was the person taken to be the devil, for the self evident fact is that the confessions all point to a living person. The confessions make no sense without a person, afterwards taken to be the devil. And if this be so, no other person is qualified as he is so manifestly and in so many significant ways.

(xxxi) Master Robert Stewart at Kilchattan

This person is mentioned on the jury at the Assize of 1673. He is unlikely to be identical to Master Robert Stewart of Scarrell. No one would associate with anyone who had been excommunicated (or ostracised) nor were such associations allowed. This means that Master Robert Stewart of Scarrell could not be on any committee or jury for that reason. Besides, no one would want to serve with him on it. Since the records have been lost we do not know for sure whether he was excommunicated or not. Reasons have been advanced which may have saved him: his not being a minister on the list at Edinburgh; he was not a minister but a schoolmaster, or had been until he demitted the post and was a schoolmaster at the time of his adultery with Nancy. Since he himself, as reported by Nancy at the Kirk Session, minuted on 4th July 1661, expected to be executed, the seriousness of his crimes must have ensured his utter ostracism, even if it stopped short of excommunication. All his life, his father was known as Master Patrick Stewart of Roseland, despite the fact that he occupied a manse first in Kingarth and later in Rothesay, at the Old Bishop's House at the top of Castle Street. So the appellation 'of Roseland' was for life. Master Robert Stewart of Scarrell is probably the same: known by this name all his life. In the Town Council Records he is mentioned in 1673, the year of the Assize, as 'of Scarrell'. Unless he removed to Kilchattan within a few months of the date of this mention and wanted to be known differently, there must be another Master Robert Stewart. Even so, people would be very slow to make the change; some would never make it and would continue to refer to him as 'of Scarrell' no matter where he lived or what he did. Indeed, the very reason for the location is to distinguish men with the same name. In Bute, there would be several Robert Stewarts: one farming at Kilmory and another at Kilwhinleck, for example, as we have seen, amongst others. But there were so many Stewarts on the island that it is quite likely that there was another Robert Stewart who had graduated at university. If this Robert Stewart were identical to our Robert Stewart it means that he was on the jury who condemned Jonet McNicol. And that is not impossible. He might have been against it, might have argued against it and been outvoted. He might even have been co-opted onto the jury because of his association with her, if, as argued in the novel, he was the person referred to as the devil— at least by the minister and elders in the dittays. But that event is quite unlikely. A man as well educated as that who had the temerity to behave as he had done, might have caused a lot of trouble at the trial. Instead, this different Master Robert Stewart at Kilchattan is probably a young relative of Robert Stewart of Scarrell like Master Patrick Stewart who became schoolmaster around 1665, a brother perhaps or a son of Dougal Stewart, son of Sir James, the Sheriff at that time.

(xxxii) Deceased Rev Mr. Patrick Stewart's Estate

Rothesay Town Council Records p38/39

2nd Nov 1659: 'Forasmeikle as the Collectour of the Cesse within the brughe of Rothesay declaires that he has great difficulty in exactioun of the cesse of the deceist Mr Patrick Stewart his lands in respect of severall heretours thairof and some of them absent quherby he is prejudget and damnifiet, thairof and for remead thairof that the collectour may have the readier payment, the magistrates and counsell ordaynes that the said Collectour exact the said cesse from Mr William Maxwells tenants and possessours of the lands belonging to him in particular according as the land is valued or utherwayes of the maist responsibill of the said tennants of quhom he may have it readiest as he thinks meitt and als muche as may defray and pay the cesse imposed for the tyme and lykewayes for riding merches betuixt Mr William and Mr Robert Stewart heretours thairof hes authorized Allexander McConochie and Allexander Wode to value the said Mr William and Mr Roberts lands particularly according to the proportioun of thair lands for the cleiring the collectour in the exactioun in the said cesse with all expeditioun and give a particular note of valuatioun thairof to the Collectour betuixt   (sic)and nixt as lykwayes of the lands of those that hes bought certane parcells of the samyn lands.'

This is taken to mean that Mr William Maxwell is the same person as Mr William in this paragraph. He, then is a heritor and he is probably away from the island on other business, may live elsewhere. That is, the cess for Patrick Stewart's lands is to be borne by Wm Maxwell and by Robt Stewart, as heritors in proportion to their land holdings. It looks as if the two are related but not siblings.

(xxxiii) BUTE in 1662

(a) The Maps

Unless we can understand what the island and its people were like in 1662, we are unlikely to be able to understand the witch hunt. For a long while this seemed very difficult. There is a map of 1780 in the local museum from which inferences can be made and the statistical surveys of the island in 1792 and 1845 tell us something about the population. Then there is the Pont map, made probably around 1590 which shows the sea encroaching upon the land to within a short distance of the Castle. Unfortunately, this map is not very accurate. So one might doubt that this was so. The shape of the island shown by Timothy Pont is very different from the reality. And yet Pont made some very good 'maps' of other parts of Scotland which appear in the Blaeu atlas of 1654. Strictly speaking, they are not maps but chorographies for they reflect his interests and, made by a man working very probably alone, geometrical accuracy was not a viable concern for him.

What settles the issue is the Roy map of c1750, printed herein. This is beautiful, brilliantly accurate in nearly every detail and it confirms that the sea came close to the escarpment on which the castle is built. But far, far better, Roy has shown us the town of Rothesay in magnificent detail. Every building is drawn just as it was. This will enable us to compute the population very accurately for it happens that I have been studying the Roy maps in other places for nearly a decade and, at the time of writing, appreciate Roy's genius as few others do.

It is easy to show that Roy is worthy of this description. In 1747 at the age of about 21 he was appointed to the task of making maps of Scotland by Colonel David Watson [later Lt General Watson] of the Corps of Engineers. The purpose of the maps was to improve the knowledge of the terrain of the country for, just before, the Jacobite Rebellion had been put down by an army without the assistance of proper maps—something in retrospect seen to be necessary. Indeed, the act of pacification thereafter depended upon detailed knowledge of the country: where were the streams that must be crossed and their fords, the hills and woods in which rebels might hide, the swamps in which an army might be enmired, the houses in which men might be billeted and, of course, the roads along which troops might travel? The idea for this may be Roy's, Watson's[178] or even the Duke of Cumberland's, as reported[179]. Col David Watson was well pleased by Roy's early efforts and assigned him altogether about 50 men in six teams during the next 8 years. Of those involved, 5 later became generals, including Roy; and two artists, the brothers Sandby, who afterwards became founder members of the British Academy, were appointed to produce the finished articles.

But this is an inadequate measure of Roy's excellence. He became a Fellow of the Royal Society and won the Copley medal, its highest award, which puts him among the ablest men of the age. He was the leading advocate of the Ordnance Survey and the first to make a triangulated map possible by measuring an exact distance on Hounslow Heath as a base line.

However, none of this is really necessary. Any native of Bute has only to cast his eye upon this map—made in 1750 or thereby!— to appreciate its excellence.

Are the buildings in the town of Rothesay mere impressions? Not at all! I have seen this all before in the maps of Stirlingshire south of Stirling where every building is shown accurately, even to its shape and orientation as well as position. How do we know? Because there are some gap sites in the villages shown there, some houses even stand back off the site line of the street—utterly impossible had these been impressions. Why would you invent such things? No! This is the real McCoy. This is what Roy and his team saw. The villages of St Ninians and Newmarket are shown with brilliant precision by Roy. Every road and stream is confirmed not only on the ground—the work of a decade to me—as well as by the first OS map surveyed in 1860. The accuracy of the Roy maps is more remarkable than the reader can possibly appreciate.

In the Carse of Balquhiderock[180] at the time of writing there is a stretch of woodland along the old disused railway and a pond close to the Knoll. Neither has been shown on some of the best maps of modern times even though they have been present in the

---

[178] Watson himself paid £4000 towards the cost of the work and there is no sign that he ever received reimbursement from the King. That is, Watson saw it was a great idea to make these maps and was willing to finance it himself. See *Bannockburn Proved* p216. The fact that he allowed Roy to have the credit for the work is another sign of his unusual decency. Many would have taken it themselves.

[179] by John Watson. The Duke had been interested in maps for his earlier campaigns on the continent. Col Watson made a map of the battle of Dettingen at this time.

[180] Where I proved, as many able people who have read the work agree, that the Battle of Bannockburn took place.

landscape for well over 30 years! How can maps with aerial surveys omit such obvious features? God knows. But they have! Roy would never have made such errors. Anyone can go and check, maps in hand. Historians, in the subject of Bannockburn at least, never check anything so deeply which is why in the past they made such little progress. One of the modern maps[181]—the best known—by Harvey was aerially surveyed in 1988 and yet these errors remain in the editions of the year 2005. If the map is better now—at long last—the reader will understand why it is. I pointed out the error. The Ordnance Survey maps from 2005 on, should likewise have been corrected for the same reason.

Just south of Cambusbarron in one of the Roy maps c1750 I noticed a thin dark line which emerged from the wood on Gillies Hill. What was it, I asked myself? The problem is that the line stopped. It could not therefore be a stream. So at least I thought. Unlike our medieval schoolmen who prefer to argue about the number of teeth in a horse's mouth (there are still a lot about) I decided to go and look. I found a stream an inch deep in ordinary weather and a foot wide. It stopped because, in 1750, it fell into a hole and disappeared—a property of streams on Gillies Hill, as further investigations easily showed[182].

Moreover, none of the *modern* maps show this stream accurately! All show it stopping within the woods. Not so! It goes right to the edge of the woods where it is now culverted under the gardens and houses built about fifty years ago.

Between 1750 and 1860 this stream was led around the hole so that it supplied water near Cambusbarron. Roy has therefore shown on his map a feature that hardly any other person in the locality would have known existed, for it is a tiny stream far from every habitation at the time and mostly within woodland.

It follows that not only was Roy a good map maker who was at pains to get things right (though without the benefit of triangulation), he was accurate as to detail in ways that have hardly been equalled even yet. Close study of the maps for years by myself, while making my own maps of the Bannockburn area extrapolated back to 1314, and another enthusiast who has been making a scale model of the battle area from mine, has convinced us that Roy has shown us every tree as well as every house, every fence and every stream as well as every slope. Every road is at exactly the correct angle to every other that crosses it. Villages, like Rothesay (and St Ninians and Newmarket, near Bannockburn[183]) are shown slightly larger than perhaps is warranted by maps that are

---

[181] The ISBNS are on BP p217, PS5; p49-50 etc

[182] There is another at the back of Firpark, the house occupied for many years by Wm Taylor on Gillies Hill. It disappears down a hole and then reappears further down the slope.

[183] Roy shows that there was no village of Bannockburn in 1750, 3 houses 150 yds apart do not make a village. In 1314 there would have been no houses at all at Bannockburn because there was no bridge across the burn until 1516 and no ford for half a mile. Indeed, even after the bridge was built the village that grew up was at Newmarket, half a mile south of the burn for that was the first place flat enough to build on which had a good water supply. Building at Bannockburn meant carrying water every day up a very steep hill. Thus by 1750 there are a dozen buildings at Newmarket and only 3 spaced out at Bannockburn. Of course this means that the battle took its name from the stream and not the place, for there was no place there in 1314. Since historians had been showing Bannockburn as a place in 1314 for centuries on their maps—some of them as a town!—(and fouling up our understanding of the battle) their only answer to this revelation was

1000yds to the inch. Even so, this is an advantage for it enables us to see them more clearly.

There are occasional errors of distance on the Roy maps which matter, at least in Stirlingshire. Balquhiderock Wood, for example, is narrower than it should be shown at its maximum: the OS map of 1860 tells us it should have been 264 yds and not 150yds[184]. Why is this? Because it is very difficult to measure a distance accurately on a

---

to dismiss the Roy maps as 'stylistic devices and should not be interpreted as replicating the exact situation on the ground' [p23 of the Report for Stirling Council by Fiona Watson and M. Anderson in May 2001] . **Any Brandane** can immediately see that this is rubbish. The Roy map of Bute is brilliant and that it was made in 1750 is astonishing. The much trumpeted Pont Maps are not in the same league. Of course had they accepted the accuracy of the Roy maps it would mean changing their own maps of the battle and even their own understanding of it. Since they had not done their work properly—had placed the battle in the wrong place—this was a mistake they are still not willing to own up to. Because of their defects of scholarship the battle area is under continual threat from developers who care nothing for the history. The facts about Bannockburn are made completely clear in *Bannockburn Revealed* and *Bannockburn Proved*. Contrary to all the rubbish handed down and imbibed without sufficient careful examination and still believed by most historians, the tactics of the Scots were in the genius class: they dismounted their cavalry and, on foot, attacked the English in their camp, penning them in between the bounding streams of the Carse of Balquhiderock. This result is very important and the history community is unwilling to yield it to an outsider. Of course many of them do not think the matter can be proved which is why they do not bother to read it. Unused to studying a subject like this for years because they do not have the time, having lectures to give and prepare and papers to publish for brownie points and other self promotions, they do not understand anyone who does, full time, for a decade, at unaffordable expense and without any sort of advantage in mind beyond the passion to discover the truth. Since I saw some mistakes in historians work when researching *The Bannockburn Years*, a national prizewinning novel, it was my duty to clear up the mess. This was achieved by translating all the written reports of the battle and printing them in one volume for the first time where they could be analysed, issue by issue, a novel procedure; making a very accurate, well justified map of the battle area, also novel; and rating the arguments and conclusions—a fully scientific investigation which left out nothing relevant. Some historians who do not want their mistakes broadcast try to bury the unwelcome conclusions by ignoring the above books. The keys to the victory are in the ground: the two bottlenecks at Milton Ford and the Carse between the bounding streams. The Scots excluded most of the English army at these places. Is a footnote like this worthy? Of course! For the reader will have in a nutshell the facts about the greatest victory ever fought by Scots. And he is unlikely to see it anywhere else.

[184] BP p181 Section 15. Roy's maps point to magnetic north which means they must be turned about 20 degrees to match the true north of the earliest OS map. [copies are in BP] When this is done, every line and angle is nearly identical. Roy shows the wood came as far down the slope as the first bend in the mill lade. The first OS map surveyed in 1860 by Capt Pratt tells us where that bend is exactly, being a triangulated map and therefore more accurate. Thus the wood comes down the slope to the flat ground which is regularly pooled with water—as expected! Any place where trees can grow they will grow, especially when, because there are so many trees in the vicinity, seeding is

wooded slope, especially without triangulation. The reader should be able to see that Roy's rendering of the island is no mere impression. On the contrary, it is very accurate. And it is even confirmed, both by Martin Martin's description in 1695 and Pont's chorography of c1590 and even by the map in the local museum c1780, the core of which is the same as Roy's, with additions. This means that we are able to make very accurate deductions from Roy's map about the number of buildings and even the length of them. Indeed, given that in Stirlingshire each building represents about 3 houses on the far larger OS map of 1860 which is 6 inches to the mile, we will be able to formulate a very accurate idea of the population in 1750 from the map alone.

Roy's map [use a magnifier] is shown on the cover in two parts that enable every feature to be clear. It reveals that Rothesay is a very small town clustered around the Castle, the main building being in the block holding the Tolbooth, immediately to the east of the High Street, a ring of buildings around the Castle; some buildings east of the Watergate in what would be called the Balskyte district because of the burn that ran down Watergate to the harbour (which Roy does not show, perhaps because of dry sunny weather and the flat stones[185] that covered the street, to ease passage over the burn); buildings along the south side of Castle Street, turning the corner into the High Street and continuing south as far as Russell Street and a little beyond and that is the limit of the town. There are 4 buildings on the shore near the Albert Pier of today and 4 across the Lade to the west—and that is it! Rothesay in 1750. In 1662 it would be little different. A few less houses only: those on the periphery would be added last.

Notice the stream that comes off the Water of Fad near Russell Street and Colbeck Place. This is the Lade [the mill lade] and it follows roughly the line of John Street—confirming, then, the idea in Whyte's Lectures that a stream went down John Street. For this to be possible, given the ground elevations, the cutting for the lade must have been deep. Now, all the Water of Fad is known as the Lade, the original lade which gave it the name, having been filled in, because disused. Today it follows the line that the elevations all suggest; with the curves removed[186]. Roy shows us the original line of the Water of Fad.

And yet, there are aberrations. Townhead appears twice on this, the fair copy. Examination of the Protraction, from which it came, shows the same apparent error. And the position of the Kirk is unclear. St Blane's is shown in Gaelic, an understandable mistake: the language of the person telling it to the surveyor. The Statistical Survey of

---

widespread; but they do not grow on ground that is regularly pooled with water, for the roots rot. They seed everywhere, of course. Most historians believe there was no woodland in the Bannockburn Area in 1314 when the written reports make 17 references to it, every map shows an increasing amount as we go back in time, even today there is a lot of it—miles of it— and the ground itself shows it never could have been cut down.

[185] These flat stones were in general use from an early time. They can be seen today in the Forum at Rome, Julius Caesar's forum where they may be original.

[186] Why take the curves out? To increase the speed of flow to the cotton mill. Curves slow the water by friction. Dig them out and you get a straight channel and more speed. The maximum speed is achieved when the minimum distance is run.

1792 reports that 'the language principally spoken in the parish is the Gaelic.'[187] In 1662, this language is known as 'the Irish.'[188]

Since the island is about 15.388 miles along its main axis, this being 39 ins on a map of 1 in 25,000 we can confirm the scale. On the Roy map the equivalent distance is 19.625 ins which means that an inch on Roy's map is 15.388 miles /19.625 = 1380 yds. Measuring from burn to burn and high water mark, Ettrick to Kames, gives 1410 yds. More variation occurs elsewhere. Though the Roy maps are generally taken by scholars to be 1000yds to the inch, this one is very roughly 1400 yds to the inch and it varies because of inaccuracies in the geometry which are inevitable without triangulation.

Notice that the Kirk of Kingarth in 1750 is shown north of Mount Stuart. As the Statistical Survey makes clear, there were three kirks in the Parish of Kingarth: near Mount Stuart, at St Blanes (a ruin in 1792) and, according to Roy, across the road (or bridle path, all there was then) from the cemetery of today. That kirk, Middle Kirk was the main Kirk, the northerly kirk being used, in 1692, only when the Earl of Bute was in residence. Notice that in 1750 there is 'an island of Ascog', which suggests that landfill for the purpose of industry, possibly salt making, caused it to disappear. Pont also shows this island in c 1590.

Finally, there is a more obvious flaw in the maps which had to be joined in pieces. Because there is no triangulation, the geometry is inexact which means that a perfect match on the line of join is impossible. The join has been matched at the top which means that there is a hiatus from the centre downwards. Very many trials with the maps of Stirlingshire had to be made by me to make the very best joined map obtainable; even then, the match is not perfect. It would be possible to improve the Roy map of Bute, so far as Brandanes like me are concerned by cutting the map and rejoining. I will consult his ghost[189] overnight some time and ask his opinion. However, that this map of Bute should have been made in 1750 or thereby is a magnificent achievement. Nothing as good would be seen for a full century when the Ordnance Survey maps began to appear.

(b) The Population of Bute in 1662

Historians do not usually justify the populations of earlier times[190], any more than they justify the maps they provide (always full of errors) in medieval subjects. They are not mathematicians of course. But the matter is easy. If you compute the population by several methods which are essentially independent and get answers which are very similar, you have a very good idea of the population at that time, even though it is not completely accurate. Since no census is ever completely accurate, this is no loss. It is even possible to state upper and lower bounds which makes the process fully scientific. [The reader who does not like mathematics can pass over this section to the conclusion.

---

[187] p464

[188] Note: it really is Irish and not Scottish Gaelic at least according to those 'experts' consulted..

[189] I have spent so much time with his maps and writing him up, for he is even yet not appreciated by Scottish historians, some of whom have too much to lose thereby, that I think of him as one of my friends and feel that he casts an affectionate eye upon my struggles, partly on his behalf.

[190] Prof Barrow, eg, gives no reason for his figure of 400,000 for the population of Scotland in 1314 in 'Robert Bruce and the Community of the Realm of Scotland.'

APPENDICES

To quote a number as the population and ask the reader to take it on trust is simply worthless. The following calculations are necessary in any book that seeks the truth and they have been made as simple as possible.]

Given the success already achieved in estimating the population of the 6 sq miles of the battle area[191] at Bannockburn and Scotland itself in 1314 which occupies a whole chapter in *Bannockburn Revealed* and another in *Bannockburn Proved* (in the appendix) it should be easy to estimate the population of the Island of Bute in 1662 using the figures from the two Statistical Surveys. The essence of that method was to calculate the figures in several independent ways, using growth factors worked out from Statistical Surveys and even by counting houses on maps, etc. The outcome was several independent sets of results so close together that the upper and lower bounds of the actual figures got by extrapolation were also close which meant that they were very nearly certain. This remarkable degree of certainty was achieved by starting with slightly larger and smaller initial figures, applying the computed growth factors and observing the effects upon the actual numbers given for the years of census. Where the forward extrapolation produced figures very much greater than those actually achieved, the initial figure had to be too large. Indeed, when the computed figure, based on actual growth factors, exceeds by 10% the actually achieved figure, what we have in the estimate is an upper bound for the figure for the early period in question, for it is very unlikely a given initial figure could produce such an increase when the growth factors are known. This analysis was especially valuable in enabling the number of houses shown in the estimated map[192] of 1314 to be confirmed, thus making every feature on that map a thoroughly well-justified, scientific production— a small miracle.

In this case, there are several valuable tools: the Statistical Surveys in 1792 and 1845 written by ministers of parishes, Dr Webster's survey of 1755, Martin Martin's account of visiting Rothesay in 1695 and the various maps: Pont's c 1590, Roy's 1750 and the 1780 map in the local museum. Roy's is particularly useful as the houses can be counted. Martin's is useful because he counted fishing boats and families.

We have the following figures, among others:

Kingarth[193]   1791   727
Kingarth[194]   1776   957
Kingarth[195]   1755   979 (Webster, Pop stats, gives 998)
Rothesay[196]   1766   2658 [1500, country, 1158, town]

---

[191] The battle area is defined by a map made by me and entitled RMJ: short for Roy Maps Joined, a matter of considerable difficulty. It and my own triangulated map of 1314 include the burn, the Pelstream (drawn accurately, at last!), Gillies Hill, the four great bogs which defend the approach to Stirling from Falkirk, the Dryfield of Balquhiderock, 3 great carses and St Ninians village. The population of Scotland in 1314 is also worked out by several independent methods.

[192] This map took a year and a half of full time work to make and to justify fully, involving hundreds of visits to the battle area. An earlier version based on Roy's took almost as long.

[193] 1792 Survey, p459

[194] ibid deduced from p459, second sentence.

[195] ibid p459. There is an apparent error here, though small. The version written by a minister in 1792 is likely to be less accurate than that given in a book which incorporates Webster's Census published in 1975.

Rothesay[197] 1783 3389 [1485, country, 1904, town]
Rothesay[198] 1790 4032 [1425, country, 2607, town]
From the Statistical Survey of 1845 we have the following:
p88/89
Kingarth 1791 727
Kingarth 1801 875
Kingarth 1811 854
Kingarth 1821 890
Kingarth 1831 746, the fall due to migration to Rothesay where better employment is available.
Kingarth 1840 840
Rothesay 1837 6089 [4924 in the town itself, 300 Port Bann, 865 rest of country]

It is immediately clear that a reliable growth factor cannot be got during these periods for Kingarth because there has been a population migration to Rothesay because of better job opportunities in 1831. A cotton mill and herring fishing are the source of this change. In that case, we must take the figures for the two parishes together and deal with them. This sort of aberration will be removed then. Where useful, simple interpolations between known figures will be computed to make the extrapolations easier. Since the periods between figures is relatively small there should be little in the way of error because of this.

For the whole island, then,

1837 6898 [6089, Rothesay + 809, Kingarth: 746+ (6/9x{840-746}=746+63)]
1766 3545 [2568, Rothesay + 977, Kingarth: 998-11/21x(998-957)=998-21]

In 71 years the population has increased by 3353. If this were constant, the factor by which the population must be reduced as we go back in time in steps of 71 years is therefore 3545/6898 =0.5139 approx.
Thus we have:

1837	6898
1766	3545
1695	1821
1624	935

This means that, based on these figures alone, in 1662, the population should be: 935 + 38/71X(1821-935)= 38/71x(886) = 935+474 = **1409** of which about 700 or slightly less should be in the Kingarth parish, based on the figures given. And thus, about 700 in Rothesay Parish., figures to be improved upon, for these assume higher growth rates than would apply in early years.

What does Webster give us in 1755? For Kingarth parish 998, for Rothesay parish 2222, a total of 3220 for the whole island in 1755[199].

---

[196] 1792 Survey, p463

[197] ibid p463

[198] ibid p463

[199] Scottish Population Statistics (including Webster's Analysis of Population 1755), edited by James Gray Kyd, pub Scottish Academic Press, Edinburgh, 1975, p32.

APPENDICES

Thus we have, for the island as a whole,

1766   3545
1755   3220

In 11 years we have an increase of 325 i.e. about 27 per year. Any growth rate computed from years later than these is likely to be greater due to the gradual improvements because of the industrial revolution etc. So this growth rate is as good as we are likely to get and as we go back to 1662 it might even reduce in size. It is 1.1009 approx [3545/3220] per 11 years
Assuming this growth rate is constant, we get:

```
1766   3545
1755   3220
1722   2924
1711   2656
1700   2413
1689   2192
1678   1991
1667   1808
1656   1642
```

whence 1662 gives 1642 + 6/11 x [1808-1642] = 1642+ (6/11)x166 = 1642 +90 = **1732 for the whole island.**
What is the growth rate between 1662 and 1755? For the island as a whole it is 3220/1732=1.859. Assuming this is the same for town and country at this period, which is likely, for Kingarth in 1662 there should be about 998/1.859 = **536** in the parish. Since there are 1732 in all on the island, this means that there should have been 1196 in Rothesay Parish. Since in 1766 in Rothesay Parish the proportion in the town over the parish as a whole, See above, was 1158/2658 =0.436 approx, this means that the number in the town in 1662 should have been approx 0.436 x 1196 = **521**. And that means that in the country districts of Rothesay Parish in 1662 there were about 1196-521 = 675. The assumption here is merely that the proportion in 1766 in town and country would be about the same in 1662. However, we may be able to better this.

Readers of my works on Bannockburn should realise that this book gives the number of fighting men in Rothesay in 1755 as 444 and 2/5 out of a population of 2222 which is an exact fifth. Given the form of the statistics, this just means that Webster supposed that a fifth was the appropriate fraction. The same treatment is given over Kingarth where a population of 998 is credited with 199 and 3/5 fighting men. In my Bannockburn books, the fraction is taken to be a quarter. I defer to Webster. He should have been able to count them at the time and should have known. The force of my arguments is unaffected. However, he did not count them as he should have done; it could still be a quarter. Many modern authors think it should be a quarter eg in 'Caesar', Goldsworthy, A, 2006.

This figure, it will be seen, is not very close to the other figure got from the Statistical Surveys alone. Which is better? This figure, for it does not include statistics which occur in later times when higher growth rates can be expected.

If there were only 1732 people on the island in 1662, how many were in the town and how many in the country?

From the figures given in the 1792 Survey which is detailed, the proportion of people in the town, for the Parish of Rothesay alone, was as follows[200]:

1766 1158/2658 = 0.436 [to 3 dec]
1767 1181/2691= 0.439
1768 1254/2851= 0.439
1769 1326/2993= 0.443
1770 1470/3131= 0.469

the trend is a gradual increase. By 1783 we find:

    1783   1904/3389 = 0.562

This gradual increase in proportion in the townspeople over those in the country can be expected due to increased opportunities for work in factories and at fishing which occurred in the town.

What would this proportion have been in 1662 if the increase were constant? In the 5 years from 1766 to 1770 there is an increase of 0.033. In a year, the increase is about 0.0066 on average with 0.03 in the first year available [0.439-0.436]. This rate of increase can be expected to decline as we go back in time. And it should reach a constant very quickly. How much should this be? About 0.4. What cannot happen is a continual reduction of the proportion for if there were, if, say, it went down to 0.2, it would mean that there were 5 times as many in the country as in the town for Rothesay Parish which would imply a town that was barely a village and nothing like the Royal Burgh it had been for two centuries.

This means that a century before, the proportion would be about .4. That is, there would be nearly the same number in town and country for Rothesay Parish alone. However, the proportions would be as low as this long before we got back to 1662 and were probably constant for many years. The apparent arbitrariness of this will be resolved later.

Year	Kingarth Parish	Rothesay Parish	Rothesay
1755	998	2222	888 [0.4 x2222]
1662	536	1196	**478** [0.4]

That is to say, in the Parish of Rothesay, in 1662, living in the country, were 718 [1196-478]. In the town were 478 and in Kingarth 536. In other words, on the island as a whole, in 1662 there were 478 in the town and 1254 [1732-478] in the country within both parishes.

---

[200] 1792 Survey, p462

APPENDICES

What does Martin Martin actually say of his visit in 1695?
That the town of Rothesay 'is a very ancient royal borough, but thinly peopled, **there not being above a hundred families in it**, and they have no foreign trade. On the north side of Rothesay there is a very ancient ruinous fort, round in form, having a thick wall, and about three stories high, and passages round within the wall. It is surrounded with a wet ditch; it has a gate on the south and a double gate on the east, and a bastion on each side the gate (sic), and without these there is a drawbridge, and the sea flows within forty yards of it[201]. The fort is large enough for exercising a battalion of men; it has a chapel and several little houses within, and a large house of four stories high fronting the eastern gate[202]. The people have a tradition that this fort was built by King Rosa, who is said to have come to this isle before Fergus I. The other forts are Dun-Owle and Dun-Allin both on the west side.
The churches here are as follows[*1695*]: Kilmichael, Kilblain, and Kil-Chattan, in the South Parish; and Lady Kirk in Rothesay is the most northerly parish. All the inhabitants are protestants.
The natives here are not troubled with any epidemical disease. The smallpox visits them commonly once in every sixth or seventh year. The oldest man now living in this isle is one Fleming, a weaver in Rothesay. His neighbours told me that he could never ease nature at sea, who is ninety years of age. The inhabitants generally speak the English or Irish tongue, and wear the same habit with those of other islands. They are very industrious fishers, especially for herring, for which use they are furnished with about eighty large boats. The tenants pay their rent with the profit of the herrings, if they are to be had anywhere on the western coast.'[203]

Now we have found a figure of about 478 for the population of Rothesay in 1662. How does this compare with what Martin tells us in 1695?
First, let us correct the population figure. In 1695, for the whole of the island the population would be: $2192 + [2413-2192] \times 6/11 = 2192+6/11(221)=2192+120=2312$
Kingarth in 1695 should have: $536 + [998-536] \times 33/93 = 536+ 462 \times 33/93 = 536+164= 700$. The population of Rothesay Parish is $1196 + [2222-1196] \times 33/93 = 1196+364=1560$ of whom about 0.4 are in the town. This means that in 1695, there were **624** in the town. [Check: using the growth factor of 1.1009 per 11 years, 521 in 1662 gives 573 in 1673, 631 in 1684, 695 in 1695: the difference is due to the lower proportion of 0.4 presumed in the early years of the period studied. It should be higher by then, up to 4.2, say, in which case the 624 figure would rise to around 650]
Yet Martin says there were only 100 families in the town at that time. This makes perfect sense. It means around 6 people per family.
However, he also says that there were 80 heavy fishing boats in the harbour and of the two, this figure is more likely to be accurate, should be exact, for he is a man who counts things and boats are easily counted. There is here a contradiction: 80 heavy fishing boats implies 80 families connected with fishing. But if there are only 100 families altogether, there are only 20 families engaged in trades other than fishing. This is plainly incorrect.

---

[201] This is confirmed by Roy's map and Pont's.
[202] Where Sir James Stewart, the Sheriff, would live in 1662, the Mansion House in High St not having been built yet, still less, Mounstuart House which Roy shows in 1750.
[203] p133/134, Martin Martin, A Description of the Western Islands of Scotland c 1695, Birlinn, 1999, 2002

The records tell of 40 burgesses, the majority of whom have nothing to do with fishing. Since counting families is more difficult than fishing boats tied up in a harbour, and since some families would share a house and several share a tenement, the figure for families is probably an under estimate.

If his figure for fishing boats is correct it suggests that there are at least 160 engaged in fishing, assuming at least two to man one vessel. It also suggests another 100 female partners for the fishers. Then there are their children, say 200 more. This amounts to 460 people in fishing families which leaves too few to account for the numbers of burgesses unconnected to fishing. Maybe some fishers lived out of town. That would explain it. These would have the advantage of a farm to provide produce from the land as well as a fishery, a mixed employment which would be common. The Statistical Survey of 1792 suggests that this is the explanation: 'The farmers being employed the most part of the summer in casting and leading peats, cannot provide manure for their farms, the summer season being the fittest for that purpose; but what for some years past appears to be the greatest disadvantage to the farming interest of the parish is the bounty to the bus-fishing (sic), which is carried on to a great extent in Rothesay. Few farmers sons are bred to farming. To purchase a small share in a herring buss, and become master of it, seems to be their great ambition. It is a fact, that all the young men of the parish [Kingarth] engage in the herring fishery; and that, when once engaged, though they have an opportunity of working in the farming line all spring, and receiving good wages. few or none are willing to work. This has formerly justly raised a complaint among the farmers, and at present their greatest.'[204]

So there is the answer to the contradiction in Martin Martin's description: Many of the fishing boats are crewed by men from the country districts.

What happened to the foreshore between 1750 and 1780? Roy shows us that there was no landfill of the sea shore in 1750. As in Martin's description and Pont's map, the sea came up to within about 40yds of the Castle. That is, Montague Street did not exist as a street at all then. Yet by 1780 the land has been filled in, as the map in the museum shows.

What has happened is this. In 1695 there were 80 heavy fishing boats. These were confined to a very small harbour which stretched from the current Mid Pier to the Albert Pier, a very small space in which to manoeuvre sailing vessels of some size. As the fishing fleet expanded, the need for more docking space, harbouring and even storage for chandlery and marketing of fish made it desirable to find more space. Though the sea came up to the south side of Montague Street, as it is today, it was probably very shallow, like Lochgilphead, Arrochar and even Kilchattan Bay, now. It was very easy then to fill in the sea, extending the sea front outward into the bay. Why did it have the shape shown in the 1780 map? Probably because there were rocks further out which could be used as supports for infilling. Bringing up soil and stones and creating a sea wall to hold them in place had the effect of greatly increasing the space available for docking boats to unload fish and that space was soon built upon to provide storage.

The Roy map of 1750 tells us a great deal about the population then. There are about 17 buildings around the Castle, close to; 18 down as far as Russell St; about 11 close to the

---

[204] Stat Survey, 1792, p459

Water of Fad; about 15 in the corner join of High St and Castle St; 8 on the east side of Watergate; 4 by the sea shore near the Albert Pier; and then the Tolbooth block which has 3 shops below the Tolbooth. Notice that the Tolbooth block ends before the extreme point of the line of he moat. This means the Tolbooth block did not come as far down as Castle Hill St; and that means that the Tolbooth probably took up the entire space upstairs, the three shops being underneath and from one end to the other in the block at the south end. At the north end of the Tolbooth block there are roughly 5 buildings across and 2 deep; 10, then. A total of about 83 in the town proper.

If this is roughly correct, based on Roy's practice at St Ninians, each building represents about 3 houses, except some will be workshops and shops. We have about 250 places for living or working. However, many, as the Statistical Surveys later report, were likely to be in a ruinous condition[205]. Martin's 100 families begins to look very sensible. Assuming there was not much change in growth rate between 1662, 1695 and 1750, we should expect under 700 people in the town in 1662 and probably much less, around 500, as the statistical analysis showed. There are two sources of error: the assumption that growth rates are the same when they would differ, though perhaps slightly; and the 0.4 proportion for the town in 1662 which is very reasonable given the ratio of 0.436 a century later. Indeed, that may be taken as an upperbound for proportion in 1662 as it is extremely unlikely that it would be as great as this a century before. If 0.436 is taken as the ratio then the town held 521 in 1662 and this is an upper bound because this proportion still applied a century later, when the move from the country to the town was already happening. This is very close to the 478 got previously which is good confirmation. Thus the town population should be taken as about **500** in 1662. The number of buildings in Roy's map, the number of families and fishing boats in Martin's visit and the analysis of the available statistics all confirm this.

(xxxiv) Incomplete Research. Every work of scholarship stops somewhere for several reasons which further research might resolve. The charm in old Irish which is different from old Scottish Gaelic, evidently, was left untranslated because of the cost (£50) for 4 lines, which, even then, might not have produced an accurate result. In *Bannockburn Revealed*, a translation service was used at a cost of £192 for a few pages of the chronicles by Geoffrey le Baker and Johannis de Trokelowe and the results were unsatisfactory as judged by a few friendly academics [an expert classicist at Edinburgh and a Professor thereof at Newcastle] who later gave their versions as well as Tom McCallum's very good work. And these were better than the translation service. I have of necessity become quite good at Latin myself since then, in consequence. It has, indeed, become a hobby, enthusiastically engaged most days; as well as several university summer schools.

In the first few leaves of the Kingarth Kirk Session there is mention of several acts which clearly govern the actions of the Session: on adultery, fornication etc and their penalties. Application to the Church of Scotland produced some of the acts printed herein. However, what was provided was not all inclusive. The National Archive was

---

[205] When have there not been ruinous houses in Bute? In 1959, the author was employed briefly to survey houses in the Ladeside Area and elsewhere. If a sufficient proportion were substandard the Council were allowed to demolish and rebuild. Of course entry to many was impossible since they were holiday houses, seldom visited. Rebuilding soon took place.

applied to and the answer given was that these were not acts of the General Assembly. This is unlikely to be so. No parliamentary or judicial act would apply to actions of the Session. What was sought were the acts prior to 1641. Only determined, time-consuming and probably expensive labour would resolve this matter. Since it has no direct bearing on the cause of the witch trials, it has been left undone. It would be interesting to see these earlier acts: 1596 et al. However, they might not exist in the National Archive or anywhere else, a conclusion that would be surprising. The Session records themselves reveal quite a lot about the penalties. Acts of the General Assembly were produced almost every year, as is still the practice.

The exact connexion between Jean Colquhoun and Ninian Bannatyne of Kames and Elizabeth Stewart, daughter of Sir James, is unclear. The records are clear that Jean often travelled to Kames and it was on those occasions that Scarrell was most often free to enjoy Nancy Throw. Since Jean was married to Scarrell, it is likely that she was of the gentry, educated and wealthy. Indeed, the records show that she possessed lands which were subsequently sold. If so, it is likely that Jean was a friend of Elizabeth and that it was to visit her that the journeys to Kames were made. In 1662, there would be no one else living at Kames of that class for her to visit. Elizabeth would have made friends with anyone in the class just below her own and few would serve. Marriage to Scarrell suggests that Jean was a woman worth knowing, as well as sufficiently well off. Ninian Bannatyne would be related to many people on the island. It is suggested that he was a cousin of Jean's, though, perhaps, one several times removed which really is very likely. It is just as likely that Robert Stewart of Scarrell was a relation of Sir James, since his grandfather had been Commissary of the Isles and, more especially, because of Sir James's very generous attitude to RSS after his crimes were revealed. The fact that Rev Patrick Stewart fought Sir James in the courts in the 1650's is irrelevant: Patrick fought with anyone, often when it was about money and often when his case was unreasonable. The available records in the museum do not allow greater certainty than this.

Little has been made of the fact that Ninian Bannatyne himself was one of the men accused of fathering Nancy Throw's child. There would have been a lot of friction between the two men which more could have been made of. What there is in the reconstruction is considered just enough. The object was to understand the causes of the trials and executions and that has been completed.

10. ACKNOWLEDGEMENTS

Many people have been helpful during this research. Jean McMillan of the Bute Natural History Society very kindly let me take home the records of the Kirk Session and the Town Council for the relevant years and, at some labour, made me a copy of the appropriate Kingarth Records. Ivor Gibbs was helpful with maps, questions about maps and supplying the Lectures by Whyte, edited by himself, which were so useful. Linsae Duncan, Gregor MacPherson and the very Rev Finlay J MacDonald of the Church of Scotland in George Street, quickly sent me copies of some of the articles of the General Assembly of the Church of Scotland which bear on conduct by ministers and congregations for the year 1638 and 1648. The National Library provided a copy of the document found in the Charter Room at Inverary and printed in Highland Papers Vol 3, which was invaluable. Jess Sandeman provided a set of notes on an MA Sociology thesis

[1988] by Lawrence Donaldson of 75 pages on the subject and much helpful information about the Island and its history. The thesis itself could not be acquired by the inter library loan facilities, including application to Glasgow University which does not retain copies of work at undergraduate level. There is no evidence in the notes of any relevant originality in the thesis which would not, in any case, ordinarily be expected in an MA thesis on Sociology. The information provided is incomplete and the cause has not been looked for, still less, discovered. No distinction seems to have been made between the island and the county. The Inverary Document does not seem to have been consulted. Patricia McArthur in the local library was especially helpful. At an early stage, Mrs Mary Hoffman, whose ancestor, Susanna Parker, was the first witch burnt at Salem, kindly provided papers on the Salem Trials which were illuminating. I am very grateful to Irvine Smith who lent me some published papers of his on witchcraft and made useful suggestions. Chris Fleet of the Map Library at the National Library of Scotland was very helpful in providing copies of the Roy map of Bute and other maps like Timothy Pont's. The Roy map is printed with the permission of the British Library; the Pont map with the permission of the National Library of Scotland. Julian Goodare has given permission to make use of the alphabetical list of persons mentioned in witch trials in the Edinburgh University data base made in their survey of witchcraft. He, Lauren Martin, Jayne Miller and Louise Yeoman are joint authors; website: www.shc.ed.ac.uk/witches/, archived 2003, accessed about then. The list has been modified here in the light of this work and greatly amplified and extended. Christine Boyd, Tom McCallum, Donald Morrison and David Torrie kindly agreed to read it, made very helpful comments and proof read the penultimate draft. Tom and David gave very encouraging reviews which they allowed me to print in the document. Stephen Standaloft provided invaluable computer expertise in submitting files to the printer for which I am very grateful. This is my own original work and the responsibility for it is mine alone.

11. BIBLIOGRAPHY

There are thousands of works on witchcraft. None of them deal with Bute in anything but a superficial mention. Thus they have no relevance here. The fundamental yet very original insights made from the available records herein are sufficient. Reading through the thousands of works on this subject is a waste of time when the answer is instantly available in the local records.

I
Rothesay Parish Records, The Session Book of Rothesay 1658-1750 transcribed and edited by Henry Paton for John, 4th Marquis of Bute, printed for private circulation MDCMXXXI
Rothesay Town Council Records, 1653-1766, transcribed by Mary Bruce Johnston at the instance of John, 4th Marquis of Bute, printed for private circulation MDCCCCXXXV
Blain, John, History of Bute, edited by Rev William Ross, pub WG Harvey, Rothesay, MDCCCLXX
Hewison, James King, The Isle of Bute in the Olden Time, Blackwood, Edinburgh and London, MDCCCXCV
Statistical Account of Scotland, Gen Ed: Donald Witherington and Ian R Grant, 1792, 1st.

The New Statistical Account of Scotland, Blackwood, Edinburgh and London, 1845 by the ministers of the parishes.
Highland papers Vol III, pub Scottish History Society Second Series Vol XX: Papers relating to Witchcraft, 1662-1677.
Justiciary Records of Argyll & the Isles.
Martin Martin: A Description of the Western Islands of Scotland c1695, Birlinn, 1999, 2002, Edinburgh.
Martin Martin, Curiosities of Art and Nature, ed Michael Robson, Port of Ness, Lewis 2003.
Scottish Population Statistics, including Webster's Analysis of Population 1755, edited James Gray Kyd, Scottish Academic Press, 1975, Edinburgh.

II

Buchanan, Ann, In Search of an Alehouse at Brandsier Bog, Trans Bute Nat His Soc Vol XX (1976) p86
Bute, Marquis, Isle of Bute Charters, Trans Bute Nat Hist Soc Vol XII (1945)
Davies, G. The Early Stuarts 1603-1660 pub Oxford 1952. Ist 1937 [Ox Hist of Eng]
Douglas, Dr JD. Light in the North, Paternoster, 1964 (Minister at Rothesay, St Johns, 1958-60)
Barrell, ADM. Medieval Scotland, pub Cambridge Univ Press, 2000
Cassar, Carmel, Witchcraft, Sorcery and the Inquisition, Mireva Malta, 1996
Cohn, Norman, Europe's Inner Demons, University of Chicago, 1973,1993
Dingwall, Helen M, A History of Scottish Medicine, EUP 2003
Dow, Frances, Cromwellian Scotland, pub John Donald, 1979,1999
Jack ERDS and Rozendaal, Editors, The Mercat Anthology of Early Scottish Literature, 1375-1707
Goodare, Julian, editor, The Scottish Witch-hunt in Context pub 2002, Manchester Univ Press
Hamilton, David, The Healers, A History of Medicine in Scotland, Canongate, Edinburgh, 1981
Hay, George, Scoulag Kirk, Trans Bute Nat Hist Soc Vol XV (1963)
Kyd, James Gray, editor. Scottish Population Statistics including Webster's Analysis of Population 1755, Scottish Academic Press, 1975, Edinburgh.
Larner, C, Lee, C.H., McLachlan, H.V A Sourcebook of Scottish Witchcraft pub Glasgow, 1977
Larner, C Enemies of God, pub John Donald, Edinburgh 2000. Ist Blackwell, 1983, Oxford
Macaulay, History of England, Vol 1
MacBain, Jenny, The Salem Witch Trials, Rosen, New York, 2003
Maxwell-Stuart, PG, An Abundance of Witches, The Great Scottish Witch-Hunt, Tempus, 2005
Mackinlay, John, An Account of Rothesay Castle, Hedderwick, Glasgow, 1818
Macdonald, Stuart, The Witches of Fife, 1560-1710, Tuckwell, 2002
Melville, RD. The Use and Forms of Judicial Torture in England and Scotland Scottish Historical Review Vol II, No 7 April 1905
Newall, Venetia, Encyclopaedia of Witchcraft and Magic, Hamlyn, 1974
Paterson, Raymond Campbell, No Tragic Story, The Fall of the House of Campbell, pub John Donald, Edinburgh, 2001

Readers Digest, The Truth About History, p98-102
Sanderson, Margaret HB, A Kindly Place? Tuckwell, 2002
Scharlau, Fiona C. Burn the Witch pub Angus District Council Libraries and Museums Service 1995
Smith, Irvine J. edited with an intro Selected Judicicary Cases 1624-1650, Vol II The Stair Society, Edinburgh, 1972
Smith, Irvine J. Trial Notes in the case of Agnes Finnie, Potterrow. [5th Dec 1644: Colvile and Robertson JJD]
Smith, James, Dated Houses in Rothesay, Trans Bute Nat Hist Soc Vol XII (1939)
Smout, T.C. A History of the Scottish People, Fontana, 1998; ist William Collins, 1969
Waller, Maureen, 1700: Scenes from London Life pub Hodder And Stoughton, 2001 paperback; ist 2000
Whyte, RD Glimpses of Bute History 1654-1908, edited by Ivor Gibbs. A collection of lectures given to The Buteshire Natural History Society between 1910 and 1949 and related papers in Transactions of the Society, 1907- present, esp The McCaws of Garrochty Vol I (1907); The Old Mansion House by RD Whyte (1925) Vol IX; John Blain and his Times by RD Whyte, Vol XI (1935); Ecclesiastical Notes by RD Whyte, Vol XIII (1945).

Epilogue

No one before now has spoken up for the witches of Bute. It has seemed to me to be a duty, one I am proud to have carried out as best I can.

OTHER BOOKS BY WILLIAM SCOTT

The Bannockburn Years, published by Luath Press, Edinburgh, 1997. 'A brilliant storyteller,' said Nigel Tranter on the cover. Winner of the Constable Trophy.
A novel which set out to discover arguments to resolve the Scottish Independence question. The first insights about how the battle of Bannockburn was fought and where, are in this book.

Bannockburn Revealed, published by Elenkus, 2000.
This is a very original investigation of the battle using new procedures which demolished the false beliefs about it which have lasted centuries. Where exactly the battle was fought and how won is made clear here and shown for the first time. All the written reports of the time are translated and analysed in this work. The maps of the battle area [made by excising details added since 1314 from Roy's maps] are the first ever properly justified maps of the area, a labour of about a year full time, alone, involving hundreds of visits to the area. In future, historical questions of this kind will have to be dealt with in this way, for this procedure exposes all the errors of the past. It involves printing all the sources together in

one book where they can then be analysed fully. When every relevant source is available there is nothing more to be said. Scottish historians have erred in believing the account of John Barbour who, writing 63 years after the battle, invented what he did not know. Half a dozen English sources, mostly present, some not used before, make the conduct of the battle completely clear.

Bannockburn Proved, published by Elenkus 2005.
This work provides formal proofs of the result that the battle was fought in the Carse of Balquhiderock and what occurred in detail. There are 8 levels of proof from a sentence to a four page proof which uses quotations from all the relevant sources. The best proof is at the end where 3 simple propositions are established and these are overwhelming. Future archaeological discoveries are shown to be irrelevant. The maps in this work are different, are triangulated and the finest ever seen. A year and half was spent on them alone, with many more investigations at the area. These maps show the elevations, the woodland, the streams and slopes etc as they would have been in 1314, very accurately. Without a good <u>fully justified</u> map of the area at the time, the battle cannot be understood. Once you have all the reports and the map, it is easy to understand. The books contain copies of every relevant map right back to Pont c1600 and Roy c1750.

Reviews:

'You should get a doctorate from every university in Scotland for this.' Irvine Smith, Advocate and Sheriff.

'William Scott's work is the best piece of research on history— not just Bannockburn—of that period that I have ever encountered.' Roger Graham, The Greenock Telegraph.

'This book, like its predecessor, *Bannockburn Revealed*, is the result of dedicated, exhaustive and patient research and, for one reader at least, settles the vexed question of the site of the Battle of Bannockburn.' Irvine Smith, Advocate and Sheriff.

'William Scott brings to this sequel to his previous book, *Bannockburn Revealed*...his further reasoned consideration of the subject, attacked with the thoroughness and cold logic one would associate with a consummate mathematician.

As a classical scholar and student of Ancient History I particularly appreciate his evaluation of evidence, sifting the dross from the gold. He has challenged the historical establishment and in so doing ruffled many a feather. **I would put him on a par with the young Michael Ventris whose work on the decipherment of Linear B confounded the Classical establishment of his time.**

Hopefully, William Scott will in the end gain the same acceptance.'
>Tom McCallum, M.A.Hons St Andrews.

'I found Mr Scott's account quite fascinating....As regards the site of the battle, he demonstrates conclusively that it must be the Carse of Balquhiderock...Indeed, he demonstrates that [the Dryfield] would have been impossible.' Patrick Cadell, historian, ex Keeper of the Records of Scotland. In *Scottish Local History*, Spring 2006.

'There are two reasons why *Bannockburn Proved* is one of the great publications of the early 21st century. The first is the combination of historical scholarship and painstaking on the ground investigation which shows clearly the true site of the battle, and how the Scots achieved such a notable victory in 1314. The second is that the author has found himself, in a modern context, engaged with the same kind of opposition that faced King Robert, in the guise of a coalition of intellectuals and town councillors who now find their superiority challenged and overthrown by a man who understands the battleground.' Rev Jock Stein, Minister and Theological Publisher.

'Thank you for *Bannockburn Revealed*. It's quite a while since I felt overwhelmed by a book—especially non fiction. A whole week-end was wiped out for me—engrossed in reading and map referencing, with the occasional twenty-minute trip out in the car to check out this landmark or that. Perhaps it was the enthusiasm of the style; maybe the pace and very compelling argument. Certainly I found myself delighted by your invaluable meta-analytical approach. It's a storming piece of work. Thank you.' Dr David Simpson, Stirling.

'The starting point is a close consideration of the original sources, all of which are printed together, in full, for the first time. This gives you a full opportunity to read them all and form your own views. This in itself is sufficient justification for buying the book...you will learn that there were not four schiltroms but three and why...that there was no Scottish cavalry charge...because none of them fought mounted. There was no heroic appearance by the Small Folk, waving their laundry...and even had they appeared where they are supposed to have done, no one on the battlefield would have seen them. And, most surprising of all, the basis on which the size of the Scottish army has been computed is wholly falacious. Mr Scott has, I believe, definitively established that the main action took place in the Carse of Balquhiderock. He has reached this compelling conclusion as a result of an in-depth study of old maps and photos of the area, particularly a map of 1750 by General Roy and a team of cartographers who went on to great distinction....All this is combined with an unrivalled knowledge of the ground. The many photos of the area will leave you in no doubt that the maps you have seen in other books are at best simplistic and underestimate its complexity. This is an excellent book which I whole-heartedly recommend.' Review by Chris Jackson, Principal Crown Prosecutor, in *Slingshot*, no 230.

"I do believe that the battle area lay undiscovered for nearly seven centuries until William Scott walked the ground, year in year out, for nearly a decade! He alone studied this ground in minute detail making many remarkable discoveries in the process and I am convinced no one else has ever done this. I believe that no one else has made such exhaustive studies of the eye witness accounts and other important works associated with this event. His book is quite unique in that he applied scientific principles in his endeavour to find out what really happened. This turns out to be <u>far more</u> astounding than the account I was taught at school. All the Scots, including King Robert Bruce, on the day of the main battle, walked to their glory! Not one Scot was on horseback! They walked up to the English camp in the early morning, made their presence known, and as the song says, 'sent them home to think again!'"
How did they do this? All is made clear in *Bannock Revealed*, a book of truly amazing scholarship, the first 'scientific/ history book I've ever come across. The facts, the evidence, are all presented with great clarity and one is compelled to accept that here is the truth and because everything fits into place and makes sense. Sadly, what is truly astonishing, is that this book has not been properly read understood or accepted by any historians from the academic community. These so called guardians of our national heritage, either through apathy or arrogance, have undoubtedly put one of our greatest national monuments, the

battlefield itself, at risk. Their lack of commitment towards upholding what has proved to be the truth is likely to lead to a desecration of the battle site for commercial gain.' Donald Morrison, 2004.

'The earlier work *Bannockburn Revealed* is such an outstanding demonstration of scholarship that every single molecule relating to the event has been exposed. In *Bannockburn Proved* William Scott has taken the molecular level to the atomic. Every minute detail has been re-examined raising the status of this book to a scientifically tested proof for all time. The medieval battle maps alone are outstanding documents justified by exhaustive scientific investigation. This proof was obtained after nearly two decades of hard labour. No ivory towers here but an intense examination of every square inch of the battle ground. No odd reference to an ancient map but a close scrutiny of all maps ancient and modern. No sporadic quote from an occasional source but a thorough searching of all the sources. No skimming of a few works relating to this event. In the process every strand of evidence has been teased out. Having studied W. Scott's work for many years I have to conclude that unlike many discoveries in mathematics, physics, medicine, astronomy, genetics etc, this work is not a theory but is the absolute truth simply because no other facts will ever be discovered which will discredit this truth. What a wonderful challenge for all the academic historians from every Scottish university to dissect this work and try to find fault with it. They will find none and only conclude that W. Scott should be appropriately recognized and applauded for his achievement.

'My involvement with W.Scott's work led me to undertake the construction of a 3D model of the battle area based on his maps in *Bannockburn Revealed*, which forced me to focus on the Roy maps. Mr Scott has been examining every line and mark on the maps for almost two decades and I am convinced that he is in a class of his own with regard to Roy's maps. I concluded that Mr Scott had confirmed, one hundred per cent, everything of importance on the ground by an exhaustive study of the Roy maps supported by other useful maps of the area and the ground itself.' Donald Morrison, 2006, 118 Alexander St Dunoon, PA237PY tel 01369703006